Digital Life Together

The Challenge of Technology for Christian Schools

David I. Smith, Kara Sevensma,
Marjorie Terpstra, and Steven McMullen

W0009571

WILLIAM B. EERDMANS PUBLISHING COMPANY
GRAND RAPIDS, MICHIGAN

Wm. B. Eerdmans Publishing Co.
4035 Park East Court SE, Grand Rapids, Michigan 49546
www.eerdmans.com

Published 2020
Printed in the United States of America

26 25 24 23 22 21 20   1 2 3 4 5 6 7

ISBN 978-0-8028-7703-1

Library of Congress Cataloging-in-Publication Data

Names: Smith, David, 1966– author.
Title: Digital life together : the challenge of technology for Christian schools / David I.
    Smith, Kara Sevensma, Marjorie Terpstra and Steven McMullen.
Description: Grand Rapids, Michigan : Wm. B. Eerdmans Publishing Company, 2020.
    | Includes bibliographical references and index. | Summary: "Walks educators,
    leaders, and parents through some of the big ideas that are hidden in our tech-
    nology habits. The book draws from interviews, surveys, classroom observations,
    and school records to examine the impact of technology on Christian learning"—
    Provided by publisher.
Identifiers: LCCN 2019054749 | ISBN 9780802877031
Subjects: LCSH: Educational technology. | Technology—Religious aspects—
    Christianity. | Church schools.
Classification: LCC LB1028.3 .S58 2020 | DDC 371.33—dc23
LC record available at https://lccn.loc.gov/2019054749

Contents

Acknowledgments

The process leading to this book has been long, complex, and deeply collaborative. Many individuals and organizations have contributed along the way. We would like to express here our gratitude to the Issachar Fund for assistance in securing funding, and to the several schools that were the focus of this research for their unfailing hospitality and willingness to support research into their educational work. Many individuals who cannot be named here because of the need to preserve school anonymity contributed enormously to the success of the project—you know who you are, and we are grateful. We have also enjoyed the support of Calvin University and Hope College in terms of both facilities and time to complete the work well. Several of us have cause to thank Calvin University for sabbatical and research fellowship support and for its support of student research assistants. The Center for Social Research (CSR) at Calvin University provided excellent and extensive support in everything from database construction and software troubleshooting to coding advice and transcription services. We are grateful to all the CSR staff and research assistants who helped turn the mountains of raw data into a body of information that could be efficiently analyzed, and we are particularly grateful to Neil Carlson and Laura Luchies for their collaboration and support. Colleagues in the grants office and financial services at Calvin University also provided necessary administrative support at various stages. We have drawn on the assistance of a number of students at various stages during the work, and we thank Katlyn Hettinger, Jack Gibson, Isabella Napitupulu, Elle Quist Nieuwsma, Meri Fuji Siahaan, and Yoolim Song for their contributions. Teachers at a range of professional events have responded to our provisional findings with thoughtful comments and questions that have fed back into the work. Outside readers, including Beth Green, Paul Marcus, and Jim Peterson, provided invaluable feedback on penultimate drafts, and Kevin Den Dulk, Todd Steen, and Deborah Van Duinen provided helpful input as advisors to the research project. The Kuyers Institute at Calvin University conceived and hosted the project, and Michele Rau has contributed a great deal to processes of coding and detail checking, as well as to the editing of the manuscript. We thank the editors at Eerdmans for their patience and care with the manuscript, and The Sparrows for a welcoming and congenial setting where a large portion of it was written or edited. It is no small thing that each of us has enjoyed the care and support of our families across the five years of work on this project, and we thank them for their forbearance.

CONTEXT

This book presents a wide range of research findings about how faith, technology, and learning are interacting in Christian schools. We hope that these findings will help educators in other schools to reflect well on their own technology practices. To make the material easier to navigate, we have kept chapters brief, divided the book into themed sections, and provided an introductory overview and a summary at the start and end of each section. This is the introduction to the first part, which offers an orientation to the rest of the book.

In this part, we first describe the changes in schools that prompted our research, sketching the day-to-day experiences that are pushing educators to improvise with new ways of doing things (chapter 1). We then describe the range of strategies that we found educators using to connect faith convictions with technological choices (chapter 2). These will serve as the broad categories around which the rest of the book is organized. Next, we pause to briefly consider the nature of technology—what is it we are looking at when we study educational technologies, and what kinds of questions should we be asking (chapter 3)? The following chapter explains how our research was conducted, the kinds of knowledge it can provide, and why the results might be regarded as valid (chapter 4). Finally, we describe the schools we studied, looking at the history and the faith tradition that have laid the foundations of their identity (chapter 5).

Each of these chapters provides a necessary layer of context, putting the various findings in the subsequent chapters into perspective and suggesting how they should be approached. We hope that this introductory section will help the reader navigate the rest of the book with an awareness of how the parts relate to the whole.

CHAPTER 1

A Shifting Landscape

Continue to improve on integrating Christian perspective and technology.

School goals document

Day by day, we are shaping new technological practices that in turn are shaping us. The rhythms of our daily lives are increasingly pulsing to a digital beat. Schools are very much a part of this new dance. New technologies are reshaping learning even as we struggle to understand their possible effects on children's formation.[1] The particular mission of Christian schools does not exempt them from this process; they, too, find themselves forced to react in one way or another to a rapid process of change. The pace of change demands reflection on how to carry forward their core vision as the landscape shifts. The same pace of change makes it challenging to carve out time and space for such reflection. How might digital technologies change the lived experience of Christian education? What new possibilities, challenges, risks, and responses are emerging? Is digital technology helping or harming the project of nurturing children and contributing to their formation?

These are big questions. While there is a growing pool of resources attempting to articulate Christian perspectives on technology, few of them offer a well-grounded empirical picture of what is happening in Christian schools.[2] In this book we approach key questions about digital technology and Christian education through close attention to the day-to-day practices of actual schools. We draw on extensive data from classroom observations, focus groups, surveys, and school documents. From this data, we will be tracing the ways in which Christian teachers, learners, administrators, and parents are seeking healthy connections between new technologies and the task of maintaining a discerning Christian learning community. Their experiences and challenges offer needed resources for reflection on emerging learning practices, resources that we hope will help other schools make wise choices.

The Changing School Day

On a crisp fall day, you walk through the doors of a private, Christian high school in the American Midwest, part of a school system that, for the purposes of this book, we will refer to as Modern Christian Schools.[3] In the spacious entryway, Scripture passages and the mission statement adorn the walls amid modern, stylish decor. The glass partitions, clean lines, open space, and bright colors convey a sense of clarity and transparency. A digital display screen shows a montage of images of smiling children engaged in sports, chatting during break time, and working alone and together with laptop computers. Another screen displays the day's announcements, including today's chapel speaker.

In the welcome area a parent is in conversation with a staff member, following up on an issue that she had raised in an email late the previous evening. She wants to know more about what the school is doing to keep students away from harmful websites, having heard stories at a recent prayer meeting about students bypassing internet filters. Across the hallway, students can be glimpsed through a wall of windows working in the library. Just around the corner, two groups of students, four or five to a group, sit clustered on the floor with laptops open and, for the moment, no teacher in sight. They are independently researching a topic for their group project and collating their findings in a shared online document. All students appear engaged, alternating between working online and talking with peers about their research findings. One pauses to take a brief call from a parent, then returns to the conversation.

A little farther along, there is a brief commotion: three students seem to be imprisoning a fourth beneath some hallway furniture while a fifth captures the ruckus on video using a phone. They are working on an entry for a schoolwide competition to make a creative promotional video for the school and seem to be going for some kind of metaphor involving confinement and liberation. A passing student, not involved in the group, grins and snaps a picture, perhaps already contemplating a witty caption.

In a nearby classroom, an English teacher is sharing a student project with the class, who sit with books open to a poem about how we see others. The classroom has screens on two walls, dual projectors, and movable furniture, a combination intended to nudge the room's inhabitants away from a fixed "front" of the classroom from which lectures might be delivered. For this project, an interpretation of the poem, students have the option of creating a video or essay response. The teacher has had help from colleagues and students in learning how to work with video-editing software. The student composition that excites the teacher today is a short film that combines words and phrases from the poem with an evocative montage of images. The student has poignantly woven the faces of classmates together with the poem's reflections on how we see other people. The teacher takes the chance to raise questions about our responsibilities to those around us when we capture them in digital images and share those images online. When the video ends, some students turn to shopping online or working at other homework on their devices as the teacher talks.

Students in a social studies classroom down the hall are video-conferencing with leaders in nonprofit community organizations from across the city. Students will learn about the organizations' missions, services, and needs. They will volunteer over the course of the semester and will eventually work with the nonprofit leaders to create promotional videos or webpages for their organizations. Just across the hallway, students are painting in the art room, with their phones by their sides. As their compositions progress, they pause at intervals to record the process in digital photographs. As the teacher circulates, she reviews the history of students' paintings with them and draws their attention to the choices they have made. She pauses mid-class to email a student who is absent and to jot down some ideas in an online document for her class blog.

In religion class, students are discussing the ethics of online comment sections. They describe cruel language that they have seen posted to online debates by commenters who profess a Christian identity. The discussion focuses on how to take part in internet interactions in a way that stands by strongly held beliefs but does not descend into invective. A few students are taking handwritten notes, some out of personal preference, one out of necessity, having lost the right to use a laptop in class through addictive behavior that left him lost in the screen and oblivious to the classroom process around him. Others are using laptops and recording notes in Google Docs. An English language learner checks her phone app frequently for translation assistance to help her keep up with exchanges in her second language. After quickly looking up a couple of words, she contributes a comment to the discussion. Later, several students who have finished the assigned task early play a video game or check sports scores. Another checks his chemistry grades in the online gradebook. A poster on the wall lists the discipleship practices that are intended as a Christian framework for engaging in learning.

Faith, Technology, and Schooling

The behaviors just described are a composite, sketched on the basis of many visits to several schools, but they offer a picture of the kinds of things that might be encountered on any given day. Few of them were happening in quite this way before the schools became early adopters of a one-to-one technology program and the process of technological evolution that came in its wake.[4] These behaviors reflect developments in our wider culture, which is passing through a period of unusually rapid change in its technological practices. A host of portable devices, online platforms for e-commerce and social interaction, and tools for generating media content have achieved massive familiarity in North American culture in a short span. Not too long ago, most learning was mediated by the teacher and limited by what the teacher knew and what the school library held. School textbooks were not typically thought of as carrying dangers of addiction, there was little worry of harmful material being accessed via learning materials, and shopping had to wait until after school. Students worked largely in the medium of handwriting, with little audience beyond the teacher, and the community was not interconnected from dawn to well after dusk. All of that and more has changed.

Christian schools are typically committed to intentionally nurturing and working out of a particular set of stories, values, and commitments. They seek to shape a school culture that honors God and contributes to students' spiritual and moral formation. They are often concerned to avoid drifting from their faith and mission as time goes by. In recent years, the influx of new technologies has been provoking far-reaching changes in how a school community functions and how students experience schooling. These still-recent and still-changing technologies are reshaping how community members process information, interact, inhabit their surroundings, and relate to the wider world. Schools, including Christian schools, are in the process of adapting.

The pace of change dictates a degree of improvisation in schools' responses to new technologies, whether they have invested heavily in technology programs or are simply responding to students' increasing connectivity. As often happens with new technologies, digital technologies have rapidly become part of the new normal, passing from the initial rush of enthusiasm and concern into a taken-for-granted toolset used to navigate each day. The pace of innovation creates pressure for this to happen before there has been a chance to reflect clearly on what normal should look like, or on the unintended side effects of change. The rapid spread of new devices and capabilities challenges a community's ability to articulate, even to itself, how it wants to live with them. It also brings a sense of excitement and possibility, of perhaps being able to move beyond some of the traditional limitations of formal schooling. One teacher at the schools studied in this book (schools that have worked hard to articulate their Christian vision for digital learning) vividly expressed this sense of uncertain improvisation:

> I don't feel as though we really know yet, because it is relatively new and how do we best use this? And is there too much? These are questions we are in the process of asking and finding out kind of trial and error.... So it's hard to say "here's how to be a good steward of technology, here's our philosophy of technology in connection with our mission statement." I don't think we're there yet because we don't know. We've got to play with it a little more and see what goes well and what doesn't.... What is education now with this new tool? ... And not just school, I think church also.... So [we have] all those questions, like "What exactly is school again? Why are we here?"

Why indeed? What ideas about student formation and flourishing might guide Christian schools' technological practices? This book sets out to explore the relationship between a faith-based vision of education and the rapid technological change that is reshaping schools. It is not an addition to the various books that have articulated Christian theological or philosophical accounts of technology.[5] It is instead a detailed account of how the process of technological change is playing out in some actual Christian schools, ones that have worked to be highly intentional in their adoption of digital technologies. The book paints a picture of the faith-meets-learning-meets-technology process from the vantage point of those intensively engaged in living it out—the administrators, teachers, parents, and students of Christian pre-K–12 schools.

The research presented in this book dives deeply into the life of a few specific schools rather than collecting aggregate data across many schools.

This means that the results are not a set of lawlike generalizations, and the conclusion will not be that "technology always causes X." At least some of what we find may unfold differently in a different school with different contexts, priorities, and strategies. What we gain, however, is the ability to step down from generalizations to describe particular, rich examples of how things are working out and the decisions being made as communities respond to change. We hope that this approach will provide insights to school leaders, teachers, and parents as they process similar challenges in their own schools. Readers can make their own allowances for the ways in which their schools are different from the ones studied here. Even where there are significant differences, a closer look at other schools' experiences can help us interpret our own. This book will not set forth clear-cut, universal solutions, but instead looks for fruitful questions, fresh possibilities, and wise strategies for action. The best way to read the book is with this goal in mind.

In sum, this book focuses on what happens in a Christian school system when digital technologies begin to transform how leaders, teachers, parents, and students learn and interact. We examine how technological change is affecting the schools' understanding of their mission, the processes of teaching and learning, the effort to teach Christian discernment, the formation of students, and the nature of the learning community. How are Christian educators working to meet the challenges, mitigate the risks, and realize the potentials of learning in a digitally saturated environment? What pitfalls, solutions, and tentative ways forward are they finding?

In this opening section we will first take a closer look at the various ways in which faith connects to technology, the assumptions about technology that have informed our work, the kinds of data that we will present, and the background of the particular schools under study. Getting these matters clear at the outset will provide the necessary context for understanding the story laid out in the rest of the book.

Questions to Reflect On

The examples of the faith-meets-learning-meets-technology process presented in the book encourage readers to reflect on their own schools, asking questions like:

- Do we see any similar trends and challenges in our own school setting?
- How do we need to respond?
- What are we not addressing?
- What motivates and inspires us?

For Reflection and Response

- What questions do you have about the impact of digital technology in schools?
- What possibilities or risks related to new technologies do you think might be of concern to Christian schools in particular?

CHAPTER 2

A Faith Tapestry

How [does providing digital tools to students] integrate with faith and Christianity? I don't know that it necessarily does, but I'm sure that somebody's had to have thought it through.

Parent

In this book we are setting out to understand how technological change might be reshaping Christian schools. We are therefore particularly interested in questions about how technology, education, and faith interact. How might the presence of overarching Christian commitments influence the process of technological change, and how might technology influence faith?

The authors of one recent survey of existing research on technology in religious communities note that "when deciding how they will engage technology, religious groups often prioritize communal and spiritual values above technological affordances or advantages."[1] Understanding how technology functions in a Christian school entails close attention to communal values, not just to what devices can do or whether they affect test scores. Our focus is therefore not primarily on questions about academic performance, nor do we assume that technology is an inexorable force and look primarily for its harmful effects. Our central focus is on understanding how the mission and self-understanding of a Christian school and the formation of its learners interact with new technologies.

Faith and Technology

Schools as we know them are absent from the pages of the Bible, and the tablets mentioned in the biblical story did not come with apps. Most theologies have little to say about technologies of learning. Nevertheless, members of Modern Christian Schools spoke often, in both formal documents and informal conversations, of the importance of keeping their technology practices tethered to their Christian faith. They had invested significant time and resources in the effort to think through and articulate what this might mean in practice. This endeavor implies the ability to identify some points of contact between Christian convictions and technological practice. How might "education" and "technology" be rooted in "Christian"?

A range of frameworks for understanding how faith relates to learning have been proposed and debated in the wider literature surrounding Christian education.[2] Our interest here, however, is not in identifying the right philosophical answer to faith-learning questions but in identifying how the schools we studied actually connected faith to their technology program. Even within the cohesive Modern Christian Schools community, we encountered a variety of ways of making the connection.

Some of these ways of talking about faith and technology turned out to be ways of gesturing toward rather than defining a faith-informed approach to technology. In our conversations with school community members, we encountered recurring phrases that functioned like memes, passing from mouth to mouth and serving as shared points of reference. We heard regular references to the need to "honor God" with technology or to use technology "in a God-glorifying way." Some also spoke of using technology to "further the kingdom of God," or of "redeeming" technology. Language like this expressed shared Christian aspirations, yet we rarely heard these phrases unpacked or explained. Such signpost phrases tended to be used as if their meaning were self-evident. This allowed them to be implicitly filled with the more specific assumptions of any given speaker. They were used to gesture toward a shared faith horizon and moral imagination and may play a significant role in sustaining a shared sense of mission and orientation. But since they were not typically used to point to any specific choice or action, it was hard to glean much more from them than the desire to live faithfully.

We also heard a range of other ways of connecting faith to technology choices that were unpacked in more detail and related to particular choices and practices. As we examined focus group transcripts, school documents, survey responses, classroom observations, and teacher case studies, a cluster of key themes emerged from the data. These themes often overlapped and mixed together in the words of individual community members. Together they offer a rough map of the community's variegated sense of what it means to be a Christian educational community engaged with new technologies. We can think of them as a range of complementary strategies for intentionally keeping technology use tethered to faith commitments. Five such strategies played a pervasive role in the thinking of the various members of Modern Christian Schools.

One prominent strategy pointed primarily to the schools' *Christian mission* and how technology might serve it. The schools' mission statement was very familiar to community members, and there was evidence that, in the minds of school leaders, a focus on meeting the mission drove the adoption of new technologies. The schools understood their Christian mission in terms of preparing and nurturing students to bring change to their world for Christ. There was strong awareness in the school community that the world in which students lived and would serve in their adult lives was an increasingly digital one. The effort to teach students to live responsibly with digital technologies could therefore be understood as a direct contribution to the mission. Technology connected to faith by offering a tool for putting a Christian mission statement into practice. We explore this thread in part 2 of the book.

A second strategy involved excitement about how new technologies could *help serve student learning*. This excitement lived alongside concerns about whether some aspects of learning might be damaged, leading to the challenge of choosing when to use digital tools. Teaching and learning are at the heart of the schools' task. The evident desire of teachers to serve their students well was both an outworking of their sense of calling as Christian teachers and a reason for selectively embracing technologies that might help them to meet the needs of each student. Technology connected to faith by promising to help teachers work out their call to teach and their care for students in a more engaging pedagogy with opportunities for individualization. We investigate this thread in part 3.

A third strategy centered on the language of *Christian discernment* with technology. For some community members, this involved a focus on managing the risks of online learning, with a concern for safety and protecting moral and worldview boundaries. Parents especially worried about access to pornography, over-absorption in social media, and distraction in class. Teachers faced the challenge of a porous curriculum, with students now having immediate access to a vast range of helpful and unhelpful ideas and material. Discernment also involved a focus on teaching students to use technology ethically. Technology connected to faith by acting as an arena for concern about students' moral safety and growth. We examine this strategy in part 4.

A fourth strategy for connecting faith and technology focused on *practices contributing to student formation.* The schools' conversations extended beyond guarding boundaries to include an investment in discipleship practices intended to help lead students into a concretely lived faith. This included efforts to actively train students in constructive patterns of Christian living with technology. How might students be helped to engage in Christian ways with the world beyond the school? How might the risks of distraction through online media be countered? How might disciplines such as contemplative reading, media fasts, or sabbath help students live well with their devices? Teachers' pursuit of such questions reflected an effort to actively shape students' technology use through practices chosen with spiritual formation in mind. Technology connected to faith by acting as an ingredient in the practices that contributed to students' formation. We probe this thread in part 5.

> **Questions about Faith and Technology**
>
> • How is the mission understood and does technology serve it?
> • Is technology helping teachers to serve student learning?
> • How can we make discerning technology choices?
> • How does technology relate to student formation?
> • How is technology affecting the fabric of Christian community?

Finally, a fifth strategy reflected concern about relationships and how to foster *Christian community.* There was a resonance here with wider societal concerns about the impact of digital technologies on our social skills, quality of our relationships, and connectedness with those in our immediate surroundings.[3] The New Testament emphasis on mutual care and a common Christian school emphasis on partnership between school and home served as the backdrop for explicit efforts to use digital devices and media in ways that might enhance rather than damage community relationships. Technology connected to faith by generating attention to how relationship patterns might be changing in a digital environment. We consider this strategy in part 6 of the book.

Strategies for Wholeness

These five ways of relating faith to technology are strategies for wholeness. They are attempts to allow core beliefs and spiritual commitments to animate professional activities that might not seem obviously related to faith.[4] Although we distinguish them here for the sake of analysis, we often heard them interweave and overlap as members of the school community talked about their experience with technology. Together, they offer a tapestry of interrelated approaches to thinking Christianly about technology. If we aim to relate something as richly textured as Christian faith to matters as complex as education and technological change, we should not be surprised to find something more like a tapestry than an equation. The various threads are not mutually exclusive, as if each offered a single, fixed Christian response to technology. What we found as we watched and listened to the parents, students, and educators in our study was a complex weave of strategies for linking education, technology, and faith.

As the book unfolds, we will trace how each of these strategies informed educational decisions and practices in the schools under study. We will also consider the synergies and tensions among the various emphases and look for evidence of them being worked out in the learning process. Having described in general terms the most prominent faith strategies that we encountered, we turn next to questions about technology. What do we mean when we talk about educational technology, and how might our assumptions about technology influence the questions we ask?

For Reflection and Response

- Do you tend to think of your use of technology as a matter related to faith? Why or why not?
- Why might a range of strategies for connecting faith and technology be needed?
- If you teach in a Christian school, how is your school making the connection between faith and technology?

CHAPTER 3

What Is Technology?

You can avoid the [computer] labs, you can avoid the [laptop and tab-let] carts. You can't avoid thirty devices walking into your room each day.

Administrator

Our society seems unsure what to make of its technologies. We are flooded with mixed messages. Some assure us that the newest technologies will connect us to the world, foster democratic participation, transform education, unleash our creativity, pull back the veil of ignorance, make us productive, and provide us with ever more immersive leisure experiences. Others suggest that the same devices may erode our relationships, keep us from sleep, drown us in fake news, destroy our privacy, undermine democracy, damage children's development, or harm our health. From day to day, from article to article, we are invited to see our latest technologies as saviors or scourges, as powerful tools at our disposal or as dangerous forces reshaping us against our will. This dance of gloom and euphoria overshadows many conversations about schooling, where new learning technologies are hailed and mistrusted with equal fervor.[1]

This book sets out to contribute to the ongoing conversation about how to handle our devices, but it does not set out to prove that technology is the answer to education's ills or that it is a danger to be resisted. The goal of the book is not to take a side in the daily debate between boosters and detractors of technological culture, but rather to understand more clearly how technological change is affecting schools, in particular Christian schools. One important step toward clearer understanding is to take a look at our assumptions about what technology is and how it works.

Defining Technology

First, then, what does the term *technology* mean? It is tempting to think of technology in terms of cutting-edge devices. Yet scholarly definitions of the term encompass far more. They identify technology as the application of knowledge and effort to create tools, means, and processes that help us achieve a specific end.[2] The smartphone in your pocket is an example of technology, but so are the factories that made it and the techniques that went into its design. The complex distribution systems that brought the phone to a store near you and made you aware of its existence are also part of technology. Technology includes the ballpoint pen that might sit alongside your laptop, the spoon stirring your coffee, and the fan cooling the room. We lean on a host of technologies whether or not we have bought the latest gadget.

Now add education to the picture. Talk of educational technology might again lead our minds immediately to digital devices, but paper, pencils, books, and bookshelves are familiar examples of educational technologies, so familiar that we hardly think of them as devices.[3] Educational technology in the broad sense is not just a specific set of recent devices. It includes the various tools and techniques that we develop and apply to try to enhance the learning process, from erasers to e-readers and from paper to pixels. As we will see later, current educational technology encompasses not just laptops in the classroom but systems for reporting grades, monitoring homework tasks, and communicating with parents.

Inside or outside education, the tools and techniques that we develop have a habit of developing us in turn, changing how we live. We invent the automobile and in time find that we have changed not only the ease of getting from A to B but the layout of our communities, the likelihood of meeting our neighbors, the quality of our air, and the sources of our pride, among other things. We adopt smartphones and find that we have reconfigured not only the ease of talking to others at a distance but also our levels of distraction, our sleep habits, our awareness of the people around us, and our stress levels. We shape technology and we are in turn shaped by it in often unexpected ways.

Because technology affects us so broadly, we often experience major technological changes, especially sudden ones, as disrupting our way of life. Such changes face us with complex gains and losses and force us to rethink how to live well together and to decide whether to rush ahead or hit the brakes. We are in the midst of such changes right now. Over a very short time, digital devices and the media they access have moved to the center of our lives and many of our classrooms. Digital technologies and the practices associated with them therefore loom large in our cultural and educational conversations. That is why we focus in this book on digital technologies in schools, yet with the awareness that they are not the only technologies involved in learning.

Three Views of Technology

This broad sketch of what technology is and why it matters risks falsely implying a single, uncontested story. In fact, it is not only the impact of particular devices that is up for debate, but also the idea of technology itself.[4] Following some existing accounts, we can distinguish three broad views of technology. Technology may be understood as a tool, as a medium, or as a practice.[5] While there are many other ways of characterizing technology, this basic set of distinctions helps to highlight issues that will remain in view throughout the book.[6]

> **Three Views of Technology**
>
> • *Technology as a tool.* Technology provides an efficient means for getting things done, and we choose what to use it for. We wield it. The key question: Does it work?
> • *Technology as a medium.* Technology provides an environment we interact with. This environment shapes us and biases our choices. The key question: How is it influencing us?
> • *Technology as a social practice.* The particular practices that we adopt as we work with our technologies will shape what technology does for us and to us. The key question: What technological practices does our community adopt?

Technology as Tool

Seeing technology as a tool suggests that it is simply a means for getting something done. It is something to be taken up or put down at will and used for one purpose or another. It is neither good nor bad in itself; the user determines whether it will be used to help or to harm. A hammer can be used to hit nails or to assault a neighbor, but the difference in outcome is not the hammer's fault. This tool perspective sits easily with an optimistic view of technology as something that lets us do more as long as we choose the right goals, though there may also be concern about how our tools increase our capacity for harm when we choose badly. Social media can be used to bully or to encourage. A laptop can be used to research for an assignment or to play video games in class. In the tool view, each of us controls whether our tools are used for good or ill. Technology itself is seen as a neutral conduit, indifferent to our choices. The main question for the technology itself is therefore whether it works. Is it effective at achieving what we set out to do?

Technology as Medium

Viewing technology as a medium, as an environment within which we move, points in another direction. This perspective suggests that when we work with a particular technology, we are shaped by the technological medium. Painting with brushes and watercolors, spray cans and stencils, or fingers and acrylics will shape the kind of picture that emerges, and a person with a paintbrush will look at the world differently from a person with a digital camera. Technology is here seen as playing a role in predetermining the kinds of outcomes that flow from its use. The implicit biases inherent in our technologies shape our thinking and behavior and nudge us toward particular outcomes with or without our conscious awareness. Unlike the tool perspective, this view of technology as a medium results in an emphasis on how technology shapes and controls us. Regardless of our constructive intentions, perhaps communicating via email shapes our relationships differently than when we rely on writing letters or talking face-to-face. The question for technology in this perspective is how it influences us.

Technology as Social Practice

The third view approaches technology through the lens of social practice. This view shares with the technology-as-medium view the recognition that technology has inherent biases, but also notes that tools and techniques are taken up within patterns of practice that make a difference to how they function in particular communities.[7] Technology is something we do, and we can do it in varying ways. Perhaps one family has a television in each family member's bedroom, while another restricts television to the family room and limits media consumption to two hours a day, while a third uses the television only for viewing educational videos and Skyping with Grandpa. Here technology is neither just a neutral tool nor a medium that always pushes us the same way. Intentionally or unintentionally, we build patterns of practice that have a big say in what technology does for us and to us. The central question here is about what technological practices we build and what convictions inform them.

The persistence of all three views might suggest that each has hold of at least some truth about how we experience technology. When we pick up a screwdriver to extract a screw, it is hard to sense more than tool use. It may well be true at some broad level that humankind-with-screwdrivers has been reshaped, but it is hard to sense picking up a screwdriver as a challenge to our commitments or our ability to live with integrity. In such cases the technology-as-tool story seems to make intuitive sense. Social media impinge on us in a rather different way, triggering widespread concerns about their effect on our happiness, our ability to relate well to others, our chances of knowing the truth, and our use of time. For many of us, it would take effort to see them as simply one tool among others for passing idle time; they seem more obviously to offer a medium that shapes us. Yet we do more than just give in; we also push back. Attempts to structure technology use through internet filters, family curfews, technology fasts, limited hours for online play, and the like witness to our ongoing attempts to responsibly shape our experience of technology. We seek life patterns that allow us to domesticate technology within our beliefs and values, and here the third view feels plausible.

Each of the three perspectives also carries risks: naïveté about the degree to which our tools shape us, exaggerated pessimism about the value of new tools, or an overestimation of our ability to conquer our own formation through intentional choices. While there are important debates here about how technology relates to society, it may be practically helpful to sustain an awareness of all three possibilities. Technology comes to us as a tool that lets us get things done, as a powerful shaper of our identities, and as an important ingredient in our social practices, bound up with our choices about what kind of community we want to be. Perhaps keeping all these pictures of technology in play can help us ask good questions, moving us past a simplistic "Is technology good for schools?" or "What is technology doing to our kids?"

Key Questions

We will find echoes of these three perspectives in the reflections of Modern Christian Schools community members as they describe their experience of teaching and learning with digital technologies. We will be tracing the various answers that they have found to the questions that these perspectives generate: What do digital tools enable us to do? How do they affect our formation? What practices should we develop to channel their use? Administrators, teachers, parents, and students alike wrestled with these questions as their schools developed the technology program.

We will be examining in later chapters some of the things that digital tools have allowed teachers and learners to achieve in Modern Christian Schools classrooms. This book is not, however, primarily concerned with the success or otherwise of digital tool use. We will not be pursuing questions about whether learning with digital tools has increased academic performance. Our main emphasis will fall more on how digital technologies are changing the environment within which Christian learning is taking place and on how the Christian commitments of Modern Christian Schools are shaping their technological practices. At the heart of our account are questions about how technological change is both affecting and being affected by the pursuit of Christian mission, learning, discernment, formation, and community. Such questions are more enduring than questions about whether a specific device is effective as a learning tool, given the speed with which devices come and go. They also allow us to explore not only how digital technology is reshaping schooling but also what it might be that makes Christian schools Christian.

Before turning to the data, one last preliminary task remains, and that is to describe the research methods that have shaped what we were able to discover and ground its reliability. What kind of data might allow us to do some justice to questions about faith, technology, and learning? And what research methods might provide us with such data?

For Reflection and Response

- What is an example from your own experience of technology functioning as a tool, as a medium that shapes you, or as an intentionally chosen pattern of practice?
- Which of these three views of technology most instinctively appeals to you? Why?
- How might our basic view of what technology is influence how we think about its role in education?

CHAPTER 4

What This Book Offers

We will truly need the power of prayer. Have you ever been traveling
so fast that you didn't realize you were moving?

Teacher

Teachers at Modern Christian Schools have sometimes felt that their world
has changed so fast that it is not easy to gain a clear perspective on what is
happening. The pace of change challenges our ability to rethink what we
are doing. How can we gain an accurate understanding of how technological change is affecting faith-based school communities, and of how those
communities are managing the process of change? Tackling this question
faces us with choices about what lines of inquiry to pursue, what data to
gather, and which research methods to apply. This chapter explains the
choices that guided our research design and the kinds of things it allows
us to know. The chapter also offers some advice on how to read the various
kinds of data presented in the book.

As we have already mentioned, even though there is a large literature
on educational technology, there has been very little empirical research
about new technologies in Christian schools.[1] There are few existing models for research that examine educational technology use in relation to specific faith commitments and mission emphases.[2] It is at this nexus that the
Technology and Educational Flourishing project (TEF) was formed. The
TEF project, supported by Calvin University's Kuyers Institute for Christian Teaching and Learning and with funding secured through assistance
of the Issachar Fund, drew together a multidisciplinary team of four scholars who recognized a crucial need for research that could probe the gap in
research on technology and faith-based education. The TEF research team
knew it was important to develop a robust research design that would allow
us to explore the complex, multifaceted realities of technological change
in faith-based school communities.

CONTEXT

Such designs begin with conceptualization of the research study, and we began by asking ourselves a series of key questions. Could we identify one or more Christian schools with a mature one-to-one technology program? To what extent would such a program be intentionally designed around the schools' Christian mission? How might we design a project that could answer multiple research questions? Could the design examine technological shifts over time? What methods might capture the ways various individuals within the school community thought about and used technology? How might we be able to compare and contrast what members of the school community say about their beliefs or practices and what they actually do?

The conceptualization phase led to the selection of schools. We selected a pre-K–12 Protestant Christian school system in the American Midwest with over 1,500 students and over one hundred teachers. This is the school system that we refer to as Modern Christian Schools. This school system was an enthusiastic early adopter of digital technologies, beginning with a one-to-one laptop program in the middle school and then expanding over five years to all grade levels. Selecting a Christian school system with a mature technology program was purposeful. It helped ensure that the school system was beyond some of the early implementation hurdles that are often reported in the first years of one-to-one programs.

We wanted to study a school system that was living intentionally with new technologies and already thinking through and responding to their strengths and weaknesses. The selected school system was articulate and intentional about the goals of technology integration from the start. Before choosing to invest in a full one-to-one program, school leaders visited other technology-rich schools. They held discussions with leaders, board members, and teachers and ran a pilot program in the middle school. Using what they learned, school leaders established a vision for the program. The school system eventually expanded technology integration through new hiring, extensive professional development, and investment in technology infrastructure and building renovations to support the vision.

School leaders shared with us several features of their initial vision for the program. They wanted to transform teaching and learning in a more creative and student-oriented direction by integrating digital technologies into educational practices. Several of them expressed a commitment to "fundamentally changing education." At the same time, the school leadership clearly emphasized that their investment in technological change was being driven by the schools' mission, not by the attractiveness of new devices per se. This missional focus reflected a well-established history of the schools placing teaching and learning within an explicitly Christian frame. The desire to innovate educationally as an outworking of a specifically Christian mission shaped technology goals. Over time, the high school won recognition for its technology program and provided leadership to other schools seeking advice as they moved ahead with digital technologies. This setting offered us the opportunity to study the dynamic changes brought about by new technologies within a Christian school system committed to thoughtful engagement and marked by highly capable practice.

Most of the research focused on this school system, but we selected two additional groups of participants to provide comparisons in the survey data. One group included high schoolers from an American Midwest, Protestant Christian school influenced by similar traditions as our focus schools, and just a few years into a one-to-one technology program. We refer to this school as Western Christian School. A second group included students at a nearby Christian liberal arts college (henceforth Liberal Arts College). Including college students in our study allowed us to compare the alumni of the schools already mentioned with students who had not been enrolled in a high school with a one-to-one program.

The conceptualization phase also led to the development of specific research questions. Among the many possibilities, we chose to pursue questions that led into rich description of how technological change is playing out within specific Christian schools. We developed multiple research questions with input from the school community itself. These included questions such as the following: How do new technologies interact with the schools' mission and core values? How does this

> **School Research Sites**
>
> Primary
> *Modern Christian Schools.* A pre-K–12 Protestant Christian school system. Mature one-to-one technology program. Research participants included administrators, parents, teachers, K–12 students, and alumni.
>
> Secondary
> *Western Christian School.* A Protestant Christian school system. Relatively new one-to-one technology program. Research participants included high school students and alumni.
>
> *Liberal Arts College.* A nearby Christian liberal arts college. Research participants included alumni of our research schools as well as college students who were not alumni from a one-to-one technology program.

interaction shape institutional and individual beliefs and practices? How are new technologies influencing teaching and learning? In what ways are student development and formation shifting in response to the schools' broader changes?

The very choice of questions calls for particular ways of approaching the research. With an emphasis on dynamic change and understanding practices in context, no single research method or paradigm would capture what we needed. The strength of the research design would come from drawing on multiple paradigms and methods to understand the complex nuances of technological practices and beliefs across the school system and over time. The resulting research design is referred to in social science as a fully integrated mixed design.[3] This design incorporated multiple research methods over three years.

Classroom Observations

We used classroom observations to investigate the teaching and learning practices in action across the school system. Our research team observed seventy-five teachers randomly selected from kindergarten through twelfth grade and across all schools in the system. Teachers were observed for a period of 30 to 45 minutes each over the course of one year. The observations offered a baseline of sorts, a view into the everyday practices of teaching and learning. They also offered a point of comparison to see if what community members described in focus groups, school documents, and surveys aligned with what we observed in practice.

Surveys

We designed and implemented surveys of students, teachers, parents, and alumni. We surveyed students and teachers multiple times and also surveyed students and teachers from the comparison groups described above so that we could compare results from within our target school system to those from another school and other alumni. We designed survey questions to be comparable across surveys of parents, teachers, students, and alumni. The content of the surveys included basic demographic and academic information, as well as questions about school practices, the effects of technology, and individual beliefs and practices.

Focus Groups

We conducted thirty-six focus groups with administrators, parents, students, and teachers spread across the three-year research project. The focus groups consisted of four to ten members. Focus group questions were semi-structured, beginning with an established set of questions, yet allowing researchers the opportunity to extend or add questions on the basis of participant answers. The focus groups provided space for school members to give voice to their perception of how new technologies were shaping school practices. These focus groups also allowed researchers to pursue emerging questions in years two and three in response to data collected and emerging analysis. Including a wide sampling of school community members in focus group conversations allowed us to compare whole-school positions with a range of individual perceptions and concerns.

Case Studies

We conducted unit-long case studies in six classrooms (second-grade social studies, fourth-grade science, seventh-grade math, high school chemistry, high school English, and high school Bible). The classrooms were selected on the basis of multiple factors, including their identification by administrators and colleagues as being led by teachers who "thoughtfully" integrated technology and learning. During each case study, we observed and recorded field notes; video- and audio-recorded the lessons; collected teacher-developed materials, student work samples, and other relevant artifacts; interviewed the teacher before, during, and after the unit; and interviewed groups of students. Like the classroom observations, the case studies provided insight into actual teaching and learning practices but did so in a way that allowed us to capture the intricacies of how day-to-day life in a classroom unfolded over time.

Document Analysis of Digital Files

We asked the schools for any digital documents and artifacts relevant to understanding their engagement with technology since the beginning of the one-to-one laptop program. The schools provided 28,184 electronic files covering more than a decade. The initial files included much that was irrelevant to our research questions (software manuals, travel receipts, apps, etc.). After reviewing all files, we identified 815 as meriting closer analysis. These included meeting minutes, professional development plans, policy documents, course proposals, communications to parents, school magazine articles, records of presentations, promotional material, handbooks, discussion notes, and individual journals. The artifacts range from polished public statements to informal reflections. The 815 core artifacts offered insight into how the schools' ideas and policies had developed over time and allowed us to compare the findings of observations and focus groups with official stances and the gradual evolution of whole-school perspectives.

As data was collected, the research team began the process of analysis and interpretation. We applied unique analysis methods to each set of data guided by best practices in social science research. For example, survey data was cleaned and then analyzed through descriptive, univariate, and multivariate statistics. Focus group data was transcribed into a written text, and then researchers developed and applied codes (discernment, community, etc.) to explore recurring themes in the data. The detailed description of the analysis for each individual method is beyond the scope of this chapter but is available in the appendix for those who wish to examine the methods of data analysis in more detail. For now, the concluding stage of data analysis, the ways in which the findings informed one another, is more important. We used a set of established social science analysis techniques (e.g., triangulation, constant comparison, exploring outliers) to interrogate emerging themes within and across data. So, for instance, if teachers in a focus group speak of students using technology to interact with the world outside school, we need to check other data sources before arriving at general conclusions about how much this happens. Do teachers across subject areas share the same perception? Do parents or administrators? Is this emphasis reflected in school documentation, or noticeable in the classroom conversations we observe? What do surveys tell us about whole-community perceptions? Through this continual process of integrating and examining findings and themes both within and across data sources, we were able to increase the extent to which the study's reported findings are valid.

From conceptualization through analysis and interpretation, the research design supported the Technology and Educational Flourishing research team's end goal. We wanted the study to shed light on the lived experiences and changing beliefs and practices of members within a Christian school community embracing new technologies. It was the very choice of multiple methods that generated the breadth and depth of data necessary to describe change within a dynamic, complex system.[4]

How to Read This Book

The research design just outlined has implications for how the findings in the following chapters should be read. Especially those less familiar with the various kinds of educational research should pause here to get clear about what these kinds of research can and cannot tell us.

At times in the chapters that follow, we will provide statistical data drawn from surveys and observations. These statistics provide the most reliable indication of the degree to which specific beliefs are held or practices are reported consistently across the school system. They do not, however, provide nuanced insight into how various different community members are thinking. That is why we will also frequently provide quotations from individual administrators, teachers, parents, and students drawn from focus groups, documents, and open-ended survey questions. These give us a more nuanced sense of what individuals are wrestling with and how they are connecting faith, technology, and learning. Coding the data for repeating themes across multiple focus groups provides confidence that the quotations from individuals are variants on thoughts shared by others across the school community, but this does not show that everyone shared the idea expressed. The quotations offer insight into the varied thought processes of the community, not a broad statistical generalization. We have indicated where appropriate that "many" or "some" participants expressed an idea, but the nature of the data does not allow turning this into meaningful numbers. Statistics and more textured samples from community members' own words each offer a different window into what is happening. It is when they are combined that we gain a richer and more robust picture of what is happening. Each kind of data should be read as a jigsaw piece building toward the whole picture, rather than as an isolated proof.

This applies to other methods too. School documents, for instance, let us see what ideas were felt important enough to be recorded, and how they were articulated as policy. They do not tell us how many people in the school system shared a particular idea or read a specific policy. Nor do documents tell us whether what is described in them really reflects daily practice. Conversely, simply watching classroom practice does not on its own tell us whether what is being done reflects what was intended when programs were designed (school documents can help with this). Case studies, on the other hand, offer a rich understanding of classroom practices and perspectives, including a teacher's rationale for a particular pedagogical design and students' understanding of what is going on in a specific curricular unit. Yet case study data represents a select handful of

CONTEXT

classrooms at the schools and cannot on its own be generalized to all classrooms. Randomized observations help here. Here again, the documentary analysis, classroom observations, and case studies are each part of the jigsaw, helping to build toward a more accurate overall picture. Drawing too many conclusions from one data source would be a little like completing the sky portion of a jigsaw puzzle and concluding that the whole picture will be blue.

Given these realities, we debated how to structure the book. Long, multi-threaded chapters might help keep in view the importance of waiting for the whole picture to emerge from multiple kinds of data. We decided, however, for shorter chapters focused on particular issues, given our hope that the book will be useful for practitioners. We hope that this structure will make it easier for readers to digest and reflect on specific issues. The reflection questions at the end of each chapter are meant to help with this process of taking each particular zoom into the data and making connections to your own context and responsibilities. They may also be useful for discussing the material with others.

Remember, though, that no chapter aims to reach definitive and comprehensive answers by itself. Instead, each chapter offers a research-based glimpse into the life of a particular set of schools, and aims to provoke fruitful reflection to inform other educators' work. Other chapters will fill out the overall picture. The society-wide nature of technological change means that you are likely to face many of the same questions and concerns, though the results may look a little different where you live. We hope that this book will help you to think about current changes more clearly and to learn about constructive ways forward from the efforts of the teachers and administrators at Modern Christian Schools.

For Reflection and Response

- This chapter describes five kinds of data collection that have fed into this book. What might each be able to tell us about what is happening in schools that the others might miss?
- How might you be able to use the findings in this book to constructively inform the work of your school or educational context?

CHAPTER 5

Modern Christian Schools in Context

Recognizing that technology and the use of the Internet are one of the most impactful things changing our world today, the future direction of the technology program at Modern Christian Schools became increasingly clear. If it was the mission of the school to prepare the minds and nurture the lives of a student body that will bring change to the world for Christ, then students needed to be equipped and empowered through a one-to-one initiative where each student would have 24/7 access to his or her own laptop or tablet. A one-to-one initiative would allow students to harness the collaborative and creative power of . . . technology. Learning has changed forever at Modern Christian Schools.

School document

The decisions that have shaped technology use at Modern Christian Schools were not made outside time and place or against abstract criteria. They have taken shape within a tangle of tradition, context, and conviction that has complex roots. We begin, then, by exploring those roots. Modern Christian Schools have a specific sense of purpose, are rooted in a particular community, and draw on a tradition of curricular choices. How have these shaped decisions about digital technologies?

Vision: Multiple Currents

Modern Christian Schools began in the first half of the twentieth century as a single, parent-run, K–8 grade school,[1] backed financially and philosophically by Reformed churches and led by a Christian school society. Supporters desired a school with a thoroughly Christian curriculum that could compete with the quality of the public schools. Classes were initially taught in Dutch and English, to help students understand the Dutch sermons and catechisms of their Dutch-immigrant churches, and to keep the faith relevant to English-speaking young people. To maintain doctrinal purity, parents and faculty were required to commit to the historic Reformed confessions.

Two currents within this focus on Reformed identity have been influential since the schools' inception. The first was concerned with preserving piety. Personal piety and a desire to remain faithful to God's leading compelled the first Dutch settlers to leave the Netherlands and settle in the area where the school would later be founded. With their emphasis on the Dutch language and Calvinist beliefs and their concerns about American culture, the settlers insulated themselves from outside influences.[2] Establishing a school focused on Christian teaching further separated families from those who attended public schools. A second current flowed more in the direction of cultural transformation. The influence of Dutch theologian Abraham Kuyper's view that every square inch of human existence is open for Christian transformation and under God's care and control motivated some immigrants as they pressed for Christian education.[3] They believed that they could culturally transform society on the basis of Calvin's ideas about life in community.

These two currents, with their inward (community piety) and outward (cultural transformation) trajectories, could work together. Faithful piety could be sustained if children had Christian schools and teachers to shape their ways of living and thinking. Influencing society could happen if children were trained in Christian schools to engage in all spheres of society in ways rooted in their faith. The two emphases could also be in tension. The pietistic emphasis inclined toward separation and purity, while the Kuyperian emphasis pushed for engagement with the world in order to influence and transform it. As this dynamic unfolded, a further emphasis emerged that connected learning how to engage the broader society with functioning well economically. This was seen as another way of being faithful to God's call.

These currents were channeled by the experience of immigrants working to preserve their faith identity while engaging their new cultural context from out of that identity. The varying emphases that resulted continue to shape present discussions, as we will see in later chapters. For instance, the concern for preserving boundaries influenced conversations about filtering and access to inappropriate content on the internet. At the same time, part of the appeal of laptops was their offer of tools for engaging the world, interacting with ideas, people, and places beyond the school walls. Laptops, it was felt, might allow students to come to know and influence the varied square inches of God's world, as well as provide skills needed for good employment.

Context: The Local Community

During the 1920s, Modern Christian Schools had considerable presence in the community, enrolling 20% of local children. Its role was tested when a proposed amendment to the state constitution called for abolition of parochial schools, but the amendment failed statewide, with a large majority opposing it in the Modern Christian Schools locality.[4] Today the area supports a Christian college and seminary and public, charter, private, and parochial schools. Modern Christian Schools remain a visible and respected option within the local educational culture. Nevertheless, the process leading to their adoption of new digital technologies was framed by several significant changes in their relationship to their community.

One important change has been in the composition of the student body. The number of students coming from Reformed churches declined from 90% of the student body in the 1970s to 54% by the early 2000s, though the percentage seems to have grown again in recent years, with 76% the most recent figure reported to us. This led to an adjustment in expectations, with parents and teachers no longer expressly required to adhere to the historic Reformed confessions. Teachers are still required to be members of Reformed churches, and at least one parent in each family is expected to be a member of a Bible-believing church. Now the more than 1,500 students come from over twenty denominations and 160 churches.

The size of the student body has also changed over time. Trends in enrollment have reflected national birth rate trends. Less than a hundred students attended in the schools' first year. The 1960s saw a high of over 2,500 students, but from the 1990s to the early 2000s there was a 30% decline. Besides demographics, this downward trend reflected a growing homeschool movement and interest in public charter schools. It was during this time of numerical decline and increased competition that school leaders began exploring facility renovations and a one-to-one laptop initiative.

There have also been changes in the surrounding population and how Modern Christian Schools are positioned relative to it. At the time of our study, Modern Christian Schools were part of a thriving small city and drew from a broader urban area of over 100,000 people. Hispanic and Latino immigrants made up nearly one-fourth of the city's population. The Modern Christian Schools student body was mostly white. Less than a tenth received a free or reduced lunch, compared to nearly two-thirds in the more diverse public schools. When Modern Christian Schools began their laptop program, 97% of school families had internet access in their homes, with high speed internet access in 65% of the homes.[5] Many families at Modern Christian Schools seemed to do well economically. This helped set the stage for the arrival of costly digital technologies.

Curricular Choices

Approaches to curriculum and instruction at Modern Christian Schools have always evolved in interaction with state requirements, religious beliefs, and national trends. Early in the schools' history, the state attorney general ruled that parochial and denominational schools could not receive free textbooks from the state. The principal responded by writing a distinctively Christian curriculum plan that strove to match or exceed the public-school curriculum. He also authored teacher and student guides that reflected an American patriotic tone. During World War I, English became the language of instruction, further encouraging the process of Americanization and acceptance of American pragmatism and materialism.

In the late 1900s, lecturing and study of prescribed textbooks were the most common instructional activities. Additional activities such as experiments, learning stations, field trips, and community speakers supplemented the curriculum. Digital technology use appeared in the mid-1980s as high school teachers began to use digital calculators and computer-assisted learning. By 2000 the schools had established computer labs and laptop carts for accessing resources and creating small projects and presentations. This expansion of digital technology use happened alongside a multiphase facilities renovation plan spanning nearly twenty years. This plan focused on updating and remodeling facilities to meet future teaching and learning needs, build community, and be "equipped for tomorrow."[6] However, substantial changes to teaching and learning did not result, leading to a felt need among leaders for further innovation.

In the early twenty-first century, Modern Christian Schools moved toward full immersion in a technology-rich environment where every student had a device. This move began at the middle school, where grading software was piloted schoolwide, and teachers and school administrators received laptops for teaching and learning. School leaders decided to adopt a one-to-one laptop program for grades 6–12 with the conviction that this would serve the schools' mission of preparing students to "bring change to the world for Christ." With a shift of the primary focus from content to pedagogy, teachers in grades 6–12 received laptops first for their instructional and managerial tasks. They were encouraged to employ the laptops as much as possible in their teaching, with the expectation that in the following year implementation of student laptops would begin.

One-to-One Technology

Sixth graders received their laptops in the first year of the one-to-one initiative, in the mid-2000s. According to the schools' own reports, "the tremendous success of that pilot program—an assessment shared by teachers, parents, and students—let the Board expand the program." In the second year of the program, additional middle schoolers received laptops for use at school and at home. Each year another grade or two was added, and three years after full launch all of grades 6–12 were participating, with grade 5 added soon after.

The next major shift involved tablets at the elementary level. In the sixth year of the one-to-one initiative, grades 2 and 4 piloted the provision of a tablet for each student for use during the school day. The following year all students in kindergarten through fourth grade received tablets.

These shifts involved teachers in a wave of professional development, starting with large-group sessions and evolving through weekly after-school sessions and individual technology coaching. The training focused on technology skills and curricular applications and evolved from a "just in case" focus on learning technologies that might be used to a "just in time" approach focused on helping individuals learn to use technologies in their own courses. When the curriculum director left and was not immediately replaced, there was less pressure for curriculum mapping, and the technology administrators stepped in to use the professional development time for training in educational technology integration. In the same year as the tablet rollout, work on curriculum and technology was administratively combined with a focus on integrating faith, teaching, and technology.

As the schools' technology practices changed, so did their relationship to the wider world. The one-to-one initiative soon caught the attention of the education division of a computer company. Modern Christian Schools allowed the company to schedule visits for groups from other schools considering one-to-one laptop initiatives. Visitors could observe and talk with school technology leaders, teachers, and students about their work with technology. As one of about one hundred schools in the nation at that time employing laptops in a one-to-one manner, Modern Christian Schools had a conscious sense of leading the way in exploring pedagogy in the digital age. This awareness reinforced their belief that forging ahead with digital technology would support the Kuyperian emphasis on Christians contributing to and transforming the wider culture.

Technology in Context

Discussions of educational technology sometimes give the impression that change is driven simply by progress, a steady march out of the past into the realms of twenty-first-century learning. Yet the decision to move to a one-to-one technology program at Modern Christian Schools was not simply a decision to move on to the newest devices. The initiative evolved amid a complex set of influences. Contextual constraints such as changing demographics and declining student enrollment played a role. So did a particular sense of mission and the Kuyperian emphasis on claiming every square inch as belonging to Christ. Other factors included community priorities, such as the desire to ensure that students function well economically after graduation, the desire to maintain standing in the wider community, a concern for faith formation, and a felt need for pedagogical change. By the time of this study, the schools had been developing and refining their technology program in the context of their Christian goals for learning for about a decade. Modern Christian Schools offer a rich context in which to examine how technological change is unfolding within an evolving Christian understanding of educational mission. With this context in place, we turn now to that data, beginning with a focus on the schools' mission.

For Reflection and Response

- This chapter outlines various features of the context at Modern Christian Schools (summarized in the last paragraph). What difference do you think these factors might make to how the school community views and works with digital technology?
- Consider the context of your school or a school you know well. How does it differ from Modern Christian Schools? How might those differences affect its approach to technology?

Part 1 Summary

In this first part we have described the aims, methods, and context of the research described in this book. The book focuses on how technological change interacts with the faith commitments of a Christian school system. In these opening chapters we have reviewed the following facets of the context of our findings:

- Modern Christian Schools (a pseudonym) reflect a wider societal process of change related to digital technology. School practices ranging from parent communication to the nature of student assignments are changing as use of digital devices becomes common. The rate of change pushes schools into a state of improvisation, trying new ways of doing school before we can be sure of their effects.
- In our interactions with members of the Modern Christian Schools community, we identified five main interrelated strategies for connecting faith to technology and learning. Technology was approached as a tool for carrying out the schools' Christian mission, as a way to help teachers serve their students' learning and offer individual care, as a matter requiring intentional Christian discernment to maintain moral and worldview boundaries, as a factor in students' personal and spiritual formation, and as an influence on relationships and community.
- Technology includes not just recent devices but more generally the application of various tools, means, and processes to achieve particular ends. We focus primarily on digital technologies and place them in the context of three broad views of technology. Technology can be understood as a tool that helps us achieve tasks, as a medium that helps shape how we live, and as a set of practices shaped variously by particular communities.
- This book draws on a range of research methods and types of data from a Christian school system in order to build a rich and reliable picture of how technology is affecting learning practices. We draw on classroom

observations; survey data; focus groups with administrators, parents, students, and teachers; unit-long case studies; and analysis of school documents. Each type of data provides part of the overall picture; for instance, the voices of focus group participants offer insight into how various community members are thinking, while survey data let us investigate what general views are shared across the whole community. Combining these research methods allows us to confirm findings in more than one way.

• The main focus of this study is on a long-established, Reformed Christian school system that has a history of intentionally relating education to Christian faith. The school system has invested extensively and intentionally in the use of digital technology. Modern Christian Schools had a conscious sense of leading the way in exploring digital teaching and learning as part of their Christian mission to contribute to and transform the wider culture.

PART 2

MISSION

Questions about Faith, Education, and Technology

> **How is the mission understood and does technology serve it?**
- Is technology helping teachers to serve student learning?
- How can we make discerning technology choices?
- How does technology relate to student formation?
- How is technology affecting the fabric of Christian community?

An important part of understanding human practices is attending to the goals and narratives that have framed them. Practices take shape within shared stories, moral frameworks, and implicit or explicit beliefs.[1] We noted in chapter 2 that faith connects with technology in the life of Modern Christian Schools in a variety of ways (see the sidebar repeated here and at the beginning of each remaining part of the book). The five chapters in this part of the book explore one of those ways, one that was prominent especially in the thinking of school leaders. The emphasis here is on how the appeal to a Christian mission statement shaped the technology program. New technologies promise ways to make the pursuit of mission goals easier or more effective. School leaders emphasized that it was these mission goals that drove the use of new technologies as a tool to support the schools' Christian identity. What can we learn about how this worked out in practice?

To get a closer look at this line of reasoning, we first clarify the content and function of the stated mission of Modern Christian Schools. This involves taking a close look not only at how the mission is stated but also at how community members interpret it and whether they all understand it the same way (chapter 6). We then look at what other ideals, besides the official mission, might have influenced technology adoption. Has the mission statement been the sole driving force, or have other kinds of motivation shaped how technology goals are understood (chapter 7)? Next, having clarified the explicit and implicit goals of the technology program, we consider why different understandings of those goals might have developed in different parts of the school community (chapter 8). These three chapters give us a basis for understanding how mission statement language has informed the community's thinking.

In the next chapter, we turn to the community by means of survey data and take stock of the level of confidence that mission goals are being met. How is the effort to harness new technologies as tools supporting the mission working out? A decade into the technology program, do community members believe that use of digital technology has in fact supported the mission (chapter 9)?

Finally, we begin to take a broader look at the ways in which faith informs teachers' thinking about technology and education. As the other chapters have indicated, there seems to be more going on than what is articulated in the mission statement. What other faith frameworks are active in teachers' thinking (chapter 10)? This chapter serves as a transition to the themes explored in subsequent parts of the book.

The core idea put to the test in this section, then, is that the mission statement acted as the key pivot connecting faith and technology. How do members of the school community understand the mission and how in turn does this relate to technology? Does technology serve the schools' Christian mission? Examining these questions provides a glimpse into how a mission statement might inform the technology practices of a Christian school. This will leave us with other important avenues to explore, but given the importance of this line of thinking for school leaders at Modern Christian Schools, it offers a fitting place to start.[2]

CHAPTER 6

Understanding the Schools' Mission

It wasn't really a formalized "Hey, now we're going to talk about the Christian aspect of it," but it was a "Here are some of the big projects and they align with the schools' mission, and they use technology."

Teacher

Walk through the doors of Modern Christian Schools and you will find the mission statement prominently displayed. It was regularly referred to by participants in focus groups and referenced in a wide range of school documents, attesting to its familiarity across the school community. When we asked administrators what they communicate to prospective parents who visit the school, they replied, "We start at the very beginning, and we talk about mission."

The mission statement (paraphrased here to preserve anonymity) affirms that "the Modern Christian Schools community exists to prepare the minds and nurture the lives of a student body that will bring change to the world for Christ." As explained to us in focus group conversations, the statement was developed through a process that actively involved the teaching staff a few years before the one-to-one laptop program was initiated.[1] This goal-oriented mission statement was referred to regularly in our data as a shared anchor point orienting what the schools should be trying to do with technology.[2] Administrators (especially those who pioneered the technology program) insisted in strong terms that the process of technological change grew out of the schools' mission; it was, as one leader put it, "completely mission-driven." A school magazine article from early in the technology program declared that "if we are to prepare minds and nurture lives to bring change to the world for Christ, we must use the most advanced technology available to us that furthers our mission." A school document made explicit the connection in administrators' minds between the change motif in the mission statement and technological change: "Our decision to make a commitment to technology was grounded in our mission statement, preparing minds and nurturing lives to bring change to the world for Christ. We asked ourselves what was bringing change to the world more today than technology, specifically laptops, and decided this was a tool our students needed to know when they graduated."

Components of the Mission Statement

The Modern Christian Schools community exists to

- *prepare the minds* and
- *nurture the lives* of a student body
- that will *bring change to the world* for Christ.

One of the most prominent ways, therefore, in which Modern Christian Schools seek to root technology use in their faith commitments is by linking their technological choices to a Christian mission statement. A mission statement serves, in part, to fuel a shared dialogue about the aims and aspirations of a school.[3] Technology is a possible tool for fulfilling the mission. To understand how this perspective shaped practices with new technologies, we need first to understand how the schools interpret their mission. That will be the focus of this chapter.

When teachers and administrators talked about the schools' mission, they consistently divided the mission statement into three leading ideas. The schools are to "prepare minds," they are to "nurture lives," and the result should be to "bring change to the world for Christ." Each of these names a distinct emphasis in the schools' self-understanding and plays its own role in guiding policy and practice. While the mission statement was encountered at every turn and was intended as a focal point for a unified sense of purpose, there was some variation in how community members parsed it.

Minds and Lives

The "prepare minds" idea in particular varied somewhat in the way it was used in the school community. Sometimes school documents and comments from administrators and teachers framed this idea in a way that identified it with academic achievement and contrasted it with the schools' goals of Christian faith formation. For instance, a school magazine article from early in the technology program explained the contrast between the "minds" and "lives" parts of the mission by connecting the former with general academic goals and the latter with the faith context: "The 'prepare minds' portion of our mission is the desired outcome for every school, but the 'nurture lives' focus of our mission statement is limited to Christian schools. At Modern Christian we strive with zeal to provide an academically excellent education within a Christ-centered environment. Simply put, faith formation is not one aspect of our school—it IS our school!" It seems here that "nurture lives" provides the faith frame within which "prepare minds" focuses on the kinds of academics typical of any school. This kind of division was also reflected, for instance, in minutes from a school committee looking into faith and technology:

Preparing minds—content, assessment
Nurturing lives—student centered, choice, relationship building, faith
Bring change to the world—faith, real world application

Administrators pointed to the "minds" focus as the earliest connection between the mission statement and adopting new technologies. As one explained, compared to earlier times, "we know more about engaging the human brain and what it takes to do quality learning. It's high-level thinking, it's deep engagement in the learning experiences." Digital technologies seemed to offer opportunities for deeper and more active engagement by students, resulting in enhanced learning, and so adopting them could further the mission of fostering strong academic learning.[4] The same administrator also noted that there were "parallel tracks." In other words, alongside the "prepare minds" emphasis on academics, it was important to stay focused on "nurture lives" by working to integrate faith and learning. Sometimes these parallel tracks were experienced as a tension, as when an administrator commented that "one of my goals—and it's a fear sort of goal—is to make sure we don't completely set aside the rigor of providing a quality education. We're primarily an educational institution. We're a Christian institution, we've got faith formation and all that as part of it—but again . . . those aren't, to me, having to be mutually exclusive. They can both happen at the same time."

This way of understanding the mission statement ("minds" = academics, "lives" = faith formation) was in evidence whenever community members outside the school leadership referred to it in our focus groups. Students in particular consistently interpreted "prepare minds" in terms of academic skills. Asked about connections between technology and the mission statement, one student echoed many similar comments: "I think the preparing minds [aspect] is a really big one because it actually gives us physical tools to help us learn and go deeper and explore across the Internet what we're learning."

Yet on other occasions these elements of the mission statement were read differently. In those instances, it seemed that "prepare minds" was understood to include the development of a Christian mind in particular, a specific perspective and not just a set of academic skills. Another school magazine article (also from early in the technology program) argued that "part of the responsibility to 'prepare minds' is teaching young people to distinguish the valuable from the worthless, the God-glorifying from the denigrating." This sounds less like something that is simply "the desired outcome for every school" whether or not that school is Christian. As another administrator explained, "You would expect the school to have something about the mind, right? 'Prepare minds.' But that's more than just giving them an education. It's preparing their minds to discern things in technology. It's preparing their minds to defend their faith as they enter a world that can be hostile to Christianity. So, it's preparing their minds and their lives for those things as well." Here faith belongs to the "minds" component, not just to "lives" and "change." We did not, however, hear this second way of breaking down the mission statement articulated in connection with the "prepare minds" phrase by other community members outside the school administration.

The ambiguity may stem from the effort to express four ideas with three phrases. "Prepare minds" reflects a focus on learning and academic achievement, "nurture lives" emphasizes formation in community, and "bring change" points to mission in the world. The "for Christ" qualifier could be read as referring to the whole, but when school members explicitly referred to individual components of the mission statement, "for Christ" was attached only to the third phrase. This makes it ambiguous exactly how faith is to be connected to the three main goals and makes room for references to "prepare minds" that distinguish the phrase from faith formation.

It should be noted that we are focusing here specifically on how explicit mission language was used. There was a pervasive emphasis on connecting faith and learning throughout the schools, and it was generally understood, as we will see later, that faith in some way framed both academic and personal growth. Yet the variety of focus in how the mission was read colored how the benefits of technology were described by various community members, as well as how they sensed the relationship between faith and academics. A focus on academic skills fit easily with an emphasis on technology as a tool for enhancing those skills. When the focus was more on a holistic nurturing of students' lives, the effects of technology as a medium or a set of practices raised more questions. The precise relationship between these two emphases was left open by the mission statement language and read in different ways.

Changing the World

What did seem to be generally shared was the feeling that the first two parts of the mission statement are preparation for the third, which articulates a more explicit faith connection.[5] Community volunteering and service is a significant emphasis in the self-understanding of both Catholic and Protestant faith-based schools in general.[6] As we saw in chapter 5, the Reformed emphasis in the schools' heritage emerges partly in the idea that Christian education is to be oriented toward bringing about constructive change in the world, participating in the restoration of all things.[7] School leaders saw new technologies as extending students' capacity to have an impact on their world. Administrators described how this emerged as a second major legitimation for investing in new technologies. As one administrator phrased the challenge, "How do we best prepare these minds so that they can take these tools, have one foot in the world, and change the world, right at the table with anybody else, with confidence, and with the same skill level that the world has?" Another noted that "the argument was very easy to make. The laptop is transforming the world and if we're not preparing our kids to use laptops, we are not meeting our mission. It makes no sense to have a mission that states boldly we're going to make people that bring change to the world and send them out not having prepared them to use that tool in transformational ways."

Administrators pointed to a significant shift that coincided with the introduction of digital devices. There was a move (marked by a substantial community discussion) from thinking about the call to change the world for Christ as something future, taken up after graduation, to viewing it as something that can be practiced immediately through students' use of digital media. This move reflected a desire, as one administrator put it, to "enlarge [students'] world and their understanding of how they can impact their world in the name of Christ." Digital media offered ways to interact with the wider world from within the school classroom.

This third aspect of the schools' mission was the one most frequently cited in various contexts, often without including the other two phrases.[8] It seems to have come to function at times as a kind of shorthand for the whole mission. It was regularly referenced by teachers when talking about the purpose of using technology in the classroom. One teacher echoed a widely shared theme when she asked, "How do you use these tools to make the things that we see wrong, right? How do you go about dealing with poverty? How do you go about dealing with resource use, and climate issues, and all these things, from an economic standpoint? And what's the motivation behind that for someone of faith?" While a few students reported not hearing the mission statement discussed in class or viewed the "change the world" theme with skepticism, we more commonly heard students readily echo the focus on being prepared to act in the world. A middle school student, for instance, commented, "If you think about it, with technology . . . there are so many positives that can in a sense override the negatives, and we can use our laptops to do so many different cool things that we wouldn't be able to do if we didn't have it. And I feel like we can really bring change to the world for Christ through our laptops."

Teachers and students had various ways of applying this concern for impacting the world. In planning documents and focus groups, they linked this part of the mission statement to themes that included writing for authentic audiences, building a positive e-portfolio and sharing it with family, modeling Christian values in social media use, creating art for nonprofits, learning to contribute graciously and gently in online discussion forums, learning about medical uses of technology, sharing faith online, making presentations to the local community related to environmental concerns, making Christian films, preparing to serve in business or education careers, and using technology to learn about and seek solutions to global problems such as poverty. The scope of what "bring change to the world" might mean ranged from the everyday to the grandiose and could encompass evangelistic, professional, ethical, and service-oriented emphases. It led in some instances to an emphasis on being able to fix all kinds of wrongs in the world at large, and in others to intentional discipleship through small-scale, local acts of service. What the various ways of translating the phrase shared was a sense that part of what legitimates technology use in the Christian school is its capacity to provide tools that learners can use to make some kind of difference as Christians in the world. Technology was valued as a tool that might serve this mission emphasis.

Overlaps and Tensions

It was largely within the overlaps and tensions among these three ideas—extending student learning, nurturing students in faith, and making a Christian difference in the world—that the schools' thinking about faith and technology unfolded. The influence of the mission statement was strong and pervasive, yet not rigid. We found strong community awareness of the mission statement and, as we will see later, a strong shared sense that technology was supporting the key emphases of the mission. Given the concentrated nature of the mission statement and the breadth of its themes, it is also not surprising that we encountered more than one interpretation of it within the community.

Taking a closer look at some of the different strands within the school community's understanding of its shared mission can be helpful in several ways. It can open up possibilities, revealing how the same core commitments can be unpacked in a number of directions, with the mission emphases acting as a creative stimulus rather than a fixed template. It can give us a sense of whether community members can clearly articulate to one another the shared emphases to which they have committed. Finally, it can help to identify places where there are potential tensions, where community members might be committed to the same broad points of reference while actually associating them with different ideas. With these interests in mind, we turn in the next two chapters to what we learned from focus group interviews about how various members of the community remembered the role of the mission statement in the founding of the technology program and the ideas that they associated with the mission.

For Reflection and Response

- How might digital technology serve or hinder the goals of preparing minds, nurturing lives, and bringing change to the world for Christ?
- Review the stated mission of your school or a school familiar to you. In what ways might there be similarities or differences in the way community members interpret the statement? How might this affect the school's approach to technology?
- In your own educational work, what mission, vision, or orienting frameworks guide decisions about the ways which you and your students will use technologies?

CHAPTER 7

Why Technology?

> Focus on the mission and focus on getting teachers to see that it's not about the technology. . . . I've said it before: technology is not a tool. It is fundamentally revolutionary. It's not even just an evolution, it's whatever is bigger than an evolution. But it is not about the technology. It's about doing better—it's about doing better what you were supposed to be doing all along.
>
> *Technology manager*

As we saw in chapter 6, school leaders, especially those involved in starting the one-to-one technology program, were adamant that the major technology decisions had been driven by the schools' mission rather than by the lure of new devices or marketing pressures. Our focus groups with administrators, teachers, parents, and students allowed us to explore how the general phrases of the stated mission were interpreted within the specific contexts of various community members.[1] Foundational vision is formally articulated by school leaders but lived into action by the entire school community: teachers, students, parents, and staff. So how does the formal mission statement compare with what we heard from community members about the reasons for having a laptop program? What reasons did they articulate themselves, and what reasons did they recall having picked up from the schools' promotion of the program?[2] In this chapter and the next, we approach these questions by examining focus group findings. We look in particular at responses to questions about why Modern Christian Schools initially adopted one-to-one technologies. What messages from the launch were strong enough to stick and become part of the remembered story? In this chapter we will explore the range of rationales that we heard and how they might relate to the mission statement. In the next we will examine how those in different roles within the community came to understand the mission.

Transforming Teaching and Learning

One rationale for moving forward with digital technology that was re-membered as centrally important was not stated explicitly in the mission statement, though it implicitly connects to "prepare minds." It focused on the potential to shape new ways of teaching and learning. One administra-tor recalled, "[The driving motive] was not about the device, it was about learning, and we wanted them to understand that obviously the device was necessary, but it was not the outcome we were looking for. It was an educational tool, another way for kids to learn and be participating in their learning." A central goal was to leverage technology as a tool for transform-ing students' experience of learning.

This emphasis was clear in the reflections of the technology adminis-trators, who worked closely with the superintendent and board throughout the adoption of the technology program. The technology administrators were responsible for establishing the technological infrastructure, profes-sional development, and curriculum. Their understanding of the schools' motives for investing in the technology program therefore filtered down to the entire school community. The goal of transforming teaching and learning was on their minds before the one-to-one program began and was reflected in efforts to redesign learning spaces in the school. They recalled with disappointment "a big technology push" at Modern Christian Schools to incorporate laptop carts and update infrastructure several years before the one-to-one program was launched. They had hoped on that earlier oc-casion to create pedagogical change but reflected that despite the additional computers and greater access "there was not a lot of change going on."

As administrators made exploratory visits to other one-to-one schools while considering their own pilot program, pedagogy was a key focus. One recalled that during those visits "we just saw lots of technology and very little change in teaching and learning. You know, a few glitzy things that they were doing but no real change. And we said, 'You know, if that's the best we could do, then we better not do it.'"

There was a conscious effort not to be dazzled by new technologies or trends but to focus on pedagogical transformation. A few teachers also spoke broadly of the transformation of teaching and learning made pos-sible by technology. One reflected on the chance to redefine curriculum in his subject area: "I think, blow the roof off the discipline right? ... So I started just a couple of years before the launch, and at that point it was a really dated textbook that we had.... We were thinking about replacing the textbook and then thought: 'Well because of the content area, is it better to just blow the roof off of the discipline and use all of those resources that are out there.'"

This focus on transformation informed the effort to convince the Modern Christian Schools community to move ahead with the technology program. We see this in an expansion of a comment partially quoted in chapter 6:

> I also think when it came to the K–12 level, the sell—and I don't want to shortchange this because I think this is what moved it in the community and everywhere else. And so even though it might not have been the initial motivator, when we look at the decision to go one-to-one through the eyes of the mission of Modern Christian at the time—you know, "preparing minds and nurturing lives of a student body that will bring change to the world for Christ"—the argument was very easy to make. The laptop is transforming the world and if we're not preparing our kids to use laptops, we are not meeting our mission. It makes no sense to have a mission that states boldly we're going to make people that bring change to the world and send them out not having prepared them to use that tool in transformational ways.

The technology administrators, like other administrators, regularly wove additional rationales through the language of the mission statement. More often than not, when describing the technology program, they returned to the mission statement or connected a further rationale to one of its phrases. The mission statement provided a key rhetorical frame for articulating vision and obtaining consent, and through this process it became linked to a broader rationale that could be argued to be consistent with it.

Twenty-First-Century Skills

Others in our focus groups articulated reasons for adopting new technology that appealed to frameworks other than the mission statement. One of these was an emphasis on the importance of twenty-first-century skills. In contrast to the handful of teachers who spoke broadly about pedagogical transformation as the driving motive, most teachers recalled hearing this more specific rationale for the new technology program. They described Modern Christian Schools' adoption of new technologies as fueled by the need to prepare students with specific twenty-first-century skills and dispositions. Teachers gave examples such as increasing opportunities for collaboration, enhancing creativity, communicating effectively, and learning to use technology safely. When they spoke of these skills as the motivations for the technology program, they did not tend to connect them to faith concerns or to mission statement language unless specifically prompted to do so by researchers. The emphasis on preparing minds and pedagogical transformation fostered attention to the forward-looking pedagogical emphases of the twenty-first-century skills movement, and created space for the ideas of that movement to frame how learning goals were talked about.[3]

Mixed Motives

Administrators emphasized that the technology program grew out of the mission, which is "to prepare the minds and nurture the lives of a student body that will bring change to the world for Christ." Technology was to serve as a catalyst or tool that would further this mission.

Other motivations articulated alongside the mission statement included the following:

- Transforming pedagogy
- Gaining twenty-first-century skills
- Preparing for a digital future
- Improving learning
- Getting ahead

Preparation for the Future

A variant of the twenty-first-century skills theme focused more generally on preparing students for the future. This theme was articulated with two emphases: ensuring students' success in college, higher education, or a career, and preparing them for life in a digital age. Some teachers believed that Modern Christian Schools' one-to-one program was established, in part, as "preparation for work force and college." Far more teachers told us that the school embarked on the program to prepare students for a digital age, "a world of tomorrow." In our surveys, 82% of teachers and 85% of parents agreed that the use of technology at Modern Christian "helped prepare students for future education after high school." One teacher recalled, "There was a lot of talk in the beginning about the twenty-first-century learner and that we had to prepare our kids for what's in the future for them. And we don't necessarily know, but [those] technologies will for sure be an important part of their futures, so we had to get ahead of that or try to get ahead of that."

Time and time again, we heard variations of a theme that could be summarized as "we live in a digital world, students will need to succeed in that world, therefore Modern Christian Schools should adopt technology to prepare them." Parents also echoed this theme. Multiple parents suggested the schools' technology investment was rooted in twenty-first-century learning and preparation for the world of tomorrow. This theme reflected an implicit narrative about which changes matter in the wider social context.[4]

Academic Progress

Teachers and parents clearly understood that preparation for the future was contingent on students' academic progress in the present. Academic achievement in school was not mentioned often in focus groups as an explicit rationale for adoption of the one-to-one program, but it was implicitly present. Discussions of technology as an avenue for the transformation of teaching and learning were qualified by terms like *better* and *more effective*. Such language suggests that the point of the transformation is ultimately to improve students' learning in school. The initial decision to adopt technology was not framed by a concern for raising test scores or increasing academic performance, but talk in focus groups of "doing better what you were supposed to be doing all along" implied the background hope that technology would enhance academic learning.

Getting Ahead

We quoted above a teacher's comment on the need to "get ahead" of technology trends, and the desire of the technology administrators to "do it better" than other schools. In our surveys, 77% of teachers and 81% of parents agreed that "the schools' use of technology has remained at the forefront of technology and innovation."[5] Metaphors of competitive technological progress informed the community's imagination. The desire to keep up or be ahead, with its implied underlying image of a competitive race into a technology-rich future, recurred in focus groups. Parents noted that the technology endeavor was necessary to "keep up with the local schools and technology," wanting their children to be prepared at least as well as public school children for the digital age. Some teachers voiced the belief that Modern Christian Schools invested in one-to-one devices to remain ahead of the curve. For example, reflecting on how the new technology program was framed, one teacher recalled that "we were going to be cutting edge, and I think we were." At the outset, at a moment in the United States when schools were just beginning to invest more in digital technologies, it was felt that the move to a full one-to-one program with a fiscally supportive donor base might distinguish Modern Christian as an innovative leader in technology.

Completely Mission-Driven?

It is not difficult to see how these emphases could be experienced as out-workings of a mission focused on preparing students and bringing change. The desire to bring change to the world implies an idea of what kind of world is unfolding. Preparing minds and enabling students to bring change to the world have been taken to imply a set of cutting-edge skills, strong preparation, academic success, a desire to lead more than follow, and a fo-cus on social success. We heard community members joining these dots. At the same time, the broad aspiration of preparing for the future and bringing change to the world leaves space that can be filled in community mem-bers' imaginations with cultural narratives about the digital future and the competitive imperative that are less clearly connected to Christian faith.[6] When this occurs, we begin to understand how community members might become vague about key narratives, revealing that they don't know how technologies intersect with faith or mission but hope that "somebody's had to have thought it through." The fact that other rationales tended to be articulated without appeal to faith or mission statement language suggests that the idea that everything simply flowed from the schools' mission is too simply stated. These additional emphases suggest that if technology adop-tion was driven by the mission, the way the mission was understood in the wider community was also shaped by broader social aspirations and im-plied stories about success. To what extent might an expansive statement of mission such as that adopted by Modern Christian Schools function at once as a conduit for harnessing faith to transformative practice and as a screen onto which secular aspirations can be projected?

This question points us back to a distinction noted in chapter 3. On the one hand, we have a picture of technology as a tool that can be pressed into service to deliver the priorities of the mission. On the other hand, we see signs that broader social narratives about technology that tie it to future competitiveness may have provided an influential environment within which the mission was heard and interpreted. Christian schools should be asking how digital technology contributes to their mission, and also what role might be played in that mission by Christians who are less academically gifted, less economically well placed, or less technologically cutting-edge. Digital technology is easily associated with the desire to get ahead socially through educational success. We also need to consider how such desires relate to specifically Christian virtues such as charity and humility. We will see how community members worked to make these connections in later chapters. For now we simply note that the schools' mission has been interpreted, and the reasons for adopting new technologies have been remembered, amid a complex of motivations. Whether we view them as part of the rich variety of perspectives or as potential points of tension within the community's vision, these varying versions of the story of why digital technology came to Modern Christian Schools have helped shape community members' sense of what the technology program was about. In the next chapter we will look a little more closely at this process of diffusion across different community groups.

For Reflection and Response

- Which of the additional motives for foregrounding digital technology described here fit best with the schools' mission?
- In what ways would you modify or extend the schools' statement of mission to guide technology use?
- How should the mission of a Christian school and the aspirations of the wider community relate to each other?

CHAPTER 8

Communicating the Mission

> Our mission statement is different. That's who we are. We try to stay true to that.
>
> *Teacher*

The administrator who was superintendent of Modern Christian Schools at the time of the technology program launch reflected in a focus group conversation that he "led the charge off the cliff to step into this [digital] environment with some passion and purpose." He worked with other administrators, the schools' board of trustees, and a select group of teachers to begin the process of considering whether Modern Christian Schools should invest in one-to-one technology. From his perspective, the process had a single driving force:

> Our mission. The mission to prepare minds and nurture lives, and we really felt that this was a tool, if we were preparing kids to go make a difference, this was a tool that they absolutely had to have at their use, but also to help them understand how important it was to be a part of the digital world that they were going to live in and bring a faith perspective to that. So, it was mission driven. It wasn't "boy, this is a pretty cool gimmick," or "this will save money," or "this will bring in new students," it was totally mission.

This way of articulating the mission draws in some of the themes present in the last chapter—notably, preparation for an imagined future in a digital world—and places them in a Christian frame as part of how the mission is understood. One school principal actually suggested that the new technological developments "brought that part of the mission [bringing change to the world for Christ] back into a live . . . approach." The fact that it was the superintendent and principals who were most articulate about the schools' mission is not surprising given the centrality of the mission to their leadership roles. We saw in the last chapter that recollections of the rationale for adopting technology were more varied and diffuse in the wider community. What can we discover about the range of perspectives present in the school community if we take a closer look at what different groups remembered about why the technology program was originally adopted?

Administrator and Teacher Perceptions

While administrators generally guide vision and policy for new initiatives, it is teachers who are tasked with the daily realities of integrating technology into practice. Teachers are instrumental to the success of full-scale technology integration in a school.[1] Research about technology adoption and how innovations are diffused across systems reminds us that each individual within a system varies in when, how, and to what extent they choose to adopt "new" technologies.[2] The process of technological diffusion across a system is complex, slow, and shaped by multiple factors, including individual dispositions and provision of resources, training, and support.[3] In Modern Christian Schools an additional layer was the attempt to connect the process of technology adoption across the community to a particular vision of Christian mission.

We glimpse the challenge of this process in the way the various kinds of rationales described in the last chapter were distributed. We found wide familiarity with the mission statement, which was central for administrators and regularly referenced by teachers, and we also found a strong, shared desire by teachers to connect faith, technology, and learning. Yet when teachers were asked about the messages they remembered hearing regarding the rationale behind the initial adoption of one-to-one technologies, they tended to shift away from mission-specific language.[4] They opted instead for phrases that emphasized Christian commitments broadly related to the mission, but without referencing the specific mission terms. Teachers described the schools' investment in technology for the purposes of "teaching discernment, wise use of the technology," and teaching students to use technology "with a Christian perspective" and "for God's kingdom." Separately and in parallel to this they spoke of the technological changes needed to develop twenty-first-century skills. While administrators articulated connections between digital-age skills and mission-specific language, teachers generally did not articulate any such connection without further prompting by interviewers. In fact, the idea surfaced in conversation with some teachers that the emphasis on the mission had come after an initial focus on preparing students for digital skills so as to keep up with the digital world. One teacher commented, "I think originally, if I remember correctly, it was more . . . 'the technology is there, we want our students to be able to use it and be part of that world,' but I think what I hear more now is 'this is a way that they can impact the world for Christ. This is a tool they can use, one of many.' Whereas at that point it was: 'This is cutting edge. We've got to get on this.'"

Several other focus group members voiced their agreement with this account. While it was not encountered across multiple focus groups, the presence of this version of the story in the minds of some suggested some slippage between administrators' stories and at least some teachers' stories about the program launch.

The teachers' emphasis on digital skills aligned closely with frameworks for twenty-first-century skills like those emphasized by the International Society for Technology in Education or the Partnership for 21st Century Learning (P21).[5] These frameworks do not include any focus on the particular faith-informed concerns of Christian education, and so do not naturally prompt connections to the schools' mission language. As we will see further in chapters 19–20, part of the challenge of technological change for faith communities concerns language. New technologies come with new patterns of speech that may have little connection to the language used to reflect on faith. This is one of the limitations of thinking of technology simply as a tool for achieving existing goals; a new technology may come wrapped up in new ways of talking about what we are trying to do that tug us away from past speech habits and the values rooted in them. When teachers spoke of twenty-first-century skills in their responses to questions about the technology launch, connections to mission language or specific Christian concerns were infrequent. Teachers were certainly invested in connecting faith and learning, but their discussion of Christian themes usually happened separately from mention of twenty-first-century skills. Mission statement language, more general Christian themes, and talk of twenty-first-century skills seemed to function as separate clusters of talk. This might be reinforced by the ambiguous relationship between themes of academic excellence and faith formation in the mission statement noted in chapter 6.

Parent Perceptions

When parents were asked what messages they had heard about why the one-to-one initiative was launched, their responses varied widely in their recognition of the role of mission or Christian commitments as a foundation for the technology initiative. Some parents did reference mission language, speaking of "better preparing [students] to bring change to the world for Christ" or providing students with "a Christian perspective on how that technology should be used." Some parents clearly recognized mission as an original motivation for the one-to-one program. However, other parents seemed largely unaware of the role of the mission. Take, for example, the following parent response to a question about why the school originally committed to the technology program: "The only thing I can think of is the thought process behind it would be to make sure that they're prepared, so that when they do get out into college . . . they've got all the tools that any other school system would have provided their kids. How that integrates with faith and Christianity, I don't know that it necessarily does, but I'm sure that somebody's had to have thought it through." It is clear that this parent, like others with whom we spoke, believed someone had considered the way the mission shaped the technology initiative, but they were unable, even with input from other members of the focus group, to expand on the idea.

It seems, then, that as the vision for the technology program traveled from administrators to teachers and parents, the message was transformed. Much like the childhood game of telephone, in which a message is whispered ear-to-ear around a circle, losing clarity and accuracy the further it is passed, accounts of the rationale for the technology program became more diffuse the further we moved from leadership circles. This dilution and transformation of any initial vision in the vagaries of daily communication is unavoidable and even to be anticipated in schools as ideas move into actual practice.[6] That is part of what makes it important to understand the lived rationales circulating in the community and not just the official, formally articulated ones.[7] Subjective understandings of the rationale for the one-to-one program offer insight into the role of beliefs and values that extend beyond mission language. They also suggest the range of visions of what would count as success for the technology program. The mission statement clearly plays an important role, but daily community awareness of the purposes and success criteria for using technology are complex and varied.

Mixed Messages

There were, however, signs that more was at work than simple problems of signal decay as the attempt was made to spread a consistent message through the community. We also need to consider how community values might have influenced the articulation of the mission. In the early years of the technology program, parents were asked to attend orientation meetings before laptops were distributed. Various individuals remembered the initial message itself as mixed,

> **Motives for the Schools' Investment in the Technology Program**
>
> • To teach students to use technology wisely or with discernment, from a Christian perspective, and for God's kingdom
> • To develop digital-age or twenty-first-century skills
> • To prepare students for college/career
> • To ensure the school remained on the forefront of technological change

appealing to a variety of motives in the effort to secure commitment from the community. A teacher recalled concerning the program launch, "It also felt [like] a little bit of a marketing push, that this is something that we can provide that maybe other places cannot. So just another feather in our hat a little, but it was definitely to prepare [students]. This is the new wave of education and we want to be at the beginning of it and not riding behind it."

This teacher noted that distinguishing the school in its market was secondary to preparing students for the future, and yet the marketing theme still resonated enough to be remembered as an emphasis. A school principal recalled that during the original push for technology "we did unashamedly leverage the fact that Modern Christian likes to be first. . . . It's a resource-rich environment, and if they were presented a case that this could mean that our students would have a leg up, that was not a bad thing." A series of publications to school alumni and supporters reflect this intertwining of rationales, with the emphasis on mission joined with statements about how "integrating the best educational tools into the classroom has been a hallmark of Christian education since the founding of Modern Christian Schools." Appealing to existing community desires and values, including those focused on material advantage, was a way to build support for the program. As we have seen in chapter 7, the focus group data suggest that this strategic communication choice left its mark.

This suggests another dynamic in the attempt to build a shared vision for technology use. As the principal above noted, the themes of competitiveness, liking to "be first" and wanting a "resource rich" educational environment as a "leg up," already marked the culture of the school community. This culture allowed leaders to "unashamedly leverage" these themes to secure community commitment to an expensive and disruptive new initiative. This could be seen as part of the necessary politics of educational change. Yet it also points to risks. The pattern of recollections about the reasons given for a new technology program plausibly suggests that if the language of Christian mission is attached to motives of self-advancement that are strongly rooted in community culture, there is a risk that mainly the latter will be remembered as having guided the choices made. The challenge of building shared understanding of mission seems to have been not only that messages get lost in transit but that the messages in the first place made strategic appeal to a range of motives, leading to different themes being heard and remembered.

These mixed messages have persisted across a decade as rationales for continuing to invest in technology, with the emphasis on particular themes shifting over time. Perceptions of shared goals and rationales help shape professional development, teaching practice, policy development, assessment of the program's effectiveness, and communications between the school and parents, donors, and the larger community. In a community of any size, we should expect these perceptions to be varied. It is also to be expected that more visionary emphases on changing the world and forming students in faith will be intertwined with the basic tasks of preparing students for a perceived economic future and trying to help them do well in school. School leaders were more articulate than teachers and parents about the connections between skills for the digital age and Christian mission. Teachers and parents were more likely to associate the technology program's goals with values that administrators may have seen more as strategic levers or concessions to culture than as connections to their positive vision. The diversity of perspective is not surprising, but there may be questions here for other school leaders to ponder about how different sectors of the community interpret their vision, and how arguments used for more pragmatic purposes might help shape community perception and memory. What unintentional or strategic messages might be in play? Do those messages reinforce the core mission and values?

We have spent some time building a picture of how the schools' mission was understood in the school community. How confident were community members that digital technology was indeed serving as a tool that helped the schools to meet their mission? We explore this question in the next chapter.

For Reflection and Response

- Reflecting on this chapter, what glimpses do you see of how technological change might be affecting these Christian schools' sense of mission?
- Consider your school, or a school familiar to you. What motivations are commonly appealed to when changes are promoted?
- How might the way we talk about technology make it challenging to connect it to faith perspectives?

CHAPTER 9

Do Laptops Support the Schools' Mission?

I can remember the first couple of years at the high school.... You had to
help students to see past the gimmick of the computer in the classroom
... to help them to think about that as a tool for their learning, and again,
something ... driven by mission. We're learning how to use this tool
just like any other tool that comes our way in a way that will honor God,
create that positive digital footprint; we talk about that often.

Administrator

We have seen in the last several chapters how a Christian mission frames
the way many members of the Modern Christian Schools community think
and talk about the technology program. We have seen technology pictured
as a tool for carrying out the schools' particular mission. Do community
members in fact experience the schools' use of laptops as an aid in their
pursuit of the mission? In this chapter we begin to explore this question
by turning to data from surveys of teachers, parents, and students in the
Modern Christian Schools system.

While we turn to focus groups, classroom observations, case studies, and
school documents for rich and detailed accounts of how school members
think about the mission, the survey data support other kinds of investigation.
By asking very similar questions to people across the school community and
across time, we can gauge overall consensus and disagreement in the community regarding important elements of the technology program. The qualitative data from focus groups and case studies let us see the more detailed
texture of how various groups and individuals are thinking, while the survey
data allow us to check whether the focus group data are really representative
of larger patterns. The survey data also allow us to make good comparisons
across groups and between schools within the school system. In this chapter we will focus in particular on questions that we asked students, teachers,
and parents about the impact of the technology program and whether it sup-

ported the schools' mission. As we will see, student and parent perceptions on this point are generally positive, with some interesting variations.

Overall Perceptions

A first thing to note is that the school community is in broad agreement that the technology program has been helpful for the Christian mission of the schools. A large majority of parents surveyed (70%) agreed that "overall, the school's use of technology has supported the school/district's broader mission." Among teachers, the agreement was even larger (77%). This consensus also held when we asked the inverse. Only 2% of teachers and 16% of parents agreed that their school's use of technology "diminished the school's ability to fulfill its mission/vision" (see table 9.1).

Table 9.1. Technology and the mission of the schools

	Teachers	Parents
	Percentage agreement	
Overall, the school's use of technology has:		
Supported the school/district's broader mission	77%	70%
Diminished the school's ability to fulfill its mission/vision	2%	16%
Number of respondents	65	101

This level of agreement is probably to be expected given the maturity of the technology program and the substantial investment the schools made in bringing teachers and parents up to speed at its inception. Moreover, most of the parents and many of the teachers entered the community after the laptop program was already in place and well established. Teachers who resisted the technology program are likely to have left the school before our study began, and parents supportive of the approach were drawn to the school. As will become clear after this tour of survey results, while parents and teachers were quick to discuss specific concerns regarding the technology program in face-to-face conversation, the vast majority were, on balance, supportive of the kind of education that the laptops enable. More specifically, they believed that it helped the schools' mission.

Minds and Lives

We saw in the last few chapters how different members of the school community emphasize distinct aspects of the mission. How strongly was technology felt to support the mission in response to survey questions that broke down the mission statement into its constituent parts? We asked participants a number of questions related to "preparing minds," "nurturing lives," and "bringing change to the world." When we break these questions down by category, we start to see some noticeable differences between the views of teachers, parents, and students. Participants were optimistic about the impacts of technology for the intellectual and the world-changing goals of the school, but they expressed mixed views about the impact of the technology on students' faith formation. We will take a closer look at each aspect of the mission statement in turn.

Table 9.2. Technology's impact on the goal of preparing minds

	Students	Teachers	Parents
		Percentage agreement	
Overall, the school's use of technology has:			
Improved students' inquiry skills		72%	83%
Helped develop students' critical thinking and problem solving		69%	63%
The use of digital technology at our school has:			
Helped me/students understand difficult ideas in my/our class	71%	72%	
Helped me/students develop ideas that went beyond what was presented in class or assigned materials	83%	88%	
Number of respondents	533	65	101

As we saw in chapter 6, the goal to "prepare the minds" of students was widely taken to refer to academic goals. Survey questions asking about the impact of technology on this component revealed solid approval. The use of digital technologies was felt to have had benefits for students in terms of problem solving, critical thinking, and inquiry skills (see table 9.2). Students shared the view that the new technologies had helped them both to understand material and to extend their learning beyond what was assigned or explained in class. These results echo the strong emphasis on improving learning that informed the connections made between the mission and technology early in the schools' technology program. When the schools invested in training teachers to integrate digital technologies into teaching and learning, there was a substantial focus on these academic goals.

Table 9.3. Technology's impact on the goal of nurturing lives

	Teachers	Parents
	Percentage agreement	
Overall, the school's use of technology has:		
Enabled an effective focus on character formation	35%	31%
Contributed positively to the formation of a spiritually enriching learning environment	51%	40%
Encouraged the exploration of the world from a biblical perspective	51%	47%
Number of respondents	65	101

The goal to "nurture the lives" of students was more closely associated by community members with aspirations for students' faith formation and spiritual health. When we asked questions probing the relationship between technology and this specific part of the mission, parents and teachers saw far less complementarity between technology and mission goals (see table 9.3). Teachers and students agreed, in similar percentages, that technology had benefits for classroom learning. Teachers and parents did not widely agree with the statement that the laptop program "contributed positively to the formation of a spiritually enriching learning environment" or "enabled an effective focus on character formation." When we asked about the relationship between technology and "exploration of the world from a biblical perspective," arguably both an intellectual and spiritual prompt that may span the first two mission statement ideas, teachers and parents offered only mild agreement. Overall, then, community members were much more hesitant to affirm that technological change had supported the "nurturing lives" goal. Community members seemed more positive when viewing technology as a tool for achieving academic improvement than when thinking of its role as an environment for student formation.

MISSION

Changing the World

As we have seen, the mission statement of Modern Christian Schools includes a strong mandate to "bring change to the world for Christ." Noting the importance of information technology in the worlds of business, media, politics, and entertainment, the schools are keen to prepare students to be responsible participants and a force for good in the broader culture. Overall, survey data suggest that school participants have embraced this narrative as a guiding reason for embracing technology and are optimistic about the approach (see table 9.4).[1]

Table 9.4. Technology's impact on the goal to change the world

	Students	Teachers	Parents
	Percentage agreement		
Overall, the school's use of technology has:			
Helped the school impact the world for Christ in ways that were not possible before		75%	57%
	Percentage rating "Well" or "Excellently"[*]		
In your classroom, how well do teachers:			
Encourage students to talk about how they think technology can be used to change the world for Christ		24%	
	Percentage greater than monthly		
How often do teachers:			
Encourage students to talk about how they think technology can be used to change the world for Christ	86%	41%	96%
Number of respondents	533	65	101

* Each question had five possible responses; the scale here was "poorly," "fairly well," "well," "very well," or "excellently." No teachers responded with "very well."

Teachers in particular saw ways in which the world can be changed through this technology: 75% of teachers at Modern Christian Schools agreed that the technology program "has helped the school impact the world for Christ in ways that were not possible before." Parents agreed, though with less consensus across participants. When we probed teachers about what happens in the classroom, however, they reported only infrequently connecting this element of the mission explicitly to classroom technology use. In fact, only 41% reported making this kind of connection in their classroom more than once per month, and even fewer (24%) said that they did this well. No teacher responded that they make these connections "excellently."

The perspective of students and parents, however, is different. Students and parents both overwhelmingly agreed that teachers frequently helped students think about how technology can be used to change the world for Christ. It is likely that the difference in perspective drives this difference. Students and parents may well encounter memorable examples several times a week in the students' classes and the chapel program. These connections need not be made by all teachers for students to encounter them at some point in the school week, and as we will see in chapter 28, specific one-time encounters may stand out as memorable. Teachers, however, primarily experience their own teaching, so if they are not addressing this theme often in their own classrooms, or if they lack confidence in how to make the connections, they might give a more muted response than students who see multiple teachers each day and remember the most striking examples.

It is also possible that teachers are holding themselves to a higher standard. Our experience talking to the teachers in focus groups was consistent with this. They were, as a group, extremely thoughtful about the integration of Christian commitments with their teaching, but at the same time experienced this element of their teaching as a real challenge. Very few teachers were confident that they had it all figured out. The expansive language of changing the world heard whenever the mission statement is discussed may reinforce a hesitation to see modest forms of engagement as valid examples. Since this aspect of the mission has been talked up in connection with the technology program, students and parents may be primed to see any example as evidence of the mission being worked out, and so they may perceive these examples as being far more frequent and relevant to the mission. We will explore more concretely what is happening at the classroom level in part 5.

As we might expect, then, the connection that the community drew between the technology program and the schools' mission was mixed but broadly positive. While there was agreement that the laptop program supports the schools' mission, when we drill down a bit deeper, it was the intellectual ("prepare minds") and missional ("bring change to the world") elements of the mission that were strongly associated with the technology program across the community, and teachers were more hesitant about the latter. Conversely, there was more skepticism from both parents and teachers about the impact of the technology on students' character formation and spiritual growth. We glimpse here concerns about the relationship between technology and faith that we will explore further in later chapters, concerns that focus more on technology as a formative environment and the kinds of practices it promotes. When any significant new technological tool is adopted in the hope that it will meet a core goal, it is worth asking whether certain aspects of that goal are less well promoted by the new tool and how the new pattern of emphases might shape us over time. It may not always be clear how to balance success in one criterion against weaknesses in another area, and considering only one part of the story can fuel one-sided optimism or pessimism. Approaching student formation responsibly requires a careful breakdown of both the strengths and the weaknesses of new technological strategies.

For Reflection and Response

- Which of the three aspects of the schools' mission (prepare minds, nurture lives, bring change for Christ) would you have anticipated being best supported by digital technology? Why?
- Why do you think Modern Christian Schools' community may perceive that their technology program supports academic learning but is less beneficial for character formation and spiritual growth?
- Think of your school or a school you know. What aspect of the school's mission statement do you think is best supported by digital technology? Why?

CHAPTER 10

Reaching beyond the Mission Statement

My understanding was that they would take the technology and [ask] from a biblical perspective, or from a Christian perspective, how do we handle that responsibly as a Christian?

Parent

In this part of the book we have been examining the idea that it is the schools' explicit Christian statement of mission that guides technology choices and practices. We have looked at how mission concepts have filtered unevenly through the school community. We have noted varying levels of confidence that digital technology serves as a helpful tool for achieving mission goals. The explicit mission is an important strand in the schools' identity, yet the interface between faith, teaching, and technology is not made up of a single strand. It is more like a tapestry, with threads of different colors running in multiple directions. Before we begin to examine other threads in more detail, we consider here some reasons why things are more complex than simply using technological tools to work out the mission. We will take a look in turn at how changes over time, differences across roles and departments, and the difficulty of keeping multiple ideas in play all had a part in weaving the tapestry.

Shifts over Time

A first reason for complexity is that the schools continue to evolve over time. Neither faith nor technology are a static target. As devices have changed, there has also been turnover in school leadership, bringing fresh emphases and accents. Shifts in wider Christian discussions of faith and culture have brought new influences into the school community through books, speakers, articles, blogs, and other media. More than one vision of Christian education has left its imprint. As one senior staff member put it, "I think it reflects the journey that Christian education has been on. I'm by far the oldest in the room, and watched Christian education move from 'What do you know?' to 'What do you believe?' and finally 'So, how are you going to live differently?' . . . I think that that's been the journey we've been on as a school as well, and adding technology has been a part of that too."

At different times in the schools' development, there have been emphases on securing strong Bible knowledge, learning to think in terms of a Christian worldview, and living into discipleship practices. Different generations of teachers within the schools have roots in one or another phase of this development. The changes in the composition of the community, described in chapter 5, have likely contributed to some diversity of theological idiom and instinct. New technologies have entered the school and been integrated not with a static, unchanging set of faith commitments but with a developing understanding of what it means to do Christian education. Some parts of the overall tapestry have been picked apart, others show evidence of earlier patterns, and significant areas are still being woven.

Role and Subject Area Differences

Differences in role between administrators, teachers, students, and parents also affect which faith emphases they most readily resonate with. In focus groups, administrators were by far the most likely to refer to the schools' mission when connecting faith and technology. Parents were the most likely to raise questions about purity and moral boundaries.[1] Among teachers we saw some hints that those working in different subject areas may find different models of faith and learning more or less congenial to their thinking.[2] We heard teachers wrestling with how the general faith project relates to the emphases of their particular subject area.[3] An art teacher, for instance, commented in a survey response,

> My faith flows through all my teaching. As an art teacher, I can't help but point back to the Creator Artist. When I do art, and when my students do as well, we are worshiping him. I find it comes out in my attitude, my treatment of my subject matter, and in the foundations of why we do

what we do. I don't like art projects that are super didactic in their basis on a certain Bible verse, but I find my faith comes out more authentically as we are drawing something and gain an appreciation for the intricate beauty in creation—that feels more real to me.

A strategy focused on biblical references felt like a less natural fit in art than one that focused on themes of beauty and worshipful response. Articulating a different unease, a psychology teacher described their struggle to make a schematic Christian worldview framework fit the complexities of their subject matter. They instead offered their students a metaphor of wrestling toward *shalom*:[4]

> I'm really, really bad at the creation, fall, redemption framework. It does not make any sense to me. So that's probably something I should figure out, but I like to just invite kids into the wrestling match . . . with God and how he intersects with our lives. . . . This is difficult stuff we're wrestling with as we look at abnormal psychology or whatever the case may be. But how are we wrestling with it so that we may be shalom-bringers? . . . For me, that's kind of the intersection point, a wrestling match.

Our interactions with math teachers offer further glimpses of this quest for the line of best fit. There was a striking moment during a focus group with math teachers when we asked how Christian faith informed their teaching and one participant eloquently raised his gaze to the ceiling and exhaled in mock-dramatic despair. When answering this question, the teachers in this group focused on the context in which math problems are placed. They described, for instance, how mathematical work can be related to stewardship through economic examples. This was, however, clearly accompanied by a sense of struggle. As one teacher confessed,

> Those things can come up when you're in the context of solving math problems, and that's what we kind of hang our hat on, and it can be frustrating. . . . We've been down this road before, I've been doing this for a long time, and okay! We give up, we surrender. Tell us, because we can't . . . and yet . . . it might be simpler than we're making it in some ways. And yet, 2 + 2 is 4 whether I teach here or teach there . . . and I don't know if that's what it's about. I think the context, at least for me, that's the bent where I come from. The context will help me, you know, discern.

These teachers found applying a Christian perspective to curriculum content difficult in mathematics, and yet remained focused on this strategy despite their apparent frustration with it. By way of contrast, another (younger) mathematics teacher offered a different angle in a survey response. Here the focus was less squarely on curriculum content and more on communal practices such as seeking beauty, offering grace, and fostering community:

> In mathematics I have found [connecting to faith] more difficult for content integration but easier in my methods of teaching. I try to teach in ways [that] promote a safe learning environment where students are free to fail. I focus on building relationships and being a teacher [that] students feel comfortable talking to just as much as relaying the content. Sometimes this means we talk about current issues over math. Within my educational focus I really try to teach students how to help one another in love. We have completed a number of projects aimed to take us outside the classroom and thinking about our impact on the world. We also often discuss the beauty and complexity of creation and math as a part of that.

Another survey respondent also found an approach that focused on relational practices more intuitive: "I believe my specific Christian practices teach students lessons about faith and life. For example, by making my math students read story problems to each other and have the listener write down information they find important, I am teaching students that listening to one another is important and that all information doesn't necessarily need to come from the teacher."

Different teachers tugged at different threads in the faith tapestry as they worked to make their own connections. Sometimes they may have limited the potential for rich connections as they fixated on a particular thread. All were seeking congruence between their faith commitments and the contours of their particular area of teaching, a process that resisted the application of a single faith template.

Seeing in Part

Another kind of shift in faith and learning emphases became visible at times during the research encounters themselves. Despite the schools' intensive history of training and conversation around technology, for some teachers the experience of participating in this research led to awareness that they had not yet joined up different fragments of their own thinking. As they answered survey questions or participated in focus groups, the prompt to reflect on their practice resulted in fresh realizations. These came in the form of dawning awareness that a way of linking to faith that had been learned in a particular context had not stretched to accommodate further developments. This sometimes left parallel tracks in their minds rather than rich connections.

The effort to relate new technologies to the schools' mission accompanied a shift from focusing

Faith and Teaching with Technology

Reasons why the relationship between faith, teaching, and technology is complex:

• The continuing influence of various stages in the schools' faith journey
• Ongoing change in leadership and faculty
• Changes in technology
• Changes in the confessional makeup of the wider school community
• The influence of different subject areas on teachers' strategies and identities
• Lack of time for sufficient reflection to connect elements learned at different times or in different contexts

mainly on worldview and knowledge perspectives to foregrounding Christian practices.[5] For some teachers, these changes were still in progress, as one teacher's survey response illustrates:

My Christian faith deeply impacts my teaching and course content. I'm frequently thinking about how I can get students to grapple with class questions from a faith perspective. This survey made me consider that while I often think about my faith in connection with my course material, I don't often link those two pieces with technology and how it [is] used in my classroom. I've seen many ways that technology has helped my communication with students, but I've also seen how it can be used in hurtful ways among peers. I rarely (if ever) challenge my students to think critically about their technology usage and how it might be assisting or hurting their Christian walk. It's been powerful to consider this.

Where teachers have learned to question their course content in terms of a Christian worldview, this does not automatically lead to sensitivity to the role of practices. In fact, the very emphasis on applying worldview thinking primarily to the ideas conveyed in courses may allow classroom technology to remain simply a tool for accessing those ideas, with the formative impact of technological practices relatively unquestioned. A laptop is not an idea; perhaps having a perspective is not an adequate response to its impact. When we recenter our view toward technology as a medium, new possibilities become visible. We shift the frame to focus not on what we use the device to access but on how using the device might shape us.

A similar moment of realization emerged as science teachers talked together in a focus group:

> One of the things that struck me as you asked about the faith-related things, when you asked about how does faith affect the way we use technology, and we talk about being discerning, and using it in a Christian way, and being responsible . . . and then, when we talked about how does faith relate to science we talked about awe and stewardship, and then when we talked about how science relates to technology . . . there was a disconnect. If you think of it as a triangle, the "how we teach technology as Christians" was totally different than "how we teach science as Christians," but somehow the technology . . . Do you see what I'm saying? It struck me that we talked about those in really drastically different ways.

What this teacher sensed was that they and their colleagues had learned strategies for thinking about the content of science education in light of faith (connecting to ideas like wonder and stewardship). They had also learned strategies for thinking about responsible, ethical behavior with technology in relation to faith. What emerged in the discussion was that these two scripts remained distinct and had not really been integrated.

Teachers often had articulate ideas about connecting faith to their subject, or about Christian use of technology, or about how technology could help their teaching strategies. Yet as a social studies teacher pointed out in a different focus group, what was still needed was more of a "trialogue," a connecting of faith, the ideas that inform the curriculum, and technological practices. This remained elusive: "How are we having . . . that *trialogue* happening, as opposed to 'All we need is technology now' or 'Oh, I've got to remember to do faith a minute' or 'Oh, this is my content area standards that I'm trying to meet.' How is that trialogue of those three components always happening?"

Part of the challenge, as expressed by another teacher, is the tendency in a busy school, with initiatives that shift over time, to think about issues serially, one by one as they arise. There is a focus, say, on Christian world-view. Then on digital citizenship. Then on Christian practices and for-mation. Each comes with its own training. Where can time be found for the kind of conversation that might connect the threads into a whole that shapes the overall integration of technology and Christian education? "It would be nice—because I feel like, now we're moving on. This is done, this has been integrated, so now we're doing discipleship practices, now we're doing [curriculum mapping], now we're doing . . . So this kind of gets left. And I don't have time to do everything, and it would be nice to talk with other people. How are we using it? How can we use it? When would be the best time to use it? Integrating it with faith. But there's never enough time to keep talking with each other." This lament that there is not enough time for genuinely reflective conversation on how to connect faith, technology, and teaching was echoed by others. Connecting faith *and* curriculum *and* practices *and* technology is a rich and variegated task, one that calls for professional development that has an integrative focus and ample space for dialogue and reflection.

Multiple Threads

The literature that has debated the nature of "faith-learning integration" in Christian education has wrestled with the tension between the actual diversity of approaches and the impulse to elaborate one true model over against less trusted alternatives.[6] The goal has often been to clarify philo-sophically what really ought to be happening when faith meets knowledge, or to lay out clear alternatives. What we see in the lived experience of this school community is a dynamic, shifting complex of faith motifs and un-derlying assumptions about how they might connect to education. There are multiple approaches in play, and they are all happening at once, some-times in parallel, sometimes in moments of creative interaction, some-times in a sudden realization of disconnection.[7] The immediate concern for teachers is to find ways of flourishing amid a complex set of pressures and constant changes, not necessarily to boil things down to the single cor-rect approach. Being locked within a single approach can feel frustrating. Keeping multiple approaches in play offers chances to make fresh connec-tions and expand unexplored possibilities. Yet teachers express a need for the space, time, and support to really explore the interconnections among their various partial strategies for weaving the faith-technology-teaching-

learning tapestry. The overall process is more complex than can be captured by the idea of a progressive, linear outworking of the mission with
new tools. As Modern Christian Schools found, significant investment in
professional development is needed to maintain a rich conversation that
connects faith, teaching, and technology. Even then, important parts of
the tapestry are still constantly being woven. We will examine a number
of strands in more detail in the remaining parts of the book.

For Reflection and Response

- Consider some basic elements of what happens in schools: curriculum
  content, teaching processes, behavioral expectations, classroom environments, resources and technologies. Which are you most or least
  likely to think of as being connected to faith? Why?
- Consider the various subject areas in the school curriculum. Which are
  you most or least likely to think of as being connected to faith? Why?
- How might schools create the space and opportunity for maintaining a
  rich conversation that connects faith, teaching, and technology? What
  might this look like over time?

Part 2 Summary

This part of the book has focused on one prominent strategy at Modern Christian Schools for connecting new technologies to Christian education. The idea is that Christian faith shapes a statement of mission, and this mission then guides technology choices. An overarching set of questions thus arose: How do members of the school community understand the mission, and how in turn does this relate to technology? Does technology serve the schools' Christian mission? From our research we learned several things:

- The mission was familiar and often mentioned throughout the schools, yet administrators were most likely to refer to it to explain the schools' technology choices. There were also divergent interpretations of one of the key phrases ("prepare minds"), leaving some ambiguity about how it related to other elements of the mission.
- When members of the school community were asked to recall what motivated the technology program, they offered a range of reasons, some compatible with the mission and some reaching well beyond it. This reflects slippage as the message was communicated to different groups. It also reflects the effects of a strategic appeal to parent and alumni self-interest to help sell the initial program. In some cases, a competitive emphasis on achievement, future-readiness, and getting ahead of others infiltrated the transformative Christian emphases of the mission statement.
- Survey data show that the school community largely believed that the technology program supported the schools' mission. However, there was significantly less confidence that technology enhances the "nurture lives" part of the mission than that it helps to "prepare minds." Confidence that technology helps to "change the world for Christ" was higher among parents and students than among teachers.
- When we look more closely at teachers' thinking, we find more complex struggles with relating faith to teaching with technology. The

idea of wielding technology as a tool to implement mission goals is too simple to capture the landscape. Ongoing changes in leadership, understandings of Christian education, and technology, together with differences across generations of teachers and subject areas, make for a complex tapestry of faith strategies.

- A recurring implication of the findings reviewed in this section is the need for more time for teachers to reflect together on how the various aspects of the schools' mission and of their complex task as Christian educators relate to one another. School community members need intentional time to revisit and clarify their understanding of the mission and its theological moorings. They also need intentional time to reflect on how they are connecting faith to ever-changing technological practice. The constantly changing nature of the landscape means this must be a repeated investment, not just an emphasis at the outset.

PART 3

TEACHING AND LEARNING

Questions about Faith, Education, and Technology

- How is the mission understood and does technology serve it?
- > Is technology helping teachers to serve student learning?
- How can we make discerning technology choices?
- How does technology relate to student formation?
- How is technology affecting the fabric of Christian community?

Expanded opportunities for teaching and learning and a promise to bring fundamental change to schools are among the "technocratic dreams" that often drive investment in new technologies.[1] In part 2, we examined how Modern Christian Schools' articulation of their Christian mission provided broad categories within which their technology program was understood. We also began to see how teachers drew from a wider range of reference points in their own efforts to relate their work with technology to the goals of Christian education. While administrators helped establish visionary goals and drive a process of institutional change, the work of experimenting with how to change daily teaching and learning was the province of teachers. In this part of the book we focus in particular on the pedagogical benefits that teachers found in new technologies as they sought to serve their students' learning well.

Our study includes no observational baseline for what teaching and learning looked like prior to the integration of technology, a good decade before our research, nor do we focus here on measures of academic success or overall academic standards. Our research methods do, however, offer a picture of how pedagogical practices match up to the schools' vision. In this section we explore the impact of digital technology on teachers' practices and students' learning.

We begin with teachers' decision-making processes. What choices are they making for and against technology in the classroom? We look first at those teachers who seem most fluent at integrating technology into teaching and learning, sketching the importance of play and experimentation for their own development (chapter 11). We then broaden out to consider the beliefs and values that inform teachers' decisions about when to teach with digital technology (chapter 12).

The next three chapters take a deeper dive into the "preparing minds" emphasis in the schools' mission. One hope bound up with the Modern Christian Schools technology program was that students might become more actively engaged in their learning. What can we discover about whether teaching with technology has helped foster student inquiry (chapter 13)? Do digital devices foster a focus on rote learning or on higher-order thinking (chapter 14)? Does teaching with technology make it easier to differentiate learning for diverse students (chapter 15)?

After examining the potential benefits of learning with technology for students' thinking and engagement, we consider some more pragmatic benefits. Teachers and learners describe the benefits of enhanced speed, access, power, and efficiency offered by new devices. How are these benefits experienced (chapter 16)? Do they come with downsides, fostering a focus on efficient task completion rather than actual learning (chapter 17)?

Teachers at Modern Christian Schools express a strong commitment to enhancing their students' learning. These chapters offer some insight into how digital technologies are helping to reshape teaching and learning.

CHAPTER 11

Pursuing Pedagogical Play

I found the biggest role . . . that technology plays with me and my teaching is me experimenting, me having fun, utilizing the computer specifically to create and to make. . . . I've not found a ton of great resources. . . . I utilize all the tools that most other teachers are using, but beyond that I haven't found an incredible website to use for all of our Bible stuff. Every once in a while, I'll use a site that utilizes maps, or something like that. For the most part, the tools that I use are not tools I'm giving to the students; I'm playing with them myself. . . . I used some technology to create, basically, the way we introduce a unit.

Teacher

Administrators at Modern Christian Schools associated the aspiration in the schools' mission to "bring change to the world for Christ" with a goal of using new technologies to transform teaching and learning. This involved teachers in new pedagogical challenges as they sought to harness digital devices to enhance student engagement and creativity, promote student inquiry, and adapt learning to students' particular needs. In the following chapters we focus on the pedagogical benefits that teachers saw in teaching with technology and take some steps toward examining how they were realized. We begin, however, with a brief look at teachers' own learning processes. How did teachers begin to develop the capacity to make wise pedagogical choices in their use of technology? How did they begin to choose for or against device use for particular learning tasks?

When it implemented its one-to-one technology program, Modern Christian Schools made significant investment in professional development.[1] The teachers whom we saw succeeding with technology pointed to the benefits of this training. Focus group teachers suggested that both whole-school and grade-level or disciplinary-focused professional development were crucial in learning to use technology to enhance student thinking. The recurrence of this theme in focus group conversations suggests that the schools' professional development efforts were effective in creating shared aspirations in this regard. Teachers also found that external frameworks and standards offered ways to think about how they were using technology.[2] These frameworks and standards promoted questions that moved teachers toward focusing on higher-order thinking skills, questions such as how technology use might be shifted from consumption to creation, or how to avoid using technology simply as a substitution for something that could have been done without it.[3] Other teachers pointed to the pedagogical maturation that simply comes with time and experience with applications that had been tried and found wanting. Teachers viewed this growth not as a sprint but as a long-distance event where the finish line keeps moving. This required school support for intentional learning time spent designing and refining technology-enhanced lessons. In all these forms of teacher learning, a recurring theme was the importance of play, for teachers as well as learners. Finding space to explore, to experiment, to play with possibilities beyond the routine seems to have been an important factor in teachers' pedagogical engagement. Play is an important step on the road to wisdom.[4]

Playing with the Bible

Imagine yourself a student in a high school Bible class (one of those taught at Modern Christian Schools). The teacher announces that today's lesson is an introduction to the city and people of first-century Corinth, a foundation necessary for the Corinthians unit. The lights dim, the unmistakable sound of a FaceTime call rings through the audio system, the projector reveals an incoming video call, and the Bible teacher accepts the call with a knowing grin. The video call reveals two teachers dressed in robes along with fake beards and haphazard wigs, accompanied by digitally added background sound effects like neighing horses, carriage wheels, and milling crowds. These humorously costumed teachers are evidently first-century Corinthians. They open a conversation with the class:

Two Corinthians: "Oh, hello! Hello, students!" (waving and smiling) "So nice to see you. Welcome! Welcome to Corinth!"

Bible teacher: "Hello! It is nice to see you too!" (waving to Corinthians on screen)

Two Corinthians: "We are so happy this worked out." (nodding, smiling)

Bible teacher: "This is great. We are hoping you can tell us a bit about Corinth."

Two Corinthians: "We'd be happy to tell you about the city of Corinth..."

The scripted dialogue between the Bible teacher in the classroom and the Corinthians on screen continues, providing a contextual overview of Corinth. It becomes apparent that the teacher has prepared a prerecorded video with purposeful pauses so that he can engage in a choreographed exchange. As a student, you laugh along with other students, enjoying the creative approach to the unit. You are imaginatively invited into first-century Corinth, establishing a sense of context that frames the remainder of the unit. The title of the New Testament epistle becomes a concrete city, inhabited by real people. Textual study becomes a dialogue.

The Bible teacher's experimentation in this lesson simultaneously hooked students' interest and promoted understanding related to specific learning goals for the unit. While teachers sometimes experimented with already-developed content, this Bible teacher found readily available digital content lacking. The quotation at the head of this chapter is drawn from his description of this lesson. He reflected that "I've not found a ton of great resources." So he experimented with developing his own content and then creatively harnessed the available technology applications to deliver it in an innovative way. The content itself was not novel; the same information about Corinth could have been delivered with or without technology. Yet the technology-assisted delivery invited students into the content in a fresh way. The teacher reflected that in this instance the emphasis was not on the students using technology in creative ways, but rather on his own use of the technology to deliver content more effectively with an eye to student engagement. He also hoped that modeling play extended an invitation for students to follow his example. "For the most part, the tools that I use are not tools I'm giving to the students," he noted. "I'm playing with them myself.... The technology that I use has been more playful ... as a way of inviting them into doing the same thing."

Playing with Technology

This teacher's creative approach to teaching with technology was echoed in the stance of several teachers selected for in-depth case studies. Case study teachers were selected not because they used technology the most but rather because they were seen by colleagues and administrators to be using it particularly thoughtfully and effectively. They all shared an eagerness to innovate, to adapt and enhance their teaching, and to support student learning. They voiced excitement about playing with technology and approaching teaching strategies or content in varied ways. This open stance was reflected not just in their innovation with technology but in their teaching more broadly. Technology offered a new medium in which to be creative, a fresh playground in which to explore new possibilities. As one teacher described the process, "I think that's what makes me a better teacher. . . . I keep learning new things. . . . I think a teacher has always got to continually work at getting better at what they do. If you ever stop and think, 'Yeah, I got my canned lesson plan' and just go with it, it's time to get a different job. I really believe that." These teachers already wanted to enhance their teaching and were not daunted by exploring new technologies as one possible way to achieve their goal. They also understood that investment in a fallible process of experimentation was necessary to ultimate success.

The case study teachers knew that pedagogical play comes with potential risks. Approaching a new lesson or unit while using technology may not always go as anticipated. As they described their efforts, they noted the perils of technology crashing, students failing to participate as expected, or the content or lesson delivery falling flat. As one teacher put it, "You have to go through some bumpy, hard things to figure it out." Teachers often voiced uncertainty about the possible success of a redesigned lesson or unit, but they embraced the risk of trying something new. At times they described their in-the-moment decisions with verbs like "experimenting," "jumping in," and "calling audibles." They were ready and willing to adapt and were prepared with alternate plans for any given lesson. They embraced vulnerability, knowing that potential failure was on display for all to see but willing to use such moments as learning opportunities. Such vulnerability plays a role in creating hospitable classrooms, inviting students into their own learning without fear of failure.[5]

The teachers' readiness to adopt this approach pointed to the existence of a school culture in which some level of risk and experimentation was encouraged in the interest of eventual pedagogical change and learning gains. A professional development plan for the high school noted that "we expect teachers and students to try new things and fail. That is great! That is part of learning." An administrator described this ethos and its importance for both teachers and students:

> If you don't have an invigorated teacher, your students lose in the end, so if they bring energy, excitement, fresh ideas, and to have fresh ideas you have to feel fresh, if you feel beaten down, overwhelmed, burdened . . . that plays out quickly. The air that kids breathe is the air that teachers put out, so if they put out excitement and freshness, that's a great learning environment—it's engaging, it's [important] . . . for teachers to know that we embrace the risk. Take it. I'll celebrate your failure right along with you. If you stuck your neck out and you tried it and if it makes you pull your head in your shell, recover, but do it again, and I'll be there to celebrate your failure again.

In part, the success the case study teachers experienced as they played with technology in their teaching was due to their intentionality. They were not embracing the newest content or latest technological trends or tools arbitrarily, as we will see in the next chapter. Instead, they were allowing their pedagogical goals and knowledge of the content, classroom, and students to guide their technological decisions. When asked about technological choices, teachers reflected first on curricular goals, teaching approaches, or particular challenges related to teaching a lesson. Only then did they highlight how they experimented with technology as a potential resource. Their openness to experimentation went together with selective technology use. Their intentionality was not immediately visible simply from observing their classroom teaching, but it became readily apparent when the case study teachers spoke about their process of designing lessons and units.

The case study teachers' descriptions of their work offered a glimpse into processes whose value existing educational research has confirmed. Pedagogical play, including both experimentation and risk-taking, is critical for learning to teach with technological tools or digital content. This openness to change, to adapt the curriculum or try different pedagogical approaches, supports the effective use of technology in teaching.[6] In fact, research on expert teachers has found that experimentation and risk-taking are crucial elements that lead to innovation and creativity.[7] Expert teachers are willing to play with technology, but they never fail to consider it in light of educational content, teaching approaches, and learning outcomes.

It seemed that the emphasis in the schools' mission on bringing change helped open space in the schools' culture for the kind of experimentation that leads to expert teaching with technology. Certainly, administrators were pushing for pedagogical transformation. Yet despite some of the pressures that teachers sensed toward maximum technology use early in the one-to-one technology program, the end result was not blanket, uncritical adoption of new technological means. When teachers discussed their work with us, they regularly focused on the challenge of making discerning choices informed by their beliefs and values. Schools seeking to foster creative, pedagogically engaging uses of digital technologies would do well to focus on the role of the professional climate within the school. Do teachers feel free to play with possibilities and feel supported when they take risks, or do they sense a drive to lockstep conformity? Are they helped to find time and confidence to explore what is possible? When teachers do feel empowered to make discerning decisions, they can approach choices about technology in ways that reach well beyond the pragmatic, as we will see in the next chapter.

For Reflection and Response

- How might schools foster safe spaces for risk-taking and pedagogical play when integrating teaching and technology?
- What might students gain from seeing teachers embrace pedagogical play?
- What pedagogical approaches or frameworks support an openness to experimentation with teaching?

CHAPTER 12

Digital or Not?

> I have to weigh every day what's the best, what's my teaching target, what's the best way to get to that teaching target, and what's going to work for most of the kids, and sometimes there is a choice. What's a good use of their time and our time?
>
> *Teacher*

In the early years of the technology program, some teachers felt pressured to use digital technology as much as possible. "There was a push to use it for every class for everything," one teacher recalled. Another went so far as to suggest that "technology for the sake of technology was how it first started."[1] This rather stark judgment was, however, immediately qualified by a fellow focus group participant, who agreed that there had been pressure "for the first two years, but it relaxed and got more organic." Others described a growing sense of experimentation in which "we guinea-pigged it a lot." Over time, a shared awareness developed that a key skill was knowing when to use technology and when not to. As one administrator put it, "Teachers when they begin this process feel they have to use technology all the time because this expensive tool is now in front of my kids, and so they use it inappropriately. They use it too much and it takes as much discipline and boundary to not use it, and we have to permit that, ... expect that there are times that it needs to be closed and gone."

In the last chapter we found the case study teachers, those recommended to us as being particularly thoughtful in their integration of technology into learning, successfully experimenting. Yet the change process has left teachers in general in various places. We heard confidence from some that they had learned how to make choices about when to use digital devices. Others expressed a preference for using digital technology as often as possible and discovering its failings by trial and error. Still others found that principled choices remained difficult. One wrote in an internal school survey, "I enjoy change and learning new technologies, but sometimes even for me it is overwhelming how much I could still learn. New products come out so often it is hard to discern which ones are valuable." Many reflected a more focused approach, selecting specific units or lessons each year to revise or enhance and using them as opportunities to think more about technology use. If technology is a tool, there was still uncertainty among the faculty as a whole about when to use it.

The idea of making discerning choices about when to use technology implies having reasons to hesitate about going all in. In this chapter we use case study and focus group data to examine how teachers made their decisions and why they hesitated. We saw individual teachers making principled choices motivated by a range of considerations, some of which reflected the Christian school context.[2] Examining these choices opens a window into how beliefs and values ground efforts to discern the day-to-day boundaries of technology use.

> **Considerations Informing Teachers' Choices at Modern Christian Schools**
>
> - *Effectiveness:* Does the technology increase learning?
> - *Embodiment:* Does the technology detract from direct engagement with creation?
> - *Imperfection:* Does the technology hide the imperfections of reality?
> - *Interaction:* Does the technology enhance or detract from the social dimension of learning?
> - *Distraction:* Does the technology distract the individual or others nearby?
> - *Associations:* Does the technology evoke helpful associations?

The Right Tool

Sometimes teachers' decisions grew out of trial-and-error judgments about effectiveness. Many teachers at Modern Christian Schools happily chose new apps and devices when they offered greater power and efficiency—for instance, by allowing students to write more quickly or simulate many repetitions of an experiment. The same teachers were willing to reject technologies that did not fulfill their promise, such as math apps that provided fun but little substantial learning. Several teachers voiced awareness of research suggesting that typing can diminish retention, and had adjusted their teaching to emphasize taking notes by hand.[3] As one summed up, "You have to look at it, what are we gaining from this, and what am I gaining from doing it this way, and kind of look at the benefit to the kids based on which way you're going to do it." This kind of judgment frames technology as a tool and asks whether it is the right tool for each task.

More often, however, motives for choosing nondigital avenues were more complex and value-laden. When talking about how they made these decisions, focus group and case study participants made unprompted connections to their faith and values. These reflections often framed technology more as a medium that might influence student formation.

Embodiment and Imperfection

One recurring hesitation focused on the value of embodied experience. Various teachers saw a tactile relationship to the material world as important for certain kinds of learning. An art teacher declared, "I want their hands messy with paint." A chemistry teacher emphasized "actually making a chemical reaction and knowing what it looks like." Science teachers described how creating virtual circuits seemed to diminish the sense of wonder and satisfaction experienced by students who made a real light bulb glow as they completed a physical circuit. The real circuit "gives them ownership of their learning. . . . It's not just the tablet is doing this for me or showing me how. I figured this out!" Teachers praised the usefulness of digital simulation yet also noted a need for students to be in touch with real-world texture. As they attempted to explain why, a web of considerations emerged:

Participant 1: What does it look like when you form a gas? It doesn't just disappear into the air. You see bubbles forming. Or titrations, when you have an acid and a base mixing together. And you're trying to figure out when they're mixing together perfectly, having a color indicator and watching the color actually change, and how it's not just perfect and happy and nice. Some of the imperfections you really do have to see.

Participant 2: I do think, speaking [of] the imperfection, to try, and fail, and have things not turn out the way we expect them to, adds to our Christian perspective of teaching and the whole concept of sin and the fall. And this is a piece of real life. It's not always going to go perfectly the way the computer screen showed it should.

Participant 1: And just the natural experience of experiencing God's world, rather than just seeing it on the screen or touching it on a tablet screen. They need to have those hands-on experiences too because, I mean, at home, a lot . . . revolves around screens.

This conversation reveals several layers. There is a sense that deep learning in chemistry means having a tactile sense of the different ways things can turn out. As one teacher put it, "I would not want a doctor to have only done simulations before they showed up." Reality exceeds our simulations, and so laboratory work requires nondigital experiences. Underlying this is an implicit idea of mediation versus immediacy. Chemicals are felt to be an immediate part of "God's world," whereas screen images are mediated representations, in some sense second-hand. This connects the decision about how to teach with a Christian sense of the worth of creation. The teachers feel that appreciating God's handiwork demands that they reduce technological distance.[4] Simulations also feel too tidy, failing to fully capture the unpredictability and imperfection of reality. The teachers sense that facing imperfections can deepen learning and perhaps guard against absorption in a glossy facsimile of the world. Here a belief in the fallenness of the world becomes relevant. Teachers wonder whether sin and imperfection may be obscured in the sleek contours and sophisticated programming commonly associated with digital devices. The considerations in play are complex, connecting ideas about learning, the nature of reality, and theology.

Interaction

Another hesitation, perhaps the most common, concerned interpersonal interaction. This concern tugged teachers in multiple directions. One described the deep satisfaction of realizing that having students work in groups around a shared computer led to rich learning conversations where students had previously worked alone. The teacher was able to listen as students' reasoning emerged, calling it "one of those moments you get to go home and be happy about." Another teacher was less positive about the role of digital tools when describing a class on the structure of the brain:

There's a [digital] 3-D model and I did that one year, but then later I just bought a bunch of junk from Hobby Lobby and then they built brains out of little boxes, and puff balls, and pipe cleaners. And those groups, they're all having these conversations about the different parts of the brain, what do they do, and how they're going to represent that. And then they make brains. And that worked better for their learning the parts of the brain, and what those parts do, than doing a 3-D model on-line. They just played with it more. . . . They were looking those things up on the technology, but then they were just playing with glue sticks.

In this case, choosing against digital technology meant more experimentation, reflection, and conversation. The shared hands-on task generated interaction that might enhance learning and was valued for that reason. Another teacher described a similarly motivated choice in an English class:

We use our laptops a lot for writing. This unit we're not going to pull our laptops out and we're just going to use notebooks. And if you want to, rather than doing tons of writing, you may sketch, just as a different way of responding to things, and it was amazing. They loved it. Kids that normally didn't listen are much more into it. Then when we did our group work, it wasn't on Google Docs sharing docs, it was on paper with sketches, and then they had to explain the results of their sketches, and so on. It really changed the dynamic in the class, and the kids, I think, saw the difference in their own interactions and in the class atmosphere. I think from time to time it's really, really important to change it up and to keep kids aware and keep talking about how this affects us, what happens. . . . Our joke is computers are the one-eyed hypnotist.

In either kind of instance, we see teachers concerned about the social, interpersonal dimension of learning, and using it to guide technology choices.

Distraction

Sometimes, by contrast, teachers were more concerned to limit interaction and enhance student focus. A social studies teacher explained that a digital medium was almost always best for collaboration or sharing work with an audience. However, "if it's going to be an individual time, if it's going to be annotating sources, I don't like them to use technology as much. If I want them to be taking notes, I don't want them to use technology." Pushed to articulate a rationale, this teacher noted that "memory retention is better" with handwritten notes and that students sometimes drifted away from the task when working online. "The way they did that with technology is almost always distracting to those around them. So, they're watching ESPN instead of paying attention to what's going on in class, and that distracts everyone else around them. And I don't want to give them that option."

A colleague added that "we've had lots of conversations about that. Kids focus better if it's listening and processing on paper, because of the distraction issue, I think."[5] Another teacher described having students create documents digitally, because of the efficiency of typing, but then print the results, because

> when they read each other's research, again, it is too distracting for them to go look at everybody's Google Doc. Honestly, it might not be that interesting the whole time. It might be very easy to get distracted and go to other websites that you have opened and not do what you are supposed to do. So, this way they will have it on paper, one paper in front of them, just read certain parts. I think it is just easier to navigate it too. If they have a huge long Google Doc of somebody else's work, just finding what they are supposed be looking at could be more difficult.

The challenge of harnessing social interaction for learning while reducing the potential for distraction informed technological choices.

Associations

A further factor involved the connotations that clung to particular devices and media. An elementary school teacher worried aloud that patterns related to specific devices used outside school might influence student attitudes in school: "I think the tablets the kids see as a toy, not a tool; no matter how much we drill it, no matter how much we use the language, it's handled in a different way, but primarily outside of school it's used as a toy and you see that wherever you go.... It's used to play games.... Most of the kids are using it for entertainment purposes, not for educational purposes outside of school, so therefore they carry that over and think that that's what it looks like in school."

This was felt to be less likely with laptops, which students associated more with schoolwork. Students also reflected on the associations attached to particular media. In a case study interview, a student expressed appreciation for one teacher's insistence on using paper Bibles, because "for me, going forward in my life I want to be able to say, 'Oh, I know where Judges is,' and flip to it instead of being, like, I need to scroll through this until I find it or click it to get to it." This connection of paper Bibles to learning goals led to a more extended reflection on the connotations of the chosen medium:

> I kind of like it because I like . . . how he forces us to use paper, because now it's just not on the computer and it's not one-dimensional. It's actually in your hands and you are actually reading it on paper. Sometimes I think there's stuff that a computer can't really replicate. For me, reading it on paper, in your hand, is a lot more spiritual than actually just reading it on a screen. Well, I kind of feel like on a computer you have all these distractions and you get pop-ups and all that stuff and it kind of disrupts you and it's very easy to lose your focus, whereas when you have a book, it's in your hands, you feel it, and you actually go and open it up and be, like, this is God's word and it's actually in your presence, not just on a computer screen.

Another student concurred:

> What I would probably say is that using a computer feels very high tech and new, and when you think about the Bible stories, you don't always think about them as super new. So when you get out a real book, a huge textbook kind of, you look at it—you feel like, you get the sense of this is God's word that someone wrote down specifically for me to read, like this is a big deal that it's sitting in front of me right now because these are God-breathed words. . . . It's no less important when you read it on a screen, but you don't get the same . . . there's been generations and generations of believers before me and this is an older way of doing things, but a way we should preserve.

Felt associations with particular media informed the preferences of individual teachers and students. In these particular students' comments, we see again the sense that tactile experience is less "one-dimensional" than digital media, and that digital devices might bring distraction and loss of "presence." We also glimpse a wrestling with what happens when we read a weighty, ancient text in a modern medium. These are the reflections of only some students, not all, but they invite us to wonder what is happening when a student works in a medium they perceive as less "spiritual."

A recognition of the efficiency of note taking on the laptop sits together with reflection on spiritual formation, in which efficiency may not be a primary value. Here again, technology choices are experienced as part of a richly layered experience of learning, and not simply as a matter of effective technique.

What we heard from both teachers and students was often not a simple vote for or against digital devices and media. Nor was it simply a pragmatic matter of choosing the best tool. The same teachers who enthusiastically described new efficiencies and broadened horizons also described occasions when they chose nondigital media. This was not because they were opposed in principle to technological change. It was, at least in the most thoughtful cases, because of a rich complex of values that they brought to understanding their classrooms. Choices were sometimes about what worked, but also reflected an effort to locate technology within concerns for classroom community, student formation, a healthy relationship to the material world, and the framing horizon of Christian faith. Talk about these choices rarely involved explicit appeal to the mission statement; rather, teachers were trying to apply their own process of discernment.[6] The teachers in our study approached technology not just as a tool for getting things done but as a medium that might shape our choices and experiences and therefore needs to be approached critically in light of concern for student formation and basic beliefs and values.

These reflections did not lead to uniform choices, or even choices that always pointed in the same direction. Indeed, not all teachers were able to articulate their grounds for choosing as clearly as the ones quoted above. Figuring out what it means to be discerning with technology in a Christian context was a challenging part of the learning curve for teachers at Modern Christian Schools, one that many teachers still found something of a struggle. With the technological landscape continuing to evolve, it seems unlikely that this struggle will go away any time soon. The task of teaching now includes the need to be able to make decisions about technology use that are not based merely on convenience or the attractiveness of new devices, but rather reflect wise appropriation of technology in the service of students' learning and overall formation. This suggests that Christian schools need to consider what kinds of support can make the struggle a fruitful one and equip teachers to clarify the values and commitments that inform their choices.

For Reflection and Response

- What specific beliefs and values most often guide your own decisions about when to use digital technology?
- How do the questions we need to ask about learning change if we shift the lens from technology as a tool for achieving goals to technology as a medium within which we are formed?
- What kind of professional development support might help teachers feel confident in making principled decisions about when to use digital technology for learning?

Pursuing Inquiry and Lifelong Learning

But you know, is that something I need to sit there and do rote memorization? [Does] that make me a better learner, a better citizen? Absolutely not. . . . My students will always have access to any answerable rote memorization questions that they need. There are definitely skills that prepare us to be successful lifelong learners, but this is a different type of preparation process: to prepare kids to learn always; to be invigorated; and to be engaged. . . . Therefore, it becomes our responsibility to prepare them to know how to navigate and be comfortable with failing and not knowing the answers, but knowing how to find the answers and being excited about that process.

Teacher

The "prepare" and "nurture" verbs in the mission statement of Modern Christian Schools imply a focus on learning that goes beyond grades. The intention that this should result in learners who "bring change to the world" helped ground a desire for students to become lifelong learners and more active participants in the learning process. School leaders connected the need for a transformed pedagogy explicitly to the mission, as we see in a focus group exchange:

> Administrator 1: We looked at it and said, "We want to change teaching and learning. We think we need to do a better job of that to meet the mission."
> Administrator 2: And the world. We want to change the world.
> Administrator 1: Yeah, and in order to do that, we need to change how we do teaching and learning. In order to change teaching and learning, we . . .
> Administrator 2: We need a catalyst.

Administrator 1: We think this [digital technology] is going to be the catalyst that's going to push that.

The desire to establish new patterns of teaching and learning was grounded in a shift from thinking about schools as places where teachers tell students *what* to learn, to emphasizing instead *how* to learn. In focus groups, educators described using technology to allow students to "lead," "ask questions," "choose their projects," tailor learning to "their areas of interest," or "craft a bit of a learning path on their own." As one administrator recalled, "We were trying to fundamentally change education so that it was about learning and not about sorting, so that it was about . . . true engagement, so it was about transformation." Another reflected,

> I think there's a lot of responsibility, obviously, that comes with being an educator and preparing the minds of kids, and when I look at what we knew about education when I was being taught, I think there are two critical changes. We know more about engaging the human brain and what it takes to do quality learning. It's high-level thinking, it's deep engagement in the learning experiences. So, we begin to look at how do you engage a learner well so that the learning . . . number one, sticks, and that that child grows into a person who wants to learn for the rest of their life because they've been so engaged.

This comment suggests another strand in the thought process. Alongside the mission language and its image of active engagement with the world, we see an awareness of recent trends in how learning is understood. Emphases on higher-order thinking, active learning, and individualized engagement helped frame how mission goals were interpreted when it came to transforming pedagogy. Students who are learning to change the world, it was assumed, will need skills of inquiry and high engagement with new ideas. Digital technology could provide tools for provoking change and help create an environment in which inquiry skills might more readily be fostered. This seemed, at least, to be how administrators understood the matter. Teachers were also invested in the idea of increasing active learning and inquiry skills, but did not talk about these in mission language. Over the next three chapters we describe what we were able to learn about how this pedagogical vision was being realized. We begin in this chapter with the idea that using digital learning technologies might promote a stronger emphasis on inquiry and lifelong learning skills.

Fostering Inquiry

Technology's role in enhancing student inquiry was a common theme that Modern Christian Schools teachers mentioned when asked about the benefits of the technology program.[1] Teachers shared a range of examples, like the following one from an elementary teacher who promoted deeper student understanding through inquiry-oriented lessons in a historical fiction unit:

> One of our teaching points was being able to envision. It was during kind of a historical fiction unit, and I wanted them to be able to envision these very specific situations, and that's challenging; to go to the library, find a book, open it up, and see a picture, multiple pictures, to . . . be able to form that mental movie. To have the internet at your fingertips, and to be able to look up pictures and put yourself there, to be able to step into the character's shoes, it's just amazing. I had them make slide shows, so they could glance at that to get their mindsets into that period of time. . . . We could take them all to the library and open up books, and we do do that multiple times, but for each individual, forty-two different topics, it's very amazing and . . . it would spark a lot of conversations.

In another example, at high school, a technology-enhanced science unit emphasized the experimental design process that aligned with related science goals.

> Students can choose a natural spot of land anywhere that's easy access for them, and then they track seasonal change from when school starts in August through December. They create a blog where they're . . . basically documenting, and they run one experimental design that they design, and plan, and carry out themselves. They're amazing, some of your photographers, some of your writers, oh my word. . . . I had a student come to me initially and say, "Can I combine this blog with a project I'm doing for creative writing?" and I said, "Yes!" One of those moments of "That's awesome!" So, I have more and more students who are starting to combine them with something they are doing in Spanish, and something they are doing in creative writing. It's really cool. I had a student make a book . . . [about] her grandfather's land. She made a book of all her photos for him for Christmas. Then she brought me the pictures in, of when she gave it to him, and I was bawling. . . . Ah! It was amazing.

These teachers invite us to imagine deep student engagement that is built on some degree of student choice combined with technological resources. Their accounts suggest opportunities for students to develop lifelong learning skills such as critical thinking, self-direction, and communication. They also, at times, related course content authentically to the world beyond school. Existing research suggests that technology can increase inquiry-based learning in classrooms, and that these experiences can indeed increase academic achievement and prepare students with relevant twenty-first-century skills.[2]

However, research also points to the high level of pedagogical skill and commitment necessary to effectively design inquiry-based learning,[3] which can make carrying it out difficult. If Modern Christian Schools teachers did indeed manage to regularly integrate technology with inquiry-based pedagogy, then they achieved at least one kind of transformation of teaching and learning. We can draw from what teachers report in surveys, together with observational data, to get a clearer idea of whether such teaching and learning was actually happening.

How Much Inquiry-Based Learning Is Happening?

Our survey data indicated that about 45% of teachers believed technology had made their own teaching more inquiry-based.[4] This percentage was similar across grade levels. These survey findings are promising but do not tell us whether teachers' beliefs were echoed in actual classroom practice or where inquiry-based learning was most fully implemented. For this we turn to data from our randomized classroom observations.

It is important to recognize that the vast majority of Modern Christian Schools teachers varied the type of activity throughout a lesson (see table 13.1). Amid this variety, we can look for how often inquiry-based learning occurred relative to other activities.[5] At the high school, inquiry-based learning was observed about 16% of the time in random observations. To understand this in context, researchers recorded twelve distinct types of teaching and learning activities, and only direct instruction and/or lecture (22%) and sustained periods of reading, writing, or viewing (20%) were seen more often in high school classrooms. The middle and elementary school findings reflected a different picture, with inquiry-based learning observed during only about 1% of the total activity time at the middle school and 3% at the elementary school. At these two grade levels, inquiry-based learning activities were among the least observed of the twelve teaching and learning activities. From this vantage point it seems that inquiry-based teaching was relatively common at the high school but rather limited at the other grade levels.

Table 13.1. Frequency of observed teaching and learning activities in random observations

High Frequency		Low Frequency	
High school		*High school*	
Practice and/or drill	22%	Assessment	2%
Sustained reading, writing, or viewing	20%	Devotions/prayer	1%
Inquiry-based	16%	Technology management	1%
Middle school		*Middle school*	
Direct instruction or lecture	28%	Kinesthetic activities	1%
Practice and/or drill	21%	Discussion	1%
Sustained reading, writing, or viewing	20%	Inquiry-based	<1%
Elementary school		*Elementary school*	
Sustained reading, writing, or viewing	34%	Inquiry-based	3%
Practice and/or drill	22%	Devotions/prayer	1%
Classroom procedures or management	14%	Technology management	<1%

Does the picture change if we turn to case study observations, where researchers observed entire units over longer intervals of time in particular classrooms?[6] In case studies, we see slightly different findings, but ones that reinforce the grade-level distinctions seen in random observations (see table 13.2). The activity time spent in inquiry-based learning at the high school was nearly double that of random observations (30% compared to 16%). Inquiry-based learning was by far the most frequently observed of the twelve activity types in the high school case study classrooms, followed by direct instruction and/or lecture (near 20%) and sustained periods of reading, writing, or viewing (near 10%).

Table 13.2. Frequency of observed teaching and learning activities in case study observations

High Frequency		Low Frequency	
High school		*High school*	
Inquiry-based	30%	Discussion	2%
Direct instruction or lecture	20%	Other	1%
Nonacademic social interactions	14%	Technology management	1%
Middle school		*Middle school*	
Practice and/or drill	56%	Kinesthetic activities	1%
Direct instruction or lecture	18%	Sustained reading, writing, or viewing	1%
Assessment	9%	Inquiry-based	<1%
Elementary school		*Elementary school*	
Direct instruction or lecture	32%	Inquiry-based	4%
Sustained reading, writing, or viewing	28%	Devotions/prayer	<1%
Simulation/role-playing	16%	Technology management	<1%

Combining random and case study results suggests that in high school, inquiry-based approaches to learning were indeed a significant part of the overall learning picture. Was this connected to technology use? Our data also show that when inquiry-based activities were happening, they were supported by one-to-one learning technologies over 70% of the time, strengthening the likelihood that these technologies were contributing to the implementation of inquiry-based learning, at least for high school teachers. If we view the desire for "fundamental changes in education" in terms of increasing student engagement through this kind of learning, and take into account the research evidence that inquiry-based approaches are difficult to achieve, then the commitment to pedagogical transformation appears to be a fruitful one in the high school.

At the elementary and middle school, however, the case study observation findings were similar to random observation findings. Inquiry-based learning happened less than 1% of the time in middle school and nearly

4% in elementary school. Since research suggests that inquiry-based learning designed by knowledgeable teachers is possible at all grade levels, and that technology should enhance such learning experiences, what should we make of these findings?[7]

One possibility is that there may be differences in how teachers at various grade levels understand and implement inquiry-based approaches to teaching and learning. The research team set a specific and stringent standard to identify which observed activities were inquiry-based, and this standard may have aligned best with high school teachers' implementation of inquiry-based pedagogies.[8] Although elementary and middle school activities did not meet the research criterion for being inquiry-based, there are wide-ranging conceptions of inquiry-based learning, and teachers may have designed units and lessons aligned with those conceptions but not with our working definition.

A second possibility relates to the focus of Modern Christian Schools' professional development efforts. One administrator highlighted a distinction between an emphasis on inquiry training at the high school and differentiation training at the elementary school. Targeted professional development in inquiry-based learning at the high school may have bolstered the grade-level distinctions seen in random observations and case studies.

A third possible interpretation is that inquiry-based learning may be somewhat harder at the elementary level and easier in high school. Adolescents may be developmentally more capable of navigating somewhat self-directed learning opportunities using digital technologies. Most high schoolers have developed a stronger repertoire of both cognitive and technological skills (e.g., for researching and digitally presenting knowledge). High school teachers, in turn, can minimize the time spent on teaching students cognitive strategies to support inquiry and ways to use specific technologies. They can then maximize the time spent on actual engagement with course content.

Finally, related to the fact that inquiry-based pedagogy is difficult to sustain, it may be that high school teachers have relatively more time to plan such lessons. Since high school teachers generally teach fewer distinct subjects and classes than elementary teachers, they may be able to devote more time to a single unit or lesson plan, which may make it easier to plan for inquiry-based learning.

So while our observational findings at the elementary and middle school level suggest that inquiry-based approaches were limited, it may be that these teachers were nonetheless adopting inquiry-based pedagogical approaches that looked different from those in the high school. The focus group data seem to support, to some extent, this possibility. The data above, then, should be interpreted with some level of caution.

Other Pedagogical Transformations?

In the chapter to this point we have been looking specifically for evidence of inquiry-based learning at Modern Christian Schools. As we have seen, teachers may have been overestimating the amount of inquiry-based learning in their classrooms in survey responses, or possibly interpreting inquiry-based learning differently than the researchers. Yet an increase in student engagement or development of skills related to lifelong learning can come in forms other than inquiry-based learning as defined in this chapter. Other survey results pointed to a high level of confidence that more general inquiry skills were being enhanced. More than 70% of teachers reported that technology use increased students' inquiry skills, helped students develop initiative and self-direction, promoted students' critical thinking and problem-solving skills, and engaged students in course content. Furthermore, more than two-thirds of teachers felt that the use of technology had made their own teaching more student-centered.

Collectively, these responses suggest that something is leading teachers to believe that new technologies fostered student engagement and lifelong learning. This is a part of the landscape of teacher decision-making that we began to explore in chapter 12; teachers are putting digital technologies to work out of the conviction that they can enhance student engagement and investment in their learning. What else, in addition to inquiry-based teaching, might be informing this conviction? What other pedagogical transformations might lead teachers to report that technology positively shaped students' initiative, self-direction, critical

> **Teacher Perceptions on Technology Use**
>
> Percentage of teachers who believed that technology promoted students'
>
> - Inquiry skills—73%
> - Initiative and self-direction —78%
> - Critical thinking and problem-solving skills—71%
> - Engagement in course content —91%
>
> Percentage of teachers who believed that technology made their teaching more student-centered —66%

thinking, problem solving, engagement, and inquiry skills? Could it be that teachers were more focused on what one administrator referred to as "higher-order thinking" opportunities? Perhaps technologies offered a shift from designing lessons focused on lower-order skills to an emphasis on higher-order skills. Or could technology's perceived ability to enhance differentiation have been a key factor? The next two chapters will explore these possibilities.

For Reflection and Response

- Why might teachers at a Christian school believe that inquiry-based learning contributes to the goals of Christian education? What view of learners and their future callings does it imply?
- In later sections we will explore concerns about Christian discernment, student formation, and community. How might an emphasis on inquiry and lifelong learning skills relate to these other concerns?
- In your own teaching, what do students most often do with digital technology? What kinds of learning are involved?

CHAPTER 14

Promoting Higher-Order Thinking

> The desire is always to enrich students' learning with technology and
> what does that look like? What are tools that are going to promote
> higher levels of thinking?
>
> *Teacher*

In chapter 13 we found evidence of significant amounts of inquiry-based
learning at the high school level, yet we also saw a high level of confidence
among all teachers that technology was enhancing student inquiry, engagement, and skills for lifelong learning. Another factor mentioned by
Modern Christian Schools educators was a shift from lower-order toward
higher-order thinking. Perhaps this shift was promoting skills like inquiry,
initiative, critical thinking, and problem-solving without moving fully into
an inquiry-based pedagogy. In one administrator's words, the "quality
learning" that the schools strove for required "high-level thinking" and
"deep engagement in the learning experiences." Teachers spoke of moving from "drill and practice" to "creation," or of shifting toward specific
higher-order skills, particularly "inquiry" and "creativity."

This concern with moving students toward higher-order thinking
skills is often associated with new technologies in schools and twenty-
first-century skills, so it was no surprise to hear it echoed at Modern Christian Schools.[1] This emphasis was another facet of what Modern Christian
Schools educators associated with transforming teaching and enhancing
engagement, though, as with inquiry-based learning, teachers did not tend
to associate it with mission language or other theological rationales. What
can we learn from our data about this facet of technology's possible contribution to teaching and learning?

Higher-Order Thinking

We found evidence of an emphasis on higher-order thinking in both focus group discussions and classroom observations. Consider, for example, the band teacher who digitally recorded sections of the entire band playing music and then played it back for students to hear and analyze in class or as homework. He remarked, "Rather than me just being the guy always saying, flutes are out of tune, trumpets, it's too long, trombones, you're too loud . . . you can give them examples." He used digital recordings to push students to evaluate what they heard and make critical suggestions, rather than relying only on the teacher's judgment. This teaching move turned what could have easily been a lower-order thinking task (responding to the teacher's analysis and corrections) into a higher-order thinking task (students analyzing their own playing). According to the teacher, this one pedagogical move allowed students to develop ownership of their analysis, critique, and response over the course of the year. Or consider the elementary classrooms in which teachers and students used drones to take aerial images of their school structures (building, playground, parking lot, etc.) for the purpose of learning about scaling, perimeter, and area. Students then compared results to direct measurements of the physical zones, analyzing and evaluating the various methods while reinforcing math concepts. These examples of technology-enhanced lessons that encouraged sophisticated thinking processes could certainly be seen as avenues toward increased engagement and twenty-first-century skills. Previous research has related using technology for learning tasks that draw on advanced cognitive skills (creativity, inquiry, critical thinking, etc.) to a reported increase in student engagement.[2]

Again, we turn to our observational data to check whether emphases in focus group comments really reflect daily life in classrooms. In both random and case study observations we evaluated learning activities on the basis of whether they engaged students in lower-order thinking or more sophisticated levels of thinking, whether technology was in use or not.[3] At Modern Christian Schools overall, learning activities demanding lower-order thinking skills made up nearly 69% of total activities in random classroom observations and nearly 51% in case study observations. Conversely, more sophisticated thinking was required for nearly 31% of total activities in random observations and 49% in case study observations. Taken alone, these figures do not yet tell us very much, for there are no clear evidence-based benchmarks or specific guidelines about the right balance of thinking skills in classrooms. The presence of lower-order activity is not a bad thing, because lower-order skills do matter. What these figures offer us, however, is a context in which to examine whether technology played a role in promoting learning that transcended lower-order thinking.

The findings in table 14.1 help us answer this question. They show the percentage of time that students spent at each level of thinking when engaged in learning activities that involved use of one-to-one technologies.

Table 14.1. Percentage of activity time students spent at various levels of thought by presence or absence of one-to-one technology use

Random observations

	Lower-order thinking with tech	Lower-order thinking without tech	Middle-/ higher-order thinking with tech	Middle-/ higher-order thinking without tech
Elementary	20.87%	79.13%	45.41%	54.59%
Middle school	34.02%	65.98%	74.84%	25.16%
High school	27.11%	72.89%	78.92%	21.08%

Case study observations

	Lower-order thinking with tech	Lower-order thinking without tech	Middle-/ higher-order thinking with tech	Middle-/ higher-order thinking without tech
Elementary	23.96%	76.04%	66.27%	33.73%
Middle school	57.54%	42.46%	95.33%	4.67%
High school	61.64%	38.36%	73.23%	26.77%

We see a convincing trend: one-to-one technologies like laptops and tablets were in use more often in the activities with more sophisticated thinking processes than without. In random observations, digital technologies were used for about 21%–34% of the lower-order thinking activities, but they were used far more often for middle- or higher-order thinking activities. Technologies were used comparatively more during sophisticated thinking activities in the elementary (on average about 45%) and middle and high school classrooms (about 75%). The case study observations confirm and extend these findings. In case study classrooms, one-to-one technologies were used for more than 66% of the activities requiring more than lower-order thinking skills. These findings confirm that technology was not just being used as a "drill and kill" device but was being used to foster skills like critical thinking, problem-solving, analyzing, and creative thinking.

These findings gain weight when understood in context. Recall that for Modern Christian Schools students, activities requiring advanced cognitive skills (with and without technology) made up a third to a half of the school day. It would have been easy, therefore, for teachers to focus on using laptops and tablets for activities (basic skill practice, mastery of information, etc.) that made up the majority of the school day. Instead, we see comparatively more laptop and tablet use for lessons requiring more sophisticated thinking skills. This points to teachers intentionally designing lessons that use digital technologies for more than lower-order thinking.[4]

Given this evidence of technology supporting learning activities that push students to use more advanced thinking skills, we have gained another perspective on how Modern Christian Schools teachers might also believe that technology fostered student engagement. When education focuses on tasks that encourage deeper thinking, students are often more interested and engaged in the learning process.[5] Teachers at Modern Christian Schools reported experiencing technology as a catalyst that promoted educational experiences that require advanced thinking skills. Their reports were supported by observational data. This shift probably contributed to the sense that students were more interested and engaged in their own learning.

Pedagogical Transformation?

So, are we seeing a wholesale pedagogical transformation in the wake of the arrival of new digital technologies? We cannot say for certain. Our study does not include longitudinal observation data. Without a baseline, we cannot measure whether technology adoption at Modern Christian Schools actually increased opportunities for higher-order thinking. Perhaps the overall levels of higher-order thinking are similar to where they were in the past, but just attached to new learning activities using technology, or perhaps there has indeed been an increase. What we can say is that the teachers we observed were harnessing digital technologies to promote learning activities that extend and deepen cognitive skills. At this point in their technology journey, they were using laptops and tablets comparatively more for lessons that promote higher cognitive skills, and they were doing so more often than the overall pattern of activities might lead us to expect.

This finding allows us to affirm that these teachers have cleared a common hurdle for schools adopting new digital technologies. It can be tempting to use digital devices mainly for drilling and low-level practice. Yet teachers at Modern Christian Schools were not using technology mainly to replicate lower-order thinking tasks that could easily be done without technology. This resonates with what we heard from teachers in focus groups. One teacher commented, "I feel like using it just for drill and practice isn't the best use of the gifts that we've been given." Another emphasized, "My biggest phrase is 'we use these for creation, not consumption,' because we're not there just to take in apps and play apps all day. It's . . . a learning tool." While some acknowledge a learning curve in terms of discerning which technology applications were not offering rich learning, a commitment to moving beyond drilling was clear: "We didn't want this to be turning classrooms into educational arcades." Our observational data suggest that this aspiration was being constructively worked out in practice.

Faith and Higher-Order Thinking

How does this trend relate to the schools' broader Christian goals? We have seen that administrators associated a transformed pedagogy with the "bring change to the world for Christ" motif in the statement of mission. We also heard an administrator connect an emphasis on enhancing students' creative skills with the image of God: "I think early on the easy starting point . . . was recognizing [the] image of God and recognizing that students can use that device as a device, as a tool, of not only reflection but also of creation, of expression, of things that they've learned, allowing them to personalize and give expression, and so I think that does spring out of a thought of teaching Christianly, approaching students from the Christian worldview." Students who are made in the image of God, the thought goes, should be helped to unfold their capacity for reflection and creativity, so that emphasizing higher cognitive skills might itself be an outworking of a Christian worldview.[6]

Teachers for the most part talked of these pedagogical changes simply in terms of serving students well and enhancing their learning. There were occasional glimpses of larger connections. A case study teacher described a fourth-grade extension lesson about human impact on loggerhead turtles that included a digital component where each student tracked and analyzed turtle migratory patterns. As the teacher described the rationale for adding the lesson to an already-developed animal adaptations unit, she connected "higher-level thinking" with "challenging students in their thoughts" and helping them realize that "what you do and the decisions you make impact life." She continued, "I think there's a big faith piece there. . . . We talked about that responsibility that God calls us to care for his earth and . . . we don't really do that in the ways that we should."

Such overtly articulated connections between higher-order thinking and Christian formational goals were, however, rare. This may be connected to the tendency noted in chapter 6 to think of "preparing minds" as the generically academic part of the mission statement. It may also be that connections to formation are implicitly assumed in matters such as course content, relationships, or devotional practices, but teachers are less used to connecting faith language to their thinking about instructional processes.[7] Even in school settings where a framework of Christian faith is an active ingredient in shaping how education is approached, teachers may be more practiced at relating faith to some issues than to others. Nevertheless, a focus on higher-order thinking is another part of the broader teacher conviction that digital technology can enhance student learning. In the next chapter we turn to a third possible factor in student engagement, one that showed more connections in teachers' minds with theological themes. Perhaps technology also enhances the tailoring of teaching and learning to the individual needs of students made in God's image, allowing for new kinds or degrees of differentiation. Is this also happening at Modern Christian Schools?

For Reflection and Response

- How do higher-order thinking skills contribute to Christian discipleship?
- In what ways are students at your school encouraged to use technology for "creation, not consumption"?

CHAPTER 15

Differentiation and Inclusion

I've found that [technology] just offers more choice. So, there's choices in how to present the material, there's choices in how to get the material—to listen, to read, to watch. It makes differentiation a lot easier. And that's the billion-dollar word in education. But I think it's still a lot easier. This enables student choice. This enables student autonomy in that choice. They can be creative in the way that works best for them.

Teacher

We have explored whether technology is contributing to inquiry-based learning and the development of higher-order thinking skills, and we turn now to whether it is helping teachers to meet individual students' needs. Teachers, administrators, and students at Modern Christian Schools shared a common belief that one powerful benefit of digital technologies was differentiation. Differentiation refers to adapting teaching and learning to meet the varied experiences, knowledge, skills, and interests of different learners in a single classroom.[1] When teachers differentiate, they adapt content and instruction to meet the needs of all learners[2] and establish a connection between students' own life experiences or affinities and the curriculum.

Differentiation is widely embraced at Modern Christian Schools whether or not technology is in use. In surveys, a full 90% of teachers report differentiating instruction at least a few times a month, with 62% doing so on a weekly basis. Is technology enhancing this process? Members of the Modern Christian Schools community described digital technology as helping them to enhance student learning, treat learners as image-bearers, and include all students. We will take a look at each of these in turn.

Enhancing Student Learning

Unlike individualization, which focuses on enhancing and adapting instruction for a single learner, differentiation seeks to simultaneously reach all learners. Embracing this philosophically is easy, but actually achieving differentiation in the classroom is more difficult. Teachers across focus groups and case studies spoke of digital technologies as tools that enhanced their ability to help all students achieve academic success. They found that using digital technologies allowed for "more choice" in the resources available to students, "more methods" for helping students understand challenging concepts or extend learning, and "more [student] ownership" over which resources would best support their learning.[3] Technologies also provided effective ways to track individual or whole-class progress and grades and provide faster feedback on student work. Teachers who put technology to use in these ways reported finding more means to reach students at different levels simultaneously. As one put it, "I think [technology] allows for that differentiation that you need in any classroom when you have to provide the reinforcement for the students that didn't get the concept but then on the same day you need to provide activities for the kids that already understand the concept and are ready to move on."

In our survey data, 59% of teachers believed that technology integration made them more effective at reaching high-achieving students and a similar percentage reported it helped them reach traditionally struggling students. Furthermore, as we saw earlier, 66% of teachers felt that technology integration made their teaching more student-centered. Even if some teachers did not believe the technology made them "more effective" at reaching particular groups of students, an

---

Teacher and Student Perceptions on Technology Use

Percentage of teachers who believed that technology made them more effective at

- Reaching high-achieving students—59%
- Reaching low-achieving students—66%
- Reaching all students (range of ability levels)—89%

Percentage of students who believed that teachers allowed students to use technology (one to three times per week or more) to

- Help students that have a hard time learning or understanding lessons—78%
- Offer students opportunities to go beyond what is taught in class—82%
- Make choices about when and how to use technology to understand content—81%

---

overwhelming 89% of teachers affirmed that they use technology well to reach all students, across the range of academic ability. After nearly a decade of technology integration, a majority of teachers at Modern Christian Schools perceive that technology is enhancing their ability to meet a range of learning needs. This focus on differentiation might be another factor contributing to teachers' sense that digital technologies enhance student engagement.

As usual, when interpreting survey data, we wonder whether teachers' perceptions reflect students' experiences in the classroom. Turning to student data about student choice and technology use to support or extend learning, we can generally confirm what teachers reported. Over three-fourths of high school and middle school students reported that teachers allowed students to make choices about when and how to use technology to help understand course content one to three times per week or more. Further, students overwhelmingly agreed that teachers used technology one to three times per week or more to help students that have a hard time learning or understanding the lessons and to offer students opportunities to extend learning beyond what is taught in class.

Students' recognition of differentiation was also evident in our focus group data. A high school student, for instance, described a chemistry class: "I also like [that] there [are] various levels of how much help you want. So, the lectures are probably the most in-depth, but then if you think like I think, I have the basics, the videos. [They] are usually good. He preps it for different people, so if you need to be having a lecture and [need to] ask questions, you have that available for you. But if you are the type of person who can figure it out more based on a video, that also is available."

Classroom and case study observations added further evidence of differentiation in action. Take, for example, an elementary classroom where students were learning strategies for solving multistep word problems. Students were clustered at various centers, some working as individuals, some as pairs, and others in larger groups. Half of the students were sitting or sprawling around the teacher on the rug where she was leading guided practice. Some worked with paper and pencil, some with whiteboards, and others with various drawing or calculator apps on tablets. The teacher occasionally recorded notes or logged student work into digital records that tracked individualized math goals for all students in the classroom. Students who completed the core set of problems before others moved to another center, choosing between solving "challenge" problems written on the board or extension word problem activities loaded on tablets. They took photos of their work on paper or screenshots of their completed work on the tablet and uploaded them to the teacher. One group of four students practiced multiplication and division facts independently on an app designed to adjust levels according to student performance and generate a digital progress report for the teacher. The teacher, monitoring real-time reports of student progress on her app, looked up and offered a verbal "Way to go!" to a student at the math facts center. When they had finished practicing multiplication facts, two students chose to join the group on the carpet, and the other two used their tablets to watch a tutorial video about order of operations prerecorded by the teacher. Two students who received targeted math support in a separate room returned to the classroom and joined their peers on the carpet solving multistep word problems. Assignments were already adjusted in difficulty or length to meet them at their current ability level. The teacher was leveraging technology, in addition to other resources, to differentiate instruction for all students.

Such classrooms illustrate the potential of technology as a tool for enhancing differentiation. Differentiation could be achieved without digital technologies. However, the addition of digital technologies extends the range of resources available and provides new possibilities for real-time tracking of student progress.[4] While these technologies are not essential to the work of differentiation, they offer teachers a sense of greater capacity to make differentiation practically viable. We may question whether this supports the idea that technology will radically "change how we do teaching and learning," but technology has undoubtedly offered additional ways for teachers to effectively carry out differentiated instruction.

Nurturing Learners as Image-Bearers

For some teachers, the opportunity to use digital technology to enhance differentiation in their classrooms was linked closely to their Christian views of individuals as image-bearers.[5] "Image-bearer" language appeared regularly in articles in the school magazine over a ten-year period in the context of unfolding students' individual gifts and abilities, and the theme also appeared in professional development presentation materials. We heard teachers and administrators draw on "image of God" language to describe students as uniquely formed with "individual gifts and abilities and eventual callings in life." This theological reference point helped frame an emphasis on seeking each student's flourishing.[6] As one teacher put it, "The Christian mission part is (and I think . . . we've been talking more about that even this year again) just, each individual that comes through our door has value, has purpose, has gifts. And those gifts don't always equal intellect, but they have gifts, and it's our job to help find those and help develop those to their fullest potential, so that would be the mission part."

This type of teaching demands that teachers know each learner and adapt their pedagogy and curriculum in response. If technology could be used to help with this, then it was contributing to the effort to treat students as God's image-bearers and contributors to Christian mission, as another teacher reflected:

So, I always think, "Alright. How will this tool help me to meet all these kids at different levels?" Sometimes that's within the apps, and also I think about how do I take what I'm using or whatever app I'm using, how do I use it to create something instead of just drill and practice? . . . And then for a wider audience, to impact the world for Christ. Because . . . that's always a piece of it. I think even it's in the differentiation too because everybody has a different skill set, so you're teaching the whole child right where they're at, because they're an individual child created in the image of Christ with their own personal strengths and weaknesses.

As teachers found that technology made differentiation easier, they felt more successful at "teaching the whole child" and helping students reach "their fullest potential." These outcomes were closely aligned for many teachers with their Christian beliefs and practices related to students as image-bearers. Technology, differentiation, and Christian ways of teaching and learning were interconnected in a manner consistent with the mission statement's emphasis on "nurturing lives," yet they were also expressed in theological terms drawn from outside the mission statement. The focus here was less explicitly on working out the mission and more on seeing students with Christian eyes.

Promoting Inclusion

The benefits of this kind of technology-enhanced differentiation extend even further. Teachers often reflected on how meeting a range of learners' needs ultimately promoted inclusion. One reflected,

One of the things I'm seeing, especially for students that we would call "inclusion," and so they have more significant needs, is utilizing technology. So, if in class they're reading a certain book, finding it in a lower-level reader and [having] them follow it on the tablet. Or I know we have a couple students in third grade right now that are significantly behind their classmates, but then, using different apps to help the students to be able to participate at a certain level with their classmates. And that's been, I think, a little easier process to implement than before.

Technologies became a tool that opened up new ways to support student learning in the general education curriculum, thereby enabling more students to remain a part of the classroom with their peers. As another teacher pointed out, "I think technology is an equalizer." She found that technological possibilities allowed students with particular needs "to do what everybody else in the room was doing, at the same time, staying in the room." The power of this inclusion was frequently praised in relationship to the benefit it brought to students who may be marginalized in schools, which included students receiving special education support, but also those with limited English proficiency or those considered advanced or gifted learners.

Inclusion at its core, though, should not be reduced to a practice or framework to be implemented for the academic benefit of marginalized students. It is a relational state of affairs, one that resonates closely with Christian concerns about interdependent community. Truly inclusive communities are not primarily about the benefit for marginalized students. They are spaces where mutual care and respect are fostered, where the gifts of *all* students are recognized, where *all* students embrace vulnerability, and where *all* members are in relationship with one another and with God.[7] Articulations of the connection between inclusion and community were infrequent at Modern Christian Schools, despite the teachers' certainty that technology enhanced both. Case study teachers were closest to connecting these threads when drawing on professional development themes of community-building or life together. Many described how these themes were exemplified in classroom spaces that promoted interdependence and embraced vulnerability. Such examples were only loosely tethered to inclusion or differentiation.

The data suggest that Modern Christian Schools teachers readily point to how technology opens academic possibilities, thereby promoting inclusion. Less explored, though, was why technology-enhanced inclusion might be valued in Christian schools beyond academic benefit. Perhaps this disconnect between inclusion and Christian community was an artifact of the tendency to separate out missional elements, with the benefits of inclusion related to "preparing minds" and with community related to "nurturing hearts." Modern Christian Schools teachers were certainly thinking deeply about technology and community relationships, as we will see in part 6, so could this relationship to inclusion have been overlooked or underexplored? We do not know for sure. Unlike technology-supported differentiation, which teachers more clearly and explicitly aligned with their Christian beliefs and practices, inclusion lacked clear and explicit connection points. Nonetheless, for Christian educators striving to create inclusive classrooms, it seems the most compelling rationale may be found within the biblical emphasis on mutually supportive Christian community in which each seeks the good of the others.[8]

Technology and Engagement

If we step back to review what we have learned in the last three chapters, we see three factors that may be supporting the sense that using digital technology has enhanced student engagement and active learning and has changed pedagogy for the better. There are signs that digital technology is supporting student inquiry, albeit only at the high school level. Across all school levels, activities using digital technology are on average more likely to involve higher-order thinking than activities without digital technology. The reports of teachers and students as well as classroom observations suggest that technology is helping to make differentiation in support of all students' learning more practically feasible and providing an increased palette of options for learning. It also contributes to the ability to promote inclusion.

These strands are, of course, interwoven. Inquiry-based learning serves, among other things, as a tool for differentiation, allowing a stronger focus on particular student interests. It is also likely to promote tasks that focus on higher-order thinking. The focus on using technology to differentiate instruction for all students may perhaps reinforce the determination not to use it mainly for uniform low-level drills. It is likely that all three emphases are felt in some measure to be part of respecting and unfolding students' gifts and creative capacities, an attitude that teachers and administrators associated with students' being made in the image of God, though this connection was most explicitly made in reference to differentiation.

All three strands make possible the goal of creating inclusive communities, but this was largely unexplored in missional or theological terms.

By examining each of these threads separately, we have been able to tease out some different pieces of evidence with which to understand talk at Modern Christian Schools of technology transforming teaching and learning and increasing student engagement. The hope that technology will transform learning calls for consideration of what facets of learning will be enhanced and how, for learning is not a simple process. If we seek to understand the pedagogical results of technological integration as a journey rather than measuring it by aspirations of radical transformation, we can affirm signs of technology enhancing inquiry-based learning, differentiation, and inclusion. More broadly, we can plausibly associate evidence of technology enhancing facets of instruction with enhanced student engagement and the promotion of lifelong learning skills. This does not complete the picture of how these technologies might be affecting instruction, and we will be exploring other aspects of how students' development might be affected in later sections. It does, however, lend some credence to teachers' feeling that digital technologies have benefits to offer in these specific areas.

For Reflection and Response

- What implications for technology use did Modern Christian Schools educators draw from the idea that students are made in God's image? Are there any other implications that they should consider?
- What elements of Christian community should create a foundation for inclusive classrooms?
- What further concrete examples can you identify of how digital technologies might help adapt instruction to the needs of an academically high-achieving student, a student with learning difficulties, or a student who might benefit from different approaches to learning?

CHAPTER 16

The Benefits of Efficient Tools

> While education at Modern Christian is focused on a carefully crafted curriculum, it is also necessary to use the best available tools to help our students absorb their lessons. We consider technology to be an important tool (like a book, a chalkboard, or movie projector) that helps teachers be effective teachers and students be effective learners.
>
> *School magazine*

For several chapters we have been tracing evidence for whether teaching and learning with digital devices promoted inquiry, a focus on cognitive skills, and differentiation or inclusion. These themes reflect the influence of the wider push for "twenty-first-century skills" and were also related by teachers and administrators to their desire to honor the gifts and callings of students as image-bearers. Powerfully present alongside these themes, however, was a more pragmatic reason for choosing digital tools: new devices were valued for their promise of greater efficiency.

Efficiency is an undeniable preoccupation in modern North American culture. We place high value on productivity and time or energy well spent. We are drawn to devices that promise help in getting more done or arranging our tasks more efficiently. It is therefore no surprise that students and teachers were especially vocal about how digital tools increased efficiency in teaching and learning. Even as they applauded the technological efficiencies that support learning in a digital world, however, a thread of underlying questions and concerns was woven through their praise, forcing our gaze past the technology-as-efficient-tool model. This chapter and the next will explore how a focus on technological efficiency shapes teaching and learning for good or for ill.

Efficient Learning

What do teachers and students mean when they say technology is efficient? Members of the Modern Christian Schools community did not identify efficiency only with doing things more quickly. One student, for instance, commented, "I think the use of technology and laptops makes everything so much faster ... projects, explanations. You can also go at your own speed too, because you know the resources are on your laptop. If you're behind, or if you're going to miss school next week, you can always go there. I just really think it's a great thing. Communication too ... it makes everything go faster and more efficient." While clearly emphasizing speed, this student also highlights access to resources and the ability to organize one's own learning. Focus group participants praised technology for its productivity benefits. Their praise at times reflected the optimism implicit in a view of technology as simply a better tool for getting things done. More often, though, they found the value of efficiency in recaptured time that could be put to better use in supporting learning. Both teachers and students associated efficiency gains with speed, access, organization, and power. We will take a closer look at each in turn.

Speed

Time and time again, focus group participants described technological efficiencies in terms of speed. Many students appreciated the speed with which they could access resources, process data, receive feedback on homework, complete schoolwork, or communicate with other community members.[1] The connection between efficiency and speed was most evident in discussions of the benefits of typing over handwriting. Middle and high school students believed their faster typing speed was an asset for school assignments. Some described the benefit in terms of productivity: typing fast translated into completing assignments faster than students who do not type. Others saw the benefit in terms of using the time saved to focus on incorporating more ideas or increasing the time spent editing, with the goal of enhancing the final product.

Access

Although speed was often highlighted first, in nearly all the examples offered, speed depended on internet access.[2] A student noted, "You can do so much research so much faster on a computer ... [because] we have so many databases connected to our [school's] homepage that we can just go to." While focus group participants rarely directly named the connection between efficiency and access, in most cases new technologies that students applauded for speed were effective as tools only because of internet access.

Modern Christian Schools teachers had a different reason for valuing increased access to information. Knowing that information stored online was (almost always) available 24/7 from any location appealed to them, since students could more easily work beyond the physical and temporal boundaries of the school day.[3] Constant access to the course page meant students had fewer excuses for failing to turn in homework or falling behind when absent. This access, along with speed, is a facet of technology often praised in an educational era where the pursuit of information reigns.[4]

Organization

Another central feature of efficiency was increased organization.[5] Students often spoke of organization and speed going hand in hand:

> Note-taking in general is just so much faster, and with paper and notes ... I don't always ... keep track of all my papers, because we've had laptops. So, my binder, sometimes I lose papers here and there. ... Having it all organized and ready to go, and I can quick click on it and quick take notes, because typing for me is a lot faster than handwriting, it's easier to read. I just feel like taking notes overall has been so much more helpful, so you organize it better—how I like to do it.

Cloud-based storage systems like Google Drive and Dropbox, classroom or learning management systems like Google Classroom or Moodle, and digital note-taking software like Evernote were among the technologies seen as increasing organization. Students highlighted systematic consistency, knowing where to store and locate information so that it could be quickly and easily accessed later. They often contrasted the benefits of knowing where everything was online to the chaos of trying to keep track of loose-leaf papers and binders.

Related to organization was the searchability of online systems. Instead of having to search by hand to find specific notes, sections of papers, or documents, a remembered word or phrase enables a digital search of the filing system. A student described sorting through all of her English notes and assignments: "Google Docs ... helps because if you remember the title, you can just type it in and then it'll find it for you, where you don't have to go digging through [everything]."

A handful of teachers also praised the benefits of cloud-based software for organization. Those in the middle and high school found that consistent use of systems like Moodle or Google Classroom helped some students organize and turn in assignments by offering a predictable channel of communication. They liked a shared online system where students could find assignments and resources quickly. The elementary teachers used classroom blogs or webpages for similar organizational purposes. For instance, one teacher made a single classroom blog entry that included all the links to websites that students would need for their research. Rather than asking her young students to painstakingly type in four web addresses, a skill that was not the focus of the research project, the teacher allowed students to navigate via the classroom blog. Teachers at all grade levels who spoke about time saved because of organizational tools felt that saved time created opportunities to extend or deepen students' learning.

Power

Sometimes praise for technological efficiency was connected to power. This was explicit in descriptions of statistics projects, where laptops and powerful statistical tools allowed students to focus on analyzing and interpreting large data sets, instead of spending time generating data, entering raw data into spreadsheets, plotting graphs, or calculating statistical measurements by hand. As software handles the representational work and the repetitive calculations, the ability of students to analyze information increases significantly. In the words of one teacher, "The laptops have blown that up even more with the CPMP-Tools and the different visualizations and the different things we can do—I mean the histograms and creating a thousand trials of something—you couldn't do that [before]; it just wasn't feasible."

Students also made this connection. One noted, "[In] college statistics, I took it last year, and I found it was really nice. ... You could analyze and replicate large amounts of data and it was nice because you could

... make the graphs and then find from there the quartiles, the ranges, the standard deviation, and all that. It was just nice, so you could visualize such a large amount of data without having to individually put in each plot. ... Instead of flipping a coin five hundred times, you could simulate that in five seconds." The learning objective in this statistics example was not creating visualizations of the graph by hand but rather analyzing large data sets, a task the student could focus on and take further because of technology.

Facets of Efficiency

Technological efficiency has multiple facets:

- Getting things done faster (e.g., typing speed)
- Accessing resources (e.g., online research, 24/7 course access)
- Organizing learning (e.g., searchable notes)
- Gaining power (e.g., analyzing large data sets)

These facets may be pursued for different reasons:

- Productivity, simply getting more done
- Saved time that can be reinvested

Why Value Efficiency?

Increased speed, access, organization, and power were key components of the efficiencies that teachers and students saw in learning with digital tools. Their comments suggested two underlying rationales for valuing these efficiency gains. The first was efficiency for the sake of productivity. Why take a long time to complete something that could be done more quickly? Like many others in the digital age, many students at Modern Christian Schools believed that completing tasks faster was simply better in and of itself.[6] This may prove valuable in some instances, a fact that should be recognized. Yet speed does not always lead to deeper or more effective learning, a caution that teachers shared across focus groups. We explore this caution further in the next chapter.

The second rationale was recaptured time that could be leveraged for other purposes. Saved time could be invested to enhance student learning, often in ways that focused on deeper engagement rather than just getting more tasks completed. The teachers and administrators were most articulate about this pedagogical benefit and typically described it as more important than productivity. They aimed to leverage efficiency gains to stretch the space for deep and engaging learning.

Designing Curriculum

There were signs that efficiency gains might sometimes be connected to efforts to relate Christian faith and learning. A case study math teacher discussed an emerging idea for a new lesson relating justice and accessible drinking water to existing work on scaling, percentage, ratios, and fractions. He described reading an online article about the realities of access to clean drinking water around the world, which began to spark ideas for a new lesson. The combination of speed and access to resources about accessible drinking water allowed him to efficiently locate potential resources for a quickly approaching unit. While showing an online image of a woman in a developing country laboring to carry an enormous bucket of water, the teacher described the possibilities of connecting it to math. "These women . . . carry [the water] three kilometers one way. They do it nine times a day . . . and they get paid 900 birr, and I think a birr is a nickel. I don't know, maybe it's not, it's not much." As the math teacher continued to develop his tentative ideas aloud, the beginning threads of a connection between justice and math were taking shape. Just two weeks later, the same teacher was asked about the intersections between technology, faith, and content:

> Well, [technology] gives you that real data that's current. The other day . . . I was looking at just the percentage of people that . . . have access to clean drinking water, and which country's the poorest and the richest. You're changing from one day to the next. It's that live. It's not like a book, "Well, ten years ago . . ." It's now. You can get videos about it and show them. . . . I had one where they don't have water, and then they walk two miles every day to get their water. . . . You can watch that. It's pretty cool actually. You know, back in the day, they still used technology. We had to find some film, remember to order it a week ahead of time. Remember those days? And then sometimes it would get eaten by the film projector. If you remember all that, it's so much easier nowadays.

The ability to access up-to-date, relevant, real-world data enhanced the teacher's ability to create a justice-based connection to the math curriculum that was grounded in faith commitments. The teacher capitalized on the spark of an idea and drew on the speed and accessibility of digital resources to quickly research material to meet the multiple criteria taking shape in his mind (e.g., data for calculations, sites/organizations with an emphasis on action, age-appropriate introductions to the issue). When all the pieces came together, students used real-time data to calculate how many people lack access to water and the related infant mortality rate. They made comparisons and extrapolations to the Modern Christian Schools population. They answered reflection questions about what God calls us to do in response and followed this up with whole-class discussions about the Christian moral responsibility to respond to injustice. The lesson did not reduce justice to a series of decontextualized math problems supporting only math goals with biblical glosses. It promoted a deeper exploration of justice issues related to accessible clean water. Such exploration was possible because rich, relevant resources were easily available to the teacher, who could make them immediately available to students through Google Classroom. This lesson joined others that served a similar purpose in the overall teaching sequence.

As Christian schools shift away from sole reliance on printed curriculum toward a curriculum constantly being reshaped by resources available online, this teacher's work highlights new opportunities. The efficiency of technology makes it easier for teachers and students to draw on broad resources to make rich connections between faith and current disciplinary content.

Such, at least, is the positive side of the story. The examples just discussed underscore a general sense of optimism among teachers about the academic benefits ushered in when the efficiency-related promises of new technologies are fulfilled. The same teachers are quick to report that understanding how to best leverage these efficiencies did not come easily. It took time to sort the valuable technologies from those that were touted to be the newest, best, or greatest but ultimately did not serve learning. Teachers who succeeded at this had to adopt a mindset that focused on the nature of the content and pedagogical goal rather than the device, and applied any efficiency gains toward that goal.[7] This kept efficiency in and of itself from masquerading as the goal.

A critical approach to the pedagogical usefulness of technologies helps us move beyond a view of technology as simply an efficient tool for getting more done. The appeal of efficient tools often opens the door to the broader effects of technology. We seek a more efficient tool for completing a task, and using the new tool builds new habits, expectations, and patterns of behavior. In time, the new tool helps shape a new culture within which we develop, influenced in ways that we did not anticipate when we first adopted the tool. Teachers at Modern Christian Schools sensed this dynamic, for in the same breath that they described the benefits of technological efficiency, they shared concerns about the ways that these same technologies could serve as a medium shaping beliefs and practices. We turn to these concerns in the next chapter.

For Reflection and Response

- Compare the findings in this chapter with the discussion of differentiation in the last chapter. How might the efficiency benefits of digital technology described here help in raising the success of all students?
- What signs do you see in this chapter of technology functioning not just as a tool for completing tasks but as a medium that helps shape our values?
- Are there any downsides to increasing efficiency and productivity in learning? When might efficiency and productivity not be virtues?

CHAPTER 17

Completing Assignments
but Cheating Ourselves

It's more addicting than I thought it would be. Also, I think that it tempts people to do things that they aren't supposed to be doing—like instead of doing your homework you could be instant messaging.

Student

A recurring theme in discussions of the nature of technology has to do with how new tools help foster new patterns of practice that change how we live.[1] Particularly with tools that take up as much of our time and attention as digital technologies, it is worth wondering whether, as well as helping us complete tasks more efficiently, the new medium is also influencing our relationship to those tasks. In fact, even as teachers and students applauded the efficiencies of technology, they showed a simultaneous awareness of causes for concern. Their worries focused on how the practices and behaviors taking shape in a digital environment might be forming us in unhelpful ways.

The Temptations of Efficiency

Students themselves were quick to tell us that technological efficiencies heightened temptations toward distraction, laziness, or academic dishonesty.[2] They recounted many examples of shortcutting or even cheating: seeking quick answers with Command-F instead of reading an assigned article, using the "three-finger tap" to reveal definitions during a vocabulary quiz, plagiarizing sections of a paper from an online source, using cell phones to take a picture of a test and send it to a friend, and more.[3] Each of these is in one sense an efficiency gain, but not one that actually aids learning or integrity.

Focus group conversations left no doubt that students were aware of temptations and knowledgeable about specific ways to use digital devices toward unethical ends. However, once students started describing actual behaviors, they distanced themselves. They described "other students," maybe friends or other high schoolers, who fell victim to the temptation, but rarely did they implicate themselves. This is understandable in a focus group setting, answering a stranger's questions in front of peers. It also suggests awareness that the behaviors in question are problematic.

In our surveys, students' responses about using technology to shortcut learning were generally reflective of middle and high schoolers across the United States. For general school populations, more than 75% of students in various studies report engaging in at least one instance of shortcutting learning.[4] At Modern Christian Schools, more than half of the students reported that the way technology was used in the school allowed them to find answers without understanding them. Nearly three-fourths agreed that technology use led them to look for quick and easy answers to problems. Approximately a third agreed that they were more likely, as a result of technology use, to skim over material when they knew they should be reading it deeply (see table 17.1)

Table 17.1. Student views on using technology to shortcut learning

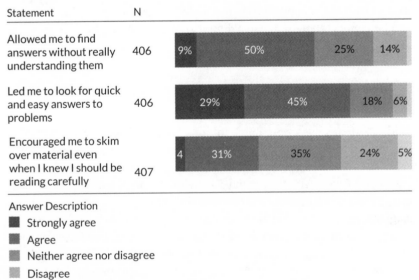

How much do you agree that the way technology is used in school has done the following?

Statement	N				
Allowed me to find answers without really understanding them	406	9%	50%	25%	14%
Led me to look for quick and easy answers to problems	406	29%	45%	18%	6%
Encouraged me to skim over material even when I knew I should be reading carefully	407	4	31%	35%	24%	5%

Answer Description
■ Strongly agree
■ Agree
■ Neither agree nor disagree
▨ Disagree
▨ Strongly disagree

While we did not directly ask students in surveys whether using technology led them to cheat, we did ask questions designed to provide a picture of regularly occurring student behavior, with or without technology. We asked students how often in the past year they cheated on schoolwork. Seventy-eight percent said they almost never cheat, 14% said they cheat one to three times per month, and the remaining 8% reported cheating at least once per week. So even though the focus groups demonstrate that the students knew technology made cheating easier, the survey data may suggest some limits on the percentage of students that were using technology to cheat on a monthly basis or more. It is worth noting that Modern Christian Schools students report cheating less often than high school students in some national studies.[5] The survey responses also suggest that more students find it acceptable to use technology to shortcut the learning process than to cheat.

Addressing Temptation

These temptations and shortcuts have not gone unrecognized. Modern Christian Schools administrators and teachers were clearly aware of undesirable behaviors related to technological efficiency. They also understood that similar temptations have always been present but are "far easier with the technology" and therefore warrant special attention as use of digital technology increases.

One response was to block the technological feature itself—for instance, by trying to disable the "three-finger tap" on students' laptops. Another was to increase monitoring and then intervene with specific students—for instance, by using software that scans for plagiarism and creating a plan to address the problem with offenders. The schools also worked to explicitly raise students' awareness of these temptations, integrating discussions or assignments on the topic into classes. For example, English teachers and students described lessons about plagiarism and contracts that students sign promising not to plagiarize content. In Spanish, where students try to use Google Translate to shortcut the work of translating English to Spanish, teachers have whole-class discussions about what happens when students use technologies in ways that bypass learning goals. A Spanish teacher describes this conversation as helping students understand "how you can get away with completing the task but cheat yourself."

Teachers also applied educational research about technology to their own classrooms. One told us, "I've been reading a lot of research about memory, and it's in the research that you remember things better when you write them down."[6] Others shared how similar research guided them in deciding when students should write or type notes, weighing efficiency against depth of learning. These teachers' reasons for making specific technology choices were shaping students' ideas. A middle school student described a teacher who made them take most notes by hand "because he's seen [from] scientists . . . that [you] can remember better if you write [it] down." Another student added, "And I do find that true." The same group of students also described some teachers letting them choose how to take notes, "which is nice because some people prefer writing it down, and it gets stuck in your memory better so that's nice that they do that." High schoolers likewise described sometimes choosing handwriting over typing if they wanted to recall the information better. Such responses suggest that teachers were finding some ways to help students think about their learning processes in relation to the choice of medium. Students saw teachers questioning technological efficiencies and making informed choices. They could rearticulate the teachers' rationales and at times showed insightful reflection about the ways that technologies like laptops, tablets, and phones may be shaping them. This is no small gain and reflects an important step toward discerning use of technology.

Focusing on Task Completion

Despite the schools' attempts to address the temptations of laziness and cheating that come with certain technologies, the survey data show the related behaviors persisting. Data from the focus groups and case study interviews with high schoolers suggest some possible reasons why. They also suggest a different kind of concern, one not focused on individual breach of ethical boundaries.

Hovering behind specific instances of shortcutting or cheating is a broader task-completion mindset. A number of high school students were especially focused on the efficient completion of assignments. While occasionally useful, a focus on the time it took to finish work often overshadowed attention to the content or learning process. The point was simply to get things done efficiently. Such a mindset tempts students to reduce the very purpose of education to the swift and successful completion of tasks. Several influences help fuel it.

A task-completion mindset is linked to the ways schools have historically rewarded student learning. Learning in schools has commonly been measured by course-based grades. Research evidence across four decades suggests that many common grading practices lead students to preferentially choose the easiest possible task.[7] Students have learned that achieving a high grade on a task is equivalent to success in school, and that choosing the most demanding path is not the most efficient way to secure high grades. When grading is poorly designed, completing the task and banking the grade as efficiently as possible become more important than the learning that the task was meant to facilitate.

The task-completion mindset is also linked to values of speed and individual productivity promoted in Western cultures. Individual measures of success understood in terms of productivity favor those who complete work, even when the time required to complete the work comes at the cost of a healthy balance between work and other aspects of life. This produces a cultural push toward speed of execution in which time is experienced as scarce and the focus is on not getting left behind.

These influences are amplified by increased digital connectivity. Access to work tasks beyond the physical and temporal boundaries of the workplace has expanded. When our tasks are constantly within reach of the nearest phone or computer, there is a heightened sense that we should be able to complete more of them. Virtually never disconnected from the demands of productivity, we allow work to seep into time that once was devoted to family, sleep, and pastimes. We experience a heightened sense of the need to complete tasks because our technologies make it possible to do so. This recalls some of the very features of technology described by teachers as gains in chapter 16: students can now access tasks at all times, increasing productivity. Various scholars have also argued that it is part of the character of modern technology that devices tend to present themselves to us as instruments of mere technique, distracting our attention away from the goods they were meant to serve to the mere efficiency of the process itself.[8]

Another influence comes from the appeal of digital media. In contrast to the teachers and administrators, who saw the value of technological efficiencies in reclaiming time for deeper learning, some high school students viewed the reclaimed time as a legitimate opportunity for recreation. Students openly justified finishing an assignment swiftly in order to use laptops or cell phones during class time to text friends, shop online, watch live sports, finish other homework assignments, and more. As we observed in case study classrooms, students were not often using the reclaimed time to extend or deepen learning opportunities unless required to do so by the teacher. Instead, they were opting for digital diversions. As one student commented, "You know, my go-to is to go to my phone. If I have an extra five minutes in class, that's just what I will do." A significant part of what makes this behavior feel justified is the task-completion mindset; as long as the task has been efficiently completed and logged, the obligation to the school has been fulfilled. What is left is free time, which can be maximized by completing the task quickly.

Ironically, this mindset promoted procrastination. Students justified putting off work that could be completed in class, promising themselves they would finish it later so that they could enjoy technological diversions now. A student explained, "A lot of times if you have the entire time to just work, sometimes you're like, oh, I have time; once I'm home I'll do it then if something's due the next day. Then you'll mess around for those 45 minutes and go, oh, I can do it later—procrastinate. So, then that just stops you from doing work."

If the goal is task completion, and the task can be completed later, then turning to entertainment in class feels justified, something not really at odds with the underlying goal. Combined with 24/7 online access to assignments and resources, this helps erode boundaries between school time and leisure time, expanding the boundaries of the task-completion zone later into the evening.

In some cases, students described teacher expectations about technology use in class as a factor that unintentionally endorsed a task-completion mindset. Teacher expectations were widely varied, but according to high school students, some teachers allowed the use of laptops and phones for nonclass purposes after assignments were finished. Others allowed use during the class period as long as the assignment was eventually completed. Some teachers completely prohibited technological devices for nonlearning use. When possible, we asked students in the case studies why they were using phones and laptops for purposes other than the classwork. They often responded with statements like "[teacher name] doesn't really care if you're on your phone." They qualified these statements with recognition that it was only acceptable "as long as you get it [work] done," or that teachers didn't police the matter because "it is your responsibility" to pay attention or complete work. Students then followed up these justifications with statements like "I don't have much of a problem staying on task." There was an underlying sense that perhaps the teachers would hold different expectations if students were not completing their work. The main thing was to complete the task.

Given the distracting tug associated with digital media, the urge to return quickly to one's own technological pastimes heightens the temptation to finish assignments too quickly, prioritizing efficiency over deep learning. Savvy students wanting to return to their diversions sought easier or faster ways to complete assignments and ended up shortcutting learning. Even students who believed they were using saved time productively by completing other work may have shortcut their own learning in one class for the benefit of another.

The Two Faces of Efficiency

In the previous chapter, we heard praise for the efficiencies offered by digital technologies in terms of speed, access, organization, and power. When intentionally harnessed for pedagogical purposes, these efficiencies can support high-quality teaching and learning. Yet the same efficiencies heighten particular temptations and lead to various abuses of technology. A majority of Modern Christian Schools students reported using technology in ways that diminished learning. The overall patterns suggest that this should not be regarded simply as a matter of individual lapses. Cultural, institutional, and social messages nudge students toward valuing efficient task completion as a primary goal of school. Even as the schools took specific steps to resist some of the effects of these messages, some teachers were contributing to their reinforcement. The result seemed to be at best rather mixed messages. Getting things done can be an important element of success in school; at the same time it is possible to get more things done and, in the end, learn less and grow less.

These concerns push us further beyond thinking of technology as an efficient tool and into the effects of technology as a medium on our practices. Technology does not just help us get things done. It also imperceptibly reshapes how we experience time, work, learning, and priorities. Yet this need not be a pessimistic or deterministic story. Responding to the downsides of efficiency requires examining the values implicit in our current practices and devising consistent patterns of practice that point in a constructive direction. We saw just this happening as teachers began to respond to emerging concerns. In later chapters we will see how intentional Christian practices have been emerging at Modern Christian Schools, practices focused on learning slowly, taking sabbath rests, and prioritizing gracious speech over efficient communication. The challenge is to weave such practices far enough into the fabric of school life that they do not simply serve as occasional interruptions of a task-completion culture.

For Reflection and Response

- Are students justified in playing games or watching videos in class if they have completed a task or think they can complete it later? Are they justified in completing work for another class? Why or why not?
- How might schools or educators shape classroom practices to encourage students to move beyond task completion as an end goal?
- What might healthy boundaries between school and personal or family time look like when technology makes tasks always accessible?

Part 3 Summary

This part of the book has focused on how and whether digital technologies are helping teachers at Modern Christian Schools to change teaching and learning in positive ways, thereby serving their students better. We addressed these central questions: How are teachers making choices about when to use technology for learning? What benefits for learning do they perceive, and are they being realized? Are those benefits tied to any pedagogical downsides?

- When we focused on teachers who seemed to be experiencing success integrating technology into their teaching, we found them emphasizing the importance of play and experimentation, both for themselves and their students. Their efforts at innovation were driven by pedagogical questions rather than by the capacities of the technologies themselves. This work flourishes, in part, as schools create an atmosphere that welcomes risk-taking and innovation.

- As we stepped back to consider the faculty as a whole, we found varying reasons for making decisions about technology. Sometimes decisions were pragmatic, based on whether a digital tool seemed to offer efficiency gains or promote twenty-first-century skills. Teachers also made decisions about when to use technology, taking into consideration experiences of embodiment and real-world imperfection, the effects on interaction among students, concerns about distraction, and the wanted or unwanted connotations that particular technologies carry with them. These bases for decision-making showed the influence of faith concerns.

- Technology was adopted in part because of its promise to enhance student learning. One perceived benefit was enhancement of capacity for student inquiry. Survey and observational data show that technology use was in fact associated with relatively substantial levels of inquiry-based learning at the high school level, yet such learning was limited at the lower grades. Nevertheless, teachers at all levels believed that technology had made their teaching more inquiry-based.

- A second perceived benefit focused on higher-order thinking skills, especially student creativity. Observational data show that device use at Modern Christian Schools was indeed associated with activities requiring advanced cognitive skills. There was resistance to using technology simply for drill-type activity. While teachers did not talk about these gains in ways that explicitly connected to mission language, some connected them to other faith themes concerning the image of God and vocation.

- A third perceived benefit concerned the capacity to differentiate instruction to enhance the success of all learners. Survey data showed both teachers and students affirming gains in this regard, and observational evidence confirmed this. The benefits were experienced not only in terms of academic achievement but also in terms of inclusion. This theme was connected in teachers' minds with the idea of respecting all students as made in God's image, with individual gifts.

- A more pragmatic benefit that was widely noted by teachers and students concerned various facets of efficiency. Digital technologies were felt to offer gains in terms of the speed at which tasks could be accomplished, the ease of access to resources, enhanced ability to organize work, and expansion of the capacity for more powerful analysis of information. Teachers saw the efficiency gains as saving time that could be reinvested in deeper learning and in more intentional Christian curriculum design.

- On the student side, efficiency gains were not an unmitigated blessing. The presence of tools for more efficiently completing tasks heightened the temptation to cut corners when completing tasks or even to cheat, temptations that remained in spite of explicit school efforts to counter them. This was not simply a matter of individual lapses but reflected a larger pattern in which a task-completion mindset was reinforced by digital connectivity. When students perceived the main goal to be task completion, their inclination to cut corners in order to turn to entertainment, or to choose entertainment first and procrastinate, was strengthened. Sometimes teacher choices reinforced this mindset.

PART 4

DISCERNMENT

In part 2 we explored the idea that technology might serve as a tool for pursuing the schools' Christian mission. Part 3 considered how the changes brought by new technologies are affecting academic learning, which is often associated in the Modern Christian Schools community with the "prepare minds" part of their mission. But "prepare minds" is joined in the mission statement with "nurture lives" and "for Christ." This invites us to explore another thread connecting faith and technology. When administrators, teachers, and parents talk about how technology should be used, their focus is not only (often not even primarily) on academic outcomes. They are also concerned about how to make *wise* decisions with students' overall formation in mind, decisions that reflect Christian discernment. This brings even more clearly to the fore reflection on technology not just as a tool but as a medium that might shape us. How might technology decisions be related to the effort to "determine what is best, so that in the day of Christ you may be pure and blameless" (Phil. 1:10)? This part of the book examines what Christian discernment with technology looks like at Modern Christian Schools.

Christian discernment is a faith practice with a long tradition. We therefore begin this section with some consideration of what Christian discernment means in wider theological discussions, and why it is relevant to technological changes (chapter 18). We then consider another concept that has played a role in the schools' thinking, sketching the similarities and differences between Christian discernment and digital citizenship (chapter 19). This puts us in a position to see more clearly how the schools' ideas about Christian discernment evolved as they moved from initial vision to planning faculty development and formulating written policy (chapter 20).

With this map of the key framing ideas in place, we turn to the concerns about wise choices with technology that emerged in conversation with community members. We begin with the question of screen time (chapter 21). We examine how much screen time students experience, and on which kinds of devices, comparing the students at Modern Christian Schools to national trends. We then move to more directly moral concerns: Will there be an increased risk of exposure to immoral and harmful material online if students spend more time with digital devices (chapter 22)? The schools have responded to this concern in part by implementing filtering and monitoring technologies. Are these proving helpful, and is students' risk level really increased by their participation in the technology program (chapter 23)? Finally, we broaden the lens to consider discernment issues that are not well addressed by worries about filtering out immoral content. Even if the filtering is successful, what might the effort to avoid bad material be missing in a digital environment suffused with pressures toward distraction and consumerism (chapter 24)? How does the goal of teaching students to think from a Christian perspective or worldview relate to discernment with technology (chapter 25)?

In this section we see faith framing a concern for technological choices that are grounded in Christian discernment. We also see the effort of Christian discernment engaged in a complex, shifting dance with ongoing changes in technology, teaching resources, and concerns about the internet.

CHAPTER 18

What Is Christian Discernment?

Interviewer: What does "discernment" mean?
High school student: It's knowing . . . the line between right and wrong.

Some research suggests that working with digital technologies can enhance academic achievement.[1] Yet once we start seeing technology not just as a tool for getting things done more efficiently but as an environment in which we learn to operate, or the focus of a new set of practices, other questions come to the fore. When our technological choices will affect the habits and choices of those in our care, our choices matter more. Whether we tend toward technological optimism or pessimism, the sense that we are experimenting not just with academic outcomes but with our children's broader formation raises the stakes.

High stakes can lead to large anxieties. Consider one prominent scholar's warnings about the dangers of uncritically embracing new technologies. Here is a summary of his key worries:

• Traditionally, wisdom was something we stored up within ourselves, something we worked to make part of our very being. Now we lean on external stores of information.
• This reliance on information storage leaves us missing out on being shaped by what we learn. We have more data but are not helped to grow morally. What we do glean we use to show off and win arguments.
• There is now so much information that no one can take in even a fraction of it, and it is very hard to know what sources to believe. Even the best of us end up confused.

In sum, we are becoming mere consumers of information, shallow and vain, instead of people formed in wisdom. Which particular technology or technologies do you think he has in view here?

The scholar in question was John Amos Comenius, an early pioneer of modern education.[2] He was writing in the 1660s and worrying about technological changes that had been under way since the mid-fifteenth century. Here are his own words:

> By what means do we transmit learning to our fellow-men? There was a time when wisdom was carried in men's hearts, but today it has begun to be put into print, and hence it is confined to books and libraries and is rarely found in the thoughts, words, and actions of men. So many books are now available that no student could read one thousandth part of them in his lifetime, and they are so diverse as to put the steadiest of heads into a spin. Bookshelves are therefore more decorative than useful, becoming objects of vanity or sources of confusion if the reader persists in poring over all the contents. This accounts for the increase in badly-taught scholars or clever men who talk nonsense. The fact is that books are taught instead of people, or at least if people are taught, they are confused.[3]

The disruptive technological innovation that worried Comenius was the invention of printing and the rapid proliferation of the handheld devices known as books. The technologies of learning were changing, and Comenius embraced the possibilities with enthusiasm, authoring many books himself. Yet he also worried about how our own flaws might shape our response to new technologies, and how those technologies might in turn form us. His worries sound eerily familiar amid our own digital revolution.

Now pause for a moment of reflection. What was your own reaction to this example of past fears? Was your first instinct to smile knowingly and reflect that people have always worried too much, that we learned how to learn from print and got along fine with books in the long run? Were you reassured that the technophobes will eventually see the same happen with our newest inventions? Or was your first reaction more a feeling of concern that after hundreds of years we still rush headlong into dangerous waters and are no closer to real wisdom? Does the repetition of similar fears across history suggest to you that we should lighten up a little—or that the dangers have not gone away? Comenius's words could be heard in either way. Your reaction may offer some indication of your own degree of technological optimism or pessimism. Knowing our own biases may be one step toward wisdom.

Regardless of which conclusion most tempts us, one aspect of Comenius's comments that we can identify as perennially Christian is the way
he frames the question. His key question was not about efficiency or productivity but about who we are likely to become. He focused on our ability
to live individually and communally with integrity. Which of our tendencies might be amplified by technological changes? This kind of concern
is a significant ingredient in the Christian practice of discernment, the
practice that seeks to discover whether our choices are consistent with
our sanctification.

Discernment seems a necessary element in any Christian consideration of new technologies. Among the administrators, teachers, and parents with whom we interacted, the desire to practice and teach Christian
discernment was an explicit and recurring theme.[4] It was a central concept in the schools' efforts to articulate what was Christian about their approach to technology. An early set of "technology belief statements" that
continued to guide the schools' deliberations affirmed that "technology
is becoming an increasingly critical part of the learning experience and
curriculum delivery as well as meeting the mission of the school." This was
followed by the affirmation, echoed in various later documents, that "as
Christians it is critical that we continue to teach students discernment and
ethical use of technology." The schools' consistent stance is well captured
in a 2007 memo: "We shouldn't hide from the technology but rather help
our children become responsible and discerning in the use of technology."
The practice of Christian discernment thus offers a third window, alongside mission language and serving student learning, into how technology
connects with faith at Modern Christian Schools.

Discernment as Christian Practice

What might members of the school community be invoking when they
talk of Christian discernment with technology? Discernment is a Christian
practice aimed at finding our way when the truth about ourselves and our
futures is fogged by fallenness and finitude. It overlaps with some other
terms widely used inside and outside the Christian tradition to refer to the
art of steering well through life, terms such as wisdom, prudence, and practical judgment.[5] Different Christian contexts and traditions understand the
practice of discernment in differing ways, bringing particular emphases to
the fore. Nevertheless, talk of Christian discernment involves some recur-

ring themes that distinguish it from practical judgment and appear across a range of Christian accounts. Discernment is connected to our relationship to God, our relationship to our neighbor and community, our calling and mission, and our engagement in spiritual practices and disciplines.

Christian talk of discernment is rooted in several New Testament passages. The opening verses of Romans 12 call on the Christian community to avoid being conformed to the pattern of the world, but instead to be transformed by the renewing of their minds as they offer themselves in worship. The result of this renewal should be that they, as a community, "may discern what is the will of God" (Rom. 12:2). This suggests an ability to make discriminating judgments and choices that is intimately connected with how we pattern our lives and the loves to which we give ourselves. Discernment is a challenge connected not merely to our understanding but also to holiness, to a state in which, as Rowan Williams puts it, "delight in the beauty of God is the goal of our action."[6] First Corinthians 12:7–10 refers to the ability to distinguish between spirits as a gift of the Holy Spirit, given for the common good. Paul prays for the church at Philippi that they may "determine what is best, so that in the day of Christ you may be pure and blameless" (Phil. 1:10). Similarly, in 1 Thessalonians 5:20–22 Paul urges the church to test any proclamation of the truth that comes to them, to reject the false, and to hold on to the good. In these and similar passages, discernment is positioned in the New Testament as both a gift and a discipline necessary for the Christian community. It is a matter not simply of arriving at correct mental conclusions but of living well as the body of Christ, in communion with its head, amid the potential for deception and harm.

As discussion of discernment has unfolded in Christian theology, there have been many attempts at defining the term. One recent review of the literature identifies 280 theological monographs on the topic since 1957.[7] For present purposes, a succinct description of discernment by Henri Nouwen captures some core themes as well as any: "Discernment is a spiritual understanding and an experiential knowledge of how God is active in daily life that is acquired through disciplined spiritual practice. Discernment is faithful living and listening to God's love and direction so that we can fulfill our individual calling and shared mission."[8]

Nouwen highlights several features that are evident in the biblical texts mentioned above and that stretch discernment beyond practical judgment. Discernment is rooted in learning to listen to God and to know God's character and desires. It is therefore connected with our spiritual practices and formation.[9] It requires that we become shaped as those who can engage in such listening rather than being driven only by our own motives.[10] We are to work this out not just in attempts to believe true things but also in the way we pattern life together. Discernment is not a heroic, individual quest but is deeply tied to belonging within the body of Christ; we discern in community.[11] We seek to exercise discernment so that we know not just what we should do next individually but also how our actions might embody love of God and neighbor and contribute to shared mission. Discernment is thus focused not so much on figuring out how best to achieve our personal goals as on figuring out how our actions are part of the coming kingdom of God. It is a place "where prayer meets action."[12]

> **Key Themes in Theological Accounts of Discernment**
>
> - How do our choices affect our relationship with God?
> - How do they affect our relationships with others?
> - How do they affect our spiritual and moral formation?
> - How do they affect our pursuit of vocation and mission?

Discernment is about what spirit or spirits we are serving, not just about effective outcomes. Since we serve a Spirit who is love and seeks our good, our own flourishing remains part of the picture, but in a way that points beyond itself. The practice of discernment resists a view of the world as a closed system in which we simply need to figure out the best way to get things done. It sees the world as a place where God is active and love is at stake, and focuses our attention on whether we will end up more or less connected to that activity and love.

Discernment and Technology

What does all of this have to do with digital technologies? The need to think in terms of discernment arises wherever we sense that new technological practices might affect the following:

- Our relationship with God
- Our relationships with one another
- Our moral and spiritual formation
- Our vocation and mission

All of these possible impacts push us past questions of utility (Will this device get the job done faster?) and into questions of identity and purpose

(Will this device affect who we are and what we seek?). Even with regard to mission, a focus on discernment pushes us to ask not only whether a new technology offers a tool to further our mission but whether our engagement with the technology might shift our sense of mission and the way we live.

Connecting technological change to Christian discernment places our practical judgments in a larger context. It pushes us toward questions of how our educational technologies are fitting into our spiritual formation, the well-being of all members of our community, and our ability to pursue our shared calling. Data on questions such as whether using tablets affects math scores or increases student engagement might feed into this picture at some point, but they are not yet enough to help us with questions of discernment. The task of Christian discernment includes asking how new technologies might shape the faith and life of the community and our capacity to respond to God and to the world. We have seen related themes emerging as teachers reflect on whether to teach with or without particular digital resources. Before we take a closer look at how the idea of Christian discernment informed the technology program at Modern Christian Schools, we first need to clarify its relationship to another idea that played a role, that of digital citizenship. That will be the topic of the next chapter.

For Reflection and Response

- Choose a technology that you use regularly, in the school setting or outside it. Do the facets of Christian discernment described in this chapter suggest any critical questions about how you use the technology?
- How is the outline of discernment in this chapter similar to or different from the criteria usually used to evaluate new technologies in your school or a school you know?
- In what ways might a school encourage community-wide practices of discernment?

CHAPTER 19

Christian Discernment and Digital Citizenship

[Students] were writing all about books, so informational chapter books. [One little boy] wanted to do his topic on mahi-mahi. . . . It was awesome because he and I could sit together, and I could even reiterate the digital citizenship lesson, saying, "Okay we're going to go online together because I am an adult and you have permission and we are going to Google search and we are going to find a picture. . . . And we're searching and finding information, and he actually knew more than I thought.

Teacher

Questions about discernment connect moral and theological themes to concrete, everyday occurrences in classrooms where digital media are regularly incorporated into learning. The teachers in our study described their developing strategies for navigating the unexpected hazards that can pop up in the midst of digital media use. One described working with an elementary school student who was using a tablet to research a particular species of fish online. "I got [the screen] on the spot that didn't have the bikini girls holding the fish," the teacher recalled, "because you're just searching images, you know? That's dangerous. So, I got it on the spot where it was a safe fish for him to look at." The cautionary step proved ineffective. "Then he went to scroll up and there was bikini girl and I thought, 'Shoot!' . . . So, I just scrolled back down. So, it's not perfect even with an adult; you just have to teach into that and say, 'I don't think we need to look . . . this is why we go with an adult.'" Another teacher recounted how using online resources could derail the best-laid plans. "You plan it out and there are some things that catch you off guard. Like poison ivy. I didn't know that there was a stripper [named] Poison Ivy, until we searched up 'poison ivy.'" The need to exercise and teach discernment is brought to the fore as online resources enter the classroom alongside or in place of carefully curated textbooks, and the question arises of how to build wise practices around digital access.

Engage the World, Beware the World

Concerns about digital safety are hardly unique to Christian schools, yet Christian faith can help shape a sense of what particular boundaries need to be protected. Once devices offer immediate access to an online world that offers everything from Bible study tools to violent porn with equal facility, it is not surprising that personal and moral safety emerges as a concern. Placing this concern alongside mission recalls the tension between the themes of cultural separation and cultural engagement in the faith history of Modern Christian Schools (see chapter 5). Mission language that talks of bringing change to the world offers a picture of reaching out beyond the walls of school, with the direction of influence moving outward. Yet the shift to digital technologies also punctures the boundaries in the opposite direction, creating the constant potential for unwelcome material to surface right in the midst of learning sequences, like moles in a manicured lawn. Here discernment becomes a key theme.

Discernment is not merely a challenge for teachers but also something to be taught to students. A school magazine article explained to parents that "while we teach students to harness the power of computers to conduct science experiments or create a Clayanimation of a Bible story, we have a greater responsibility to teach students discernment in their use of the technology available to them." At one level this is a truism. Students will need to be able to make discerning choices with new technologies long after current digital tools are obsolete. At another level it is a puzzle. Teaching students to use an app or crunch data is an easier process for teachers to master than teaching discernment. Teachers can download ready-made lesson plans and learning materials for teaching many technological applications. Software and devices come with manuals and tutorials. Yet how does one teach Christian discernment with changing technologies? Teachers now face the simultaneous task of figuring out how to make their own wise choices with new digital technologies and helping students to be discerning in a changing technological environment. This is no small set of responsibilities.

As we will see in the next chapter, when school leaders turned to drafting professional development plans and policies, the language of Christian discernment soon became joined to talk of digital citizenship. Since both ideas have played a role in the way thinking developed at Modern Christian Schools, we will take a little time in this chapter to explore the similarities and differences between them.

Defining Digital Citizenship

In chapter 18 we identified several themes in theological accounts of discernment. Discernment is a practice that questions how our choices affect our relationship to God and others, the ways we grow morally and spiritually, and our capacity to fulfill our vocation and mission. While discernment is a familiar theological concept, digital citizenship is an increasingly familiar educational idea. The concept of digital citizenship has occupied scholars seeking to understand technology-driven changes in how citizens participate in society. It has also attracted attention among educators seeking to prepare students for life in a digital world.[1]

In digitally networked societies, we increasingly connect with others, access information and services, and learn about our world online. The skills needed to take part effectively in society have shifted. This has in turn shifted schools' sense of how to help students grow up as constructive citizens. Knowing that online interactions have potential for both good and harm sharpens the sense that education is needed if students are to be prepared to take up their social roles safely and responsibly. New curricular frameworks and resources seek to chart a way forward, and they have increasingly done this under the banner of digital citizenship.

The idea of digital citizenship has come to cover a range of themes. Moonsun Choi's analysis of several hundred articles dealing with digital citizenship and closely related terms suggests four general emphases:[2]

- *Digital ethics*, focusing on "how Internet users appropriately, safely, ethically, and responsibly engage" in online activities.[3] Areas of concern include copyright, privacy, cyberbullying, respectful interaction with others, and freedom of speech. There is a desire to avoid harms that we might suffer as internet users as well as ways we might harm others as internet users.[4]
- *Media and information literacy*, referring to "one's abilities to access, use, create, and evaluate information and to communicate with others online."[5] The idea of literacy here goes beyond the traditional focus

on the ability to decode text. It includes the ability to weigh, critique, and contribute to online communication. This begins with basic computer skills but opens out into broader communication skills and critical awareness.

- *Participation/engagement* refers to "different types of online engagement, including political, socio-economic, and cultural participation."[6] As politics, culture, commerce, and self-expression have moved online, taking an active part in society requires the ability to engage effectively online.
- *Critical resistance* reflects "more progressive and radical viewpoints."[7] These focus on the potential of digital media to foster social change. We can use digital media to resist injustices, make marginal voices heard, and challenge the status quo.

Digital citizenship, then, is a complex concept that includes a range of information, ethical concerns, skills, and forms of participation. These are centered on our ability to take up a responsible and engaged role in our community. Digital citizenship education seeks to produce capable and constructive contributors to a digital society. It also implies helping students avoid or resist the less positive dynamics of the digital environment. Like Christian discernment, then, digital citizenship can be thought of as part of an attempt to find the safe path through a new and risky technological landscape. It offers a more secular lens through which to consider the choices we make, the dangers we face, and the selves we become. As the teacher quotation at the head of this chapter indicates, it has provided another frame for the teachers at Modern Christian Schools to think about the risks of the internet.

Connections and Differences

Since both discernment and digital citizenship appear as themes in discussions of online dangers at Modern Christian Schools, it is worth considering whether the terms are interchangeable. What happens if we place discernment, with its spiritual, moral, communal, and vocational/missional emphases, alongside digital citizenship? We can immediately see some similarity. Both focus on helping us to be discriminating, to avoid harm, and to live well in our community. Both encourage us to think critically about our relationship to technology and who it might enable us to be and become. At the same time, there are some significant differences. Two in particular are important as we trace how these themes play out in the life of Modern Christian Schools.

First, the two ideas are different in terms of where they sit in relation to professional practice. Christian discernment names a theological theme and a spiritual practice. Digital citizenship names an educational and sociological framework that is being worked out in detailed educational resources. This difference in where the two terms live is reflected in the literatures that discuss them. Searches for research on discernment tend to turn up results from theological sources, with relatively little material in educational journals. Searches for digital citizenship yield results primarily from journals in technology, sociology, education, and political science. Talk of discernment names some key Christian concerns about our formation. When these are worked out into particular practices, the focus is often on forms of prayer or counseling or types of congregational decision-making processes. Discernment has not taken concrete shape as a curricular concept. Digital citizenship, in contrast, focuses on preparation for participating in society and comes with curriculum guides, online resources, and measurement scales.[8] It is also embedded in technology standards, which further tether it to curricular planning and educational assessment. Christian discernment includes ideas such as spiritual discipline and listening to God's Spirit, which are central to its nature but difficult to formalize into programs without losing their essence. Digital citizenship focuses on specific skills that can be improved incrementally. Given these differences in the basic geography of the two concepts, digital citizenship offers a much easier path to implementation in terms of curriculum and pedagogy in schools. This is not least because more of the work with digital citizenship has already been done and is available off the shelf.

Second, the two concepts do not cover the same territory or work well as substitutes for each other. They are not opposed to each other; as we already noted, there is some common concern. A focus on truth-seeking, ethical and responsible relationships, and contributing to the community is, broadly speaking, common to both. Yet the overlap is not complete. Digital citizenship focuses on our civic selves and how we participate in society. It is primarily about who we are in public, in our capacity as citizens. Discussions of digital citizenship are sometimes connected to character education but are not usually linked to faith or spirituality. They seek to offer a framework for public participation regardless of who we are in terms of our more intimate or ultimate identities. They therefore focus on the broad parameters of safe behavior, ethical and legal boundaries, and means of access rather than on our deepest loves, our calling, or our ties to a particular community and mission. The language of discernment explicitly taps into a religious horizon that already frames moral choices for a Christian community, and so it may add weight to ethical demands that digital citizenship may not carry. Christian discernment focuses in the first place on our faith-rooted selves in relationship to love of God, love of neighbor, and vocation. It is primarily about who we are in our basic loves and commitments, and places our relationship to the world in the context of our relationship to God and to the community of faith. Christian discernment therefore has a stronger focus on specific beliefs, hopes, and virtues. This may well include reflecting on how we participate in society in light of faith; as James K. A. Smith puts it, "There is something political at stake in our worship and something religious at stake in our politics."9 But discernment cannot be reduced to societal participation. From the standpoint of Christian discernment, then, digital citizenship is part of the whole. It focuses on a subset of civic concerns that are a part, but only a part, of the life of faith. Digital citizenship resources may offer some ways of acting on concerns that arise from Christian discernment, but they do not fully translate the idea of Christian discernment itself. Christians are to be in the world but "not belong to the world" (John 17:14–15). The discerning Christian should indeed be a discerning citizen, but not merely or in the first instance a discerning citizen.

Back to the Classroom

What difference might all of this make in class? Think back to the teacher whose student has just encountered the bikini image while searching for fish. The teacher clearly enjoyed working alongside a young student to research material online that extended both of their knowledge, and also commented that "all of those lessons of digital citizenship [were] on my mind." Might an emphasis on Christian discernment or on digital citizenship prompt different responses? How does the attempt to teach healthy digital participation look different if it is framed not only by civic safety and responsibility but also by a concern for spiritual formation?10 In the next chapter we will see how these two trains of thought became intertwined at Modern Christian Schools. In the schools' documentary record we will glimpse what happens when Christian discernment and digital citizenship meet.

For Reflection and Response

- Think of your school or a school you know. In what ways does the school's culture push students to engage the world or protect students from the world? How are these impulses reconciled?
- How would you summarize the key similarities and differences between discernment and digital citizenship?
- What challenges do you anticipate as a school seeks to apply the idea of Christian discernment to its technology program?

CHAPTER 20

How Does Discernment Shape School Policy?

Students will demonstrate appropriate legal, ethical, and discerning Christian behavior while using technology.

School technology plan

Focus groups, observations, and surveys give us different kinds of evidence about the current practices and perceptions of Modern Christian Schools community members related to discernment. The plans, policies, communications, and other documents that accumulated since the earliest days of the technology program enable us to examine developments and shifts of direction that may be obscured in more recent retellings of the story. The documentary component of our research design involved examining electronic files covering more than a decade. This allowed us to compare the recollections of focus group participants to an extensive documentary record.[1] The documents offer an interesting picture of how the idea of teaching Christian discernment evolved as school leaders sought to implement it through professional development and school policy. Tracing this story raises questions about how the process of managing new technologies can provoke changes in how a school's beliefs and goals are articulated. There are lessons especially for how school leaders manage and communicate technological change.

Defining Discernment

In chapter 18 we sketched a theological account of Christian discernment that placed our choices in the context of our relationship with God, our relationships with one another, our moral and spiritual formation, and our vocation and mission. How did Modern Christian Schools define the term as they applied it to school policy around technology?

Talk of discernment spiked in school records in two particular years. These were the year in which the one-to-one laptop program began and the year in which tablets were introduced in the elementary schools. Major change created a flurry of discussion and new documentation. This contrasted with the life-as-usual years in between, during which we find key statements simply copied and pasted into new documents from earlier versions.[2] In both of the key years we find records of discussions that explicitly focused on the idea of Christian discernment.[3] In the notes from these sessions, administrators and teachers offered more than sixty distinct suggestions as to what Christian discernment with technology might entail. When analyzed for common themes, these suggestions offer us a loose map of how school members were thinking about discernment at the two technology launches.[4]

Almost half of the comments focused on issues related to digital citizenship. These included concerns about software piracy, students' social media footprint, digital etiquette, media copyright issues, proper citing of sources, information and media literacy, internet safety, pornography, understanding social media, online privacy and passwords, and integration of NETS/ISTE standards into the curriculum.[5] There was a strong focus on moral and ethical boundaries, and several comments suggested involving students in peer education during class devotions about ethical use of technology.

The next most common theme (about a quarter of the comments) connected discernment to interpersonal relationships within the community. Participants discussed the idea of collaborating with parents to teach discernment, the need for parent education, the effects on the community of changing modes of communication, and the ways in which students might learn discernment from their daily interactions with teachers.

A third theme involved questions about student formation. What habits and dispositions might be shaped by technology use? Specific issues mentioned included life balance and healthy boundaries, mental health, addictions, and media choices. These particular topics tended to be expressed as broad worries without specific action steps.

A fourth theme in the discussion sessions connected discernment directly to faith, with explicit mention of Christian beliefs and practices. These suggestions tended to be general, referring to needing a "Christian perspective," "being salt and light," viewing media "with the eyes and ears of Christ," and bearing witness through distinctive social media accounts. More specific suggestions included discussing technology during devotions and setting a Sabbath rest from technology.

Finally, some comments focused on controlling student behavior in school. Examples included basic care of laptops; monitoring student choices and online behavior, including new forms of cheating and video game playing in class; and general student discipline. In these comments, discernment was associated with good behavior and school discipline.

In sum, planning discussions that attempted to outline a shared understanding of Christian discernment reflected five themes. In descending order of frequency, these were digital citizenship, community relationships, student formation, explicit faith practices, and good behavior with technology. The range of ideas is striking and contrasts with the more narrowly focused worries of some focus group conversations (see chapter 22). The ideas also seem to overlap with the spiritual, communal, formational, and missional aspects of Christian discernment that we saw in theological accounts in chapter 18. What happened to these themes as the work of turning them into practices and policies unfolded?

> **Themes of Christian Discernment with Technology**
>
> The following themes arose in school discussions of what Christian discernment with technology involves:
>
> - *Digital citizenship:* online safety and moral boundaries
> - *Relationships:* interactions within the community
> - *Formation:* student choices and habits
> - *Faith:* Christian perspectives and practices
> - *Behavior:* enforcing school norms

Professional Development

Modern Christian Schools invested heavily in training days, summer courses, and after-school training hours during and after the launch of its technology program, leaving a trail of planning notes, course outlines, and presentation slides. Christian discernment was a regular theme. How was it presented?

Over the first three years of the one-to-one laptop program, we see a strong emphasis on internet safety and information literacy. A typical summer training plan included the goal "to give students and teachers a framework to discern the internet and information effectively." Training outlines regularly referred to third-party tools that might help with these topics, as in the following characteristic entry:

How to approach internet and information discernment?
9:45–11:15 a.m. Tools to use for internet and information discernment
- Internet safety—iSafe
- Copyright—creative commons, citing sources
- Information judgement—validation process

Training events were given a Christian frame. One began with a 15-minute discussion of "How Can We Be Christian—Biblical?" and another included the topic "Discernment & Christian Perspective." This Christian framing language appeared in introductions to training sessions, with the main content of the session then focusing on internet safety tools and "information discernment." In practical terms, then, the term *discernment* seems to have been unpacked largely in terms of internet safety concerns, information literacy, and ethical or behavioral boundaries.

By the end of the third year, the language of "information discernment" dropped away, and "digital citizenship" became a more common heading. Statements of training session goals settled on the formula "Develop and apply a framework for discernment and ethical use of technology," and this was repeated throughout subsequent training plans.[6] As wider concerns about digital citizenship began to exert an influence, a specific ISTE digital citizenship standard was adopted as a training goal, and a training event with an external trainer focused on learning about digital citizenship. By the fifth year, some draft notes on a public rationale for the one-to-one program referred in passing to "discernment/digital citizenship," suggesting that the two terms were drifting toward being treated as equivalent. In planning documents for the sixth year, talk of discernment appeared under the subheading "Digital Citizenship," and from this time forward we find places in the documentation where discernment and digital citizenship were treated as interchangeable. A draft article for the school magazine, for instance, noted that "teachers have been working with students to develop Christian discernment in the use of technology. In the summer a group of teachers developed a digital citizenship curriculum ... that is used in grades K–8 and prepares students to use technology safely and responsibly in the 21st century."

Over several years, the training focus shifted from scheduled group sessions to less formal after-school hours. By year five, lists of planned topics consisted essentially of software applications or technology integration activities that could be tried by teachers, alongside some continued focus on internet safety.[7] In forty-eight available documents, each recording multiple annual one-on-one review meetings with individual teachers, only one teacher explicitly referenced discernment, stating the goal of working on "Discernment in tech. Internet safety. Cyberbullying."

In professional development records, then, we see the idea of discernment gradually absorbed into digital citizenship language. As detailed plans began to unfold, Christian discernment was a regularly stated goal, while session content under that heading emphasized safety, filtering, and internet literacy tools. At the same time, an awareness of the need for an intentionally Christian approach remained, as we see both in the retention of Christian discernment as an explicit goal and in the formation after the fifth year of a new team focused on leading in the area of faith and technology. An agenda from this new team in year six referred to the goal of "preparing each student to live an intentionally Christian life" and the related need to "plan and provide staff development where we define and shape Reformed Christian worldview." What weakened over time in professional development documents was the original tether to the idea of Christian discernment, which gave way to standard language of digital citizenship. Ironically, language designed to articulate Christian vigilance and faith-rooted boundaries itself shows some vulnerability to assimilation to wider secular trends in educational technology. Remaining discerning about discernment is a challenge.

Vision and Practice

Why do we see these changes? The data shows us what happened and when, but does not in itself explain why, and so we offer only a tentative interpretation of what was happening. Placing the documentary evidence in the context of what we learned from surveys and focus groups, we can suggest multiple factors that may have played a role. One is the parental concern for safety and clear boundaries that we will explore in the next chapter. Discernment and ethical use of technology were mentioned especially prominently in the opening paragraphs of handbooks and policy documents published for parents and the wider community. The body of those documents commonly went on to emphasize filtering, responsible behavior with laptops, and respect for others. A strong affirmation of the value of technology combined with prominent talk of discernment may reflect awareness of parental desires for high-quality educational provision (including new technologies) and at the same time for student safety and moral boundaries. Parents seeking a nurturing learning environment for their children need reassurance amid technological change, and as private, fee-based institutions, Modern Christian Schools must be sensitive to parental concerns. This, combined with awareness of broader societal anxieties about technology and children, may be one source of pressure on the idea of discernment that tilted it toward a focus on safety and ethical behavior.

We glimpsed another likely factor in chapter 19, namely, the lack of curricular specifics attached to the idea of Christian discernment in the world at large. The language of Christian discernment often appeared primarily, or even solely, in the opening paragraphs of training plans and policy documents. These were the places where the overall vision was articulated in broad terms. The actionable sections of documents then focused on tools, rules, and boundaries with an emphasis on safety, literacy, and good behavior. Internet safety tools and digital citizenship standards offered ready-to-use ways of implementing at least some of the concerns that might fit under the heading of discernment. Figuring out what safe and responsible behavior with technology looks like, and how to observe legal boundaries, is certainly relevant to Christian discernment and an important consideration for schools. The question is whether it can substitute for the whole. It is easier to state the need for discernment as an aspiration than to translate that aspiration into specific action steps that successfully keep the full range of its themes in play. Countercultural commitments require costly investments of time and attention by busy teachers and administrators if they are to become more than aspiration. In focus groups, as we will discuss later, there was a recurring concern about time pressures that undermined capacity for reflection on core values. As periodic discussions of vision give way to getting on with practical training and daily implementation, the ready availability of workable tools is no small influence on the way things take shape.

The trail of professional development records suggests that the idea of discernment was developed over time not so much by organically extending the themes of initial brainstorming sessions as by attaching it to available resources that offered partial overlap. The process was not clean and simple. Changes in leadership, new input from external training, and the development of new faith emphases as new voices came to the discussion all complicated the picture, as we will see later. Yet the written records do suggest a tendency for the idea of discernment—as articulated in professional development and policy documents—to become secularized and narrowed over time.

Resistance to this kind of process requires regularly returning to theological starting points and looking for themes that have lost ground, rather than allowing the original leading ideas to function as repeating rhetorical figureheads. It also requires careful attention to what is communicated to faculty through professional development across time. We saw signs of a freshening of perspective during the periods when significant new technological developments (e.g., tablets in elementary school) provoked new reflection. Yet the message thinned out in training and communications between these peaks. The process of narrowing toward pragmatic frameworks was reflected in a focus group teacher's comment: "I feel like we were taught how to teach the digital citizenship and why it was important, and everything is laid out for us and what the expectation is and all that."

How might Christian schools push back against the risk of their operative worldview being shaped by their tools rather than their commitments and priorities? Perhaps increased collaboration between schools and stronger connections to higher education, as well as time intentionally set aside for discussion of key beliefs, could help address the challenge of thinking through big-picture concerns while immersed in the daily stresses of changing practice.

For Reflection and Response

- What is lost if digital citizenship takes over from discernment when we focus on teaching good boundaries with technology?
- What initiatives in your school or a school that you know well have been driven more by availability of tools than by careful consideration of principle? What are the effects of this kind of process for a school's faith identity?
- How should Christian schools go about adopting wider educational frameworks such as digital citizenship?

CHAPTER 21

Are Students Getting Too Much Screen Time?

I don't like all the screen time that they get at school. I just walked out of the doctor's office last week, and it still has this big poster up of 30 minutes of screen time a day, and I laughed out loud, because . . . they get, like, four hours at school, and then . . .

Parent

We traced in the last chapter how school documents and professional development records articulated the idea of Christian discernment with technology. We turn now to some of the concerns that arose among members of the Modern Christian Schools community, beginning with a fear that overuse of screens for learning might itself betray a lack of discernment. Should we be concerned about students' personal, moral, or spiritual growth being affected by the sheer quantity of time spent with digital devices? This has certainly emerged as a common worry in wider cultural commentary on the effects of the digital age on our development.[1] It is also a concern voiced by parents, and sometimes teachers, at Modern Christian Schools.

This worry takes various forms. Sometimes it focuses on the risk of exposure to harmful content and ideas, the increase in distraction, or the erosion of relationships. We will explore those concerns further in later chapters. Here we begin with the simple concern that perhaps the sheer quantity of exposure to digital devices may be causing harm. The popularity of laptops, tablets, and phones resulted in a worry among some parents that using devices all day in school and then for homework in the evening might lead to too much screen time. This is of particular concern for parents of younger children, but it extends to adolescents as well. Given that each student has a personal laptop or tablet to be used as a primary learning tool, are students spending too much time staring at their screens? Our data allow us to explore this question in some detail.

Healthy Screen Use

Students in the schools we studied, much like their peers across the country, are indeed spending a significant amount of time with their laptops and mobile phones. Before looking at how their device usage breaks down, we should consider concretely how much might be too much. The "right" amount of screen time for young children and adolescents is a matter of some dispute and depends heavily on the context and the type of technology. The American Academy of Pediatrics (AAP), in its influential guidelines, recommends that limits be put on media use by young children and teenagers, but does not prescribe limits on technology use for educational purposes.[2] The guidelines note substantial benefits of online media, including exposure to beneficial programming, learning, and communication with others. At the same time, excessive use of electronic media can be associated with sleep problems and obesity, particularly in young children. In extreme cases, affecting perhaps 4%–8% of children, excessive electronic media use is characterized as internet addiction.[3]

> **Distinctions within Device Use**
>
> This chapter makes the following distinctions within students' device use:
>
> - *Direct screen time* refers to time when an individual student is directly using a personal screen, such as a laptop, tablet, or phone.
> - *Device time* refers to the total time spent using devices. Since students may use several devices at once, adding up device time is likely to give a total larger than the amount of screen time. (If a student does homework for 30 minutes on a laptop with their phone also on to check messages, this may result in 30 minutes of time with screens but 60 minutes of total device time.)

In the case of older students, a further concern arises that constant access to digital devices may increase their use of social media. Excessive social media activity has been tied to mental health consequences, particularly for girls.[4] A common theme in the literature is that moderate use of electronic media is not associated with poor mental health, and in some cases is associated with good mental health outcomes. Damage seems to be limited to very frequent use. One study estimates that mental health concerns increase with mobile phone use above 2 hours per day, video game time above 1 hour and 40 minutes per day, and computer use above 4 hours and 17 minutes per day.[5]

As the AAP guidelines imply, the effects of students' time in front of screens in school may be different. Studies that document problems with excessive use of media tend to focus on personal and entertainment consumption, such as video games, TV, movies, and social media. Most of these types of media are blocked on the laptops given to students in Modern Christian Schools, and parents are given the option of having them blocked at home as well. The use of technology for learning depends heavily on the assignments given by teachers, and on how time in school is structured. In a math class where students are asked to complete graphing problems on their computers instead of paper, students will spend much more of their class time working with their laptops. The effects of this may well be different from an equivalent amount of time spent gaming or consulting social media.

Device Time in School: Survey Data

What, then, does our survey data from Modern Christian Schools and from our control group at Western Christian School tell us about screen time?[6] Given the desire at Modern Christian Schools to transform pedagogy through technology integration, it is not surprising that students there report using their devices often. High school students in Modern Christian Schools report almost four hours of laptop use in school each day (see table 21.1).

Table 21.1. Average daily screen time in school

	Modern Christian Schools	Western Christian School
Laptops	3:53	2:30
Tablets	0:12	0:13
Desktops	0:29	0:32
Smartphones	1:26	1:52
Total device time	6:00	5:07

Note: Student-reported data. Because devices can be used simultaneously, the total device time may include some overlap.

In the comparison population at Western Christian School, students report using their laptops much less in school: only two and a half hours per day on average. There are several plausible reasons for this difference. Because Western Christian School has a younger technology program, teachers have had far less time to adjust the curriculum toward increased integration of technology into learning. Western Christian also uses different devices, which may affect function and battery time. Most importantly, perhaps, the schools' different understandings of the goals of their technology programs may be resulting in different patterns of device use within the curriculum. Here again, the specific sense of mission at Modern Christian Schools may well be playing a role.

In addition to laptops, tablets and desktop computers make an appearance in both school systems, but the second most common screen-type used in school is the mobile phone. The average high school student in these schools reported using their phone for between one and two hours during the school day. Because students may use multiple devices at once, we cannot simply add up these numbers to get a total screen time statistic. Instead, the numbers represent "device time," the amount of time per device.

Device Time in School: Observational Data

Students' self-reported use of technology on surveys provides one useful picture of how students are spending their time, but we can turn to other methods to fill out the picture. Classroom observations across many Modern Christian Schools classrooms allowed us to observe technology being used by students and teachers. The technologies we observed ranged from personal laptops and tablets to teacher microphones and classroom projectors. Given the particular concerns surrounding screen time, understood as students' direct interaction with personal screens, we look only at direct screen time use (see table 21.2) and not other types of technology use in the classroom (e.g., teacher microphones, projectors).

In elementary classrooms, the personal technology used most often was a tablet. The extent to which students were using personal technologies varied widely by classroom, with some students not using any technology and others using it for the entire class period. However, randomized observations of thirty-one elementary classrooms suggest that on average in a 30- to 45-minute observation, elementary students spent 12–18 minutes in learning activities requiring direct screen time.[7] Much of this time was spent engaging in digital reading, writing, and viewing activities, or in practice and drill exercises. Although we have no specific observational data about screen time use over the course of a day, we can extend the above data to make an informed estimate.[8] Elementary students likely spend from 1 hour and 36 minutes to 2 hours and 24 minutes per day using their tablets.

Table 21.2. Direct screen time observed in schools

	Average direct screen time in a 30- to 45-minute random observation	Average direct screen time estimated per day
Elementary school	00:12–00:18	1:36–2:24
Middle school	00:15–00:21	2:00–2:48
High school	00:18–00:26	2:24–3:28

We see an increase in technology use as students move to higher grades, as focus group conversations also suggested. During our random observations in eleven middle school classrooms, students spent approximately 15–21 minutes in learning activities using their personal devices. Our observations of technology use in thirty-three high school classrooms found similar patterns to those in middle school, with students engaged in direct screen time for 18–26 minutes. In-class use of technology for these older students was more likely to take the form of reading, writing, and note-taking using laptops, although phone use was also noted. If we again extend the above data, we can estimate that middle schoolers spent from 2 hours to 2 hours and 48 minutes and high schoolers spent from 2 hours and 24 minutes to 3 hours and 28 minutes hours using one-to-one technologies during the school day.

What can we learn from these observational findings? First, students incrementally increase their technology use as they transition from elementary to high school, an anticipated finding. This aligns with what we know from trends in scholarship examining technology use more broadly and Modern Christian Schools students' perceptions of use shared in focus groups.

Second, if we compare the estimated time high schoolers spent on devices per day to survey findings above, it provides reassurance that students are not on their technologies for the entire seven-hour school day. At approximately three and a half hours of maximum screen time use during instructional activities, high school students use technology, including their phones, closer to half of the day. The self-reported survey data revealing students' use at nearly six hours is either due to the way students reported use by device (see table 21.1 note) or due to students overreporting technology use. It is here that multiple research methods again provide important insights. Fears of the technology program leading to students plugged in all day long can be somewhat tempered.

Finally, given the varied nature of the technology use that we observed in classrooms, and the largely productive uses toward which it was put, our data did not show specific cause for concern about negative consequences from in-school screen time viewed purely in terms of quantity of exposure, though the concerns about behaviors associated with screen time that we explore in other chapters are clearly associated with increased time spent with screens.

Device Time Outside School

Much of the scholarly literature about the consequences of excessive technology use, however, is not about screen time in school but about screen time at home. Parents expressed some concern that students were using laptops and phones excessively. Students themselves were quick to note that they were sometimes too attached to their technology. It is not implausible to imagine (as some students actually suggested in focus groups) that the schools' use of digital devices might be indirectly increasing student attachment to them outside school. To see whether these students in fact end up with more screen time than others, we have to look to some broader data about technology use and media consumption nationwide. When we make this comparison, we see some noticeable differences.

First, while all the students in the high schools we studied have access to a laptop that they can keep with them in school and at home, this is not the norm. Only 45% of teenagers nationwide report owning their own laptop. Even among teenagers from high-income families, laptop ownership is only at 62%.[9] Moreover, students in our study report that their schoolwork often assumes access to a computer and requires they use their laptops. Across the country, using computers for homework is common but far less frequent. Less than half of teenagers nationwide reported using a computer for homework on a weekly basis in 2015.[10] It is not surprising, then, that students at the high schools we studied reported more frequent overall computer use.[11]

Table 21.3. Average daily interactive screen time outside school

	Nation	Modern Christian Schools	Western Christian School
Computers	1:37	3:20	3:09
Tablets	0:45	0:30	0:42
Smartphones	2:42	2:35	3:23
Video games	1:21	0:30	0:45
Total device time	6:25	6:55	7:59

Note: Student-reported data. Because devices can be used simultaneously, the total device time may include some overlap. Nationwide data drawn from Vicky Rideout, *The Common Sense Census: Media Use by Tweens and Teens* (San Francisco: Common Sense Media, 2015).

At the same time, students in our study spent less time on average playing video games than other teenagers (see table 21.3). This might be because the school-issued laptops afford them other avenues for media consumption and entertainment outside of video game systems. Some of our students, for example, reported using their laptops for games, complicating these comparisons. It might also be that the typical family ethos at Modern Christian Schools is less supportive of video game use than the national average. Even if these differences make comparison difficult, screen time as a whole ended up somewhat higher for the students in our study, compared to teenagers across the country.[12]

Table 21.4. Average daily screen time by gender at Modern Christian Schools

	Boys	Girls
Laptops	2:29	2:59
Tablets	0:43	0:31
Desktops	0:41	0:19
Smartphones	2:26	2:43
Video games	0:59	0:14
Total device time	7:18	6:46

Note: Student-reported data. Because devices can be used simultaneously, the total device time may include some overlap.

It is also worth noting that there are some real differences between the technology habits of male and female students (see table 21.4). Both in our study and in another recent study of teenagers' media use, boys spend noticeably more time with video games, while girls spend more time with social media.[13] This echoes the trend for teenagers nationwide: while boys and girls get very similar amounts of screen time overall, boys nationally reported spending 56 minutes each day playing video games, while girls reported only 7 minutes. Girls, however, reported spending 1 hour and 32 minutes each day using social media, compared to only 52 minutes for boys.[14] In the schools we studied, we saw a similar trend, with girls spending more time with laptops and smartphones, while boys spent far more time with video games.

Here again, one difficulty in interpreting these statistics is that students will often use more than one device at the same time. A student may be working on an assignment on their laptop while exchanging texts with a classmate on a phone and streaming Netflix in the background on their television. There is substantial evidence that teenagers are very prone to multitasking and that doing so hurts their academic performance.[15] The productivity afforded by access to these devices, therefore, does not eliminate the need to develop careful study habits. In fact, the American Academy of Pediatrics recommends avoiding any entertainment media while doing homework.[16] The seven hours of device time daily outside of school reported by students in our surveys strongly suggests that at least some of this time involves multiple device use, and this may be cause for concern regarding their learning.

Another factor to consider is whether different kinds of students are affected in different ways by access to devices. Students with higher grades were much less likely to report that they struggled with time management related to device use, and far more likely to report that the technology program helped them create healthy boundaries or helped them learn to balance their technology use.[17]

Turning to alumni, we find that all the college students that we surveyed were more likely to report difficulty setting aside their devices, but the alumni of Modern Christian Schools were far more likely than other college students to report that the technology program "made me learn how to balance my technology use." Modern Christian Schools alumni also reported less technology distraction and much more confidence that technology, on balance, made them more productive. These findings suggest that the technology program at Modern Christian Schools may be having some positive impact in terms of helping students manage their screen time responsibly, especially for academically successful students.

Too Much Screen Time?

Are these students spending too much time in front of a screen? The answer is not straightforward. Given that many of these students are spending a significant amount of time using their laptops for school work, and not solely for entertainment, they may not experience the negative consequences that the literature suggests. The heavy use of smartphones among the high school students might be excessive, but smartphone use is similar to that of other students not in one-to-one programs, according to national data, and research suggests that children's screen time may be determined in part by parents' screen time patterns.[18] The level of personal device use is therefore likely not attributable specifically to the schools' technology program. Moreover, using their devices in the context of a school community where there are limits on entertainment and social media may offer these students opportunities to practice good technology habits.

On the other hand, the broader culture, especially among young people, may tend toward overuse of computers, tablets, and phones. The strong pro-technology emphasis at Modern Christian Schools pushes students toward daily use of these technologies at younger ages and in a larger swath of their activities. It may be more difficult, in this setting, for some students and parents to set healthy limits on screen time. It is possible that some students are using their devices excessively, but our data do not offer support for the idea that the schools' technology program itself is a cause of harmful quantities of screen time, and there are some signs that it may be helping to teach responsible choices. The data do raise the possibility that multitasking should be more of a concern, especially outside of school (we take this up in chapter 29).

Even during the time that it has taken to complete our research, parental concerns about device use have continued to shift, with the role of smart phones moving to center stage. A general takeaway from our data for teachers and parents is that if we are concerned about quantity of screen time, we should be thinking about the matter from several angles. Sheer quantity of screen time can matter in terms of eye strain, but perhaps more important in learning terms are questions about how screen time is shaped. If there are concerns about too much screen time, what patterns of device use are being modeled by parents and teachers? How much multitasking is going on? How is responsible screen use being taught? What is the screen being used for, and what kind of content is being accessed?

For Reflection and Response

- How should limiting time with new technologies and learning to use them for good purposes be weighted in a school's approach to teaching and learning?
- How might students be helped to think about the time they spend on their devices and the benefits or drawbacks to the ways they are put to use?
- How do the figures reported by students in this chapter compare to your own device use, or that of your colleagues? What are adults modeling in terms of screen time and multitasking?

CHAPTER 22

Keeping the Good from the Bad

We definitely stress the safety and discernment piece. . . . If we're preparing their minds, that means, what do they need to be prepared for? And this is a different world than it used to be. If we ignore that, I don't think we would be preparing them where they need to be.

Teacher

Raising concern about the moral risks of technology use is justified in a world where, as we saw in the last chapter, students are spending increasing time on devices both in and out of school. Most of the moral risks surrounding the journey to adulthood are not new. What does seem new is the degree to which harmful material and behaviors have become instantly accessible through personal pocket devices, even through the very devices provided for learning. This shift undermines any temptation to conceive of the Christian school as a tightly bounded space. The curriculum and the voices that frame it are becoming more porous. A school that might once have relied on a Christian curriculum, perhaps with carefully chosen texts offering Christian perspectives on learning, now encourages students to draw resources from across the internet. Students can fact-check teachers in real time with devices in their pockets, comparing what they are told with the views of others outside the community. They can interact online with people from very different communities and perspectives, and sometimes do so as part of their learning. We are unsurprised, then, that 72% of teachers at Modern Christian Schools reported that technology has forced them to shift the way they think about curriculum content.[1] Alongside these curricular trends, sustaining moral boundaries also seems challenging when plagiarism or harmful content are a click away. If digital technology offers a medium within which we are shaped, our responses to the risks inherent in that medium also become part of our formation. It is not surprising, then, that community members voiced concerns not simply about the amount of screen time but about what is coming through the screens.

"Bad Things" on the Internet

We heard evidence of such anxieties among some parents at Modern Christian Schools. These parents hope for a degree of moral and spiritual safety for their children, and a degree of distance from manifestations of popular culture that do not resonate with their values. For some at least, this hope frames their choice of a private, Christian school. As one parent put it, alluding to immoral online content, "That's one reason why we have them here. At least in my mind . . . one reason why I have my daughter here is not to have to engage in that type of world." Another expressed the hope that in a Christian learning environment, students will "be able to discern better, what's right and what's wrong" because "we're going to teach that there are sites there that shouldn't be used, and [sites] that will not glorify God, so that they're given a straight path." A teacher spoke similarly of the need to have a focus on "keeping the bad from the good."

The language of protection, straight paths, and good/bad distinctions suggests a world of clear boundaries and safe spaces. This approach depends on the idea of sorting digital resources, practices, and environments into the bad and the good and establishing mechanisms to exclude the bad as much as possible. Some referred to this as "redeeming technology." Another teacher framed the concern as a question: "What do we need to help [students] pull back from?" If the schools' mission language reflects the New Testament call to "go into all the world," this concern for specific kinds of disengagement echoes the accompanying warnings to not follow "the course of this world" (Mark 16:15; Eph. 2:2).

Along with social media, sexual temptations and the dangers of pornography and sexting were prominent among the anxieties voiced by parents. Sometimes this was expressed in terms of seeking "purity" in the context of technology, a term that in evangelical culture often has moral or specifically sexual overtones. A parent recalled, "In middle school, I remember having discussions about purity with technology and how do you integrate all that stuff, how do you talk to your child about these things, how do you take your faith and the world and make . . . good decisions?" An instinctive connection between "bad things" online and sexuality appears to animate another parent's observations: "This is a perfect time in fifth grade to talk about bad things on the internet because they talk about health now and we start talking about sex. So, this would be a good layer, in fifth grade, to address internet pornography, internet bad things. . . . If we're going to teach them to abstain, if we're going to teach them to value their body . . . then technology is a part of that. If they're doing booty shakes on Snapchat, that's not good purity. So that should be talked about."

We heard students reflect awareness of these concerns and associations in their own comments about internet dangers. A student commented, for instance, that students using technology as Christians means using technology "responsibly in a way that honors God through their actions, not seeing things that are inappropriate or that show some pornography perhaps." Here again we see that quick step from "inappropriate" to "sexual." Younger students had learned strategies such as closing their laptop and calling for a teacher if a website that was "really bad" appeared on the screen, and they were aware that bad websites were blocked by filtering software. When students referred to examples of discernment with technology being taught about in chapel, they referred to themes of safety and sexual ethics. Students were clear that the main purpose of chapel was worship, and that it was the exception when chapel was used to teach a specific boundary. However, on those occasions when "there's a message they want to get across," the themes recalled by students and teachers were plagiarism, sexting, and pornography.

Parents looked to the schools for reassurance on this score, and that reassurance was regularly offered in communications from the schools. Scripts for parent evenings as well as prominent sections in parent handbooks emphasized the schools' filtering policies and safeguards. This emphasis was welcomed, for instance, in a parent's comment that "they talk to the kids. If it looks scary, don't go there. If . . . something's sketchy, don't go there. They monitor that, but they were very reassuring about [how] this is something that's really important."

Some parents still worried, however, that the very presence of laptops and what they assumed to be a widespread student ability to bypass filters and protections was leading to an increase in problem behaviors. Parents feared that their students were crossing boundaries and wondered whether enough was being done: "When I hear that kids are on porn—I know my child is doing things during class time that she shouldn't be doing, but how are we handling that? And where are we looking at the fruits of the Spirit

171

and actually instituting those in the school system? Where is self-control coming in? Where are we professing to our children and praying over them God's best?"

In general, parents referred to themes of protection and safety much more frequently than teachers, administrators, or students.[2] While there was clear awareness of safety themes across all groups, only parents focused on the language of purity, with its connotations of strong and specifically sexual boundaries. As we will see later, teachers' concerns are more complex.

Discernment Emphases and Responses

Parents

Primary concerns: maintain student purity and promote safety

Responses: teach students to avoid what is inappropriate (e.g., pornography, sexting); monitor and filter moral temptations on devices

School Personnel

Primary concerns: prepare students to respond to temptations heightened in a technological age

Responses: teach students to recognize technological temptations (e.g., control, perfection, immoral content); create opportunities to wrestle with tensions (e.g., perfection/imperfection, engagement/protection); provide a grace-filled space to respond to failures and limitations

---

"We're Not Perfect"

While a few parents spoke in a way that suggested the school should be able to get the temptations of the online world under firm control, administrators and teachers were often more sanguine. One administrator reflected, "We're not perfect. If you're looking for the perfect school, we aren't it. We'll talk about how we've got seven hundred and fifty students, and fifty teachers, and that's eight hundred sinners in one building. When you have eight hundred sinners in one building, then you're going to have some sin."

This comment draws another theological emphasis into the mix: students are sinners, and some sin should be expected. An emphasis on purity can of course go together with a lively awareness of sin, yet here there is a sense that awareness of sin should qualify the pursuit of control and perfection.

The two theological accents (maintain purity; all are sinners) suggest some possible differences in pedagogical tone. We have already seen some examples of the purity focus in the concern about controlling student exposure to inappropriate material when searching online and holding teachers accountable for helping students avoid bad things. This focus pointed toward an emphasis on sustaining protective boundaries and a tendency to be concerned about sins related to personal morality, especially related to sex.

The emphasis on pervasive sin and grace seemed in our data to be associated more with reflection on living and wrestling with imperfection across a broader cross section of experience. Some teachers connected sin to topics that reached beyond individual morality, such as how humans treat the natural world, "how we sin and how we don't treat creation the way that God called us to." The idea also surfaced that a Christian school could be a place where students could make their mistakes with technology in a supportive environment that could offer grace and Christian mentoring. In an internal school survey, one teacher described the school as "a safe place to fail" and a place that can "begin to help students." A high school teacher questioned the tendency toward perfectionism that could be augmented by digital media, suggesting that, as well as offering grace to students, "we can help them give themselves a little grace as well." One science teacher took this thought a step further, suggesting that students needed to learn to question the implied perfectibility of digital environments: "I do think, speaking [of] the imperfection, to try and fail and have things not turn out the way we expect them to adds to our Christian perspective of teaching and the whole concept of sin and the fall, and this is a piece of real life. It's not always going to go perfectly the way the computer screen showed it should." While a focus on purity was associated with anxieties about avoiding online moral temptations, an emphasis on grace in the face of failure offered the seeds of a way of resisting technology's temptation toward perfectionism and excessive control.

Part of the challenge facing teachers working with digital learning tools is the need to figure out how to connect and balance engagement with the world, protection from the world, moral boundaries, and acceptance of failure and limitations. In this way, some central Christian themes become intertwined with how the community thinks about Google searches and technology policies. The ways in which we combine in our practices a concern for moral safety and good choices and an awareness of sin and grace will say a lot about the shape of our operative theology. A concern for purity alone can easily turn isolationist or judgmental, and the moral questions arising from digital technologies reach well beyond matters of access to sexual material.[3] Boundaries are needed, but so is walking alongside students on a shared learning journey. The concerns aired in this chapter lead to some further, very practical questions. Do the schools' efforts to provide protection through filtering and monitoring work? Are students emerging from this technology program with some ability to resist the temptations of the internet? We look at some data that helps answer these questions in the next chapter.

For Reflection and Response

- What do you believe students need to be helped to pull back from in the realm of digital technology?
- What are the most commonly voiced fears in your school community about the risks of digital access? What messages might students be taking from these emphases?
- What other risks might be underestimated or downplayed as a result of focusing on the dangers of sexual material online?

CHAPTER 23

Filtering and Monitoring Internet Use

The filters only do so much.

Teacher

As we saw in the last chapter, parents were especially concerned about exposure to harmful material such as pornography online. Their concern is not an isolated one. In a recent study, the Barna Group surveyed teenagers across the United States and found that 50% of teenagers aged twelve to seventeen reported coming across pornography on the internet sometime in the last month. Moreover, 37% of teens reported actively seeking out pornography in the month prior.[1] Against this background, how can a school open classrooms to the potential benefits of digital technologies while still limiting access to offensive or harmful media? In what ways might schools provide oversight, and how might this shape students' technology practices in school and beyond?

Filtering and Monitoring

Modern Christian Schools used software to filter and monitor internet use, yet as we have seen, both teachers and students were quick to recount incidents in which they accidentally stumbled across inappropriate images or content while doing school research. These cases created opportunities for teachers to actively model responsible use of technology and address themes of discernment, failure, and grace with students. Opening up the school to the internet carries risks, but it also creates opportunities to address an important challenge head-on. In this chapter we will examine technological strategies for limiting access to inappropriate content, and then describe the degree to which students in our study sought out and consumed sexually explicit content.

Modern Christian Schools and our comparison school system, Western Christian School, responded to this challenge in slightly different ways. Both school systems used an internet filter to block the most offensive material. If a student stumbled upon inappropriate websites or images while using the school internet connection, software would usually detect this and block access. These filters are common in schools and some public internet connections.[2] However, Modern Christian Schools went further and installed additional software on all laptops that blocked access to social media, video sites, and games during school hours. The schools then allowed parents to decide which kinds of internet use should be available on student laptops outside of school hours. As an extra layer, beyond filtering out certain content, the schools also monitored the content accessed on each laptop. If any student sought out objectionable content using their school device, even while at home, the school would be alerted, and parents notified.

The value of this filtering and monitoring to the schools was evident in multiple ways. First, it provided a way for the schools to clearly express community standards for internet use and to communicate their commitment to addressing the risks that concern parents. Given the risks of exposure to harmful content, parents and teachers likely derived comfort from the boundaries created by the software. Information about filtering and monitoring formed a prominent part of parent handbooks sent home each year. Second, these technologies served to decrease the amount of active in-class monitoring that teachers had to engage in when students were working independently with their laptops. Most importantly, perhaps, these monitoring technologies could give parents and teachers a valuable teaching tool, particularly with younger students, as their children were learning to navigate the internet.

While it is difficult to be certain what the schools can do that will have the most positive impact on student behavior, there is some evidence that these schools and families were doing something right. School administrators reported almost no cases of students caught viewing pornography while in school (though there were regular instances of students being caught with such content in their device histories), and in our surveys, only 11% of high school students at Modern Christian Schools reported seeking out sexually explicit content at least a few times each month on any device.[3] Students in these schools, when compared to those in the Barna study, reported seeking out pornography far less than their peers across the country. Given that these students all attend Christian schools, this might be expected. The Barna research indicated that practicing Christians were somewhat less likely to seek out pornography than the overall population. Even so, 36% of practicing Christian teenage boys and 5% of teenage girls reported seeking out pornography at least once a month.[4] In contrast, in our surveys of students and recent alumni of similar ages from Modern Christian Schools, only 20% of males and 3% of females reported seeking out explicitly sexual content at least monthly. This figure does not tell us whether the effective ingredient is the schools' filtering and monitoring or some other practice or characteristic of this particular Christian community, but it does indicate that the schools' investment in digital technology is paired with lower, rather than higher, incidences of such behavior. Apparently, having a one-to-one technology program does not have to lead to increased accessing of explicitly sexual content.

Our data allow us to dig deeper. Because we surveyed students at two different schools—one with monitoring software on every laptop (Modern Christian Schools) and one without (Western Christian School)—we can compare the behavior of similar students in these two schools. If students at the school with monitoring software reported seeking out pornographic or violent content less often than those with only in-school internet filtering, it could be evidence that the monitoring of laptop use has a positive effect. Because these schools might differ in other ways, the comparison is not perfect; the difference may also be because of other school practices. However, it gives us one method of exploring the effectiveness of these technologies.

In our surveys, we asked students how often they accessed sexual content, violent content, content that they knew was inappropriate, and content that made them feel guilty.[5] In each case male students and students with low grade point averages were more likely to indicate a higher frequency of these behaviors. However, when we compared the frequency between students in two Christian high schools—one with device monitoring and one without—there appeared to be no difference between the two groups of students. Those who were subject to the monitoring of school devices reported the same frequency of consumption of sexual and violent content, content that they knew was inappropriate, and content that made them feel guilty.[6]

Faith in Filters?

While our data indicate that students at these schools were comparatively unlikely to put their laptops to inappropriate use, confidence in the filtering and monitoring system at Modern Christian was mixed. In their laptop handbook, Modern Christian Schools cautioned, "While Internet filters provide an important level of protection, no filter program provides 100% protection. [Parent] monitoring and supervision are still very important." Likewise, students and parents expressed concern that these technologies were unable to fully prevent students from accessing objectionable content. In our surveys, 13% of middle school and high school students expressed confidence that they could easily bypass the schools' internet filtering. Less than 40% indicated that they thought getting around the filtering would be very difficult.[7] It is likely, then, that some students either know how to get around the filters or know friends who have done so. In the context of these schools, bypassing internet filters does not necessarily mean viewing pornography in school. Social media and video sites were also blocked during school hours, so students might have found ways around the filter merely to post selfies, watch sport clips, or update social media profiles. That said, when we compared responses within our survey data, we found that those students who were confident in their ability to bypass the restrictions were also far more likely to report recently viewing sexually explicit or violent content, content that made them feel guilty, and spying or stalking others online.[8] It seems likely, then, that for this minority of students at least, the filtering systems were not completely effective.[9]

Concerns about these filtering and monitoring technologies also arise when we consider the proliferation of mobile devices, particularly smartphones. In the early years of school laptop use, the number of students with internet-capable smartphones or tablets was small, but more recently, in the high school at least, these devices are used by the vast majority of students. The ubiquity of these devices has made it easy for students to shift any technology use that they want to hide from the school laptops and networks to their personal devices. It is likely, in fact, that students who seek out particularly offensive material do so when outside the school network.

Sending students home with school-issued laptops creates a space in which responsibility for student behavior is not always clear. Parents often look to the school to monitor technology use and to help students avoid pitfalls. Yet most student media consumption happens outside school, and students often use other devices. Teachers and administrators sometimes expressed the wish that parents would take responsibility for guiding their children in these areas and not expect more than the school can deliver. Yet the technology-rich curriculum is leading students into competences and practices that may push beyond their parents' technological literacy. The result is a technology-saturated environment that requires cooperation between parents, teachers, and students to navigate well.[10] Filtering and monitoring are only one ingredient.

A further challenge with internet filtering and monitoring that emerged in conversation with administrators had to do with the human cost of monitoring student internet use. There was a cost not only in terms of the financial and time investments necessary to set up and maintain the filtering and monitoring systems, but in terms of the work of reviewing what students had accessed. When this becomes the responsibility of a few administrators, they may be put in the position of regularly having to review violent and sexually explicit content in the process of verifying what students have inappropriately accessed. This raises questions about the effects on their own well-being and whether appropriate support, or even counseling, is in place. An administrator who reviewed this chapter reflected that with hindsight this role of monitoring what students had accessed had been taken on too lightly, without sufficiently considering the stresses it could create.

Do Ethical Habits Persist beyond School?

The goal of Modern Christian Schools is to prepare students to make discerning choices after the watchful eyes of the schools and parents are gone. School members noted that the opportunity to learn technological discernment was one of the benefits of introducing devices to students at a young age. What can we learn about whether the schools' technology program influences students' technology practices after they leave school? To investigate this, we surveyed students of Modern Christian and Western Christian School after they graduated, as well as a comparison group of students at Liberal Arts College. This latter group may have included a small number of alumni from the two Christian school systems, but no students appear in both samples. If alumni from Modern Christian Schools reported better behavior than their peers, that would provide some positive evidence for the view that the technology programs can help students to learn responsible technology use.

This comparison gives some evidence that the students at Modern Christian Schools were well served by the technology program overall, particularly in terms of their preparation for making moral technology use choices. A couple of pieces of evidence point in this direction. First, it appears that students were tempted less by inappropriate content while in high school, even with the strong technology focus, than when they went off to college. We asked students in both settings if the technology program in their school tempted them to access material online that they knew they should not seek out. While in high school, 21% of male students and 14% of female students (18% overall) agreed that it did. In college, however, once outside the influence of the school, agreement with this same question increased, with 40% of male students and 19% of female students (26% overall) reporting being tempted.[11] These alumni did not report seeking out inappropriate content more frequently, but their experience with technology in the college context created more temptation to do so.

Table 23.1. Intentional and ethical use of technology among college students (percentage agreement)

	Modern Christian alumni	Western Christian alumni	Liberal Arts College students
I am intentional about using technology in an ethical manner	84%	70%	74%
The school technology program tempted me to access online material I know I should not access	26%	27%	43%
Total responses	137	95	195

Second, it appears that these laptop programs are preparing students for better use of technology after they graduate. Our surveyed alumni of Modern Christian Schools reported less frequent consumption of inappropriate online content than did our comparison sample of college students at Liberal Arts College.[12] They were also far less tempted by such content than this comparison group. As table 23.1 shows, the Modern Christian graduates were more likely to report that they "are intentional about using technology in an ethical manner." It is difficult to be certain which characteristics of this school population make the difference. It may be that the population of students from Modern Christian Schools have different cultural expectations than college students overall. It seems likely, though, that these schools' broad investment in Christian education with technology helps prepare students to live with the technology differently.

By using these online technologies in a structured and productive manner, students are able to develop positive technology-use habits. Moreover, it is possible that the constraints on technology use—and the monitoring—train students to use that technology more responsibly when they are on their own.

Concerns about dangerous online content reflect real risks. However, it appears that a carefully run school laptop program such as the one at Modern Christian Schools is not doing harm in this regard. Students reported less pornography use than their peers nationally, less temptation in school than in the college environment, and more responsible use of their laptops once they were outside the school restrictions. It seems that perhaps they have learned some degree of discernment with technology, which suggests that schools can and should aspire to more than policing the boundaries. Although this particular data does not show us which elements are decisive in the formative shaping, our research points toward likely factors. Thoughtful modeling of ethical technology use, monitoring and filtering technology use, and intentionally emphasizing Christian discernment and engagement in faith-formative practices all appear to make a positive contribution. These factors are supported when schools view student failure as an opportunity to provide a grace-filled response that enables students to learn how to live better with technologies.[13] Students can be helped to grow into more responsible digital choices through an intentionally structured life together in school.

For Reflection and Response

- Did any of the data about the result of increased technology use in this chapter surprise you? Why or why not?
- Having read the chapter, what do you see as the strengths and weaknesses of technological solutions (such as filtering and monitoring software) to the risks of digital access?
- The chapter suggests that healthy technology use "requires cooperation between parents, teachers, and students." What strengths or weaknesses do you see in your own school with regard to the effectiveness of this cooperation?

CHAPTER 24

Discernment and Consumerism

There are also restrictions. If there's a website that has more inappropriate content, then it's blocked for us, and I think that's reasonable, but . . . sometimes some bad stuff comes up, and [we] mainly either exit out of the tab, or we scroll so we can't see it.

Student

For the last two chapters we have been exploring an emphasis visible in school documents and parent interviews on maintaining moral boundaries. Yet Christian discernment is more than this, and there are risks to reducing Christian education to successful moral boundary maintenance. Christian Smith, in his extensive study of the spiritual lives of American teenagers and young adults, emphasizes that the forces eroding clear-sighted faith commitment among young people are not just moral dangers and lack of a well-formed theological worldview. The context in which formation is taking place is mass consumer capitalism, which shapes a sense of the human person as "an *individual, autonomous, rational, self-seeking, cost-benefit-calculating consumer.*"[1] In other words, the daily practices of mass consumption influence us to see ourselves as individual consumers of products at our own convenience and to serve our own comfort. Teenagers, with their high level of disposable income and high influence on their parents' spending, are prime targets of marketing that tends to appeal to impulsiveness, insecurity, and vanity more often than self-control, humility, or selflessness.[2]

Asking questions about discernment from this angle leads us into challenges not met by filters. Consider the following comments from a student on why it was helpful to have laptops available as a tool in Bible class: "In some ways it's good . . . because you can obviously type faster on your computer, and you can take notes faster, you can share them faster, and email faster. . . . Also, in that class, because once you get your notes done, and [the teacher] is talking, you can go shopping or do whatever you want." We have already explored some implications of doing things faster (see chapters 16–17). Here we want to focus on another issue. This student was not accessing what is most commonly thought of as harmful online material, but they were acting out the script of the autonomous consumer in the midst of Bible class, with the aid of their school-issued device. The same device that enabled faster note-taking enabled shopping in class, which was framed by the student as simply a matter of individual choice.

Distraction and Learning Devices

One of the most striking changes that wireless digital devices have brought to the classroom has been to change learning materials into shape-shifting environments. Students of previous generations may have smuggled a magazine into the pages of their textbook, but no one expected the pages of the textbook to suddenly morph into a shopping mall. A digital environment is more protean. A web search projected on a screen for the class or conducted by individual students can pull up not only inappropriate images but a seductive array of advertising and clickbait built around suggestive visual triggers. A student can skip from the day's quiz to a text from an absent friend to a video of events in another country to a deal on shoes and be nimble enough in doing so that the learning task is back on screen whenever a teacher passes by. A learning device can more or less instantly become a distraction engine or a storefront.

Some intrusions into the digital learning space are uninvited and unexpected. Both teachers and students described to us the need to have strategies ready for when sexual or violent images occasionally pop up in the middle of an image search for a classroom project, or when an inadvertently clicked link redirects to an inappropriate page. As one student put it, even with filters and internet restrictions in place, encounters with distracting or disturbing material are "kind of hard to escape." The insistent attempts of internet pundits, marketers, and vendors to titillate the eye and ear pursue students right into class, invited or not.

Other intrusions are chosen, even positively pursued. The student comments quoted above suggest a conscious trade-off: my notes for Bible class are complete, and I can go shopping without leaving my desk, without even giving the impression that I am no longer working, so why not? At moments like these, the issue is not unexpected mishaps. Students are positively seeking distraction and gratification. This need not mean that they are exercising some sovereign act of free will. Digital media are often specifically designed to capture and hold the eye, to appeal to personalized interests, and to evoke and intensify desire for possessions, for social affirmation, for sexual gratification. Their designers leverage such desires to foster habits of engagement and gain a captive, or at least a captivated, audience.[3] Referring to an electronic game as "addictive" has become a common marketing boast in app stores rather than an admission of a possible defect. An important change happening through the proliferation of digital devices in classrooms is that even during the school day the objects of consumer desire are never more than a click away. They are on offer right in the midst of class, and few students are good at resisting.

One convenient heading under which to file these calling cards from the world at large is distraction, and they certainly fulfill that role. The benefits of digital technology in terms of information access come packaged in a high-distraction medium and create new variations in the long-standing dance between teachers and students around the matter of staying on task.[4] Teachers and parents rightly fear that as devices proliferate, students may end up wasting time pursuing matters that have little to do with their learning tasks.

While teachers and parents worry about student choices, some students cast the spotlight back on the teacher's pedagogical strategies. Students sense that if taking notes with the laptop is more efficient, if the goal of being in class is to complete assignments efficiently, and if the teaching strategy allows tasks to be completed with less than full engagement, then surely filling the dead time with other stimuli is an acceptable part of the bargain. If the notes have been typed and filed, there is time to go shopping, even if the teacher is talking.

Shopping and Formation

Distraction is an important and ever-present issue in classrooms, but the porous boundaries of digital learning resources raise further questions about student formation. As we saw in the last chapter, pornography and abuse of social media were concerns mentioned by a number of parents. Some were reassured by the schools' provisions for filtering, blocking, and monitoring internet use, but concern remained that the boundaries were not watertight. Parents feared that "students are smart, and they know how to get around those things." As one put it, "It's wide open. I mean these kids can go absolutely anywhere they want to go, and they are going!" Wider parent concerns included the influence of social media, sexting, song lyrics, and exposure to the values of secular media. One parent summarized the general feeling of concern: "I think my biggest fear is . . . that they would just be exposed, and especially in these walls where it's supposed to be safe, as much as it can be anyway, be exposed to some of that pop culture."

Some aspects of parents' concerns may be somewhat exaggerated—as we saw in the last chapter, far from all students are evading filters or accessing harmful material. In other regards, however, parents' concerns might be too narrowly targeted. Parental anxieties about digital technology gravitated toward a concern for sexual purity and safety amid social media. However, none raised shopping as an issue. An administrator reflected that the community's perception of the range of concerns meriting vigilance might have blind spots:

> I was always surprised—every time we'd get a complaint about porn or that kind of stuff, I was always shocked that . . . I don't think I one time fielded a complaint about materialism. And if the laptop truly degrades the Christian walk, I think materialism is a far greater danger to the vast majority of the Christian school crowd. And I caught—I don't know how to say this right—we literally, in my time there, what, one time caught a kid with porn at school? The porn incidences almost always happen at off-site, off-campus. But catching kids shopping during class, all the time. Right? All the time.

Students and teachers lend credence to this concern at the high school level, though not at the middle and elementary levels. High school students told us that in class "there's always the temptation to go on what you're not supposed to . . . so we have filters on our laptops." However, despite the filters, "it's really hard to regulate. . . . A lot of people will be shopping, or on Pinterest or Facebook." A substitute teacher echoed this, lamenting, "The things that I see on the screens during math class—you've either got kids doing math or you've got kids shoe shopping." Although such comments showed awareness that shopping in class is included among the things the school might want to regulate, there were also signs that it was perceived differently. Younger students knew to close their laptops, exit from browsers, or call a teacher if "some bad stuff comes up." Yet while students spoke to us of strategies for avoiding "bad stuff," some at least saw shopping in class as more benign. Students displayed none of the sense of wrong in talking about this that was evident when bad websites were referred to. It was presented more as an area of discretionary choice. As one summed it up, "I go shopping a lot during class, but I know that's kind of my deal, so if I miss out it's just like, oh, I won't go shopping anymore." Some students cheerfully continued shopping for tires or clothing as we filmed class sessions for later analysis, fully aware of the researcher observing. Online stores, falling outside what we most readily imagine as "bad stuff" online, do not tend to trigger filters that are geared more to pornography and social media, or to ring the same instinctive alarm bells for students or other community members.

Identifying "Bad Stuff"

This is not to suggest that parents are wrong to be concerned about pornography or the dark side of social media. As we have seen, there are signs that students at Modern Christian Schools may be doing comparatively well in this area compared to national averages. This does, however, still leave a fifth of male students over the age of thirteen reporting that they seek out explicitly sexual content at least monthly. There are grounds for both encouragement and concern.

However, a focus on these forms of exposure alone would miss the question of what Christian discernment might have to say about the kinds of faith formation happening when the free moments in Bible class are filled with quick bouts of online consumption. Christian ethics is certainly concerned with sexuality and violence, but greed and materialism are also relevant topics. There is a "desire of the eyes" as well as a "desire of the flesh" (1 John 2:16). It is perhaps not surprising, however, that worries about exposure to shopping sites seem less quick to surface in a relatively affluent Christian community. An administrator reflected on

> the subtlety, the slippery slope aspect that technology—the dangers that are, again, also at the fingertips of our kids. So, it's there, and we have parents who I think would prefer to create the bubble and to keep our kids protected from all of this. And we have as many safeguards in place as we can to help that. Because we do have that responsibility to protect students in ways that we can. But things like filters are also—they're

false senses of security, sometimes. Sometimes parents think, "Well, they've got the filter, so I don't have to—" so parents can back off. . . . We also have this huge opportunity and responsibility to teach students discernment in how to use technology.

Addressing this broader task of discernment entails a clear focus not only on "bad stuff" and "purity" but also on broader questions of formation. It also invites attention to the teacher's design of learning tasks, and how it might encourage students to believe that as long as they turn things in punctually, their shopping excursions are not in tension with their growth as students. The focus on efficient task completion fostered by digital devices, coupled with their focus on ease of consumer access, has consequences for formation even when "inappropriate content" has been filtered out.

Students in our focus groups spoke in ways that suggested that they had listened to and understood their parents' and teachers' warnings about harmful websites and online situations that should be avoided. "If we go onto a website, and the whole website is really bad, just simply shut your laptop and tell the teacher, and she'll exit out of it for you," one explained. They also expressed at times an implicit view that their key obligation was task completion, and if tasks were completed efficiently (something that technology can help with), then using the same device for a little entertainment seemed justified. "Once you get your notes done, you can go shopping or do whatever you want." This view seems to have been gleaned not from moral exhortation but from the patterns of teaching and learning in school and the patterns of distraction and consumption in the wider culture. Here the distinction between good and bad websites becomes slippery. Are we safe if we avoid porn and get good grades, even as we flip back and forth between the Sermon on the Mount and our next consumer purchase?

For Reflection and Response

- What are the most commonly voiced fears in your school community about the risks of digital access?
- Are there differences in your school community between the leading fears of parents, teachers, and students?
- Which areas of possible Christian concern might be neglected in your school?

CHAPTER 25

Teaching a Christian Perspective

I had to write a couple papers about why technology is good and why it's bad . . . and I'm sure there was a question of "how do we feel about this as a Christian?" . . . I think that's kind of the extent. It's kind of up to us. I've heard teachers comment . . . but it's never been like a project about it. Because it's everyday life, we do it all the time.

Student

Perhaps not surprisingly, concern about the moral dangers of inappropriate online content took a different turn in the minds of teachers and administrators than it tended to for parents. We noticed in chapter 6 that the "prepare minds" part of their mission statement could refer to academics in general or to helping students to develop a Christian mind. When teachers and administrators focused on the latter goal, the language of discernment was often connected with talk of a Christian perspective or worldview. This emphasis suggests a wider frame of reference than the primarily moral boundaries that we have seen associated with discernment among parents and students. How does the aspiration to invite students to *think* in Christian ways contribute to Christian discernment with technology?

Christian Perspective

The idea that a Christian faith commitment entails the need to form a Christian mind or Christian worldview has played an influential role in Reformed and evangelical discussions of how faith should relate to learning, and we saw this emphasis reflected in our survey data.[1] When we asked teachers to select "the best description of what makes education 'Christian'," easily the most frequently selected response at the high school level (83% of respondents) was that "students develop a Christian worldview."[2] The influence of this idea was also clear in school documents. Orientation materials for parents and students regularly emphasize the desire that students develop a "discerning Christian perspective" in the way they think about technology. The same theme echoed through curriculum plans and proposals, meeting minutes, and teacher evaluations. The recurring references to "discerning Christian perspective" articulate a sense shared by administrators, teachers, and parents that an important piece of the discernment-and-technology puzzle was helping students apply Christian belief as a critical filter to the ideas accessed through technology.

In curricular terms, teachers at Modern Christian Schools are encouraged to connect what they teach to relevant Christian themes and to the wider biblical narrative, commonly expressed in Reformed worldview discussions in terms of the story arc of creation, fall, redemption, and restoration. We heard multiple examples of these connections in focus groups. A mathematics teacher, for instance, described teaching families of functions in precalculus in connection with climate change and raising the question of Christian responsibility for environmental care. A Spanish teacher spoke of framing language learning in terms of the biblical theme of welcoming the stranger. An economics teacher recalled challenging students to consider how Christian faith commitments might motivate particular responses to poverty or use of economic resources.

The focus on Christian perspective or worldview relates in complex ways to the emphasis on safety and purity that we have already explored. On the one hand, the goal of developing a Christian worldview can be seen as another form of boundary-setting, distinguishing the way those inside the community think about the world from the perspectives of those outside. Approaching life from a biblical perspective is a part of what is meant to set the school apart. It is sometimes described as part of the effort to protect students, as when an administrator spoke of "preparing their mind to defend their faith as they enter a world that can be hostile to Christianity." Yet the emphasis on Christian perspective can also sit in tension with the impulse to create protective boundaries.

Critical Engagement

Teachers in our focus groups regularly touched on this tension. A middle school teacher reflected that students will inevitably encounter an outside world of mixed virtue through digital media, and the challenge is to help them evaluate what they find in light of Christian beliefs: "I've found it hard from a standpoint of . . . the world being out there. I think it's a lot easier to have a conversation with a junior or senior in high school and say, 'This is what we believe,' but also, 'You're going to find things on websites . . .' Or: 'We're going to watch this movie. There's this scene in it and we have to sort of find the redemption in that.'"

Some very practical tensions emerge in this dynamic of inevitable exposure and commitment to Christian beliefs and ethical boundaries. Teachers have to consider what students of a given age and maturity level can handle and how ready they are for conversations about the conflicts between Christian beliefs and material found online. They have to make decisions as they plan about what should be accepted, what should be filtered out, and what should be brought in for critical discussion. They do this in a context where choices made for pedagogical reasons with the goal of critical engagement might seem worrisome to the community. The teacher quoted above wondered aloud, "How do I show them appropriate things, but that are still authentic, without them being too mature or something their parents wouldn't approve of?"

These concerns are not unique to a digitally mediated curriculum. Educators have always faced decisions about exposure to outside material that may be controversial or harmful. Yet student access to a wider range of materials via the internet is more immediate and open-ended, and digital technology has added pressure by increasing the fluidity of the curriculum. In chapter 5 we saw a Modern Christian Schools principal in the first half of the twentieth century authoring curriculum guides for all the teachers. Teachers in our focus groups described how boundary decisions become more challenging in a teaching situation where "we don't have a set curriculum . . . we're creating that day by day." One teacher reflected,

> I think my go-to at the end of the day, is always . . . as much as I can, I want them to see what's real. . . . I think I would always rather have them exposed to it and have the conversation than not expose them to it. Obviously, I mean in my position . . . that's a fine line . . . but I think it's important . . . to not shelter them from things that are real, and I think I can say that as a former Christian school kid myself. They need to see what the real world is. But they also can have a conversation about what that means and what we believe.

We saw in chapter 22 how some parental anxieties support an emphasis on protection. In the words of the teacher just quoted, we hear a desire to harness the capacity of digital media to create access to the wider world and expose students to "things that are real" while also trying to make judgments in real time about the "fine line" of what should be excluded and how the things included should be framed by a Christian perspective. Again, it is worth emphasizing that technology did not create the question of what Christian discernment should allow into the classroom, but it has increased the degree to which such decisions have to be made in the moment by the teacher. Another teacher echoed these themes: "Now, if I'm looking at a Lady Gaga video in class, okay, let's look at the Lady Gaga video then. What is the message she's trying to get across? Or whatever is showing up in that magazine, that tablet, the technology—what is that saying? Now, I'm not going to say, 'Let's watch that porn video together,' but you have to have a discerning eye at what that technology is bringing to the forefront."

Teachers' desire to help students develop a critical Christian perspective often seemed, particularly in higher grade levels, to push them toward exposure and engagement rather than sheltering and protection, even as they clearly recognized that some things were beyond the pale and that student maturity was a factor. A commonly articulated goal was to gradually broaden students' exposure to the world as they matured. This placed on teachers the complex demand of making day-to-day choices about material that may be viewed in various ways by different community members, and of setting it within a Christian perspective.

One effect of combining new technologies with a continuing focus on Christian perspectives, then, has been to intensify the demands of mediating between students and curriculum content. Teachers work amid the multiple pressures of parental concerns, learning goals, a mandate to teach Christian perspectives, the unpredictability of what students will find online, and the inevitability of eventual exposure to troubling material. As curriculum has come to be, at least in part, constructed dynamically using current online resources, teachers (rather than textbook authors or curriculum-writing school leaders) must carry significant responsibility for the discernment process from moment to moment. This places quite large demands on their capacity for bringing moral, theological, and pedagogical reflection to bear on a day-to-day basis. Their efforts to maintain a Christian perspective seem to call for the combined roles of air traffic controller, diplomat, and security guard even as they work to achieve the more mundane learning goals of the curriculum.

Teacher Variation

The delicacy of this task was reflected in the range of individual responses to it among teachers and other community members. For some, the idea of applying a discerning Christian perspective sounded like quite a clear-cut affair. As one parent put it, "Discernment—is it agreeing with Scripture, is it not?" A teacher agreed that students should be helped to "read everything through a biblical lens in order to find what truth it has in it, if it has any." Such comments made discernment sound like a one-way street where securely established Christian perspectives should be used to weed out the helpful from the unhelpful on the internet.

Many teachers, however, used language that suggested more than just truth-checking against a fixed frame. There was broad agreement among teachers that students needed to be engaged in critical inquiry while interacting with a Christian perspective. As an art teacher put it, the goal was "not turning your brain off but constantly analyzing and asking yourself, 'Is this something I agree with?'" They went on to explain, "I think often we passively take in media, and I think discernment means to be in active engagement with it." In chapter 10 we already heard another teacher drawing attention to the times when ready-made Christian frameworks felt inadequate to the range of new topics and challenges encountered. That teacher confessed to being "really, really bad at the creation, fall, redemption framework," and preferring to "just invite kids into the wrestling match . . . with God." In the end, the teacher reflected, "this is just hard."

Digital access connects teachers and students to a constantly changing landscape of new findings, issues, events, and cultural debates. Having a ready, informed, and plausible Christian perspective on all of these is a tall order. Some teachers expressed a lack of confidence when it came to relating the big Christian categories of the schools' mission to the details of their own curriculum area. Others articulated an awareness that their own worldview commitments could lead to confirmation bias and should be open to scrutiny. A psychology teacher raised the point that what we already believe may shape the very outcomes that we look for: "When we talk about confirmation bias, we talk about getting discernment in those things. . . . So that's kind of our guiding principle. Wisdom seeking throughout that is saying, again, 'How are we . . . looking for things that confirm what I already think we believe?'" Where the emphasis on safety suggests an image of clean boundaries, as teachers reflected on the need for a discerning Christian perspective, there was a stronger sense of give and take, including moments of self-critique.

Worldview and Technology

Despite the emphasis on critical reflection, when the faith focus was articulated in terms of a Christian perspective or worldview, technology tended to be positioned as a tool or a conduit, something used to access ideas that could then be examined for consistency with a Christian worldview. Put another way, when the idea of worldview or perspective was to the fore, the focus tended to be on the perspectives and ideas encountered *through* technology more than on rethinking technology itself. Teachers did explicitly mention the idea of needing a philosophy of technology, a perspective on technology itself, but they did so to point out that discussion on that topic had been lacking. Technology was most often implicitly pictured as the means of access, the conduit for ideas and media with which we might agree or disagree. The idea of a Christian worldview or perspective tended to be applied to the ideological content of the curriculum more than its technological medium.

There are several possible reasons for this bias when teachers focus on talk of Christian perspective or worldview. After the initial implementation phase of the technology program, much of the schools' professional development focused on developing expertise with devices and apps. As comfort levels increased, the new technologies moved from being the focus of attention to being a familiar resource for getting things done. Sometimes the idea that technology was just a tool was used to demystify it and affirm its compatibility with Christian learning goals. It may also have been the case that the challenges of mastering new devices while relating an influx of new curricular content to Christian perspectives was enough to leave little space for making technology itself the focus of worldview discussions. Furthermore, since worldview-oriented thinking about curriculum was a strategy for connecting faith and learning that predated the technology program, it may be that it simply carried with it existing intellectual habits that kept it focused on curriculum content more than on the practices that framed learning.[3]

Whatever the causes may be, the concern for addressing the content of the curriculum and of digital media with a "discerning Christian perspective" was talked about by teachers in ways that rarely raised questions about the formative effects of technology use itself. It is not that there was no concern about those effects, but rather, in that particular part of the technology conversation, worldview language was not readily applied. Concerns already discussed about the reinforcement of a task-completion mentality, or the temptation to use time saved from learning to go shopping, were not brought to the surface in the context of world-view talk. Yet such concerns are a reminder that more is at stake in Christian discernment than having a perspective on media content.[4] Christian discernment is also about our moral and spiritual formation. The formation of our mind is no doubt an important part of that formation, but it is only a part.[5] Approaching questions about whole-person formation with Christian discernment means adding to concerns about boundaries and beliefs an interest in practices. How do we use technology, and how might that shape us? We focus more directly on this question in the next part of the book.

For Reflection and Response

- How do you think schools should address tensions between the educational desire to help students engage critically with a wide range of material and parental desires for safe boundaries?
- In what ways might a Christian worldview encourage Christians to question their own beliefs and assumptions?
- Does your school community think in terms of offering a particular perspective or worldview? Is this related mainly to the ideas in the curriculum or also to how resources and technologies are used?

Part 4 Summary

This part of the book explored how the Modern Christian Schools community has understood and worked to put into practice the task of Christian discernment with technology. Here we looked at the interaction between discernment themes and an emphasis on digital citizenship and asked how the community has approached concerns about maintaining safe boundaries.

- The idea of Christian discernment has a significant theological heritage. According to Nouwen, discernment is "a spiritual understanding and an experiential knowledge of how God is active in daily life that is acquired through disciplined spiritual practice."[1] It is not just an individual affair, and it is not just focused on moral questions. It is a communal Christian practice aimed toward knowing how our choices might affect our ability to love God and neighbor. Thinking about technology in connection with Christian discernment requires a focus on our relationship with God, our relationships with one another, our moral and spiritual formation, and our vocation and mission.
- A second source of ideas for approaching ethical boundaries in relation to digital technology is provided by work on digital citizenship. Digital citizenship is concerned with digital ethics (including copyright, cyberbullying, and privacy), media and information literacy, the capacity to effectively participate in a digital society, and the potential of digital media for fostering critical reflection and social change. The concerns of digital citizenship and discernment overlap in their common focus on how we treat one another, yet they are not identical. Discernment draws on our specific faith commitments, our spiritual formation, and our relationship with God. Digital citizenship is more developed in terms of educational frameworks and practical tools.
- Close examination of a decade of policy documents and professional development records shows a consistent emphasis on the need for stu-

dents to learn Christian discernment with technology. Early school conversations reflected the breadth of themes present in the idea of Christian discernment. Over time, perhaps in part because of the pressure and practical accessibility of digital citizenship frameworks, the meanings connected with talk of discernment in school documents tended to narrow to a focus on ethical behavior and information literacy. A regular return to theological sources and core commitments to clarify what was intended seems needed if the scope of key ideas is not to be narrowed by the pressures experienced during rapid processes of change.

- One critical question raised by some members of the parent community concerned whether students in the technology program were getting too much screen time. Close examination of actual screen time in class suggests that students' screen time per se is not excessive. Using their devices in the context of a school community where there are limits on entertainment and social media may offer these students opportunities to practice good technology habits. Given pressures in the wider culture and the increasing use of personal devices such as smartphones, it is possible that some students are using their devices excessively. However, our data do not offer support for the idea that the schools' technology program itself was a cause of harmful quantities of screen time. There were also signs that various intentional aspects of the program may be helping to teach responsible choices.
- We heard somewhat differing emphases when talking to parents and teachers about the moral risks of the internet. Parents in our focus groups were more likely to express an emphasis on safe boundaries and avoiding harmful internet material. Teachers, while sharing an awareness of the need for protections, expressed an emphasis on recognizing that students make mistakes and helping them learn from them in a context of grace and support. Teachers felt that this emphasis on trying and failing within the context of Christian community was itself a reflection of a Christian emphasis on grace. This difference in emphasis points to the need for good communication between home and school concerning the basic stance taken toward online risks.
- One mechanism used by Modern Christian Schools to minimize moral risk is the application of filtering and monitoring tools to restrict and oversee students' online access. Filtering and monitoring tools did not generate complete confidence among parents and students that risks had been removed, and in fact school leaders wanted parents

to understand that no filter is perfect or a replacement for mentoring of students. These tools also raised questions about the degree of the schools' responsibility for a student's behavior while at home and about the personal cost to staff charged with reviewing harmful material accessed by students. Nevertheless, broader school efforts to teach responsible use of technology were bearing fruit. Students reported less pornography use than their peers nationally, less temptation in school than in the college environment, and more responsible use of their laptops after they were outside the school restrictions. Again, there were signs that the schools' technology practices were supporting responsible use of technology.

- Students seemed well aware of adult concern about avoiding bad material online but seemed much less concerned about the dangers of materialism. Shopping in class was a common behavior and one freely reported by students—shopping sites are, after all, not bad websites. This raises concerns that are more specific than a general concern about distraction in class. While the community concern for safe boundaries often focused on sexual or violent material or social media, the high level of consumerist behavior occurring during school time requires attention.

- While parents often focused on concerns about moral boundaries, teachers were more likely to foreground a concern for teaching a Christian perspective or worldview in relation to content encountered online. This entailed fostering critical examination of ideas from outside the safe boundaries of the community. The challenge of helping students to approach curriculum content with a Christian perspective while aware of parental fears about safe boundaries has been intensified for teachers by the tendency of online learning to widen the scope of the content encountered and render the curriculum less fixed and predictable. When the idea of worldview or perspective was to the fore, the focus tended to be on the perspectives and ideas encountered through technology more than on rethinking technological practices themselves.

PART 5

FORMATION

Questions about Faith, Education, and Technology

- How is the mission understood and does technology serve it?
- Is technology helping teachers to serve student learning?
- How can we make discerning technology choices?
> **How does technology relate to student formation?**
- How is technology affecting the fabric of Christian community?

In part 2 we found the Modern Christian Schools community feeling confident that the technology program was helping to "prepare minds . . . to bring change to the world for Christ," but less sure about the "nurture lives" part of the mission. This suggests questions about student formation beyond the bounds of the academic. Even if new technologies are providing powerful new tools for reaching particular goals, what kinds of formation are happening along the way? How are the new technological media and the practices that grow up within and around them shaping students?

We begin this part of the book by clarifying the relationship between beliefs and practices. What happens when teachers connect faith and technology not so much through questions of worldview as through Christian practices (chapter 26)? After establishing this framework we turn to a range of particular practices that teachers are fostering as they seek to contribute to students' formation. First, we consider practices related to the mission theme of "bringing change to the world for Christ." We examine the various ways in which digital technology is helping students to connect during their learning with the wider world beyond the school walls, and how practices such as witness and service are relevant (chapter 27). Then we take a critical look at whether the best examples of this are really representative of everyday life in the classroom at Modern Christian Schools, and we discover some obstacles limiting the scope of this part of the mission (chapter 28).

Next, we turn to the struggle with distraction. While technology provides powerful tools for learning, we saw in the previous section that it also provides tempting new distractions. Here we probe this issue further. How is learning with digital devices affecting students' ability to concentrate and practice self-control and attentiveness (chapter 29)? We then look at how teachers are responding to the risks of digital distraction with practices that focus on slowing down learning for the sake of spiritual growth (chapter 30), and at attempts to use disciplines such as sabbath and fasting to set limits on students' relationship to their devices (chapter 31).

Finally, we examine some challenging questions that face efforts to deal with distraction and efforts to build communal Christian practices. Whose responsibility is it to help when students are distracted? Is this just the teacher's job, or is there evidence of students taking responsibility for one another's technology use within a Christian learning community (chapter 32)? This last chapter points forward to the themes of part 6, which focuses on technology and the community within which student formation takes place.

This section focuses less on what students can do with technology or access through it, and more on who they are being helped to become. It explores the connections between normative Christian practices and the concrete, daily challenge of shaping student responses to technology in school.

CHAPTER 26

How Do Beliefs Relate to Practices?

Technology can be a really great thing, but it's also something that you can misuse, and so the school was being really trusting with giving us laptops. . . . The discipleship practices, like offering grace and seeking the kingdom and service, we can practice those with our use of technology. I think social media is just a really big thing, especially in high school, and so you can do a lot of damage using it or you can use it positively. And so, I think the intentional discipleship practices that they're teaching us transfer into how we use our technology.

Student

In chapter 25 we saw teachers mainly drawing on the idea of developing a Christian perspective to critique ideas and messages. They did not as readily connect worldview talk with questions about the devices themselves and how their use might be shaping us. An emphasis on worldview and beliefs did not automatically lead to questioning technological practices. Teachers were, however, drawing on other faith emphases to think about the practices associated with digital media.

The question of how beliefs relate to practices arose regularly in our focus group data. One teacher described teaching a class on doctrine and apologetics in a semester during which a minor controversy erupted in the local press. Someone had written a piece in a local newspaper arguing that a mosque should be built in a nearby community that had a strong Christian majority. The article argued the benefits to the community of drawing from various sources of spiritual wisdom and questioned whether God is concerned about the specifics of worship practices. A student saw the article and brought it up in class. The students were already engaged in writing blogs relating to their course focus on apologetics. The teacher recalled,

What bothered one of those kids was not that that piece was written, but the online responses that were coming back from the Christian community. They were harsh, they were angry, they were ugly, many of them. And we talked about that in class. First Peter 3: always be ready to give an answer but do this with gentleness and respect. That was a huge part of what we did. So, we talked about, "How do we respond? What can you do using this tool and using the internet . . . to bring some grace? To bring change to the world for Christ by bringing some grace, even to this little corner of the universe?"

The teacher emphasized to the students that bringing gracious voices to even a small, local discussion was a way of making a difference in the world. The episode stuck in his mind as "something that was really good for me to think about and to process with the students, and I think it was great for students too, and beautiful to see the things that they wrote."

This episode points to another way of putting together faith and technology, focusing on technology as a social practice. The class included a strong focus on understanding Christian belief, so the idea of developing a Christian perspective or worldview was entirely relevant. Yet in this instance the faith-technology connection that came to the fore had to do with the *how* of communication more than the ideas communicated. For comparison, when another teacher offered an example of teaching Christian discernment, they described asking students to critique the underlying assumptions of PowerPoint presentations found online. The focus in that case was clearly on critiquing the ideas that were communicated, with less focus on the how. In the present case, beliefs are not left behind; the class remains, after all, a class on doctrine and apologetics. Yet the focus is on practicing gracious speech as a response to the often ungracious world of online comments. Shaping students' communication practices using technology is offered as a key part of a Christian response to the world of blogs and online comments.

Practices and Learning

What do practices have to do with learning? We often think of practices as a kind of follow-through on learning, as when we talk about "putting ideas into practice." That picture might lead us to see Christian beliefs or worldviews as the first step, and their application to practice as a secondary move once the ideas are already straight. First think/believe, then apply/

act. Yet we do not learn only by thinking. Participating in practices draws us into patterns of engagement that have their own learning momentum, as when we start a new job and are soon adapting to "the way we do things here" regardless of whether that way is written in a formal manual.[1]

Moreover, Christianity is not just a set of beliefs but also a set of practices. A range of recent publications on the nature of Christian practices and their importance for learning have generated lists of Christian practices that include worship, witness, reading and biblical interpretation, prayer, confession, forgiveness, encouragement, hospitality, bearing with one another, giving, receiving, listening, discernment, and justice-seeking, among others.[2] Such Christian practices not only grow out of faith but help to form faith.[3] Christians believe in God, and they also seek to grow in their love for and knowledge of God through engaging in prayer and worship, community and hospitality, giving and service. We can think of practices like these not just as the application of beliefs but as themselves a form of Christian education, working from the body up rather than from the head down, potentially reshaping our thoughts, desires, and preferences.

When we link practices to formation, we are focusing on something more than isolated behaviors. Practices, in the richer sense that connects with learning to live well, are regular affairs, extended over time. They are also rooted in a community and its stories.[4] Imagine two individuals both eating bread and drinking grape juice. One is enjoying a midafternoon snack; the other is participating in the Eucharist. At the level of behavior—chewing motions, swallowing, walking over to get the bread and then sitting down again—they may be doing pretty much the same thing. But they are not participating in the same practice.

What makes the practices of communion and snacking different, despite the similar behaviors? The moves may be similar, but they fit differently into story and community. Snacking is not typically done amid recollection of Christ's death and the gathering of a faith community to reaffirm their life together as the body of Christ. It is often a more individual, spur-of-the-moment thing and is less likely to be a fixed sequence of a morsel of bread followed by a sip of wine. It could, however, become ritualized in other ways—for instance, as part of a prescribed diet. Then it, too, becomes an intentional bid to reshape our habits and desires and part of a story shared with others about health, diet, and virtue. A practice, then, in the strong sense, is a set of moves that come together regularly and embody a particular shared purpose and story.[5] This is why "Would you like to share in the Eucharist?" does not mean quite the same thing as

"Would you like to eat some bread and drink some juice?" even though similar behaviors might result. The story—the shared beliefs about what is happening and their influence on the shared rhythms that result—is part of what makes the practice what it is. Practices have to be understood as complex wholes, not as small, isolated moves.

It is important to recognize this holistic characteristic of practices when we try to describe how faith is shaping the community's actions. For example, two teens pick up litter on a beach. One wants a clean patch for the photograph that they plan to post to social media to make their weekend seem more idyllic and impress their friends. The other (a student participant in our focus groups who provided this example) is responding to their Christian school's emphasis on care for creation as part of responsible Christian living. Similar behaviors, different stories, different practices. When we focus on practices, then, we are not moving from "theory" to "practice." We do not leave questions of belief or perspectives behind, nor do we simply add behaviors as the secondary outcome of beliefs. Rather, we shift attention from how faith is expressed in beliefs to how faith lives and grows in and through the patterns in our actions as a community.

Discipleship Practices

As we saw in earlier chapters, the schools' efforts to frame their technology use in Christian ways gained some fresh impetus several years after the initial implementation of the laptop program. This seemed to be spurred by several factors. The introduction of tablets motivated a fresh flurry of discussions about Christian discernment and technology. Some personnel changes and the creation of a new faith and technology committee yielded a fresh focus on faith formation and some new lines of thought. There was also an influence from recent writings about Christian education that invited a stronger focus on practices and formation.[6]

All of this led to a new emphasis on discipleship practices, which became a theme cutting across school subject areas. This was understood as part of the schools' curriculum work, not merely as a matter of good student behavior. The words of a senior staff member, cited earlier, are worth repeating here: "I think it reflects the journey that Christian education has been on. I'm by far the oldest in the room, and watched Christian education move from 'What do you know?' to 'What do you believe?' and finally 'So, how are you going to live differently?' . . . And I think that that's been the journey we've been on as a school as well, and adding technology has been a part of that too, moving from what do you know to what do you believe to what are you going to do with it?"

The fresh emphasis on intentional, communal practice was reinforced through the choice of a related book each year to inform chapel themes and community reflections, lists of key practices posted in classrooms, and attempts to build shared, schoolwide practices into the timetable. Alongside the existing talk of Christian discernment and Christian perspectives, a focus on Christian practices became a further strategy for linking technology and faith.[7]

Practices and Accountability

By the time we conducted our focus groups, the language of these shared practices was widely familiar, and teachers were finding ways to connect the practices to their particular teaching areas. The second language teachers, for instance, spoke of wanting to frame language learning in terms of practicing hospitality to strangers. They presented language to students as an opportunity "to extend hospitality, see the other's perspective and create connections rather than isolation and fear of people unlike us."[8] This meant, for instance, including challenging intercultural themes, representing perspectives from beyond the schools' cultural circles, and creating opportunities for direct interaction with people from other communities. Attending to the practice of hospitality can provide an impetus to focus not only on transactional language or on student self-expression but also on intentionally attending to the voices, perspectives, and needs of others. Grounding the design of second language instruction in the practice of hospitality directs attention to how speakers of the target language are represented in the curriculum, how stories are used, the opportunities given to students to learn from cultural others, how gracious listening is practiced, and how students learn attentiveness to a world outside their own cultural circle.[9]

As Christian practices such as hospitality are named and woven into subject teaching, they can not only help shape pedagogical practice but also create a framework for accountability. They can be appealed to, for instance, when helping students wrestle with cultural difference. One teacher described addressing the politicized topic of immigration in Spanish class.

She had drawn students' attention to the current range of polarized views on immigration. She recalled,

> When I was talking about that, I also put on screen a picture at the border.... It doesn't say any words. It's just a picture of three people running near the highway. The first time I saw that my stomach was ... Because in Michigan we see deer crossing signs like that, "Caution: Deer" maybe. So, it really struck me, like, oh my goodness, I might be driving down this highway and there might be people running for their lives because they're trying to provide hope and a future for their kids.... One of my students, they totally laughed at that and [said], "Yeah, what do you do when you see that?" And they said, "Hit them." I was, like, really? So, I pulled out the discipleship practices and I said, "What discipleship practice does 'hit them' go with?"

The teacher appealed here not primarily to right belief (What is a Christian perspective on immigration?) but to right practice (Is this consistent with the life of a disciple?). She was certainly concerned about what students believed about migrants. Yet what she emphasized in this instance was that casual dismissal and appeals to violence, even offered in jest, suggested a practice deeply at odds with Christian practices of love of neighbor and hospitality to strangers. Rather than carrying on toward the planned lesson objectives, she altered course and invited students to reflect at some length on whether the behaviors they implied could plausibly be characterized as Christian practice. This kind of move reflects a hope that Christian practices might provide a lived framework that helps pattern student engagement, including engagement with digital technologies.

Modern Christian Schools have begun to emphasize a broad range of explicit practices, embracing themes such as beauty, service, and wonder, as well as the emphasis on love of neighbor and gracious communication that we have seen. All of these practices carry potential for shaping how teachers and students engage with technology. As we move beyond seeing technology as merely a tool for meeting discrete goals, or as a medium that shapes us whether we like it or not, and into a focus on intentional practices, we begin to see another important facet of how Christian faith might make a difference. It is not only a matter of pursuing missional goals or of clarifying Christian beliefs about technology and moral boundaries for its use. Intentional, shared, communal practices rooted in faith have the potential to discipline, at least to some degree, how technology is used and what we learn from using it. They are also a key point at which technology decisions intersect with questions of student formation—the "nurture lives" aspect of Modern Christian Schools' mission. It is within shared practices, either intentional ones or the defaults that have accrued over time, that we learn how to relate to others, choose what to take up or put down, and pattern our engagement with the world. What Christian practices are shaping classroom life in the schools we studied?

For Reflection and Response

- Did the story about the mosque unfold in the way you expected? How might it have gone differently?
- What is the difference between a practice and a behavior? Why might it be important to think in terms of Christian practices rather than Christian behaviors?
- Do you tend to think of the connection between faith and education more in term of beliefs or of practices? How might the emphasis on one or the other shape the way you think about technology?

CHAPTER 27

How Do Laptops Foster Connections to the Wider World?

> I think initially, when the mission statement was written, it was more [that] the bringing change to the world for Christ was after graduation. It was something you did when you were finished with this process. Now, it's what are you going to do today, what are you going to do this afternoon, what are you going to do this hour? And so, it brought that part of the mission back into a . . . live approach, as opposed to something in the future. I think that was a significant change for us. It was not something you were working towards; it was something you were involved in right now.
>
> *Teacher*

A group of high school students in a multimedia class are designing a promotional website about their school. They work individually and in small groups using laptops, with a variety of activities happening at the same time around the room. Students use varied software packages to capture and edit video and to record, edit, and add audio commentary. Some of the thought processes involved are quite complex. As some struggle with a layout problem, the teacher points out connections to other subject areas: "Everything you learned in math now starts coming together for a purpose." When the class gathers to check on progress, the teacher reminds students that they are supposed to promote their website beyond the class. The goal is for them to gain an audience outside the school.

In another classroom, students are watching the movie *The Kite Runner* as part of an exploration of world cultures. The movie viewing was preceded by a review of key events in the history of Afghanistan. As the movie is showing, the teacher meets outside the classroom with a smaller group of students to review their project progress. Their research question is "How should the government of Nepal handle injustice toward disabled students in their education system?" One student shares her difficulty with finding online data on government schools in Nepal (she has found private school information) and her frustration with finding a path toward a solution for students with disabilities in Nepalese schools. She comments that it is hard because of a mindset associated with Hinduism in which disability is seen as a curse or bad karma. The teacher asks, "How do you bring a bit of shalom? Are there any avenues within Hinduism you can work with?" The students seem to appreciate this new line of thinking. They return to the classroom, and another pair moves out to talk with the teacher in the hall.

These two vignettes of classroom practice, both observed at Modern Christian Schools during our classroom visits, show a significant aspiration of school leaders in action. As we saw in chapter 6, the potential for new technologies to extend the schools' capacity to meet their mission to "bring change to the world for Christ" became an important strand in school leaders' justification of technological change. As one explained to us,

> We enlarged the audience. Modern Christian Schools were stuck on [a side street] and were not extending their influence beyond the walls, and I think this was a tool that extended our influence and our opportunity, and I think that that changed the game considerably. Now that's not what's happening in first grade necessarily, but it is what's happening pretty significantly at the high school/middle school level. And I think it's coming along as first graders email material to their parents and their grandparents. . . . It's starting to enlarge their world and their understanding of how they can impact their world in the name of Christ.

At different times administrators spoke of this both as a way in which new technologies might radically transform learning and as "doing better what you were supposed to be doing all along." So what specific technological practices are arising from the view of technology as a tool for furthering the mission? The hope of administrators was not simply that students would understand the idea of mission to the wider world. They hoped that technology would change educational practice in such a way that students would begin to practice engagement with the wider world immediately, in the course of their learning. As students experienced active connection to the world beyond school through digital communication technologies, their sense of calling was to be impacted. Students were to be formed as those who might "bring change to the world for Christ" by engaging in classroom practices oriented to that end.

What can we discover about how this was working? As we studied what was happening in classrooms, we actively sought examples of students using technology to connect their learning with people and places beyond the walls of the school. We focused especially on examples that moved outside the bounds of their own families and immediate community (we discuss community connections in part 6). Has digital technology strengthened the capacity to connect learning with mission to the wider world?[1]

We saw this emphasis playing out in several distinct ways in relation to teachers' and students' technology practices. Sometimes the emphasis was on *access* to people and resources to aid learning. This was accompanied by an emphasis on *service* and by a concern for various forms of *witness* to wider audiences. Sometimes this led to significant *exchange* with groups outside the school. We will look at each of these in a little more detail before considering the role they play in the life of the school.

Access

In our survey data, 83% of teachers and 75% of students agreed that technology use in school had created opportunities to learn about the experiences and needs of people outside the community. Many of the examples that we encountered involved using digital technologies to gain access to individuals or resources—for instance, in connection with individually chosen research projects.[2] A social studies teacher commented that "if you're going to differentiate, and if each student is going to pursue their passion, you have to be able to tap into resources that we don't have access to inside the four-concrete-walled building." Students and teachers described to us research projects on issues ranging from local water ecology through disability in Ghana to ISIS in Syria. These projects were often driven by charitable or justice-oriented concerns, resonating with the biblical call to seek justice and love mercy.[3] Internet access was used to search for data and other resources such as images and videos. It was also used to seek immediate access to individuals involved in trying to bring positive change to the situations being researched. Examples included sending emails to nonprofit organizations, asking questions over Skype of overseas contacts from the teacher's personal network, and messaging the author of a novel. This kind of work harnesses digital communication to extend the range of experience and expertise from which students can learn. Such access is one of the primary affordances cited by nearly all schools investing heavily in digital technologies and aligns easily with schools seeking to connect to the world beyond their walls.[4]

Service

Face-to-face service opportunities initiated through electronic contact were common examples of engagement offered by students. In surveys, 56% of students and 41% of parents felt that technology use in school had created opportunities to respond to the needs of others outside the community. One student reported, "I [worked with] refugee children one summer. . . . I've done tutoring and I did . . . mentoring . . . one summer. All those have started through email correspondence." Another recalled making a video about a Holocaust organization and "just going there and videotaping and then showing them our project. They asked us to come back and continue helping out there." One offered an example of the skills learned in these projects extending beyond school work altogether: "For spring break I'm going to California with a bunch of my friends and we decided to focus our trip on service, so I looked up all kinds of organizations in Southern California, where we're going, and I was able to email them all and get responses from them, so we're going to do a bunch of service projects over spring break, all [set up] using my laptop and emailing."

Some students worked on projects that involved using digital skills directly for service to local organizations. One student described working on a multimedia presentation about a local environmental concern that was formally presented to a panel of local people. A math teacher described a project in which "we have the kids do an animation for a nonprofit agency. They go and learn about the agency and learn what their purpose is and then make a little video clip using matrices and math, and then they fill it in with color using matrices, and then they do sound over it, and then they send it back to that organization [so] that they can use it."

We begin to sense in these examples the ways in which students might experience multiple service opportunities throughout their school experience as communal practice that promotes an outward reach. The contribution of technology to these service experiences, however, was most often indirect. Several of the examples that we heard made no mention of digital technology, focusing simply on service projects and charitable donation drives. Technology was seen as enhancing service to the wider world by making it easier to establish contacts, and sometimes through having digital skills and products to offer. Many student comments evidenced a confidence that their technological skills could enable them not only to find out information but also to contribute something.

> **Ways Digital Technologies Fostered Engagement with the Wider World**
>
> • *Access:* increased access to resources and people beyond the school
> • *Service:* provided ways to learn about and connect to service opportunities
> • *Witness:* enhanced opportunities to share the schools' perspective and innovative work with technology with other schools
> • *Exchange:* promoted interactions that supported a mutual exchange of learning

Witness

A third emphasis focused on the idea that the school could work at extending God's kingdom by freely sharing expertise, demonstrating the potential of Christian schools, and using digital media to communicate Christian convictions. We saw this theme in comments from administrators and teachers, but rarely from students. Interestingly, the emphasis in such comments was often less on the transmission of Christian ideas through digital media and more on the idea that the schools' innovative work with technology might showcase a Christian school making a forward-looking contribution to educational practice. An administrator recalled that as the technology program developed, "it was a great way to share our story; it was a great way to help other schools thinking about transforming teaching and learning." Another added, "We shared everything. We didn't ever hold back a document or anything from anybody. It really raised our status, in some sense, in the nation." This kind of interaction occurred with both faith-based and secular schools.

A few student projects also involved broad forms of witness outside the school. Students gave examples of projects focused on topics such as stewardship of local waterways, gang membership, and caring for refugee children. Groups gathered information online and from local experts, worked together to develop a response to the issue, created a multimedia presentation, and made their argument to a panel of local community leaders.

Exchange

The emphasis on access suggests information flowing into the school from outside. The service and witness themes suggest goods flowing from the school out into the world. However, some of the most compelling examples of using technology to transcend the schools' boundaries involved a strong sense of interaction and mutual learning. Sixty-three percent of students in our surveys felt that the schools' technology use had helped them communicate with people outside of their community. Two examples in particular stand out.

A high school Spanish teacher reported a series of efforts to use online communication to foster exchanges between Spanish students and contacts overseas. Advanced students studying a unit around the theme of design interacted through Facebook and a Google Doc with a fashion designer in Spain. Beginners recorded simple video greetings to send to a school in Spain and received responses from students there. Interaction with the local Spanish-speaking community was also enhanced: "In my Spanish 3 class last year . . . we had seven sections, and so we didn't want to ask a guest speaker to come in for the whole day. So we FaceTimed with a couple people from the community, just for . . . 10 minutes in class, and they could ask questions. And that worked really well, just with our iPhones through Apple TV. They were on the screen, and I could just go around the room and show the kids asking the questions."

In another Spanish class, a teacher worked with a contact who was teaching Spanish in the Czech Republic and who collected and sent over the Czech students' perceptions of Americans (written in Spanish). Modern Christian Schools students were asked about their stereotypes of Czech people and discussed why they did not have any or know much about Czech culture. The teacher recounted, "Since we have technology at our fingertips, we just responded to everything that they said, and we kind of guided some of their stereotypes into the right direction. And then they said we were all fat. So we took a picture of our class to show them that we're not all fat and sent it to them."

Another example was closer to home but also sought to tackle stereotypes. A teacher described an initiative designed to reduce tensions between students at Modern Christian Schools and those at the nearby public school. She described a history of some "animosity" between the two student bodies, expressed particularly at sporting events, noting that "we have kind of a tumultuous relationship there, [they are] not a big fan of ours." Precisely for this reason, the idea of connecting via Skype seemed to offer a more controlled environment in which to learn from one another. A series of shared class sessions were set up in which students from the two elementary schools interacted and discussed common readings.

> So, our goal and our talking—this other teacher and I—were to work at seeing and learning from each other—what each of us needed. We need diversity. And so, seeing kids who are in your same town, very different from you are, doing the same things, because their curriculum is the same as ours—we both use Reading Workshop—that was our goal. . . . So then we connected via Skype and we sat, and we talked, and we shared, and we showed each other each other's classrooms and we did . . . mini interviews with just a few kids and a teacher and that kind of thing and showed each other what we were working on. And I think that is . . . a way to grow—I mean, we're growing God's kingdom by doing that. We're learning about our own town and people living in our own town. That was a really cool experience.

It was these kinds of practices that sustained the sense among Modern Christian Schools administrators and teachers that digital technology could be a tool that extended their capacity to fulfill their missional goal of bringing change to the world for Christ. Few of the examples were entirely dependent on new technologies. Service projects, research into other cultures, and interaction with members of the local community were quite possible before the advent of digital devices, and in many cases what digital communication offered was a gateway to physical, in-person interactions between students and others. The belief was clearly present, however, among both teachers and students, that intentional practices that depend on digital technology and online access can widen the scope of student research, allow for the pursuit of individualized projects oriented to constructive change in the world, and offer more efficient and immediate access to outside agencies and individuals. Perhaps working with digital technology can help students gain a sense of agency as Christians engaged with a wider world. This is not, however, the whole story, nor is it an accurate picture of every classroom at Modern Christian Schools. We explore some of the limitations of this vision for technology in the next chapter.

For Reflection and Response

- How might the forms of digital connection to the wider world described in this chapter serve the mission of a Christian school?
- Think of a concrete example of how digital technology could be used to connect student learning to the wider world. What exactly does the technology add that could not be achieved by other means?
- What might the practices described in this chapter be contributing to students' formation?

CHAPTER 28

Limitations of Digital Engagement
with the Wider World

> We just have a lot more skills, I feel like, than other people. . . . I have
> friends who go to [another school], they don't have a lot of technology
> there. So, in comparison with them, I feel like I have a lot more skills
> that can be used to bring change to the world. For example, I have a
> world cultures class and I just emailed someone across the world in
> Ghana, and I talked to them about my project and how we can fight the
> problem of stereotyping of people with disabilities in Ghana. So, we're
> already bringing change to the world, and we're just in high school.
>
> *High school student*

In the last chapter we surveyed some of the ways in which students are
being encouraged to reach out digitally beyond the school walls. The examples described there represent the kinds of practices seen by administrators as positive signs that the mission to bring change to the world for
Christ was being enhanced by digital technology. When students described
these learning experiences to us, their responses were very positive; such
opportunities were "cool" or "super interesting." The potential for high
student motivation is well illustrated by a student's account of a school
science project:

> A partner and I, for our biology project, we had to research green fluores-
> cent protein. It was super interesting, and it's kind of boring if you had
> surface level, but we were doing research, and green fluorescent protein
> is fairly new, so the people who discovered it and made advancements in
> it are still alive, and all of their information is online, and you can email
> almost every one of them. So, we emailed, there was this website of five
> different people or whatever and we just looked up their names, and they
> wrote a textbook on green fluorescent protein or something like that.
> And we got a response from a dude who's the head of the department

at Rutgers University, and he just went off on so much stuff, so that was just crazy that he responded, and that he was interested enough, and he invited me and my partner to one of his classes. I was, like, sorry, I can't make it out quite to the Northeast, but it was still really, really cool, and just really exciting. You don't get that in school a lot. . . . It made it really exciting to learn about, and we emailed back and forth three or four times, so it was really cool.

The impression left on this student is evident. Should we take it as evidence that this aspect of the mission is being realized?

While we certainly saw encouraging examples, a few qualifications are needed. Understandably, connection to the outside world is more controlled at the elementary level, opening up more in high school. Yet even allowing for this, we observed several limitations that provide a cautionary undercurrent to the enthusiasm for changing the world and the confidence that technology is helping. In this chapter we explore some of these limitations.

"Nobody Answered"

Students reported mixed success with contacting people in the outside world. This is hardly surprising. The need for staff at a major public aquarium to respond to elementary students' scientific questions about starfish may seem compelling to their teacher, prompting a sense of indignation when a letter came back saying that aquarium staff were unable to offer science instruction. The response becomes more understandable, however, as soon as we imagine the potential number of inquiries from school children in the region if such a pedagogy were widely adopted. The idea that everyone should be readily available for everyone else's queries is part of both the benefit and the bane of digital communication technologies.[1] Students with whom we spoke expressed both an apparent confidence that email offers immediate access to anyone and a degree of resignation about the patchy results. One reported writing letters to the president of Syria and a US group against ISIS "to see if we could get any response." In the end, "nobody answered, but it was still part of the project." A teacher recounted the process of seeking authentic sources for student projects: "I have forty-two students this year. . . . They each have to [seek] at least one. We get five to ten meaningful responses and a few form letters, and most of the time it's no response at all."

Other teachers described managing a process in which one student might get a response the next day and another not for weeks or at all. They were left needing to award credit for trying rather than for achieving a result. The exciting successes ("Last semester we had a group with a back and forth with the US ambassador in Pakistan on honor killings") stand alongside failures to elicit a response ("I know many people who've called [a certain author]. He's never answered"). This could perhaps be seen as a constructive learning opportunity, encouraging some discussion of the limits of digital accessibility and the communication demands we place on others in the age of digital media. Most often, however, we heard a lack of response from potential contacts framed more as an unfortunate failure to get results, one that sometimes left students adrift in their projects as the world failed to answer their emails.

"Better Than Nothing"

In a few interesting instances we heard teachers and students reflect on the limitations of even successful digitally mediated outreach. As one high school student commented, "There's value to real-world experiences also. There's something to be said about having a conversation with someone in Spanish in person versus over Skype." Digital access can extend geographical reach but also feel more limited than physical presence.

The sometimes complex considerations in play are illustrated by one teacher's account of changes to a curricular initiative that connected students in an introductory business class with local businesses. He explained, "I teach a management class, and kids are developing a business model for themselves, and they get paired with a local business as well. In the past I've had them go visit those businesses and spend time with the owners . . . but our transportation policy makes that a little difficult this year, so they are paired up electronically and they can share that document . . . back and forth and get some feedback from somebody who is doing what they're hoping to do down the road." His reflections on the effects of this shift from face-to-face site visits to digital communication reveal a mixed picture: "I think they get less feedback because it's easier to sit down for an hour with somebody who has dedicated time and get conversations. Getting someone on the other end to really invest in putting time in [online], it takes a lot more time for them to do that. That face-to-face conversation is better in all honesty, plus they can see things, and being at this business would spark a question in a kid and [they would] say, 'What about that, what about this, what about this?' It doesn't happen electronically."

The shift that this teacher identifies here is twofold. First, he suggests that when we meet someone face-to-face, we capture their attention more effectively than when we send them documents to review, and so there is potential for stronger personal investment from our conversation partner. This recognition echoes voices of scholars who believe there is a fundamental difference inherent in face-to-face interactions that promotes connectedness in ways nearly impossible through digital communication.[2] Second, when we meet face-to-face, we do so in a physical context that can itself raise questions for our conversation, grounding our process of inquiry in a concrete setting. It seems, then, that the original program of site visits might have been pedagogically the better plan. However, the change in transportation policy has made it logistically infeasible to get all of this teacher's students to the off-campus sites efficiently. The choice of digital communication was therefore not so much a vote for the empowering potential of digital media as a reliance on digital media to sustain in some form connections that otherwise would have been dropped: "To get them to all these different places was logistically not possible . . . so this was my second choice but a good second choice. It wouldn't have worked otherwise. There would be no pairing if that didn't exist. Better than nothing." There is a sense here of technology creating both possibilities and limitations in terms of offering access to the outside world.

"I Haven't Done It Lately"

Another pattern to emerge in descriptions of the most interactive forms of digital outreach was their often temporary nature. While online research can be conducted at any time, richer connections with external conversation partners often depend on the availability of contacts, time zone differences, the changing agendas of both parties over time, and the time and energy needed to sustain a more interactive approach. Thus, a Spanish teacher described to us how Skype was used to connect Spanish students at Modern Christian Schools with students in Honduras to discuss cultural differences, before reflecting that "that was . . . the first three years. I haven't done it lately." The example discussed in the last chapter, in which students connected with the nearby public school, was also short-lived. It "went well," the teacher reported, but "we didn't get to extend it as much as we wanted to purely because of the time of year that it is. For the four or five times that we did it, it was a really interesting experience . . . and I hope it grows in the future, but I have a little too much on my plate for it to grow right now."

It is normal for teaching ideas and units to come and go as fresh ideas are developed. There was, however, a strong hint in these descriptions of interactive digital outreach that costs in time and energy made such activities challenging to sustain or practice frequently.

"You Don't Get That in School a Lot"

A fourth limitation can be heard in the student praise for digital connections with which we began this chapter. Connections such as the one made with protein experts were said to be exciting in part because they are unlike what is normally done in school, including at Modern Christian Schools. The last chapter offered evidence that the mission focus on seeking to engage with and influence the wider world out of a Christian concern for charity, justice, and witness was indeed shaping some instances of teaching and learning. Yet on closer examination, the most interesting examples often came from a particular cluster of teachers and subject areas, and we began to hear the same flagship examples narrated repeatedly across focus groups. Could it be that a few strong examples are being overnarrated out of the desire to affirm pursuit of the mission, or simply because they are attention-grabbing? One way to approach that question is by comparing the focus group data with our classroom case studies and randomized classroom observations. Across seventy-five observations of 30–45 minutes each in randomly selected individual lessons, we saw only 6 out of 479 total activities (including those described in chapter 27) that connected directly to the emphasis on bringing change to the world or that involved interactions with the world outside the school. Some of these six activities did not include a focus on technology. In our more extended case study observations, we saw activities in three classrooms (two elementary and one high school) that primed students for future engagement through technology with the outside world (e.g., discussing how to write a blog post), but in none of the six classrooms did we observe technology used to actively connect to the outside world. The few striking examples that have emerged in particular classes were renarrated often, but we were not able to find evidence that they were common occurrences.

A Glass Half Full or Half Empty?

This does not necessarily negate the value of those examples. Perhaps much of the work that takes place in schools must inevitably consist of an everyday focus on gaining and honing skills, with ambitious, integrative projects that reach out into the world only sometimes taking center stage. However, the lack of evidence for engagement with the wider world in seventy-five classroom observations and six case studies spread across a school year suggests we should hesitate over the more sweeping visions of technology radically redefining the schools' pedagogy by engaging students in changing the world in the here and now.[3] Interestingly, in survey data, while 63% of students believed that the schools' technology use had helped them communicate with people outside their community, only 38% of parents affirmed the same conviction. Only just over half (57%) of students agreed that the technology program had prepared them "for Christian engagement in the world," with a similar 56% among alumni. The data explored in this chapter raises the question of whether even the positive responses are built on recollection of vivid but occasional, unrepresentative examples. To put the alumni figure into perspective, however, only 36% of our control group of other Christian school alumni agreed with the same statement, so 56% may be seen as a significant increase compared to the experience of students in similar schools.

What can we say, then, about the idea that laptops are serving as a tool to push forward the mission to bring change to the world for Christ? There was evidence that an emphasis on outward engagement was present, worked into practice by some of the most creative teachers and in particular curriculum areas. There was also evidence that it was appreciated by students as they engaged the strongest instances. There did, furthermore, appear to be some enhancement of this outcome as perceived by students when compared to other similar populations. At the same time, the impact of this particular mission emphasis was more limited in classroom practices than its prominence in the schools' talk might suggest. Where it did appear, there was a sense of contrast with business as usual, rather than a wholesale transformation of learning.

It is unclear exactly how disappointed we should be with these qual-ifications to the more transformational picture implied by the exam-ples in the last chapter and in mission talk. If we start from the common marketing promise that technology will bring about comprehensive life transformation, or even from some of the more visionary statements of Modern Christian Schools administrators about how technology might be transforming pedagogy and the pursuit of their mission, some skep-ticism seems warranted. External engagement was occasional and only sometimes genuinely interactive or transformational. It was challenging to sustain and unevenly distributed across the curriculum. Yet if we start from the challenges of reshaping classroom learning, we can think more in terms of partial progress. The commitment, support, and encouragement required to consistently bend learning toward outside engagement should not be underestimated. Nevertheless, even occasional interventions can create memorable experiences and so shape students' sense of the import of their learning and their agency in the world. Efforts to harness digital tools to engage and serve the world were adding a clearly discernible ac-cent to the education offered at Modern Christian Schools, and that may be an important gain.

For Reflection and Response

- How might limitations like those described in this chapter be mitigated in schools with outward-reaching visions?
- What stories are told in your school to illustrate its success at pursuing practices that express its core aspirations? What evidence is there that those stories are representative of average practice in the school?

CHAPTER 29

Are Students Really Paying Attention?

I think probably students who do well in school benefit more, because students who do poorly in school just tend to get more distracted, I think. But students who do well in school maybe use the laptops to research more or just use their laptops to research different things about colleges and stuff.

Student

The practices discussed in the last two chapters aimed to put technology to work in the service of vocation. Yet when formation was in view, we often heard a more cautious countertheme: Might technology foster the wrong kind of formation? As students harness technological tools for learning, might the digital medium be shaping them in less desirable ways? The theme of Christian discernment continued to hover nearby.

Many educators and parents asked us to explore whether students were "really paying attention" when learning with laptops and tablets. As we glimpsed in part 4, they wondered whether students' ability to focus was undermined by screen use and constantly "toggling around" between apps.[1] Such questions were not surprising. Research suggests that multitasking with digital technologies interferes with working memory, undermines sustained attention, and leads in some cases to negative learning outcomes.[2] Do new technologies increase distraction in Modern Christian Schools classrooms? How did administrators and teachers address this concern?

Distraction and Multitasking

A growing chorus of researchers have documented two facts about modern students. First, students are fond of multitasking with technology, consuming multiple kinds of media while they work. Second, multitasking tends to be unproductive, particularly in learning settings.[3] Phones are distracting for many teens.[4] One experimental study found that teens who used phones while taking notes during a lecture recorded 62% less information, retained less, and scored lower on exams.[5] In lecture settings, a recent study found that students taking notes on laptops also tended to multitask frequently during the lecture, leading to distraction and worse academic performance. Laptop multitasking also tended to distract nearby peers.[6] Young people recognize that digital media distract them but underestimate the degree to which it hurts their ability to focus on academic work.[7]

So what can we learn about these practices at Modern Christian Schools? During our classroom observations, we recorded instances where two or more students spent more than a minute on activity unrelated to the current class and noted whether technology was in use.[8] Our choices in data collection shape what the data can and cannot answer. We cannot report on momentary distractions (e.g., a quick toggle to social media and back to classwork) or on how many students were off task at any one time. What we can report concerns the percentage of classroom activity time when at least two students were off task for a minute or more. We can compare this to the total time students spent on task and we can consider whether digital technologies were in use. We can also compare patterns across elementary, middle, or high school.

Random Observations: Digital Distractions?

We rarely saw elementary and middle school students off task for a minute or more with technology or without in random observations. Elementary and middle school students were observed off task for less than 1% and 5%, respectively, of the total classroom activity time. Given that we might expect some distraction in any classroom, these figures seem quite promising.

What role did digital technologies play? In the elementary classrooms, all off-task behavior occurred during times that one-to-one devices were not in use. This changed in middle school, where students were off task about twice as often working with laptops than without. High school students were observed off task nearly twice as often as middle school students, at 8% of the total classroom activity time, but mostly when digital technologies were not in use. So as students progressed from tablets to laptops and from elementary to middle school, we saw the pull of digital distractions become stronger, yet middle school students seem to have been the most distracted when laptops were in use. This suggests that they may be the least adept at tuning out digital distractions during class.

It is here that multiple research methods offer a reality check. In these random, one-time observations, students were quite aware of researchers' presence and some were adapting their behaviors under the scrutiny of strangers. In the case study classrooms, students grew accustomed to having researchers in the room and began to reveal behaviors that might be more characteristic of true daily life in their classrooms.[9] What do case study observations show?

Case Studies: Digital Distractions?

At the elementary and middle school, the case study data confirmed what we saw in random observations. Elementary students were off task for 1% of classroom activity time and only when not using one-to-one devices. This was true even as students used one-to-one devices for 35% of the observed classroom activities. At the middle school, off-task behaviors made up about 4% of total classroom activity time even as some students used technology for nearly 80% of the observed classroom activities. Off-task behaviors in middle school occurred when laptops were in use at nearly three times the rate compared to when they were not in use. So middle school students, who were encouraged to use one-to-one devices more than twice as much as elementary students, were more prone to wandering attention when using them. Even so, elementary and middle school students were infrequently distracted for a minute or more. Such a finding may help alleviate fears that school technologies lead straight to an abyss of digital distraction. It also suggests these schools and teachers are doing something right.

The high school case study data present a different picture from the random observations, with students more distracted and technology a major culprit. High school students' off-task behavior (with or without technology) made up nearly 14% of total classroom activity time, more than three times as much as in middle or elementary school. Off-task behavior involving individual digital technologies (primarily phones and laptops) made up about 11% of classroom activity time, the majority of the total time off task. The level of distraction ramped up from middle to high school and seemed to be fueled by digital technologies. This mirrors research trends suggesting that for adolescents and young adults, online behaviors like texting, social media, and gaming lead to frequent task-switching or distraction while studying.[10] For adolescents, there are simply more ways to be distracted, and so paying attention in class becomes increasingly difficult.

Exploring the Differences

To some extent, the differences between various grade levels are related to social and cognitive developmental factors at work as students mature. Yet additional factors became evident in survey, observation, and focus group data.

A first factor was related to students' access to internet-connected personal devices through which participation in applications like social media, email, and texting were commonplace. The survey and focus group data affirmed that the vast majority of high school students had personal smartphones, and those phones were frequently observed in classroom observations as a source of distraction. This number was lower at the middle school and even smaller at the elementary school, and we almost never observed smartphone use in case study classrooms at these grades. High school students also reported much greater access to and more time spent using social media, email, and texting than middle and elementary school students, and were often seen distracted in class by all of these. We know from existing research that this increasing connectedness begins to heighten distraction for adolescents and young adults.[11] Such distractions are not fully fledged for elementary and middle school students and do not yet pull attention away from work as readily as in high school. Care is called for as educators and parents weigh choices about students' access to devices and social media as they grow older.[12]

School policy and procedures were a second factor and helped to limit digital distraction. The elementary and middle schools banned personal devices in classrooms, and teachers carried out this policy. The high school was far more lenient and less clear about personal technology devices. Some teachers thought there might be a "no phones in the classroom" policy. In reality, each teacher established their own classroom expectations around personal technologies, with many allowing varying degrees of use. It is not surprising, then, that high schoolers had phones out and were distracted by them more than in other grades. The schools' monitoring and surveillance efforts, discussed in depth in chapter 23, also played a role and may help explain differences between middle and high school. Some upper elementary and middle schoolers expressed an exaggerated sense of the schools' ability to monitor their device use. Students voiced the belief that "they can track everything . . . they can see anything we've ever done," and that "they can, like, type you a message, like, 'Stop playing games!' And then they'll . . . give you the assignment you are supposed to be working on." Students assuming the existence of an all-seeing school surveillance system may be less likely to cave in to digital distractions. High schoolers did not share this exaggerated sense of what the school could do. Many knew that while inappropriate content could be monitored, off-task behavior within limits could not.

A third important factor involved teachers' pedagogical practices. Focus group students shared explicitly that getting distracted online was simply easier in some teachers' classrooms than others, and much of this came down to the teachers' pedagogical design and classroom expectations. According to students, when it came to phone use, "some teachers will let us, some teachers are super, super strict about it. Otherwise, some teachers don't even care if you have it out. But usually the teachers who are strict about it, they still will let you use it if it has a purpose for the activity at hand, whereas teachers that are more relaxed about it, those tend to be the kind of classes that it's more abused in."

As we will see in future chapters, some teachers explicitly considered technology expectations for all students and designed instruction to minimize distraction. Several focus group students reported that their attention was higher in these classes because there were fewer opportunities for distraction. Worth special note here is a specific move made by several elementary teachers and some middle school teachers that was not seen in high school. At times, teachers structured group dynamics by encouraging students to work together on assignments so that pairs or small groups used one device. Students were even given different roles (photographer, blogger, web navigator, sketch artist). These setups promoted collaboration and increased students' accountability for attending to the assignment and avoiding digital diversions. Might stronger peer accountability or shared devices for collaborative work also be effective for high schoolers who are feeling the tug of digital distraction?

From Distraction to Addiction?

There is no research consensus about whether compulsive digital technology use can be placed alongside other well-documented physiological addictions.[13] What is clear is that a growing number of people express anxiety about being disconnected from the internet, even for short periods of time. In our surveys, middle school students were relatively unlikely to report that the laptop program made them feel addicted to their devices, but as students grew older, the level of agreement increased.[14] As teachers noted, even within grade levels technology did not affect all students in the same way:

> It totally depends on the kid. For some of them [the technology is] not good for them because the distraction factor goes through the roof. They don't know how to handle it. It takes a lot of . . . you're doing more teaching of how to handle it [rather] than learning content. But for other kids it makes it so much easier and nicer because they're able to communicate more effectively when they're typing or doing pictures or they're able to understand more effectively because you can get different ways of communicating on a laptop, but it totally depends.

Teachers reported a few cases of students for whom the technology was a real stumbling block. A teacher described one case:

> This particular student . . . with an agreement . . . with his parents, he's not even allowed to take his laptop home because it literally consumes him. . . . He's not allowed to have his laptop at lunch anymore either because he was always late for the class after lunch because, for an example, he'd be in the cafeteria during lunch on his laptop so literally engrossed, and I do mean like an addiction kind of thing, so engrossed that he neglects to notice that everyone has now finished eating lunch and left the cafeteria, the food has been put away, and now the study hall people have come into the classroom.

Adding to concern for such cases is the fact that students for whom technology seemed seriously addictive were often also students with behavioral problems or disabilities. Teachers reported that technology was a problem for "the impulsive kids, the ones who can't screen, the ones [with] ADD, the hyperactive kids . . . they can't help but, you know, play with it."

For other struggling students, teachers described laptops and tablets as "just another thing to manage," adding to all the other aspects of school they were already having trouble managing. These students, who already face challenges in the school environment, may be hindered more in a technology-rich environment. In survey data, students with lower reported grade point averages were more likely to report that the technology program made them feel addicted. Similarly, those with lower grades were twice as likely to report that the technology program had bad effects on their relationships, and reported much higher amounts of time playing video games or watching TV or movies, greater time on social media, and less time in extracurricular activities.[15]

The picture that begins to emerge is that the pitfalls of digital distraction are more of a challenge for those struggling academically.

> **Distraction and Addiction**
>
> What percentage of total class time were students off-task for 1 minute or more in case study classrooms?
>
> Elementary: 1%
> Middle: 4%
> High school: 14%
>
> Has the school's technology program made you/your student addicted to technology?
>
> | | |
> |---|---|
> | Middle school | 20% agree |
> | High school | 30% agree |
> | Modern Christian alumni | 37% agree |
> | Parents | 50% agree |
> | Teachers | 65% agree |

Some students find digital activities difficult to leave behind, even when there are significant academic and personal consequences. For these students, individual laptops and independent work, which is common at Modern Christian Schools, may substantially hinder their learning. While these cases may be outliers, it is important to have a strategy for teaching the rare student for whom technology addiction is very serious. At Modern Christian Schools, the students struggling most with this issue have individual plans to help them use their laptops wisely. The question remains, however, of how to help the most vulnerable students with learning devices that may in fact be causing them harm.

Shaping Distracted Selves?

Christian schools have multiple reasons to be concerned about distraction. Multitasking diminishes learning, reducing the amount of information retained and harming performance on exams. Simply in terms of the schools' task as schools, digital distraction is a relevant concern. If digital distraction harms learning, then care for students implies a need to address it in some way. Some normative concerns are particularly relevant to a community devoted to Christian formation. The capacity to focus carefully on texts and ideas, to contemplate and reflect deeply, and to listen well to others is no trivial matter for a faith concerned with hearing the word of God and the voice of the neighbor well. Developing high-distraction habits does not seem a promising recipe for spiritual growth. When distraction often means turning to the consumerist attractions offered via digital devices, the concern only deepens. What digital tools can do for us is yoked with what the digital medium might be doing to us. The possibility that struggling members of the community are disproportionately affected also raises challenges for any Christian community that wishes to live by the principle that "if one member suffers, all suffer together with it" (1 Cor. 12:21-26).

We began this chapter with some encouraging findings. It does not seem to be the case that use of digital devices in class automatically leads to high levels of sustained off-task behavior, especially in the lower grade levels. Again, it must be borne in mind that our data addresses off-task behavior lasting more than a minute, and so does not address the effects of rapid task-switching and momentary distractions, even though those may be significant in forming habits. And the news was not all encouraging. The risk of digital distraction increased significantly as students reached high school. Students spent significantly more time off task, and that time was strongly associated with use of digital devices. But perhaps the most important finding is that practices matter. Both the differences between randomized and longer-term case study observations and the differences that students described between classes in terms of ease of distraction suggest that the situation is amenable to positive influence. The effects of digital devices on attention are not simply a deterministic consequence of their presence. They are affected by the practices that are built around them to guide and set boundaries on their use. Where teachers do not implement clear, intentional technology expectations designed to maximize learning, increased distraction is likely. But it seems to be possible to build practices that limit distraction and turn the focus more consistently to learning.

For Reflection and Response

- What explicit policies and practices exist around digital device use in the classrooms you know? What is the basis for them?
- Why do you think we tend at one and the same time to understand that distraction is a problem, underestimate its effects on ourselves, and continue to multitask with our devices? What does this suggest about the relationship between beliefs and practices?
- What kinds of pedagogical strategies do you think are most likely to help reduce multitasking and distraction?

CHAPTER 30

Teaching Slow Learning

Everybody should have a hiatus from technology, but we know that's artificial, because they're all running around with these [devices] anyway. Their access point is not just the school—if anything, the school is helping them discern how to use the rest of their devices.

Administrator

We sit at the back of another Bible class, one observed during our classroom observations. The focus today is Jesus's Sermon on the Mount. Class begins with some instructions on how to read. The teacher tells students that they must read from a print Bible and may not use a digital Bible on their phone or laptop. They are also to take notes, just for this activity, using pencil and paper in place of their more common reliance on typing. Finally, the teacher tells them that they are to read in solitude and silence, and that to achieve this they are to leave the classroom, with its associations with tasks and testing, and find a quiet place to sit somewhere in the school building. They are to begin reading at Matthew 5 and make notes on what they notice as they read.

In an email after class, this teacher shared how he had been inviting students to connect these concerns to the question of how God speaks to us: "The day before you came we discussed possible reasons why God often speaks in the wilderness, noting too that we have fortified ourselves (culturally) against wilderness in many ways. So, we decided to attempt to create a little wilderness space in our busy day by seeking as much solitude and silence in the school as possible to allow the Word of God to come to us as well."

In an interview during our case study research, this same teacher shared with us some of his reflections on how technology was shaping the learning environment, and how his thinking about that fed into his lesson planning. In today's culture, he reflected, "there are all kinds of conveniences that are allowing us to go faster, and one of those is technology.

We can communicate to more people, and I personally noticed in my own life, sometimes I need to back off from that for health. Even the concept of a Sabbath is pushed to the fringes." He suggested that what might be seen as one of the central benefits of technology (certainly one mentioned by students in our conversations with them) could also be a drawback. "Technology does a lot of things, really great things. One of the things that's maybe a negative is that it allows us to go faster, and to do more. I've kind of noticed with my students, [so] I want to back off on that avenue a little bit. I don't always want to go faster, I don't want to always get through more of the Bible, sometimes I want to slow down and engage one part of the Bible really well, and to be slow, and to relieve some of the pressure of school." The pressures arising from new technologies, he suggested, may augment the existing pressures of school, strengthening a focus on getting more done, finishing more tasks. This results in an emphasis on velocity and productivity over depth.

And so, on this particular day, students sit silently, dispersed around the hallways. It is not unusual to see students learning in the hallways at Modern Christian Schools, for one of the intentional effects of adopting laptops has been to free students to some degree from their desks, allowing them to work on projects in any location where there is Wi-Fi. Today, though, the Bibles and notebooks are old technologies, paper only.

After a reasonable time, the teacher calls the students back into the classroom and tells them, "Raise your hand if you didn't get to chapter 7." He then asks them to move into groups based on which chapters they finished reading. It becomes visible that almost 60% of the students did not get to the end of chapter 7. At this point, the teacher pauses and asks, "Wait, you didn't get to 7?" and looks at them in silence for a full ten seconds. The students all nod. (A ten-second silence is an eternity after a teacher has asked a question in a North American classroom; for most teachers a pause of two or three seconds requires training.)[1] It is not too hard to surmise what students may be expecting him to say next. They have failed to complete the assignment.

Finally, the teacher speaks again. "Okay, I'm proud of you because you are engaging with these chapters." In saying this, he frames the learning sequence in terms of the concerns he had voiced earlier, concerns that valued slowness, wilderness, listening. He tells students that he had hoped they would read through all the chapters, but he wanted to affirm that "learning to slow down and engage the text is one of the skills I want you to be developing."

The point here is not a general vote for or against using technology; this is one learning sequence amid others in which laptops were used. What is striking is the careful intentionality of the teacher's practices in relation to goals for the students' spiritual formation. In our surveys, a large majority of students told us that using laptops for learning had helped them to understand difficult material and to develop ideas that went beyond what was provided in assigned materials. Yet as we saw from another angle in chapter 17, a similar majority affirmed that working with laptops had encouraged them to look for quick and easy answers to problems. Over half felt technology had helped them find answers without really understanding them, and a third felt it had helped them skim over material even when they knew they should be reading carefully. Teachers responded similarly to the same questions (see table 30.1). Print and digital media frame the act of reading in different ways and come associated with different practices.[2]

Table 30.1. Student academic practices (percentage agreement)

The use of digital technology at our school has:	Encouraged me/ students to skim over material	Led me/ students to look for quick and easy answers	Allowed me/ students to find answers without understanding	Helped me/ students understand difficult ideas in my/their class	Helped me/students develop ideas that went beyond what was presented in class or in assigned materials
Student % (n = 533)	35%	71%	57%	72%	83%
Teacher % (n = 63)	41%	n/a	67%	83%	88%

Speed, Learning, and Formation

Many digital media are structured to assist skim reading and swift location of data. Religious reading practices, in contrast, focus on depth of understanding and spiritual formation and are therefore associated with practices of reading slowly, repeatedly, communally, reverentially.[3] Such reading is also associated with some basic Christian virtues, including patience, humility, and charity. These entail avoiding hasty judgments. The efficiency of scanning and searching for information and moving on as soon as we have located what we need can be valuable when we need to maximize the information at our fingertips. The strategies associated with such reading can, however, nurture superficiality and premature conclusions. They are also less well suited to the pursuit of personal transformation and deep engagement that belong to spiritually nourishing reading.[4] The modes of engagement that students associate with digital reading environments may work together with the school focus on productivity and task completion to reinforce the temptation to skim even when that would not be the optimal strategy. If the default practices toward which our institutions and devices nudge us are to be challenged, we need explicit and intentional framing of learning practices and their purposes across the curriculum. In practical terms, this means framing tasks not just in terms of "read this," or even "read this carefully," but "read this in this particular manner, because of this particular way in which you might grow as a result."[5]

Students told us that this kind of framing made a difference. In a focus group conversation, a student commented that "we'll ask [our teachers], 'Can we skim it and just look for the answers?' And they're like, 'No, I actually want you to read it.' . . . One of my teachers did that, and I diligently read it and took notes . . . because I just do that. And I know a lot of people did because he emphasized that it's important to read it, whereas most teachers I get, I kind of skim it and look for the answers."

Another student chimed in, explaining that in other classes "they just say, 'Here's your reading assignment, fill out the worksheet,' and it is easy to just do Apple-F and find where the answers are to each of the questions." Interestingly, the first student's aside that "I just do that," with its suggestion that careful reading just comes from being a good student, is immediately followed by the confession that their reading practices in fact vary depending on which teacher set the assignment. The specific invitation to a particular kind of engagement made a difference. The temptation to abridge the act of reading using search capabilities was a recurring theme. Some students even voiced concern for the effects on their own formation of the digital practices to which they became accustomed when pursuing efficiency. "I think using technology like Command-F can make us more lazy," one reflected.

Shaping Practices

The teacher in the Bible class described at the start of this chapter took matters a few steps further than just emphasizing that students really did have to read the text. In fact, he wanted to erode the idea of reading the Sermon on the Mount as an efficiently completed task. He placed the act of reading in the context of Christian narrative, framing it in terms of wilderness and listening for/to God. He also supported this story with attention to several other key aspects of curriculum design. He was careful to specify not only what to read but how to read. He specified the behaviors that he was looking for and the physical media that might support them (such as taking notes with a pencil and paper). He used physical space intentionally to underline the idea of quiet and solitude and, by moving away from classroom desks, to deemphasize associations with school task completion. He attended closely to the flow of time, using not only time allocated to silent reading but also a deliberate ten-second pause to help communicate what he wanted to emphasize. He approached this learning sequence not just with a message containing ideas about reading and technology but with a considered set of practices around reading and technology.[6] He led students into both the practices and the story that undergirded those practices.[7] It was a clear example of an effort not just to "prepare minds" but also to "nurture lives."

> **Worldview and Practices**
>
> Whereas a focus on worldview often foregrounds questions of what is true and how we know it, a focus on practices more directly foregrounds questions such as these:
>
> • What patterns shape our behaviors?
> • How are we using and moving through time?
> • How are we interacting in physical space?
> • What projects and goals do we share with others?
> • How do we name our tasks and choices?
> • What implicit stories shape what we do?
> • How is all of this shaping who we become?

If we step back and look at his teaching choices in this broader frame, it quickly becomes evident that intentional choices with an eye to student formation need not necessarily involve stepping away from digital technology. An art teacher described having students use their smartphones to step back from their paintings every so many minutes to take a picture, with the goal of encouraging them to review the stages the painting went through and reflect on the compositional choices they were making. Here, too, intentional practices were being pursued, this time retaining use of a digital device. A technology commonly associated with speeding us up and making us less attentive to our surroundings was instead used to slow students down and promote careful reflection and review.

In teacher choices like the ones described above, we see an approach to Christian discernment that is not just focused on avoiding potential harms or critiquing messages. The focus is on building intentional practices around new technologies with formation in mind, so that the ways in which students grow through their learning are not determined by the default capacities of the technological medium. Technology is in these classrooms no longer just a tool for accessing or controlling information, but a medium that itself requires critical awareness and a set of intentional practices to shape its use.

For Reflection and Response

- How are changes in technology affecting the way time flows in the classrooms you know? Are the effects helpful?
- Why might slow, careful reading be an important Christian practice? How do classroom and homework practices encourage or discourage such reading?
- Does your use of technology help focus your attention or disperse it? What could change the pattern?

CHAPTER 31

Can Spiritual Disciplines Help with Technology?

> As parents choose options for their children's preferences, offer an option for the laptops to be shut down on Sundays, as an option for supporting the Sabbath. School partnering with church.
>
> *Minutes from a planning meeting*

In the last chapter we looked at how individual teachers focused on classroom practices designed to nudge student formation in a positive direction, drawing on Christian intuitions about what growth might look like as well as a sense of the risks of the digital medium. These teachers worked to design learning that pushed back against the potential for a distracted, fragmented, superficial experience of the world. Yet they still leave us with a question that arose in our examination of student distraction. Is it enough for individual teachers to make changes to their pedagogy? What happens with student formation if the patterns are not consistent? In this chapter we approach the matter of student formation from a slightly different angle, looking at how practices related to Christian spiritual disciplines are informing the collective life of Modern Christian Schools.[1] Practices related to prayer, worship, sabbath, and fasting were visible in school documents and focus group conversations and were sometimes related to the schools' efforts to respond to digital technology as a whole community.

Prayer and Worship

One regular and visible cluster of Christian practices at Modern Christian Schools revolved around communal worship. This included communal chapel several times a week, classroom devotions, and occasional impromptu prayer in class. In our surveys 60% of students reported engaging in devotions one to three times a week. As we saw earlier (chapter 22), when students talked about chapel in relation to technology, they mentioned themes associated with maintaining safe and ethical boundaries. It may be that placing such reminders about appropriate technology use in the context of worship lends them added gravity, helping to give context to the regular talk of using technology in a way that "honors God." There was also some evidence of teachers explicitly connecting classroom devotions to broader teaching points about technology and formation, as when a teacher commented in a survey response that "through my actions, devotions and prayer in the classroom, I reinforce that all of creation belongs to God and that we must love and serve Him and others."

Our data do not allow us to measure how much chapel and devotions affect ethical behavior with technology or influence students' general digital practices. What they do tell us is that devotions offer an interval during the school day that limits engagement with devices. As one teacher put it,

As a teacher, there are times where . . . this laptop is what we're doing, and this is where you should be, and there are times where I say I don't want to see . . . laptops out. . . . [I want] to try and move them toward . . . someday you'll be making that choice without a teacher giving you permission to make that choice. It still annoys me, even in the teachers, when we've got people with their computers up. When [Name] is going to do devotions, I close my laptop, not because I need to have it closed, but because I want him to know the laptop is not open when you have devotions.

This inclination to avoid laptop use during devotions was borne out by our observational data. As we tracked device use across some 80 hours of classroom time, we found that devotions were one of the activities in which device use was least likely. When prayer or devotions were happening, digital devices were used only 10% of the time, less than any other tracked activity except for activities involving physical movement. This pattern seemed likely to be related to another practice that we observed in some classrooms, whereby all laptop screens were immediately lowered if a visitor walked into the classroom. This simple practice was designed to foster a focus on people above devices and was connected to beliefs about hospitality and respectful listening.[2] The apparent sense that devotions were a time when screens should be put away appeared to draw on similar intuitions. Devotions were felt to be a time for setting the digital world aside and engaging in focused, respectful listening.[3]

The overall result was that those times in the school day that were visibly devoted to prayer, worship, or overt sharing and reflection on matters of faith were relatively free of direct engagement with digital technology. This was part of a larger pattern, for we saw similar sensibilities reflected in references to sabbath and fasting.

Sabbath and Fasting

Theologically, both sabbath and fasting have to do with turning aside for a time from our efforts to secure our own flourishing in order to celebrate the unearned gifts of creation and acknowledge our dependence on God.[4] The things set aside may be good in themselves, but the different yet related practices of sabbath and fasting pause to put them in their place so that they can be enjoyed in proper measure and with freedom from their potential tyranny. It is not hard to see the potential for these practices to be part of a Christian school's engagement with technology, especially given the awareness that digital technology can be highly absorbing, even addictive. And indeed, we find the ideas of sabbath and fasting recurring in Modern Christian Schools' conversations about technology.

The idea of a sabbath rest from technology began to appear in the early days of the one-to-one laptop program. Meeting minutes periodically recorded the suggestion that parents be offered the option for laptops to be shut down on Sundays, or that a no-email policy could be set for Sundays. Although such ideas recurred in recorded discussions, we did not find any evidence of them ever being put into practice at a whole-school level. Teachers spoke of having to negotiate their own individual boundaries around abstention from electronic communication, and students were well aware of differences in sensibility and practice among teachers. However, awareness that digital technologies could further magnify an existing Midwestern Protestant work ethic (a "culture of do, do, do, do, do," as one administrator described it) did lead to smaller-scale efforts to create technology-free pauses in the midst of school life. These represented intentional efforts to move toward a culture in which (to quote the same administrator) "we are not just what we produce" but can be "whole people." Alongside a strong affirmation of the positive potential of technology, there was a recurring sense that wholeness nevertheless required some measure of abstention, and that achieving this might involve structuring the time of the whole community rather than relying on individual initiative.

By the time of our study, once a week in the high school there was a scheduled device-free hour ("PowerDown") in which students gathered in mixed-age groups. The time was used for reading or for interaction and fun activities intended to build community across grade levels. The students with whom we spoke expressed appreciation for this innovation in the school schedule, while also reporting that some of their peers were not so keen. A student reflected,

> I think . . . it is kind of like a stress reliever. You don't need to think about your classes. You don't need to be connected. You don't find a ride after school or whatever. It is just a nice quiet time whether you read or not. It's just nice to not have anything to do. You know, my go-to is to go to my phone. If I have an extra five minutes in class, that's just what I will do, but it's just nice to be able to just read . . . to have that set-apart time, like, once a week I think is really nice.

Students were less sure that the mixed-age, community-building interaction was working well; they found it an attractive idea but reported that the reality was that "when we get together we just read." Some adults in our focus groups found this focus on reading "an actual book" a strong argument in favor of PowerDown.

Teachers identified another concern about how PowerDown was working out in practice. Several focus group members echoed the concern reflected in one teacher's comment that "I was just walking through PowerDown today because I had to have a picture taken with my students and I was struck by how many teachers were on their laptops during PowerDown." Despite the shared emphasis on holding students accountable, the periodic raising of sabbath as a topic in planning discussions, and regular articulations by focus group teachers of the importance of modeling, it seemed that there remained a powerful temptation for teachers to use the PowerDown time to focus on their own devices and get things done. Perhaps the "culture of do, do, do, do, do" is not so easy to undermine and genuinely communal practices are hard to build. "Kids are reading, teachers are on laptops," another teacher lamented. "That's really sad," a third replied.

While PowerDown was an orchestrated technology fast, a variety of classroom routines for separating students from their devices evolved more organically. These included activities such as providing a designated location for students to opt to surrender their phone during class or offering extra credit for those students who regularly did so. A handful of teachers appear to have piloted these activities, but student focus groups and observations made it clear that the idea had spread widely enough that such practices were experienced by or common knowledge to all high schoolers. We heard an explicit connection made between these practices and the idea of fasting. One teacher conducted a "media fast" with students every semester, allowing them to choose whether to fast from specific media or all digital media.[5] Students journaled as they fasted. The teacher's aim was to make students' relationship to their devices more explicit and intentional. "Kids always say, 'Yeah, the second day is incredibly hard,' and yet the third day they kind of wish they'd keep going, but they don't have the will power. But still, they see so much value in it and they have rich talks with their parents or even with their rides to school instead of having the radio on, and that kind of stuff. . . . I try to encourage them to see that the awkward moments come before rich experiences and they're getting that."

Students with whom we discussed this activity expressed appreciation for the exercise. "I also like that because after the whole media fast you kind of see how much you depend on phones or how much you depend on something. After I did that, on the last day that I didn't use any media, I actually finished my homework four hours before I usually do. So, I noticed a really big change, like, oh, well I actually use [my] phone a lot, and . . . it distracts me and leads to other distractions." Students similarly appreciated the "cell phone challenge" implemented in some classes, whereby they were challenged to consistently place their phones in a basket for the duration of class. It offered them what one described as "a good way to pay attention during class without getting distracted," and freed them from having the entire burden placed on their own self-control.

While students appreciated the boost, teachers were aiming for them to learn self-control over time. This could involve, for instance, offering students extra credit for consistency, or telling them that there would be an extra credit reward for setting their phones aside in class this semester, but that it would be up to them to continue the practice without reward the following semester. As with the media fast, students were asked to record their reflections in a journal as they engaged in the practice. A high school senior reflected in a focus group that "our general response to it was that, you know what, this is really good, and we benefit from putting our technology away for a while." Teachers spoke of receiving thank-you messages from students who had graduated from the school focusing on the benefits of some training in abstention. Survey results echo these perceptions:

65% of students reported that the schools' use of technology made them learn how to balance their technology use in healthy ways, with only 12% disagreeing. At the same time, it seemed that such practices were often the initiative of individual teachers. Students reported that norms around having their devices available varied widely between different teachers' classrooms. Overall, only 44% of students and 52% of teachers reported efforts in their classes to limit technology use. The learning about abstention described by students may have been emerging mainly from a subset of the schools' classrooms.

A Mixed Picture

The picture with regard to spiritual-discipline-related practices and selective abstention from technology is mixed. On the one hand, the devotional life of the school created zones in the school week in which devices were set aside. These zones may help foster an association between intentional technology choices and respectful listening. The positive value that Christians place on ideas such as sabbath, fasting, and self-denial, even in relation to things that may be good in themselves, offered a cultural resource for living with new technologies. The idea of setting things aside and engaging in self-examination as part of Christian practice serves as a ready-made frame for building practices of temporary disengagement from devices. Naming these practices with the language of sabbath and fasting may lend them added spiritual weight. Students seemed on the whole appreciative of the learning experience that these practices provided, and the majority believed that they were being helped to set healthy boundaries and recognize unhealthy dependencies.

Spiritual disciplines associated with abstention, listening, and reflection also provided a framework for teachers' decision-making processes. A story from one teacher's class that illustrates this is worth recounting in full:

> I think part of it too is just, besides discernment, how to use it but also when to use it and when not to, and I've been working with my students this year on that. Yesterday I took a group of sophomores to the cemetery; we walked there. It was a poetry assignment, and ... I wanted them to imagine the lives behind the tombstones and to look for details that would trigger their imagination, and they could write a monologue from

the grave. The day before they asked, because they always put their cell phones in a box when they get to my room, they said, "Well, can we take cell phones?" Because I'd said I'd like you to take notes, and, you know, just note anything—maybe it's the shape of the tombstone and certainly the words and the letters. And then they said, "Well, could we just take our cell phones and take pictures?" And the day before I said, "Yeah, sure, I guess I'll let you do that this time," because they were asking and not assuming. But then the day of I said, "No, let's leave those. Part of this is contemplation, standing by yourself in front of a tombstone and imagining and who knows how the Spirit might speak to you?" And I said, "That cell phone is just going to do what it does to you everywhere else." They were fine with that. . . . And so, we walked and talked without cell phones getting in the way, and then once they were there I at least could know that they're not off wandering checking emails, they're thoroughly present and recording details. And I just think we have to both model that and give them opportunities to see that technology is not appropriate here. You have to know when that's so. And they're getting better at it, but we have a ways to go.

Teachers were engaged in an ongoing process of reflection about when technology use was helpful for the immediate learning task and for students' longer-term formation.

On the other hand, the ideas of sabbath and fasting were often being used in a reduced sense, and participation in them by teachers was not consistent. The benefits tended to be described by students in terms of stress relief and increased efficiency and control over life, rather than in terms of gratitude, adoration, or dependence on God. In this sense, sabbath and fasting seemed to be functioning at times as a somewhat secularized and individualized language for abstaining from technology. Perhaps this weakened sacred tethering was part of why it seemed to be a challenge to implement such practices consistently as a whole community, with teachers sometimes on laptops as students powered down or as devotions were led, and "sabbath" left to individual initiative. As we have seen, the practices discussed in this chapter were part of a wider range of Christian practices that had been named as whole-school emphases and displayed throughout the schools, but their permeation through the schools' collective daily practices was still partial. There were enough glimpses to make us wonder what the potential might be if they came to be embraced in a more consistent, community-wide, and theologically grounded way as a context for student formation amid digital learning.

For Reflection and Response

- Should technology use be restricted when engaging in prayer or worship? Why or why not?
- What can students learn from engaging in spiritual disciplines such as fasting and sabbath?
- Do the schools you know focus on how to help students engage in disciplines around digital technology that might help their spiritual growth?

CHAPTER 32

Who Takes Responsibility for Distraction?

It's kind of like . . . okay, they can monitor everything we're doing, and this is so dorky, but honestly, I just imagine that they can monitor it, but God monitors my life too. He sees everything that I'm doing online anyways. . . . That's so weird, but you know what I mean? I don't want them to see it and I definitely don't want God to see it, so . . . I just don't do it. It helps to have that human person stopping . . . not that I'd do anything bad . . . but . . .

Student

It's the middle of a science class and the teacher is reviewing the chapter material before the test. Most students busily take notes on their laptops and check handwritten lab notes. One plays a video game. The student next to him peeks over periodically, but generally remains engaged with the class. Whenever the teacher moves to a place in the classroom where his game might be visible, the game player deftly switches his screen to a page of notes until the coast is clear. He intentionally looks up to connect with the teacher and then is back to his game. Seen from the front, his behavior mimics that of his classmates. From the rear, it is clear that his attention is not on the class. In an interview after class, this student reflects that sometimes he wishes the teacher would say something to get him back on track because it's too difficult to resist distraction.

Community implies responsibility for each other's well-being. In a Christian community, it is the responsibility of everyone to support each member's flourishing. "All the members of the body, though many, are one body" (1 Cor. 12:12 ESV). What does that mutual responsibility look like in a classroom? Whose responsibility is it to manage the temptations associated with digital devices?

Teachers at Modern Christian Schools were well aware of both the potential distractions and the effect that students had on each other.

A teacher new to the school noted that sometimes "some really bad things . . . happen, where people are throwing in silly, stupid, or offensive pictures into their Google documents when they're supposed to be collaborating together." A high school teacher noted that when students are "watching ESPN instead of paying attention," they keep themselves from engaging and also distract others around them. Students, too, were well aware of the issue. As one put it, "I think, just in class, there's always the temptation to go on what you're not supposed to. . . . We have filters on our laptops . . . but it's just easy to toggle back and forth." Even individual distracted behavior is noticed by others and has effects on others. How, then, should the responsibility for handling distraction be distributed?

Teacher Responsibility

An obvious first answer is that responsibility lies with the teacher. Teachers sought to manage distraction through various kinds of surveillance, making students aware that their digital work was not private or hidden. Students were aware of digital surveillance strategies; as we saw in chapter 29, younger students had an exaggerated view of teachers' ability to see everything they did on their devices. "Isn't there something they can do," a middle school student mused, "where if you're playing games during class . . . they are looking on your computer screen? I don't know how." "They can track everything, anything we do," another declared. While this is not actually true, it seems the use of filtering and monitoring software has created a perception, at least among younger students, that poor in-the-moment choices will be caught by the teacher. A sense that Big Brother is watching may promote careful digital behavior when watched, though we may wonder how it contributes to students' Christian formation and sense of personal responsibility, and how well it carries over to non-monitored contexts.

Another form of teacher monitoring was physical presence and observation. Teachers set up their classrooms in various ways to allow for quick scanning of all open screens in order to check student activity. For instance, we saw some teachers arrange desks around the outside perimeter of the class with students' backs and laptop screens facing the teacher in the center. A student reported that another teacher seated problem students in the center and trustworthy students on the periphery in order to increase ac-

countability for digital behavior. Teachers also established classroom procedures (e.g., "hands up, screens forward") that enabled them to quickly
look at students' screens.

These surveillance strategies generated a sense of accountability that
was reflected in students' comments.[1] Students reflected on times when
they evaded monitoring with phrases like "I guess we just feel guilty" or "I
know I shouldn't be doing it." Some students expressed appreciation for
the monitoring, noting how it aided their learning: "For me, some classes
do a really good job of learning on [devices], but for me it's tempting. . . .
[A particular teacher] does a really nice job of making sure you're not on
them, but other teachers just sit there, and you have freedom just to stay
on your computer and do whatever you want. . . . It's hard sometimes."
Other students argued that the matter should be left to individual student
responsibility. As one high school student explained, if students want to
pursue distractions, "I think it's best just to let them; you can be on your
phone if you want but you're not going to learn as much. . . . I don't go on
my phone, just because I want to pay attention. So, if you don't want to
pay attention, then you can go on your phone as long as you want." Several
other student comments followed this emphasis on autonomous choices
and natural consequences.

In spite of teachers' surveillance efforts, many students found ways
around physical monitoring. Students in the high and middle schools
were adept at swiping to the correct window or shrinking tabs whenever
a teacher or researcher approached their seat. "You can click off it so
fast no one ever knows," a student noted. Another explained, "You don't
want to do more work at that time and you can honestly just open a new
tab and start something, and the teachers will probably never know that
you're done, so you can just spend 20 minutes just being on Pinterest
or something."

Students, then, ranged across various attitudes. We heard talk of getting away with things, of giving way to temptation, of feeling guilty, and of
wishing for more school or classroom intervention. We also heard radically
individualistic views of responsibility tied to a strong sense of personal
autonomy. Some felt that those who were failing should be left to take the
consequences of their choices to disengage from learning, or simply that
individuals should have the right to choose freely whether to work or to
focus on something more compelling.

Student Responsibility

Another possible answer, then, to the question of responsibility in the face of digital distraction is that students are ultimately responsible. Teachers, especially in the high school, expressed a hope that students would grow into accepting responsibility for using digital technologies appropriately. One commented, "With [seniors] I was a little more laissez-faire because I felt like at some point they need to learn how to concentrate and I'd rather have them fail here than fail in college when they're sitting playing Bubble Shooter in the middle of the lecture and then they fail in college. . . . How do we gradually release them a little bit so they have more autonomy and have the ability to fail, because we know they will, you know? So that's been a constant struggle for us."

Teachers sometimes recognized their own role in students' gradual progress toward greater responsibility through intentionally designed lessons, units, or classroom practices. Some teachers encouraged their students to place their cell phones in a box as they entered the classroom, some required giving up phones, and some took a gradated approach over time. Selective removal allowed for discussion of when students might need to keep their phones. A teacher explained that "they will, on occasion, ask me if they can keep their phone today because they're expecting a call and they want me to know that mom's going to call with something and they need to answer, and that's fine. There have been a few times where I've said to them, 'I'm going to get a call at some time today and I do have to answer this one' and I just think that's teaching them. . . . I'm going to keep this thing under control, and if they can do that, I think it's huge."

Some focused explicitly on ways to encourage students to examine how their attention was drawn to their devices. A teacher explained, "When I'm grading your tests, do you want me with my phone out and checking my Instagram every five minutes? You know, that's not how I want you to work in my class. . . . So, I tell them that I put my phone away so it's not a distraction. That's what I want you to do when you're in class, working on your homework. I think that when I give them a personal example, it makes it more real to them, like, 'Hey, this is a problem for my teacher too. It's not a bad thing that this is a problem; I just have to learn some strategies for that.'"

Students reported other teachers' practices. For instance, one teacher allowed phones to be out, but if students used them, the teacher deducted points without speaking to the student.[2] A student summarized this teacher's message as "I'm not going to take it away. You're grown up so you're going to have to learn to do it yourself, but there will be consequences with it."

Students were aware of teachers' efforts to get them to take responsibility for distraction. Some students shared that they placed their phones in their backpacks during class so that they would not feel or hear the buzz and be tempted to check messages. Others reflected explicitly on the need to learn responsible use of devices: "With good also comes bad. You can send people answers, and you can send them through email, and you can Facebook them. . . . But like every bad or good thing, there's always consequences. So, if you look at your consequences before you do what you're going to do, then I think that brings more responsibility—and more credibility to your work than someone else's work." Another student commented, "I think we learn the ability to decide for ourselves when it's okay for us personally to have technology. There are classes [that] . . . move too slowly and I can take a break and check my phone, but there are classes that, if my teacher's discussing something and it's important and it's interactive and I'm really . . . trying to grasp a concept, then I'm not going to check my phone."

Other students echoed this interpretation of responsibility as deciding when to engage and when not to engage. Their comments suggested that if they were bored or tired of working, it was fine to "take a break" and turn to other digital media. Some clearly felt that this was not detrimental to their work: "Yeah, I think it does disturb work flow, but I think we've kind of adapted to that too and [are] using it efficiently at the same time. Because I'll have my phone next to me, and if I get a notification, I'll check it, or a text, I'll text back, but it doesn't really interrupt my way of thinking through an assignment or project necessarily. It just distracts me for a little bit of the time."

This statement recalls a pattern noted in chapter 29: research suggests that students tend to underestimate the effect of multitasking on their own performance.[3] Other students struggled and were aware of the fact. During the case study observation described in the opening paragraph of this chapter, we observed one student who showed great facility with switching between video games, online videos, shopping sites, and his class notes as his teacher moved around the room. This student struggled to keep up with assignments and relied on group partners for help in completing work. His expressed wish for intervention in the later interview highlighted the need to balance general approaches to teacher and student responsibility with adjustments for particular students. Our survey data in chapter 29 showed a correlation between GPA and reports of attention difficulties with technology. How might a school support those students who are expected to control themselves and cannot?

Clearly there are some complexities to the dance of student and teacher responsibility with regard to appropriate device use. These have to do not just with effectiveness (Does this strategy make students comply?) but also with meaning (How is this strategy affecting students' understanding of responsibility?). Does responsibility mean working to regulate one's behavior to meet expectations or having the right to make choices, even bad ones, and accept the consequences? How do individual choices affect others, and is this effect part of how responsibility is understood? Are students really making free choices, or do at least some students need support to be able to choose well? How should this vary by grade level, and who decides? Students and teachers in our study were still wrestling with these questions. As one student put it, "I think it's the kids' responsibility to not get distracted, but it's also the teacher's responsibility to not sit back and slack off. If that makes sense."

Peer Responsibility

If we focus on community, however, it becomes insufficient to think only in terms of the individual choices of teachers and students. The markedly individualistic bent of many student comments was echoed in what we observed. Although teachers emphasized living in community and working together in small or large groups, classroom observations rarely revealed instances of students taking responsibility for one another with regard to distraction. We observed only two instances in which a student told a peer they should not be on a game or website and called them back to the task at hand.

In focus groups, students expressed responsibility toward their peers mainly in terms of their own sensitivity to what others thought.[4] This meant, for instance, that implicit peer pressure might inhibit individual distraction when working in a group. "When there's group situations," one student explained, "you don't want to be on your phone while other people are working." This was not balanced by accounts of intervening if others were off task. In fact, some students seemed to combine a sense of needing to engage out of respect for other group members with a belief that others' right to disengage should also be respected: "[When] you're collaborating and then you are on your phone or playing games on your computer . . .

that's just blatant lack of respect for not only the teacher but also for the group. But I think I don't see a problem with it; it's the same kind of thing. If you don't want to pay attention, you have that option."

That such comments fluctuated rapidly between polar positions underscored the challenge of squaring school values of communal support, a cultural narrative of individual autonomy, and sensitivity to the peer group's values.[5] We heard from students that others should be respected, that not engaging is disrespectful, that not engaging is a right, that some should be left to fail, and sometimes several of these together. We noted in chapter 24 Christian Smith's concern that faith formation is distorted by a secular culture in which each of us senses our self as "an *individual, autonomous, rational, self-seeking, cost-benefit-calculating consumer.*"[6] When the message of student responsibility and self-control is filtered through this individualistic lens, the idea of a mutually supportive community of compassion and care seems to recede from view.

Responsibility and Community

In this chapter we have been tracing two themes that connect in complex ways. On the one hand, we see an emphasis at Modern Christian Schools on practices that help students develop individual self-control with regard to the temptations that come with digital device use. On the other hand, we see an effort to build Christian community and focus on how we treat others and live together. These two themes are not necessarily opposites. Learning to control one's own temptations and distractions is part of learning to live well with others. Indeed, we have noted awareness of the problem of some students' choices distracting others, of the need to respect others, and of the need for teachers and students to tackle digital distraction together. Such awareness is certainly a critical step toward responsibility. We found little evidence, however, that students saw themselves as having responsibility with regard to the distractions of others. More often we heard the view that if others wanted to go off task, their autonomy should be respected, and they should accept the consequence of learning less. In this sense, students did not appear to view themselves as their brother's or sister's keeper in the realm of digital practices (cf. Gen. 4:9). This view, with its implied image of freely choosing individuals, reduces the community resources available to those who are struggling to make the choices they at some level want to make, who "have the desire to do what is right, but not the ability to carry it out" (Rom. 7:18 ESV). Peer support seemed to be an underexplored avenue at least for this aspect of creating a digital learning community in which all can flourish. In the next part of the book we continue across this bridge from formational practices to community, turning from questions of how individual students are being formed to questions about how technology might be connected to community.

For Reflection and Response

* How do you understand the relationship between Christian faith, individual responsibility, and interdependent community?
* What school and classroom practices reinforce individualism?
* What kinds of pedagogical approaches might help students think of helping the growth of other students as part of their own contribution to a learning community?

Part 5 Summary

In this part of the book we brought questions of formation to the fore. Are there ways in which digital technology as a medium and the practices associated with it are contributing to students' formation? Granting that digital technology is a tool that can help us achieve certain ends more effectively, is it also affecting who our students become? What might Christian practices contribute to learning to live well with digital devices?

- In addition to the emphases already explored on Christian mission, Christian moral boundaries, and Christian beliefs or worldview, the faith identity of Modern Christian Schools was expressed through an explicit set of shared Christian practices. These functioned as another layer of accountability for teachers and students, one that focused more on how technology was used than on what was encountered through it.
- One cluster of practices related to the mission emphasis on forming students to be those who bring change to the world. Digital technology was seen as increasing access to the world beyond the walls of the school and was also associated with enhancing opportunities for service, witness, and dialogue in the wider world. These practices were rarely entirely dependent on new technologies, yet community members believed that technology could extend student research, allow for individualized projects oriented to constructive change, and offer access to outside agencies and individuals.
- A closer look at practices associated with reaching out into the world suggested that the most successful examples were not very representative of average school experience. Attempts to increase digital access to the wider world were accompanied by lack of response to many students' queries, awareness of limitations to digital communication, and time pressures. Particular teachers and curriculum areas offered successful examples, and these were appreciated by students. Yet such

practices appeared less often in classroom practices than their prominence in the schools' talk might suggest. Where they did appear, there
was a sense of contrast with business as usual, rather than a wholesale
transformation of learning.

- Another area of concern relating to student formation was digital
distraction. We did not find digital devices automatically leading
to high levels of sustained off-task behavior, especially in the lower
grade levels, yet digital distraction increased across grade levels. High
school students spent significantly more time off task, and that time
was strongly associated with use of digital devices. The harms that result from digital distraction and addictive behaviors were particularly
strong for some individual students and were more of a problem for
academically struggling students. The effects of digital devices on attention were, however, influenced by teacher practices that set boundaries on technology use. Where teachers did not implement clear,
intentional technology expectations designed to maximize learning,
increased distraction was likely.

- Students reported finding that the use of technology in school extended learning and supported understanding difficult content and
at the same time increased the temptation to skim and look for easy answers. Some teachers intentionally countered the bias toward quickly
skimming for information by building classroom practices around the
idea of slow reading and listening for God's voice. There was evidence
in such cases of clear teacher expectations, and of these expectations
affecting how students engaged with texts.

- We also saw schoolwide practices that drew from spiritual disciplines
and served to set boundaries to technology use. Prayer and worship
times were relatively free of digital device use, and the school had periodically discussed the idea of a sabbath from technology. Time was
set aside in the curriculum for reading together without screens, and
some teachers led students through media fasts. Students expressed
appreciation for being helped to put technology aside for a while. At
the same time, these practices were not always followed through consistently across the community, and they tended to be interpreted in
somewhat secularized ways.

- Noting challenges with distraction and uses of technology that detract
from student formation leads to questions about who should be responsible for keeping students responsible. The answer to this question was ambiguous within the school community. Teacher monitoring

played a role, and some teachers attempted to offer varying degrees of oversight to encourage students to take responsibility. Students tended to interpret responsibility individualistically and in terms of autonomous choice, while also reporting that some additional school or classroom oversight might be helpful. Students offered a picture in which those who get distracted should be left to accept the natural consequences and showed little evidence of prioritizing peer support. This raises questions about the nature of Christian community.

PART 6

COMMUNITY

Questions about Faith, Education, and Technology

- How is the mission understood and does technology serve it?
- Is technology helping teachers to serve student learning?
- How can we make discerning technology choices?
- How does technology relate to student formation?
> **How is technology affecting the fabric of Christian community?**

We have considered how technology, education, and faith connect at Modern Christian Schools through the lenses of mission, pedagogy, discernment, and Christian formation. An important context for all of these is the practice of Christian community. This particular Christian practice served as a focal point at Modern Christian Schools for intentional approaches to learning as well as for anxieties about the risks of digital technology. The theme of community informed the schools' engagement with digital technology through interventions (Might an explicit focus on life together help us live well with technology?), explorations (Could digital devices offer new ways of learning and interacting that might strengthen community engagement?), and cautions (Are digital devices eroding our relationships?).

This section begins (chapter 33) with a look at the main connections made by Modern Christian Schools members between technology and relationships: interaction in school, communication with the wider school community, and ways of relating to others outside the community. The third of these has already been explored in part 5, so we focus in more detail here on the first two, beginning in the classroom. What happens to classroom relationship patterns when teachers are no longer the gatekeepers for the knowledge that students can access (chapter 34)? How does collaboration become part of student learning as they work together with digital devices (chapter 35)?

We then expand the focus to include the wider school community. What role is envisioned for parents in the schools' efforts to develop Christian discernment with technology, and how do parents view the schools' efforts to communicate their vision (chapter 36)? As communication with parents shifts from paper to emails and blogs, is the change helping or hindering the effort to approach education as a shared communal task (chapter 37)? What are the effects of the expanding reach of digital communication for teachers' workload and for boundaries between school and home, work and rest (chapter 38)?

Part of Christian discernment is reflecting on how our choices and practices affect our relationships with others, including friends, colleagues, and neighbors. The chapters in this section connect discernment, technology, and the ways in which we practice community.

CHAPTER 33

Faith, Practices, and Community

I know our main theme . . . is life together, and technology helps a lot
in that, and it also can cause some problems, because you're more
interconnected everywhere, but it can also make life less personal,
and so I think that's why we chose the theme life together . . . because
technology can hurt that so we want to bring it back.

Student

One worry about digital technologies that has received significant media
coverage and scholarly attention centers on how our relationship to our
devices might shift our relationships with the people around us. Could absorption in our devices erode our capacity to connect with others?[1] Might
relationships between adults and teens tilt toward surveillance and mistrust?[2] How might the communities that have traditionally provided the
setting in which learners are formed be redefined?[3] Might digital technology, as a high school student in one of our focus groups suggested, make
us better at connecting at a distance and worse at connecting when we are
in the same space?[4] These and a range of similar anxieties are part of the
wider landscape of debate about digital devices.

Concern about the effects of technological change on relationships
was also a live topic among teachers at Modern Christian Schools. As one
teacher explained to us, the schools aimed for a balance between the "prepare minds" and "nurture lives" parts of their mission. This meant connecting faith, pedagogy, and community:

I think that for the sake of that balance we were much more intentional
about the integration of faith within the classroom. . . . We also were
intentional about creating community, because technology by its nature
can sometimes break community. We can sit next to each other and message each other instead of talk, and so there was a lot of intentionality,

including this whole building and other places, where we started to al-most demand that community still be part of us. But you know, there was a whole network of folks . . . that worked very hard to reincorporate faith integration into our pedagogy. Because it would naturally take a second place to something cool, and we didn't want it to be lost.

Sustaining strong community was an explicit priority, one that called for intentional approaches to technological and pedagogical practices.

Christian Community and Technology

This focus on community has a clear grounding in Christian theology. At the beginning of the biblical story, the triune God, Father, Son, and Holy Spirit, creates the world and a pair of humans to inhabit it, declaring, "It is not good that the man should be alone" (Gen. 2:18). This relational em-phasis echoes through the rest of the story. Jesus sums up the Law and the Prophets in the twin call to love God and to love our neighbor, and the vision of Christian fellowship elaborated in the New Testament pictures a community of mutual edification in which the gifts of each are committed to the flourishing of others.[5] The earliest Christian community is described in the Acts of the Apostles as being devoted "to the apostles' teaching and fellowship, to the breaking of bread and the prayers," and "all who be-lieved were together and had all things in common" (Acts 2:42-44). Later in the New Testament we encounter Paul's image of the church as a body in which the eye cannot say to the ear, "I don't need you," or as living stones being built into a single temple.[6] There are also the many "one another" phrases, the cautions not to let our own freedoms cause weaker community members to stumble, and the emphasis on individual gifts being for "the common good."[7] A core New Testament emphasis is a vision of community in which each member of the body is important to the functioning of the whole and all members depend on each other.

Given this background, it is not surprising that questions about the im-pact of technology on relationships and community should emerge as an important theme in efforts to practice Christian discernment with new tech-nologies.[8] Amitai Etzioni identifies two key elements of community: the web of "affect-laden relationships among a group of individuals" and the "measure of commitment to a set of shared values, norms, and meanings, and a shared history and identity."[9] We have already explored how shared values, norms, and identity have helped shape technology use at Modern Christian Schools. Here we focus more directly on the web of relationships. How might technological change be affecting the ways in which teachers, parents, and students relate to one another?[10] This was a recurring question among teachers and administrators as the one-to-one program developed. Focus group, observational, and documentary evidence revealed several distinct aspects of a concern for sustaining strong relationships.

School and Classroom Community

The deep community focus present in the schools and classrooms is a theme that has been threaded throughout the book to this point. Here and in upcoming chapters we weave together threads from prior sections and additional evidence to examine more closely the intentional decisions about community building and life together at Modern Christian Schools. Previous chapters already revealed a community emphasis fostered through schoolwide efforts to develop discernment and promote practices for living a healthy digital life. Approaches to protecting moral boundaries (e.g., filtering or monitoring online content) or teaching discernment about online content (e.g., adopting digital literacy standards or frameworks) built on communal values. We have also seen the schools create practices stemming from an awareness that "technology by its nature can sometimes break community." Practices designed to build relationships among students, such as the mixed-grade groups of PowerDown, were built into school rhythms and routines. Such practices did not always involve digital technologies, but they were an intentional response to the risk of technology breaking relationships. Although we heard varying responses about the effectiveness of these practices, the extent of focus group discussion about

> **Relationships and Technology**
>
> Three types of relationships are influenced by technology:
>
> 1. Classroom and immediate school community: interactions between students, teachers, administrators, and staff within the schools
> 2. Wider school community: interactions among members of the broader school community including families/parents
> 3. Others in the wider world: interactions between members of the immediate school community and those outside it

them revealed their role in promoting both individual and communal reflection on the way technology shapes community.

Modern Christian Schools' commitment to preparing educators for
teaching in a one-to-one program also reflected an emphasis on community. The introduction of digital learning technologies went hand in hand
with a focus on teachers working together to master new processes and
skills. Opportunities for collaboration constantly arose from the learning
curve of ever-changing technologies and applications. As individual teachers began to invest in and become expert in particular applications and
strategies, this created a need to learn from one another. Technological
change was harnessed to foster collegial interaction through both intentional and spontaneous learning opportunities. This focus on shared expertise was also reflected in classroom learning.

Teachers worked in class to help students develop discerning practices that promoted a healthy digital life together. Throughout the book,
we have seen teachers design lessons that encouraged students to reflect
on technology, reconsider the teacher-learner relationship in decentered
classrooms, and converse about the everyday possibilities and pitfalls of
living in a digital world. Practices like slow and careful reading, screens
at 45 degrees to direct attention to others in the classroom, boxes for cell
phones during class, and assignments such as media fasts were all part of
this process. Teachers also spoke of the power of reflection in unplanned
moments, as when a teacher found part of his sex education class posted
online in video form without his permission, or when the inappropriate
behavior of a student with emotional difficulties raised concerns about how
other students might post about it on social media. Teachers repeatedly
spoke of taking such events as opportunities to pause and help students reflect on how we express grace to others and practice life together in Christian community. A teacher reflected,

> As a community, how do we use these laptops so that they influence
> our community for good? How do we use them so we don't hurt others?
> What is being responsible with a laptop? How do you do that in a commu-
> nity? Because everything was phrased "in a community." . . . One thing
> that always frightens you when you give a kid a laptop is now they have
> access to email . . . and I've seen some really cruel things happen when
> kids get hold of email. I have to admit, our kids rocked laptops this year,
> they really did. Because I think life together means we're a community,
> we're brothers, we're sisters in Christ and these are the things that as a

brother and sister in Christ are not acceptable as far as technology and how we hurt each other. Constantly, whenever we would see something come back, you know, "Hey, let's talk about this in [the] form of our community—our life together. Is this life together?"

This emphasis on community and grace toward one another seemed to help teachers treat potentially hurtful uses of digital communication as learning opportunities. As a student told us, "It can be easy to maybe be mean to someone else, but I think we try to intentionally build others up through technology."

Another positive outcome of using new technologies mentioned by some teachers was a redistribution of expertise in the classroom. Some students were more expert than others, perhaps even more expert than the teacher, with regard to particular technologies and pieces of software. These were not always the students who were excelling academically. We saw instances of teachers using one student's need for technological assistance as an opportunity to draw another student alongside to support them, and to praise that student for their contribution. Teachers were on the lookout for such opportunities. As one teacher put it, "What we can say is we are community builders ... because of the way that we support each other, and we are partnering together through this. It's more of an overarching way we teach ... you know, those individual, specific [opportunities] come up, but you can't always plan for them. But you can plan the right atmosphere." Some of the best community-building opportunities were not planned; they emerged unbidden in the daily life of the classroom. It was the teachers on the lookout for these opportunities that were able to take advantage of the moment.

Communicating with Family

A second area where the idea of Christian community was applied to technology use involved intentionally fostering communication among members of the wider school community. School and classroom blogs and emails were widely used to share student work and classroom events with parents. Teachers also described how they encouraged students to use technology to connect with their family members during learning. An elementary school teacher, for instance, described emphasizing to students that if they wanted to search for something on the internet, they must do it alongside a parent. The teacher elaborated on how students communicated digitally with parents: "We've been using email for them to type a little note to their parents at the end of the week, just saying here are my two favorite things I learned in school this week. And it is using it for a positive, you know, 'I'm going to communicate with my parents and this is a good thing.' And if we're doing a service project, we'll send a note to parents about that: 'Can I please do chores to earn money for our service project.' Or that kind of thing ... using it to further God's kingdom." The intention driving such choices on the part of teachers was often explicitly the desire to use technology to support students' communication with their family and the schools' cooperation with parents.

Being Online

A third relational emphasis extended the circle of communication to include interactions beyond the bounds of the school community. As we saw in part 5, one of the ways in which a focus on Christian practices became visible was in a concern for gracious communication that extended to the world of online comments. A parent reflected that

> it's a world of comments. . . . If you get on comments, it's so disheartening, so we talk about this a lot from a Christian perspective, that you can engage in that world, and you can respectfully comment and give opinions while respecting the other person's opinion, and actually putting love out there at the same time. Because that can be really challenging to our kids when there's name calling ... and they're putting their beliefs out there, and they get shut down. So, I don't want their voices to be shut down, I want their voices, their Christian voices to come through, but it's a conversation about how to do that respectfully and still have a voice.

A teacher similarly reflected aloud that the question of whether "we comment on websites in a way that [other] people comment on websites" was a regular topic of conversation with students.

Another teacher described applying the idea of care for others to the way students used online sources for their research. Students learning about Islam were directed to conduct initial research online. The teacher first gave students time to look for sources without detailed guidance and asked them to bring what they found back to the class. The next day "we have that conversation about what was your source, and would a group of

Muslims in a room be okay with you using that source? What would they think about it?" Here again we see a focus on learning how to relate to others. Emphasizing the importance of gracious relationships within the immediate community stood in continuity with a concern for relating well to those beyond the community.

A Closer Look at Community

Attending to how we treat our neighbor in the context of digital technology was one of the most common ways in which teachers at Modern Christian Schools spoke of connecting their Christian faith to their educational practice.[11] The lens of relationships to others offers a series of contexts in which we can think about the impact of technology on love of neighbor. First, we can consider how intentional practices with technology might foster collaborative work and gracious interaction within the school. Do we use technology in classrooms with a focus on building relational care? Second, we can focus on using technology to enhance connections with the wider school community, involving family members in students' learning. Do our patterns of technology use build healthy connections between school, home, and the wider school community? Third, we can engage in intentional efforts to teach students to relate with grace and respect to those outside the immediate school community. What model of engaging with people outside our own circles do students encounter, and how might they learn to use technology for respectful, caring interaction across differences? In these three ways, a concern for the texture of Christian relationships is an important ingredient in thinking about the potentials and risks of working with digital technology. In the following chapters we take a closer look at some particular pressure points within this broad picture.

For Reflection and Response

- When you think of digital technology in connection with relationships and community, do you see mostly potential or threat? Why?
- What kinds of intentional practices might help a school community live well with one another amid reliance on digital technology?
- How might variations in expertise with technology affect relationships in a school setting?

CHAPTER 34

Shifting Relational Dynamics

Keep [the laptops], because otherwise everyone would have to go down to a computer lab . . . instead of having an all-knowing box of genius at arm's reach everywhere you go!

Student

The question of where authority and wisdom reside is part of any vision of community. This emerged as a theme in our conversations with school members about how technology is changing relationships within the learning community. Traditional visions of the relationship between teacher and student stand under scrutiny in a digitally connected environment. What happens to the teaching-learning relationship when the internet allows students to become experts in their own right? In what ways might this undermine authority structures that traditionally made the teacher the guardian of what is known?

Teachers at Modern Christian Schools described how online access changed their status as "gatekeepers" of knowledge. An art teacher, for instance, reflected, "I think before computers were in the hands of students in the art department, we were kind of like the gatekeepers. We knew . . . what was important to teach, or who were the artists. So, we would have drawers and drawers full of these posters and we would have them up and we would talk about them." Before computers, students depended largely on the expertise and resources of the teacher as the entry point for learning about content. Classroom learning was bound to teachers' choices about which content to cover and the breadth and depth with which to cover it. Internet access upsets this picture. Teachers remain the gatekeepers of many things, including pedagogical decisions about how to teach, what boundaries to set, what might be most worth searching for, and which norms will prevail in class. Yet the teachers with whom we spoke no longer believed they were the sole gatekeepers of content.

Of course, teachers were never the sole gatekeepers for knowledge and resources. Students have long drawn on resources such as libraries, out-of-school mentors, magazines, and so on. Yet such resources were limited and typically lived outside the teacher's classroom domain. In a digital learning environment such as that at Modern Christian Schools, a world of knowledge is a gesture away. A student fascinated by a topic can take the initiative to pursue it in depth. They can immediately fact-check what their teacher has to say. They can also quickly find contrasting perspectives and discover information that lies beyond the teacher's expertise. They can use social media or online forums to connect with others sharing similar passions and perhaps different worldviews, and even correspond with experts around the world. Of course, online research does not quickly yield the same expertise as those who have studied at greater length and systematic depth in preparation for professional careers. Nevertheless, students can become highly knowledgeable in their own right in ways that exceed the bounds of the teacher's knowledge. And they can do all of this from within the teacher's classroom, in real time.

Control

Depending on one's view of teaching, the changes in a digital world have the potential to shift power dynamics in the teaching-learning relationship in worrying or exhilarating ways. For teachers who see themselves as the sole expert, the reliable gatekeeper of knowledge in the classroom, the perceived loss of power can conjure fear and a sense of loss of control. For those pursuing a more student-oriented model of learning, digital devices seem to open up powerful new opportunities for engaging students in inquiry. Either way, as we saw in part 4, the shift reconfigures the challenge of teaching Christian discernment. When curriculum resources are potentially as broad as the internet, and they arrive in students' hands in real time, the slower processes of textbook publishing or the teacher's accumulation of well-considered approaches to topics become a less viable critical filter. The buffers between students and an enormous range of valid and invalid, helpful and harmful ideas have thinned considerably. This poses significant challenges to any model of Christian education predicated on having ready Christian answers to provide perspective on all curriculum content. It also changes the relational structure of the classroom, realigning student and teacher roles in ways that give more weight to student exploration.

Teachers at Modern Christian Schools who embrace these changes describe corresponding shifts in their perspectives about teaching and learning. The ways in which they talk about their pedagogy reveal a view of their role as enabling learning in a more fluid and collaborative environment. This requires that they see themselves as learners too. One teacher reflected, "I think my teaching has become more collaborative because the kids can share things that they find with me. I can also say, 'Hey, so-and-so just found an awesome link here. I'm posting it on my page. Check out what they found. That's a great image or that's a great website for teaching.' And a lot of them will come up with ways of reviewing or ways of helping themselves learn, and then I'll share [them] with other students."

There is here an openness to and celebration of students' contributions to the classroom. Students are invited to see the teacher as a learner, willing to lead but also willing to learn with and from students. This shifts the power dynamics in the classroom as students become able to actively shape learning alongside the teacher. This shared space can also be a vulnerable space, because it means sharing the role of knower with students. Students may bring content knowledge or technological knowledge that teachers do not possess, challenging the teachers' desire to be the ones in the know.

Teacher Expertise

Some of the concerns that may arise from such changes can be calmed by reflecting on the basis of teacher expertise. Teaching expertise does not arise merely from content knowledge and technological knowledge. It also stems from maturity of engagement and from pedagogical knowledge, a foundational kind of knowledge that students lack.[1] Teachers are designers.[2] They structure student learning toward particular ends and adapt curriculum to meet the needs of learners. They are best positioned to recognize when and why particular technologies should be integrated into the curriculum. They are also commonly better able than students to discern the source and motive behind online information, put things in historical context, identify the most important content to focus on, and help adjudicate contradictions. In this sense the power of teacher expertise lies in designing opportunities that most effectively weigh and harness the content or technological knowledge that they and students bring to units or lessons.[3] Teachers in Christian schools should offer greater maturity than their students in terms of their grasp of the substance of Christian faith and their ability to make discerning judgments in a shifting environment. Internet access expands the pool of knowledge but does not instantly give learners depth of character or spiritual growth. Christian teachers may think of themselves not primarily as carriers of expert Christian answers for every topic but as mature guides and designers of learning that nurtures faith and is rooted in faith.[4]

When teachers embrace opportunities to learn from and with students, they help foster students' views of learning as an ongoing, deepening process that is built on both success and failure. This offers teachers space to model the value of taking risks and failing, then trying again. One special education teacher's description of the math teacher with whom she worked offered a glimpse of this kind of approach: "I can see it coming through in the way he teaches, and the whole mindset . . . is that you sometimes just need to let up some control and be okay with kids taking risks and recognize we learn by doing and failing and that's okay for all of us, and that we are all in that same . . . we're all learners that way."

Embracing redistributed access to content knowledge can also create openings for teachers to demonstrate the power of collaborative learning. As teachers embraced a shared, collaborative approach to learning, yielding their role as sole gatekeeper of knowledge, we heard them making connections to the idea of Christian community. One teacher responded to a question about how students learn to use certain technologies for math class, stating, "Sometimes I don't even know how [students] know. It's beautiful. And then, if they don't know, you [have] the whole class talk about it. . . . My student emails me at night, 'I figured out how to do an exponent. I think they work in Google Classroom.' The kids just email me, 'Hey, I figured this out.' It's life together . . . helping each other and the collaboration and the teamwork. The things you try to instill. I'm still working on that." This teacher's comments suggest the possibility of fresh synergies between Christian commitments and the emerging patterns of interaction fostered by digital technologies. The teacher describes the new distribution of expertise as integral to Christian community, relating it to the schools' shared emphasis on life together (an allusion to theologian Dietrich Bonhoeffer's work of the same name and to conversations current in the school about Christian community).[5] Embracing vulnerability and collaborative learning and framing them in terms of life together opens space for connections to ideas such as fallibility, grace, humility, and mutually supportive community. Teachers can model and foster a self-critical approach to learning that loosens their hold on the front of the classroom yet remains grounded in their expertise as teachers and in important Christian convictions.[6]

Faith, Change, and Community

Connections between Christian community and collaboration were also an ingredient in the schools' efforts to renew the physical learning environment in ways that supported pedagogical change. The schools sought to promote community by renovating buildings to create physical spaces that might invite collaboration. This was especially visible at the high school, where on any given day students were seen working in small groups in intentionally designed collaboration nooks in hallways and in comfortable seating areas in the main lobby, media center, and other common spaces. The intentional design of physical spaces combined with the adoption of one-to-one technologies to accelerate the decentering of knowledge. Digital devices were more than a new tool for learning; they were part of a new learning environment designed to shift the community's practices around learning. These changes were accompanied by intentional professional development on Christian community, and this enabled at least some teachers to manage the shifting dynamics in ways that continued to draw on their beliefs about Christian education. In this way, rather than undermining core Christian convictions, change flowed with them.

The move toward a more decentered classroom was not generally experienced by teachers at Modern Christian Schools as threatening or as a move away from providing a Christian education. The process of Christian learning was not secured by the teacher already having all the right answers, but rather by the teacher's ongoing investment in being in close dialogue with students as their learning progressed. This created new opportunities to focus on "nurturing the lives" of students in the context of faith. Christians were seen as called into community, invited to depend on God and one another and to trust, encourage, and love one another. A classroom in which teacher and students learn to engage in mutual support, reporting what they have found and reflecting on it together, offered opportunities to live out the practices of an interdependent community that did not know everything ahead of time.

Perhaps in such spaces there is potential for discernment to become something close to what it is said to be in the theological literature, a process of listening and learning together in prayerful interaction rather than simply a controlling of boundaries (see chapters 18 and 22). This raises questions about the kinds of teacher preparation and formation that might be needed to enable teachers to work in such a context of collaborative, relational discernment while keeping the process rooted in Christian commitment to truth-seeking amid the winds of opinion (cf. Eph. 4:14). It also has implications for how the whole school functions as a community as teachers support one another amid rapid change. Successful Christian education in a digital environment may depend in significant measure on the preparation, development, and support of teachers capable of sustaining a Christian community of inquiry. In the coming chapters we will take a closer look at how this ideal of a collaborative Christian learning community is working out and at some of the challenges it presents.

For Reflection and Response

- Reread the student quotation at the head of this chapter. Do you see more potential or danger for Christian education as digital devices become primary sources of student knowledge?
- What risks might be involved in teachers maintaining a strong position of control over knowledge?
- In what ways does the vision of collaborative learning described in this chapter resonate with the idea of Christian community?

CHAPTER 35

Does Technology Use Increase Collaboration?

Accessibility to mobile technology is essential for students and teachers. We propose that each student in grades K–4 have a personal mobile device to use for their learning. The tablet is the mobile device that is accessible, media rich, powerfully creative, richly collaborative, and connected.

Administrative document

As we saw in the last chapter, teachers at Modern Christian Schools saw the potential for digital technology to create a stronger focus on collaborative learning. This sense of potential was not the limited vision of a few but a widespread belief, as evidenced by surveys. Eighty-one percent of teachers agreed the technology program at Modern Christian Schools had increased student collaboration.[1] We also repeatedly heard focus group teachers report on the importance of collaboration with their own peers in considering how to teach with technology. Enhanced collaboration echoes a common theme in external frameworks for twenty-first-century learning and digital citizenship, and we have also seen it connecting with teachers' developing ideas about Christian community. In this chapter we take a closer look at what collaboration might mean and when it is happening between students as well as between teachers.

Collaboration and Cooperation

Collaboration is commonly distinguished from cooperation, in which individuals merely work side by side. The widely used Framework for 21st Century Learning includes the following capacities in its definition of collaboration:

- Demonstrate ability to work effectively and respectfully with diverse teams
- Exercise flexibility and willingness to be helpful in making necessary compromises to accomplish a common goal
- Assume shared responsibility for collaborative work, and value the individual contributions made by each team member[2]

For work to become collaboration rather than cooperation, participants must build on each other's ideas and gifts to create outcomes that emerge from the interaction of their contributions. Collaboration requires investment from all parties in a shared product, not just coordination of their individual efforts.

Such definitions of collaboration have a positive ring for those pursuing a vision of Christian community in which individuals with varied gifts work together as mutually supportive parts of the body of Christ. A similar vision of collaboration appears, for instance, in recent writing on worship planning: "Collaborators are 'co-laborers.' They contribute from the field of their own gifts and passions. But they do not labor in isolation. Their labors are so interwoven that the final product is a composite. A group effort is genuinely the product of the entire group, not merely a modified solo plan."[3] The matter is, of course, not as simple as using a Christian account of community as a measuring stick for evaluating digital learning goals. The ways in which Christians think about community are themselves evolving as our social experience changes, partly under the influence of technological change.[4] Yet there does seem to be space here for some theological resonance. In a Christian school, collaborative work may be seen as part of developing Christian identity by developing skills and gifts to contribute to the flourishing of the community.[5]

We saw examples of students learning together at Modern Christian Schools that fell on both sides of the collaboration/cooperation distinction. Consider the following two examples. In which are students collaborating?

As second-grade students approach a learning station, they find glasses, knee-high slacks, a puffed-sleeve shirt, a dress, and grammar books. Each student chooses an item to try on. They pretend to be students from the early days of their town, taking pictures of each other with their tablet cameras. The next day, each student creates their own video about life long ago in their town by selecting pictures on their tablet and adding text to them.

Elsewhere, tenth-grade students sit around tables in the media center. Previously completed individual article summaries describing a poem lie scattered in the middle of each table. It is generally quiet as students read one another's summaries, yet students pause frequently to comment, "Here's something we can use," or "This one agrees with that one," or "This sounds like a good article." They highlight useful material and type into a shared online document to support the development of a group report and presentation.

In both examples, students work together to generate a response to new material that they encounter. The first example seems to involve more immediate interaction as students explore the costumes together, decide what to choose, and take pictures of one another. Yet the products generated are entirely individual; a given student's project requires only another's assistance in taking a picture, nothing else. The second example at first seems less relational, as students sit quietly reading various article summaries, yet their reading is feeding into a collaborative project, a jointly researched and constructed report. It is this shared endeavor, drawing on the findings of multiple students, that makes the second example in the end more collaborative.

Both collaboration (in the stronger sense intended by twenty-first-century learning frameworks) and community (in the sense that arises from Christian theology) involve more than working in the same space and interacting. Both imply a stronger degree of interdependence, supporting one another's growth and drawing on the gifts of each. How much did we see this happening in the life of Modern Christian Schools?

Student Collaboration

At the heart of the schools' vision for increased collaboration was collaborative learning among students. School leaders envisioned the redesigned high school as an environment where "student-centered, collaborative education" could be supported. Professional development included a focus on helping students "use digital media and environments to communicate and work collaboratively, including at a distance, to support individual learning and contribute to the learning of others." In a school-initiated survey early in the one-to-one initiative, 77% of teachers agreed that students' ability to work collaboratively had improved. As noted earlier, a decade later, 81% of teachers agreed that technology had raised the level of student collaboration.

Teachers spoke repeatedly of increased collaboration in classrooms during focus groups, but what did such activities look like? One project repeatedly emerged in focus groups as a paradigmatic example. Students in a World Cultures class chose topics from different global regions, ranging from persecution of Christians in Myanmar to microfinancing in Sierra Leone or the treatment of women in Taliban-controlled regions of Afghanistan. Students worked in pairs over the course of a semester to research, develop an exhibit, and present it to those who attended an evening open house. This kind of joint inquiry and product was offered as a prime example of the potential of technology to foster collaborative learning.

How Much Do Students Collaborate?

Classroom observations allowed us to see whether such collaborative work was reflected across students' experience or restricted to flagship examples. Classroom activities in both random and case study observations were coded as "collaborative," "non-collaborative," or "differs by group."[6] The first two codes distinguished whether or not students built on one another's responses, work, and ideas. For activities to be coded as collaborative, students needed to be building on one another's ideas and work, not just working side by side. The third code indicated instances when only some groups of students were collaborating.[7]

In the random classroom observations, when teachers were not prepared for being observed, 20% of the activity time was coded as collaborative and 11% as collaboration differing by group. In other words, at least some students were collaborating about 31% of the time. In the case study classrooms with teachers chosen for their thoughtful implementation of digital technology, a similar picture emerged: students collaborated 22% of the time, while collaboration differed by group an additional 4% of the time. Overall, while teachers reported that students worked together more frequently than before, and cooperative pair or small group work was commonplace, actual collaboration was not the most common pattern. Although students worked side by side and talked about their work, they did not always build on each other's work or ideas. For example, taking a cue from Max Lucado's *A Hat for Ivan*, first-grade students created pages about themselves on their tablets.[8] Each highlighted their own special talents and audio-recorded their voice-over description. The individual pages were then compiled to create a digital book of the class. While this example required each student's contribution, they worked individually, and the product was compiled from their individual components.

Given the pervasive emphasis on collaborative learning among digital technology advocates at large and leaders at Modern Christian Schools, this rate of collaboration may seem low. However, we know of no benchmark for an optimal proportion of time spent in collaborative work, and since our data does not include observation of classroom work before the technology program, we cannot measure the degree to which collaboration has increased.[9] We can, however, get a little closer to evaluating what is happening by isolating the overlap between technology use and collaborative learning.

Do Students Collaborate More with Technology?

On surveys, students, teachers, and parents showed a significant level of agreement that technology had increased collaboration. We checked this claim through observations where learning activities could be categorized by whether or not technology was used in the classroom. The technology use categories distinguished between the whole-class exposure to technology (e.g., a teacher projecting a laptop on the screen or using a voice projection system) and students accessing their own school-provided or personal digital devices (individual screen time).

There was a correlation between student collaboration and direct screen time in random and case study observations (see fig. 35.1). If we look at the random and case study observations combined, we see that when students collaborated, 71% of the collaborative activity time involved direct student screen time. When collaboration differed by group, 80% of the collaborative time involved student screen time. Screen time made up 50% of non-collaborative time. In sum, the time that students spent collaborating was also more likely to involve their use of technology. Conversely, collaboration happened more often when students used digital tools, and most often when those tools were used in the classrooms identified as showcasing thoughtful technology use.[10]

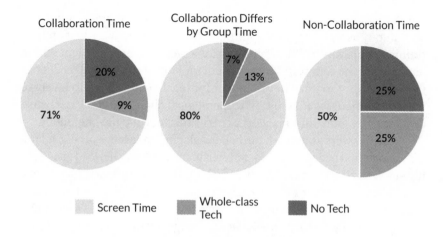

Figure 35.1. The relationship between collaboration and technology use

Collaboration in College

The effects of technology-supported collaboration on students' perceptions of how to work with technology appear to persist into college for Modern Christian Schools alumni. In surveys, 86% of Modern Christian Schools alumni felt that digital technologies helped them work better with peers, compared to 74% of alumni from other high schools. Similarly, 77% of Modern Christian Schools alumni reported that access to digital technologies led to spending more time collaborating with peers, compared to 61%. We can cautiously suggest from these findings that, in part, some aspect of the collaboration fostered at Modern Christian Schools continued to support technology-enhanced collaboration in college.

Teacher Collaboration

Another facet of collaboration involves relationships between educators within the schools. As we have seen in previous chapters, the introduction of digital learning technologies went hand in hand with a focus on teachers working together to master new processes and skills. Teachers, after all, were central players in shaping the ways in which digital technologies were incorporated into classrooms. In the earliest professional development documents, we saw concern for building a collaborative educator community as a primary goal. One document related that the first of three training goals was to "build a professional learning environment within and beyond the four walls of the school for both students and teachers." Over time, professional development for teachers morphed to leverage both the difficulties inherent in technological change and the expertise developed by individual teachers as occasions for collegial interaction.

Teachers were asked to share their developing knowledge of curriculum, technology, and pedagogy in order to collaboratively carry the load of designing new lessons and units of study in their area of responsibility. Technology coaches tailored training to the teaching needs and possibilities of the teaching teams. Platforms for online communication allowed teachers to continue collaboration beyond their face-to-face meetings and to track changes to their instructional plans. The variety of collaborative learning opportunities within the building was, as one administrator noted, "probably the most meaningful way for people to learn . . . and gain confidence." Teachers affirmed this; as one put it, "I learned the most when my own colleagues got up there, and said, 'Hey, . . . I learned about this, I'm trying this out and see if it works for you.' That was the best." In surveys, teachers identified their colleagues as the highest contributing factor in their preparation for teaching with technology and for Christian teaching with technology. School-sponsored professional development was ranked second.[11] In the later program years, coaches and teams tapered off, with many teachers reporting a desire for more community-based support. Yet teachers still found ways to continue encouraging and supporting one another. Through mentors, "go-to" individuals within the building, or grade-level teams, teachers reported seeking out and receiving valuable support from their peers. Through teachers' focus group discussions about the centrality of their peers to their learning how to teach with technology, we see glimpses of a fellowship in which members were committed to one another's flourishing. Teacher collaboration seems to have been vital to teacher learning and to keeping the change process rooted in the community's Christian commitments.

The Importance of Collaboration

What, then, have we learned? As we have seen, collaboration was an important part of the schools' vision when implementing their technology program. This was rooted in the rhetoric of twenty-first-century skills and preparation for future work environments. It also drew from ideas about students unfolding their individual gifts within a Christian community. Observation data suggests that student collaboration with technology does indeed occur, although data does not allow us to gauge whether this is an increase since the launch of the one-to-one program. Collaboration was one of several areas in which it seems clear that progress is gradual. Many activities that seem interactive are nonetheless not fully collaborative. Sustaining student collaboration, as opposed to simply working together cooperatively, requires a significant level of pedagogical intentionality.

Collaboration appeared to be a hallmark of fruitful interactions among teachers trying to negotiate the intersection between digital technology and Christian education. This strong community orientation was fostered by design, built around features like ongoing professional development, time set aside for team planning, and technology coaches to guide individuals and teams. As the school withdrew time or resources for such investments, we saw teachers lament the loss of communal time and begin to feel more isolated. Even in schools purposefully attending to community in the light of digital devices, promoting collaborative community is no simple task. Might a Christian conviction that those who make up the community depend on each other's gifts, encouragement, and correction compel a continued commitment to the resources and sustained effort required to increase collaborative work? Time will tell.

For Reflection and Response

- If students learn to collaborate with digital technology, what might this contribute to Christian community?
- Does a commitment to Christian community add anything to common emphases on learning collaborative skills for the twenty-first century?
- Can you think of a learning activity that might both develop collaborative skills and foster intentional care for others?

CHAPTER 36

Parents' Roles and Perspectives

MODERN CHRISTIAN SCHOOLS FAMILIES BENEFIT FROM TECHNOLOGY

This past year both Middle Schools used a program that allows parents and students access to grades, teacher comments, absences and tardies via the internet. This program earned extremely positive responses from both parents and students. The Modern Christian Schools website also remains an effective communication link for parents. In a recent survey parents gave high marks to our website indicating its usefulness is growing.

School magazine article

If the degree of collaboration within the schools is one facet of how digital technology might be affecting the fabric of community life, another is the relationship between schools and parents. Christian schools in the tradition to which Modern Christian Schools belong have tended to value parental responsibility and partnership between school and home.[1] Might digital technology create new possibilities for strengthening this relationship? Might the schools promote communal technology practices that enhance this relationship? These were live questions as Modern Christian Schools discussed the positive potential of digital technology. They reflected an understanding of technology as a social practice, a recognition that relationships could be molded and shaped by intentional communal patterns of technology use. In this chapter we explore the emerging patterns of technological communication between the schools and the parent community. First, we look at how the schools' view of parents as participants in the communal discernment process evolved. Then we look at some examples of how technology was used to connect student work to a community audience. Finally, we consider the matter from the parent side, asking how parents perceive school communications around technology.

School Policy Perspectives on Parents

Parental involvement in education has a positive effect on learning, and school culture can influence how parents see their own role and engagement in education.[2] As discernment with technology was discussed early in the one-to-one program, parents were mentioned in several roles. Parents might partner with the school to teach discernment, they might themselves need education about new technologies, and technology might affect how communication with parents evolved (see chapter 20). The formal policy statements and communications to parents that emerged from these discussions offer a glimpse of what the schools wanted the parent community to know.

As with professional development plans, documents written for parents tended to increasingly identify discernment with ethical behavior and relate it more readily to vision statements than to practical details. This pattern was evident, for instance, in all annual editions of the parent laptop and tablet handbooks. Discernment was prominently mentioned in the opening paragraphs but was not referred to further as the documents turned primarily to device care, behavioral policies, and other practical matters.[3]

In some communications to parents, however, a further emphasis emerged. Particularly when tablets were introduced, several documents linked discernment to e-portfolios and the creation of a positive digital footprint by students. A draft proposal for the tablet program noted, "It is important in today's world for students to create positive digital footprints to impact the world for Jesus Christ. One way to see positive digital footprints is through e-portfolios as a space for students to share and reflect on their learning. Students need to learn to navigate the digital waters with Christian discernment and understand human, cultural, and societal issues related to technology."

The idea was that the creation of e-portfolios might enable students to share their work with a controlled audience. As another document put it, "Sharing creates an audience for learning to grow deeper. When students are younger this learning circle may be smaller but [it] will expand as they get older." The hope was that students would be able to practice building a constructive online presence with a supportive community audience. Allowing student work to be viewed by family and friends should encourage students to consider the worth and wisdom of what they post in light of family feedback. In this way, the community might function as a co-teacher of discernment. This impulse was also worked out to a degree through the use of class blogs and encouragement for students to share their work electronically with their families.[4]

This picture of parents as co-teachers of discernment lived in school documents alongside another image of parents as recipients of technical information and news updates. The concrete forms of parent outreach recorded in school documents focused mainly on informing parents about the capabilities and benefits of new apps and devices, warning them about safety and the dangers of the internet, offering guidelines for device care, setting behavioral expectations, and offering options for internet monitoring and filtering. Minutes from a technology council meeting note discussion of a striking pair of questions:

> What can we provide to help students in their discernment of computer usage and the internet?

> What can we provide to help parents in managing their home environment and set up? Demo OpenDNS [a web filter]?

The focus here seems to be on broad discernment of technology for students and technical support for parents. Another set of minutes suggest some richer themes for communications to parents:

> As parents choose options for their children's preferences, offer an option for the laptops to be shut down on Sundays as an option for supporting the Sabbath. School partnering with church.

> Send a monthly tech update . . . information for parents . . . section in every parent newsletter . . .

> Maybe a question/topic of the month . . . this month we are asking questions on electronics on school trips . . .

> In general, increase communication. Talk openly and honestly about the negatives of technology . . . about what kids are being caught doing so we can help watch for the activity in our kids.

There seems to be room here for a broader focus on shared Christian practices. Generally, however, formal school documents offered minimal evidence of resources for parents that focused on building a shared understanding of discernment with technology beyond avoiding harmful material and meeting behavioral expectations.

The more recent versions of the schools' overall technology plan opened with a vision statement that summarized the technology belief statements from a decade earlier and highlighted the theme of teaching Christian discernment. The schools then included distinct goals for each of four areas of school life: curriculum, professional development, infrastructure, and parents and community. The following were the "parent and community relations goals":

> Goal I: Parents will have access to information about student learning at any time and will be given instruction on accessing that information. All . . . websites and communication will be mobile aware and ready in both form and function.

> Goal II: Information . . . including activities, programs, and offerings will be readily available and continually updated through the school website and social networking tools.

> Goal III: Parental feedback will be sought regularly to evaluate the success of technology programs including the 1:1 laptop initiative and communication tools.

These goals focus on important, concrete practices yet imply a largely receptive role for parents focused on information and assessment. Access and feedback matter but are not quite the same as becoming co-teachers of students as they learn Christian discernment in their technology practices. If we based our picture of interaction with parents on available school documentation alone, we might be left wondering what wider roles for the parent community could be identified and articulated. Turning to focus group and survey data, however, adds nuance to our understanding of parent involvement in the technology program and suggests a significant level of parent engagement.

Classroom Learning and Parents

The patterns of engagement that we heard described by teachers offered a livelier picture of the parental role in learning. Elementary teachers especially described students' enjoyment of sharing their writing and other products with a wider audience of parents and grandparents via email or classroom blogs. Parents were also the audience for persuasive letter writing, with students making a case for something they wanted.[5] An elementary teacher reported, "If I say to my kids, 'You know what, we're going to put one of the best presentations on the blog,' I mean, they are working so hard and are so excited. If I say, 'We are going to present this to [Name],' or 'I'm going to take a video so I can show my parents,' even things like that, because they know my parents and they've all come in and formed that relationship, they really get excited."

Parents and grandparents also attended face-to-face presentations in which students shared what they had learned. At the high school an external panel interacted with students and their entrepreneurial pitches in a simulation of the *Shark Tank* show. Parents and grandparents were recruited as audiences, sometimes for critique, but mainly to motivate students in their work. Teachers reflected that this effect was strongest with young students, and that sometimes students did not seem to find the idea of publishing to a more anonymous general audience online nearly as motivating.

Teachers also shared examples of digital products enhancing parent understanding of students' progress. A Spanish teacher shared Google Voice recordings of students speaking Spanish when parents were concerned about their students' facility with the language. An art teacher posted videos of students at work to help parents better understand a painting technique. A first-grade teacher described student videos sent to parents in which students showed and read aloud their writing projects as a record of their writing progress.

Such examples illustrate the genuine and articulate desire that we encountered in focus groups and case studies to see students' technology use strengthen parent connections. What seems to have been less easy was translating this desire into policies and documents that communicated an active and reflective role for parents and a shared vision of Christian discernment. We heard some reports of frustration when more vision-focused events organized for parents were poorly attended, or when parents indicated that they did not want further discussion of the mission. It was nonetheless clear that one of the attractions of digital media for teachers was the possibility of connecting student work to parent audiences in fresh ways.

Parent Perspectives on School Communications

What can we learn about parents' perspectives on the schools' efforts? Surveys revealed two broad themes in parent responses to the technology program. First, as we saw in chapter 9, there was broad support for the technology program among parents. Parents believed that laptops would help prepare students for a technology-saturated future, building skills that would offer an advantage in college and career (see chapter 7). On this point, parents were more consistently optimistic than their students, with 86% of parents agreeing that the use of technology at their school had prepared their child for their future after high school. This optimism, however, was paired with a realization of the limits of technology. High parental agreement was generally present on questions about specific ways technology supported students (e.g., prepare students for the future, increase student collaboration, make it easy for students to seek help after school), but this agreement dropped noticeably as questions focused more broadly on relationships. When asked about the schools' use of technology in making parent-child relationships deeper, only 13% agreed. In an ever-shifting digital landscape, parents paired optimism about specific outcomes with tempered aspirations about how technologies might ultimately shape relationships.

Such findings relate to a second theme of parental concern and uncertainty about how to raise their children to use technology wisely. These concerns manifested in the form of questions about filtering and monitoring, some worries about screen time, and expressions of eagerness to receive help and advice from the school about parenting in a tech-saturated culture.[6] One parent commented in a school survey:

> Although we do have concerns as parents, issues that the school should continue to address and change as the laptop computer program grows, we do feel that many important skills are being taught and developed through this program. Our child has learned a great deal about how to use the computer and some teachers are using the technology in creative and inspiring ways. Please keep working to make this program better. Don't be afraid to hear parents' concerns and address them. Computers are a great educational tool but there are inherent problems that do exist with the use of any technology, and it will take time and energy to keep working to make this laptop program better each year.

Parents also expressed both optimism and concern when asked about the schools' communication with them about the technology program. This communication included email updates, blog posts, handbooks and policy forms, school events, and orientation meetings. In focus groups some parents felt that the school could do more to communicate with them about technology, but the overall picture that emerged from surveys was more positive. Most parents were pleased with the level of communication that they received from the school. Eighty-one percent agreed that the school had provided good information about the technology program, and 72% agreed that the school provided a clear explanation about why the school invested in learning with technology. (As we saw in chapter 8, this did not necessarily mean that individual parents could articulate the schools' vision for the program.) This satisfaction with the level of communication was strong with new parents, with those who had been in the district for a number of years, and with parents who had not attended a technology-related school event in a number of years. Seventy-one percent of parents also agreed that the school had provided "adequate training" for the technology program.

This satisfaction became less consistent when we prompted for areas of parental concern. When we asked parents if the schools had provided "adequate help with the task of Christian parenting with regard to technology," 51% agreed that the schools had, and 21% disagreed. When asked how frequently they had different kinds of conversations with their child about technology, parents revealed a slightly different set of priorities than the schools. For example, Modern Christian Schools placed considerable focus on using technology to "bring change to the world for Christ," and parents generally gave the school high marks for this missional emphasis (see chapter 9). Seventy-six percent of parents thought that teachers did a good job encouraging students to "talk about how they think technology can be used to bring change to the world for Christ." In contrast, only a minority of parents responded that they discussed with their children how technology could be used to "bring change to the world" (36%) or "engage the world for Christ" (43%). This was not because these parents were avoiding conversations about technology. In fact, 88% of parents reported talking to their child "about how technology influences human relationships and communication" at least a few times a month. Likewise, 89% of parents regularly talked to their children about "discernment and ethical use of technology," and 77% talked with their children about how they "should think about and use technology in a way that reflects Christian beliefs and values." Interestingly, these reflect more of a "nurturing lives" focus, the area that we saw in chapter 9 meeting with somewhat less confidence in terms of whether parents believed the schools' technology program had enhanced it.

Parents and the schools connected Christian faith and technology differently. As we noted in chapter 22, the parents were more likely to focus on the preservation of purity or protection from negative external influences, while administrators and teachers were more likely to focus on worldview and on a Christian mission to constructively engage the world. Yet our surveys did not indicate that the schools and the parents had any substantive theological disagreement. The high levels of parent confidence in school communications and the high levels of reported parent interaction with their children about discernment and technology suggest that even though what had been articulated in school documents sometimes seemed narrow, there was a significant level of whole-community engagement surrounding students' experience with technology. Students were hearing about discernment in school and at home. There also seemed to be a difference in emphasis that might reflect a kind of division of labor. Schools focused more on preparing students for future engagement (mission and skills), while parents focused more on safety and building character.

The Challenges of Building Community

When we compare the schools' documentary record with survey results and focus group interviews, a complex picture emerges. There are several grounds for encouragement. Overall satisfaction among parents with communication about the technology program was high. Despite the impression in some school documents of a more passive role for parents, parents did seem to be actively engaged with their children outside school around questions of discernment with technology, and teachers were working to involve parents as an audience for student work. The emphasis in school documents on dissemination of information about the schools' decisions and programs was reflected in parents' report that such communication was effectively happening. There also seemed little doubt that the schools' efforts to teach responsible boundaries with regard to potentially harmful uses of digital technologies were shared and reinforced by most parents. What was somewhat less clear was the degree to which the schools had built a broad and shared understanding in the wider community of what

Christian discernment with technology might look like and how to relate it to wise parenting. In this area school and parent emphases differed somewhat, and some parents expressed a desire for more help even as some administrators lamented poor response to some past attempts at outreach.

The richer picture hinted at in documents from the one-to-one launch, of a community engaged together in practices of reflective Christian discernment around technology and of students learning to be wise within that community environment, seems still a work in progress, but with strong signs of genuine community engagement. We glimpse here once more how difficult it can be to shape shared communal practices with technology, even when a school has a vigorous vision for what these practices should/could be. Technological practices are not static but dynamic, and their meaning has to be continually negotiated as the community evolves. When schools commit to technological change alongside a commitment to building healthy community participation, a great deal of the work involved is not just technological but also relational. It involves fostering, sustaining, and revisiting patterns of communication and engagement that stay true to core values.

For Reflection and Response

- What should parents contribute to students' learning about how to live well with digital technology?
- What barriers need to be overcome in order to build strong, active partnerships between schools and parents for students' formation?
- What picture of the role of parents is implied by the communications that go out to parents from your school?

CHAPTER 37

Parent Communication
and Information Overload

> We find the same thing in middle school, trying to communicate infor-
> mation home and there are parents who don't get the messages either
> way [whether digitally or on paper].
>
> *Teacher*

Proponents of digital technology commonly emphasize its promise of more
direct communication. Digital devices are supposed to make the world
smaller, put us more in touch with one another, and increase our access to
one another's lives. When a school is founded on the belief that parents and
school should collaborate to "train children in the right way" (Prov. 22:6),
communication between home and school gains significance. Given the
influence of parent behaviors on children's technology habits, the home-
school connection seems an important piece of the overall attempt to teach
wise technology use.[1] In the last chapter we saw high levels of parent confidence that information about the technology program was being shared
well by Modern Christian Schools. Rather than stopping there, however,
we need to inquire further into how communication is happening. The
implicit messages and practices bound up with the way communication
is delivered play an important role in shaping community interactions.
What happens to school-home communication when the medium of the
messages becomes digital?

Daily school life involves an array of messages. Consider how each
of the following types of communication might affect the fabric of the
community:

> A student arrives home and unloads her backpack. She grabs the booklet
> she made in school and reads it to her parent. Her parent asks questions
> and then sets it aside for later sharing with other family members and
> guests.

A teacher updates the classroom blog, listing upcoming events and Bible memory passages, writing a short description of the students' exploration of artifacts from their city's history, and posting videos the students made about those artifacts. She emails a link to parents to announce the update.

A parent peers into the depths of her student's backpack. There, on the bottom, under shoes, old snacks, socks, and books, lies a scrunched weekly note to home from the teacher. Upon further inspection, three more crumpled weekly notes emerge.

On the learning management system, a teacher posts the homework for each night this week, including supporting resources, for student and parent access.

A parent, teacher, and student sit around a table at the back of the classroom. The student shows his completed project from the history unit and shares what he learned from it. The teacher shares what she notices about the student's learning and formation, and the parent describes what he notices about learning and formation at home and in social situations.

A parent at work opens an email from a teacher and smiles to see a link to her child's work that day. She follows the link and is amazed at the ways her child expressed her learning and articulated her faith.

A teacher sighs after completing his grading and closes the digital grade book. All the grades for the latest test are now entered and available online for students and parents to check.

These acts of communication illustrate some of the communication shifts enabled by digital technologies at Modern Christian Schools. They differ in a variety of ways. They call for differing amounts of time investment for teachers, parents, and students. They may play out differently if they are received, for instance, by single or married parents or by grandparents. They use different physical and digital artifacts to mediate communication. They suggest various levels of interactivity, ranging from broadcasting to dialogue. Some may help build a network of home-school connections. Some may miss their audience or even erode community connections. When we examined these varieties of communication through focus groups, we found both parents and teachers reporting largely positive yet mixed reactions.

Online Grades

One of the first home-directed software implementations at Modern Christian Schools involved a tool for reporting grades and attendance. In place of quarterly report cards, parents could now access grades and teacher comments at any time, even daily if desired. Having teachers input grades directly rather than working through a centralized administrative process streamlined the reporting.

Parents in our focus groups initially responded positively to this increase in access. Some parents appreciated the degree of control they now had over the information at their disposal: "I get a summary of all the classes, but then the . . . summary is just the grade. Monday morning, you have fifty new [reports], because you get them for each kid for each subject. Then for my older children, I will just click on the summary, you'll just see the grades, and then if I see a bomb in there, then I can . . . scroll down into the individual assignment, where it lists each assignment separately, so you can see exactly what they have to make up."

Poor or missing grades were followed up with emails to parents that students could also see. Parents expressed awareness of the need to interpret grade information with care. They described how the developmental and maturity level of the student informed the frequency of gradebook checking that might be required, often with the goal of slowly decreasing monitoring as students took responsibility. Some (but not all) parents were aware that automatic settings could be adjusted to reflect the frequency of communication desired as students showed progress. There was also variation in parents' beliefs about the degree to which students should be left to monitor their own work and learn from the consequences of omission.[2]

Teachers also saw benefits for working with parents and students. As one teacher put it,

> The whole trail of communication from our homework page to . . . grades to whatever else you do . . . it's all right there, so a parent can say [to their student], "You know, you're not doing a good job." . . . Before all the technology, they really don't know what we're doing. They just assume because their kid is struggling it's [the teacher's] fault. . . . Now you can

say, "Well, here's the homework page and if you do that well . . . I communicated on this date, here's the email I sent." . . . It's right there.

Teachers felt an accessible digital record reduced ambiguity for parents and students, creating an objective point of reference for whether requirements had been met. At the same time, the challenge of managing the flow of digital information led some teachers and parents to associate the new tools with increased anxiety. These tensions related to management typically surfaced after general praise for digital communication, when community members described the logistical nuances of digital life. One parent described the process of family negotiation around who should check grades and how often:

> To be honest I stopped getting the emails, because it was creating a lot of stress in our house every week. Because [I was] not sure whether the grades were reflective or not. So, I put this more on my sons to be checking constantly, and then we would sit down, actually get [online], where you can see it all at one time, and they can walk me through it. So, then I was knowing they were looking, because I had my oldest son who would never look at [online grades]. . . . So, I kind of don't look at the emails anymore, but you know it works differently for everyone.

Students confirmed wide variation among their parents in how closely they were paying attention to online grades and other school communications. Students reported checking their own grades online anywhere from once a month to multiple times daily.[3] Many students appreciated the ease with which they could check how they were doing and what they needed to do to improve their grades. We also heard occasional hesitations that hinted at the potential pressures of managing increased information. "I guess I don't really want to know what my grades are," one commented, "so I don't feel bad."

Digital Newsletters, Classroom Blogs, and Parent Emails

What about communication beyond grades? With new digital avenues of communication, the schools began leveraging mass emails to reach families in the district or those in specific schools. The format shifted as technologies advanced, with each school sending out digital newsletters to parents on a regular basis. The emails and digital newsletters were used by administrators to promote events, highlight achievements, and share other pertinent information with families.

All teachers were reliant on email as a common digital connection between home and school, but more regularized communications differed between elementary and other grades. Teachers in the middle and high schools relied on schoolwide grading or course management systems for communication with parents, as noted above. Elementary teachers, on the other hand, transitioned to digital communications to replace the weekly printed notes that most teachers had previously sent home in backpacks to keep parents up to date about their students. As the one-to-one program matured, administrators urged teachers to focus on digital means of communication with parents, especially classroom blogs, which offered opportunities to include pictures and videos of classroom life.[4]

Teacher Perceptions

Teachers expressed an appreciation for the speed of digital communication with parents and students. Emails, online course assignments, and online grades offered multiple paths of communication between home and school. Elementary teachers valued being able to update the blog quickly and share the day's work with parents without having to wait for the weekly note. They also felt that visual media offered parents a better understanding of school activities.[5] Parents, too, appreciated visual access to classroom learning. The appreciation came along with awareness of increased workload. A teacher commented, "I like the way we're doing it now. I can add pictures to my blog, I can put student work online that parents can see that otherwise they wouldn't have available to them. So even though it's more work, in that sense I like it and I feel like more of their work is out there, and the communication is more than it was before."

It is worth noting the phrase "out there," which suggests potential access but not guaranteed communication. Some teachers wondered how many parents actually read their blog posts, and a few noted that some parents now felt disconnected from the classroom because they preferred paper communication. This concern was echoed by middle and high school teachers who questioned what digital course resources parents even accessed, if any at all. The idea that "the communication is more" thus lived alongside questions as to whether posting more information always resulted in connection. Some teacher comments reflected an ambivalence about how different forms of communication should accommodate parents:

> But that's hard too, because I just received emails today from a parent who is asking me questions about things that I already have written on a blog or have already emailed out, and that's hard for me because I want to say, "Oh, I just posted about this!" . . . You want to say, "Look here for the answer because I've talked about this." But I won't do that because I don't feel like that's professional. . . . I will answer her question, but it's hard because there's a trail you can easily get to because everything has been electronic, and I feel like if she had done the work to look, she would have found her answer and instead it's easiest to type, "Here's my question." It's not easiest for me, but that's easiest for parents.

Such comments implied a sense that posting information digitally should create accountability for parents to know about everything that was posted, and thus reduce the need for parents to contact the teacher personally. Uncertain about the effectiveness of this digital communication, other teachers expressed a desire for face-to-face interactions, even if in the hallway, lobby, or student pick-up car line after school, so they might touch base with parents. Despite such efforts by teachers, sometimes ambiguity remained, and with the teacher now just an email away, it was easy for parents to generate more communication.

Some teachers wondered whether the increase in information sent home digitally might be straining connections rather than enhancing them. One commented, "I just feel like because of all the technology, that the communication is so constant, there's never a down time. And we've fed into that. . . . I don't have an opinion over one way is good and one way is bad—I'm just saying it's another piece of communication . . . because of everybody having technology." This concern found a ready echo among parents, to whom we turn next for their side of the story.

Parent Perceptions

Like teachers, parents expressed appreciation for the new digital channels of communication and the ease of information flow that they enabled, while also expressing reservations. Parents varied in their preference for digital versus paper communication, and their reasons were not necessarily rooted in resistance to digital communication in general. One parent, for instance, reflected on how receiving emails about his child's work disconnected the information from interaction with his child. When the child brought home something she had done in school on paper, it sparked a parent-child conversation in which the child could explain what she had been doing. The email, by contrast, was often received at a different time, perhaps while the parent was at work. Even if the parent enjoyed viewing what was sent, he noticed that it was less likely to lead to interaction later. The moment for interaction had passed by in the child's absence, and the email might not come to mind again at the right time.

Other parents described a struggle to keep up with the new volume of information arriving digitally.[6] As one put it, "It's through mostly email. And it does seem like a lot. . . . My husband and I don't often read the emails from the schools. We read the class blog posts for the week, but I don't always—because it's just a time thing. And then I feel guilty because I don't read it." Others found it easier to skim the emails and ignore the blog. These reactions may be driven not only by the actual scale of school communications but also by the fact that these communications were arriving through a channel already overloaded from multiple sources. As communication becomes cheaper and more convenient, it is easy to produce more of it. This risks training the receiver of high-volume communications (such as email and blog posts) to assume that they are not vital and can be ignored. It can also create stress and guilt when keeping up proves all but impossible. In either case, more is not necessarily more effective.[7]

The increase in digitally accessible information did not, in the minds of parents, reduce the importance of face-to-face communication with teachers. Nor did they feel that their access to teachers had been taken away. As one commented,

I think the face-to-face . . . I enjoy that also. It's nice to be able to do that rather than just the parent-teacher conferences and things. We pick up and drop off too, so it's nice to be able to go in and have that accessibility but I do feel like there are options, right? So, there's a lot of communication that we see in many different ways, but if we want to go face-to-face and talk to somebody directly about that, we can still do that. So, I don't think the accessibility has changed or been hindered by the technology necessarily.

Another described teachers as "super available." We will explore in the next chapter some of the implications of teachers increasing their digital communication practices while also remaining "super available" in person.

Information, Communication, Community

Digital communication generates a sense of possibility. With digital tools, more can be shared, access can be made more constant, and the sharing can happen through more vivid media. Teachers and parents certainly appreciated the newfound capacities for tracking student progress, keeping key information visible, and capturing moments of classroom learning. At the same time, the medium matters, bringing questions of time, presence, attentiveness, and well-being to the fore. Physical objects can facilitate conversation, as when a child hands a painting to a parent. The same can in principle happen with digital artifacts, yet their asynchronous nature reduces the chances of parents and children being in the same space when communications are received. When we add the increase in the sheer quantity of messages, efforts to communicate digitally can result in superficial engagement, missed messages, or even guilt and avoidance. Our conversations with parents and teachers point to some ways in which thinking about technology and Christian community requires more than quantity of communication and transparency of access. Good communication between school and home is about more than the availability of information. The key challenges have to do with our ability to remain constructively and intentionally engaged with one another. Here the effects of digital communication appear to be mixed. We explore this further in the next chapter, shifting the focus from communication to workload.

For Reflection and Response

- What strategies might a school adopt to build on the benefits of digital communication while mitigating the risks?
- Review the challenges that you experience personally with managing digital communication. How might similar challenges affect administrators, teachers, parents, and students in relation to school communications?
- How might our approaches to digital communication do to others what we would have them do to us?

CHAPTER 38

Time, Workload, and Boundaries

I was teaching a student, three years ago I think it was, and it was one of the first months. He was sitting in front of his laptop just staring at it. His mom comes in and says, "Well, what are you doing?" He says, "Well, I emailed Mr. [Name] and I'm waiting for the answer." He's just sitting there. In the meantime, I'm coaching soccer, I'm nowhere near the computer.

Teacher

One important way that technology has affected the teacher's role and the dynamics of community life is that it blurs the edges of the school day. Modern Christian Schools' attempts to be discerning with digital technology included efforts to maintain the boundaries that keep inappropriate content from students. A less immediately visible set of boundary questions concern time and space. When is "school time" if tasks and teachers can be accessed digitally late into the evening and on weekends? What are the boundaries of the home when the school has a digitally mediated presence there? When can teachers or students think of themselves as no longer "at work" or being productive? What does the way we navigate such boundaries tell us about our values and identity?[1]

Thirty years ago, a teacher's availability was defined by their presence in the school or, in rare cases, on the phone. Time in school was focused on teaching, with some preparation and grading work in the evenings. Homework and notes to parents went home in backpacks. A few times per year, teachers and parents sat down to discuss student progress during a short parent-teacher conference. In the northern United States, snow days made everything stop. When the weather was severe, students and teachers enjoyed freedom from schoolwork.

In a digital landscape, these boundaries evaporate.[2] At Modern Christian Schools, digital technology has made teachers potentially available via email, text, and video chat at any time. Students can now access school tasks at any time, including on snow days. The example described at the head of this chapter is an amusing outlier but also hints at a broader increased expectation of teacher availability outside school hours. These changes seem to fulfill a key promise of technology, allowing flexible learning and scheduling and removing limitations. They also have significant implications for workload. If we are to think of technological change in the context of Christian community, we have to ask not just about our own convenience but about whether our usage patterns are creating undue pressures for particular community members.

Blurring Boundaries

Our conversations with teachers highlighted several areas in which eroded boundaries increased workload pressures. We will take a brief look at five of them here.

Access to Teachers

One source of pressure was increased teacher availability. Students at Modern Christian Schools valued after-hours access to teachers. "It's really important with teachers," a high school student commented, "because you only see them for 45 minutes a day, so at nine o'clock at night, when you finally get to that homework and you have a question, they're still there because you can email them." Teachers, in turn, felt pressure from students to be available. "A big challenge," one noted, "is that expectation that . . . since this is so fast, you just click, and you have access, and that you're also available, and . . . eagerly willing to respond." Another concurred, "A lot of them expect the teachers are online ready to answer questions in the evening." Several teachers also felt an implicit pressure from their social environment to check email often and be constantly available. "I think that's hard to navigate," one commented, "because everybody feels like we need to be reachable at all times. Like it's not okay to not answer your cell phone."

In spite of the pressure to respond, some teachers found positive value in the increased immediacy of response. A teacher reflected,

I would say that I have lots of emails, but I appreciate them because I can address the student's concerns. . . . A student who was absent today emailed me and said, "I am trying what I'm working on, but I'm not understanding it." And I'm like, "Well that makes sense because you didn't do the lab today because you weren't here to do it." But I can still say, "Here's a link, here's a website, go check this out." I can take care of it right now. That still took me five, ten minutes because I went and searched the internet.

This teacher went on to note that emailed questions can mean "now I'm done trying to figure it out on my own." They therefore focused on teaching skills for searching online and alternative strategies beyond emailing the teacher.

Monitoring Home Activity

The new level of connection between school and home was not just in one direction. Now that homework was timestamped, patterns in students' homework habits and home supervision became visible to teachers. Some took opportunities to discuss this with students: "It's a more organic conversation for me, where a student this year, she says, 'I was watching YouTube until 2:00 a.m.,' and I'm like, 'Oh. Yeah. Sleep is pretty important don't you think?' And [she says], '. . . but this blogger and this blogger and this person . . .' So, it's more of a conversation when it comes up or when you notice, 'Hey, you were emailing me at 12:00 a.m.'" Teachers had varied policies and expectations concerning when and how students could contact them, and this created some uncertainty for students. High school students, especially, noted how they were not always certain how to best communicate with particular teachers.

Some teachers also wondered aloud about how to talk with parents about boundaries at home: "We can make suggestions to parents and we can say, even at the conference time . . . it's okay to tell them, 'I notice that they're emailing. . . . How long are they spending on their computer? Where did they have their computer when they're doing their homework? Do you notice that they're flipping between things like Facebook and homework?' And then just kind of giving some suggestions." Teachers reported being encouraged to send home suggestions concerning time use with technology. However, they also expressed uncertainty about how far their role extended. Some expressed discomfort with telling parents what to do at home. Was students' behavior at home and at night now the teacher's responsibility? Some administrators felt this to be the case. As one explained, "It just is unfortunately part of the responsibility we've taken on, and a part of it is because we own the device, and that's strong and valuable and helpful, but if it wasn't our device, we probably wouldn't look over their shoulder quite as much." Another concurred, noting that "we do own some of the responsibility because, regardless ... we are introducing things to kids at different paces than their parents might choose if it were totally up to them, so there is some responsibility that we bear." This extension of responsibility created some new pressures for teachers negotiating the interface between school and home.

Maintaining Online Presence

A further source of added workload involved maintaining an online presence to share classroom work with parents. Some teachers embraced this work with enthusiasm, some were more skeptical, but all believed it was necessary to "keep up." One related,

> I've thought about this a lot recently, the cost of—the time it takes. . . . I sat down earlier this summer and spent umpteen hours setting up my websites for this year. I thought, is this . . . really worth it? Is this valuable? Do the kids appreciate it? Is it used? . . . Is it the most efficient use of my time and their time? But I guess what I keep coming back to is . . . education isn't moving to eliminate technology. And when I remind myself of that, and that it is valuable to find efficient uses for it, and the fact that there's always going to be new apps, and new ideas, and new games . . . when I let myself pick out what is best for now, and continue to add things—and let myself remember that [I'll] have to add things later . . . [it] feels like, okay, we're doing something right.

Teachers involved with online professional learning communities also emphasized how much time reading and contributing to online groups consumed. They recognized the benefits; for example, a Spanish teacher commented that digital technology "puts at your fingertips all kinds of professional development and collaborative [opportunities] with teachers all over the world." Remaining engaged with all of these new channels of information created new possibilities for learning and also involved substantial time commitments.

Grading Rhythms

We saw signs that the speed of technology in grading tests and quizzes may be affecting students' expectations of teachers. A survey comment seen from many students early in the one-to-one initiative was their growing appreciation for taking tests and quizzes online because of the immediate feedback. Teachers, too, affirmed this as one area where time could be saved. However, they also highlighted challenges associated with the expectation of speed. "A student emails you," one commented, "and they say, 'Well, where are my grades?' We just took the quiz five minutes ago." "Someone turns in something a month late," another lamented, "and you take a week to grade it, and they say, 'Where's my grade, do you have my grade?'" Efficiency gains created increased pressures and expectations and therefore a need for developing explicit, intentional boundaries and practices to clarify what might be reasonable.

Parent Communication

The expectation of swift response also affected parent communications. Email enables more communication addressed to the teacher directly while in the classroom or at home. A teacher reported that even though school policy required appointments to be arranged through the office, parents emailed during the school day: "The communication expectation is almost sometimes instantaneous. . . . We're in a service-oriented business, so you do it and keep parents happy. But it's 3:00 and [the message is] 'I'm picking up [my daughter] at 3:05.' . . . There's an expectation, I think, . . . I don't know if it's from the school, but certainly from our parent base that I am on all the time." Some felt that this pressure toward immediacy was stronger from parents than from students: "We don't have it from kids, but parents assume that we are on 24/7." Pressures from school administration and parents to keep up swift responsiveness to parent communication added another challenge to the demands of teaching.

Developing Community Norms

As the technology program at Modern Christian Schools developed, strategies and policies for addressing risks such as pornography, plagiarism, and social media were soon considered and formalized. Guidelines for navigating the erosion of traditional time boundaries were not so quick to emerge and have remained largely up to individual teachers to navigate. There have been localized initiatives within the school day, such as the high school's PowerDown period, in which students set digital devices aside for a time. As we saw in chapter 31, planning meetings occasionally floated the idea of a sabbath from digital communication, but without moving to whole-school implementation. At the time of our study, a decade into the one-to-one initiative, stable community norms for teacher time, workload, and communication patterns had not yet fully emerged.

This lack of clear, shared boundaries created ambiguous messages and teacher uncertainty in areas where the development of thoughtful, explicit community boundaries might be helpful. Norms around frequency of communication, the degree of teacher availability, grading

> **Pressures of Digital Communication**
>
> Digital communication pressures that erode former boundaries of time and space and create workload challenges include the following:
>
> - Access to teachers at all hours of the day and evening
> - Teacher responsibility for monitoring student work patterns at home
> - Teacher maintenance of online presence
> - Increased expectation of instant feedback and grading
> - Increased direct communication from parents to teachers during the school day

timelines, the extension of learning support beyond the school day, and the degree of responsibility that should be taken for mentoring parents were all areas where teachers experienced pressures. The practice of allowing teachers to set their own norms in such areas had the merit of allowing for professional judgment. However, the awareness that norms varied, and that others might be responding more frequently to digital communications, also left teachers feeling pressure to be maximally available. When some offer more accessibility than others, it is easy for students, parents, and teachers themselves to sense the highest level of availability as an implicit best case toward which behavior should drift. Maintaining clear community expectations calls for ongoing whole-school conversation and communication.

One teacher's comment expressed a key factor informing the need for clear community conversation about boundaries: "My priority is always going to be the child in front of me, always. No matter what." Positively, this commitment relativizes the importance of digital communication: when teaching students, emails and blog posts can wait. Teachers need community permission to voice and commit to such priorities and sometimes not be immediately available so that communication does not compete with teaching. Perhaps other community members could assist with immediate parent needs, with some boundaries placed around teacher availability. At the same time, this teacher's affirmation invites some difficult questions. When is the child "in front of" the teacher? Are they present to the teacher and an immediate priority when they send a query late at night from their own home? When does virtual space (email, video chat, discussion boards) become the space in which it is necessary to be present? What if the teacher's conscientious commitment to be present combines with ever-present channels of digital communication to create unhealthy or unsustainable patterns of engagement for the teacher beyond the bounds of the working day? Such questions do not have immediately obvious answers. Perhaps they do not have correct answers, only answers that are found to contribute to the thriving of all members of the community.

Administrators were aware of the temptation to overwork. One commented that "in general we have hard-working teachers who want to do well, to their credit. They'll work themselves to the bone if that's what's put out there." Another expressed concern about a trend toward overwork in the schools' culture:

> We are inherently valuable . . . as spouses, as children, as parents, as siblings, but also as children of God. . . . You are not just a teacher. Do not believe that lie. Do not be here all the time—go home! That's a concern of mine. Because this Midwestern culture of "Do, do, do, do, do," I'm still coping with that, to be frank. It's busy here, and I do not want to create a culture where my staff believes they're only what they do, and the lesson plans they create or don't create, and the experiences they give. [We need] a larger picture of what life is—not only in Christ, but giving to their families, and their friends, and their communities. And so, do not just be the teacher who's here twelve, thirteen, fifteen, sixteen hours a day. . . . That's not good for anyone.

Administrators described some efforts to relieve workload pressures by encouraging teachers to focus on specific areas of technology imple-

mentation at a given time and adjusting the timing of collaboration meetings. Yet the broader erosion of boundaries of time and space makes the
exhortation to not "be here all the time" ambiguous, because "here" is
no longer a clearly bounded space. Digital communication reinforces the
cultural pressure toward maximum productivity by making any minute of
the day and any day of the week a time when teachers can be at work, on
call, and subject to perceived or actual community expectations regarding
their prompt response.[3] The faith-informed desire to serve others and meet
their needs may actually intensify this dynamic.

Navigating New Pressures

The new patterns of availability created by digital technologies force to the
forefront a number of challenging questions for a Christian community.
How should the relationship between school and home function now that
students can access teachers from home, the school has a digital presence
in the home, and parents can directly message teachers during classroom
instruction? How can clear, shared boundaries be defined and maintained
in the face of the patterns of engagement fostered by the sheer ease of
digital communication? How can the community form communication
practices (and the self-discipline needed to sustain them) that reflect an
understanding of the pressures created for other community members?
What patterns of digital communication might best help teachers, parents,
and students to each flourish in their callings? What implied messages and
new habits are students picking up in terms of their own use of time and
communication possibilities based on teachers' patterns of work and availability? Addressing these questions remains an ongoing task at Modern
Christian Schools.

Where such boundary questions are not addressed communally, it is
left up to individuals to find ad hoc solutions and negotiate their own truces.
For many teachers this creates pressure toward the most heroic degrees of
availability and engagement and generates uncertainty about where the
norms should be and whether they are doing well. As with monitoring student access to harmful internet content, there is a danger of unreasonable
pressure being placed on some community members for the convenience
of the rest. Navigating the pressures of the new digital medium is one area
in which the idea of Christian community may need to function not only
as the goal but also as the means: the community needs to work together

to intentionally develop and monitor shared boundaries and expectations. This is not a simple task, but it is an important one if the schools are to successfully address the human cost of increased connectivity.

For Reflection and Response

- Who should be responsible for managing the workload implications of increased connectivity?
- What is gained or lost as boundaries of space and time erode and the school reaches into the home and parents reach into the classroom?
- How might a school community go about balancing the desire to serve students well and the need to help teachers thrive?

Part 6 Summary

In this part of the book we focused on how working with new technologies has affected perceptions and realities regarding relationships and Christian community.

- There was a clear, articulate concern among members of Modern Christian Schools about the impact of technology on relationships and the life of the community. This relational emphasis was being worked out in terms of an intentional focus on nurturing grace-filled relationships within the school, with the wider parent community, and with people encountered online beyond the boundaries of the school.
- One source of pressure on traditional models of classroom relationships is the capacity of digital technology to decenter the teacher's expertise and allow students to become experts. This requires teachers to yield some control over learning, but this has not been experienced by teachers at Modern Christian Schools as a move away from Christian education. A focus on dialogue around learning and interdependent community helped teachers place Christian learning in the context of collaboration and mutual support.
- The schools hoped that working with digital technologies would increase collaborative learning. Observation data suggested that the amount of collaborative learning taking place may be lower than the best-case examples might suggest. However, collaboration and individual screen time overlapped to a considerable degree, and students were more likely to be genuinely collaborating with one another when learning with devices than when they were not.
- Although school documents sometimes positioned parents largely as receivers of information, they also revealed a vision for involving parents in the process of discernment. Teachers worked to include parents as audiences for student work. Parent satisfaction with school communication was high, and a high percentage of parents reported

talking with their children regularly about discernment with digital technology. Parents were less likely than teachers to talk with students about using technology to bring change to the world.

- Using online grade reporting, email, and blogs increased the immediacy of communication among teachers, students, and parents. Teachers were positive about the enhancement of what could be communicated, while also pointing to pressures created by their increased availability. Parents, too, were often appreciative of the new channels of communication, while some expressed reservations related to the benefits of some kinds of paper communication and the challenge of managing email.

- A significant effect of digital communication was to blur the boundaries between school and home and between the working day and leisure time. Increased access to teachers, monitoring of home activity, online communication, and pressures for swift grading all contributed to increased workload pressures. Teachers were working to find solutions individually, while feeling pressure to be maximally engaged and available. More intentional community-level work at setting boundaries may help reduce the risk of unreasonable demands created by increased immediacy of communication.

CHAPTER 39

The Finish Line Keeps Moving

Where will the future bring us? We can't readily answer that. But we do have a direction. And that direction does not lack in challenges. We are constantly challenged to stay current with technology. There is a perpetual need for funding for replacement and growth. With this staffing and training needs increase. Yet, we remain resolved to continue to provide an innovative and excellent learning environment for all students.

School document

Anyone who has stayed with us this far has seen a range of findings about how Modern Christian Schools are learning to live together with digital technology. This final chapter draws together a few major threads, though there are several reasons why we hesitate to think of it as a conclusion. The process of technological change is ongoing, and the factors involved are too complex to pretend that the data that we have presented encompass everything that is happening or lead to a neat conclusion. As members of the Modern Christian Schools community themselves pointed out when they read earlier drafts of this book, the schools and their approach to teaching with technology have continued to evolve since we collected our data. Devices and the wider context continue to change. Individual teachers speak of moving from intensive use of digital devices to minimal use and back again as they seek the right equilibrium. What was once new and challenging becomes routine, and then is placed in question afresh as teachers wonder what they have begun to take for granted. The Modern Christian Schools community is not a static specimen. It is an active community of teachers and learners that has long been invested in questioning and looking to improve its own practices. When we discussed some of the findings of the book with teachers and administrators at the schools, they immediately began talking about what they might change in response; the act of completing this study has itself already begun to change the community that we have described. Considered as a portrait of the schools, this book is like a photograph taken partway through a journey. It can capture some of the action and the current direction of travel, but we should not put too much confidence in our ability to predict what happens next, especially when the finish line keeps moving.

We also need to underline again the limitations on how far the findings that we have presented at Modern Christian Schools can be generalized. A significant part of what we have set out to show is how the specific beliefs, values, commitments, and context of a particular group of schools have played a role in shaping the impact of digital technologies. Digital media and devices are not an inexorable force, bound to have exactly the same effects regardless of our responses. Rather, they have been intentionally taken up by the school community within the context of their own mission, resources, skills, and practices. No doubt, technological change has been shaping their community in ways they might not have chosen. But they have also been finding ways to shape the process of change that do seem to be helping their students learn a responsible relationship to their devices within the context of Christian education. Other schools can learn from this process, but it will not be a matter of assuming that our findings here will play out in exactly the same way elsewhere, with different students, parents, teachers, leaders, theologies, and cultural contexts. Our research has been designed to help us get a detailed picture of what is happening in Modern Christian Schools, not to prove that exactly the same is happening everywhere.

What, then, do we hope that readers might have learned from our narrative? Another point noted in our opening chapter was that we were not aiming for clear-cut, universal solutions, but instead sought fruitful questions, fresh possibilities, and wise strategies for action. We hope that leaders and teachers in other schools can use this book in a manner similar to the way we often read biographies, not with the notion that we can live exactly the life described, but with the awareness that someone else's story can face us with questions that we need to resolve in our own context. It was to this end that we added questions for reflection to each chapter. We hope that readers will have been asking throughout the book, If this is how it happened there, do I see any similar trends and challenges in my own school setting? How do *we* need to respond? What are *we* not addressing? What motivates and inspires *us*? It would be laborious at this point to repeat the findings and questions highlighted in each chapter and already summarized at the end of each part. Instead, we will underline a few recurring themes that seem particularly important for other schools to consider. They are not the only ones we could have chosen, but perhaps they can serve to bring a few key issues into focus.

Complexity, Investment, Discernment

Throughout the book we have resisted a simple story of technology as just a tool that offers to extend our capacities for getting things done and then either succeeds or fails at the task. It is true that one of technology's functions is as a tool, but to look only at its tool-like effects and ask things like whether it improves test scores is to drastically oversimplify the landscape. The other views of technology threaded throughout this book remind us that when we adopt a new technology, it also functions as a new medium in which we work and around and through which we interact. We begin to adjust our patterns of behavior and communication to the new medium, and so we become reshaped by the very tools that we shaped. We design cars to get across cities and soon live and move in cities designed for cars. New technologies also take shape in new practices that begin to reorganize our time and energy, and the practices that we adopt around new technologies help determine what they will come to mean. This gives us a richer set of questions to ask than "Does it work?"

The trouble with "Does it work?" thinking is that more than one thing is happening at once. Technologies can stretch student learning beyond the bounds of the classroom, enable increased differentiation of learning for individual interests and abilities, help promote collaboration and higher-order thinking, increase communication between school and home, and extend possibilities for service and witness. At the very same time, those same technologies may bring consumerism into the classroom, add powerful distractions to the learning environment, push us toward information overload, and erode boundaries between work and rest and between school and home. We could pick half of this story and use it to underwrite a narrative about digital technology being the greatest thing that has happened to transform education or about digital technology being the dark force that endangers students' growth. As we have found when sharing some results from our research, both technology boosters and technology skeptics are ready with a "yes, but . . ." when presented with evidence that strikes them as a little too positive or too negative. From the beginning of our work on this book, we did not set out to bolster one side of this cultural divide, and our conclusion is not a thumbs up or a thumbs down. Instead, we want to emphasize that all of the things that we have described across dozens of chapters are happening at once, at one and the same time. The effects of technological change are complex, and reducing them to simple optimism or pessimism misrepresents what is happening. What schools have to ponder and address is multiple effects unfolding simultaneously.

One key factor that stands out in Modern Christian Schools' efforts to get their arms around this complexity is investment. Part of what drew us to Modern Christian Schools as a site for research was the fact that they had not embarked lightly on the shift to digitally mediated learning, and so offered an example of thoughtful, intentional integration of technology into Christian school practices. This process required significant investments. These included investments in the technological devices (hardware, software) and infrastructure, the renovation of physical spaces (school buildings and classrooms), personnel (technology coordinators, IT support teams, etc.), and training (professional development within school and outside school). Administrators emphasized that these specific types of investments, although well beyond the scope of what most other schools were doing at the time of Modern Christian Schools' technology program launch, were essential to success. While not every school will invest on the scale of Modern Christian Schools, it remains the case that investing in technological change in a pedagogically responsible and fruitful manner requires considerable investment, not only in the cost of devices, but in the cost of infrastructure, support, and training, and in the human cost of time and effort given to transforming practice. One administrator suggested that for any school considering a similar journey, "whatever you're anticipating for professional development, it's not enough." All of these processes absorb resources (material and human) that could have been directed otherwise, and they are challenging to sustain. Teachers who were recently new to the school suggested to us that support and training had been scaled back significantly since the early days, with some reporting limited guidance on technology use as they joined the school. Veteran teachers reported the same trend, sensing a responsibility to try to bring new colleagues up to speed themselves.

A second key factor is mission. We began the book with a focus on the schools' mission because it was a strong sense of mission that drove the substantial initial investment in digital technology and the accompanying process of reshaping the schools' practices. As one administrator put it, "You have to remember this is about people, not about devices. That becomes very clear the deeper you get into this. Everybody wants to start the conversation about 'Do we do tablets? Do we do Chromebooks? Do we do MacBooks?' and that's the wrong place to start the conversation. If they start there, they haven't answered the question 'Why?'" The level of investment needed indeed requires an answer to the "why" question. Modern Christian Schools committed to a vision of redefining what school looked like, hoping that this would further their mission of providing a world-transformative Christian education. This meant that the emphasis on investment went along with the constant emphasis on Christian discernment that we have noted in various chapters. The goal was not simply to get up to date in technological terms but to put new technologies to wise Christian use. We have sought through various means to probe into the ways in which this was happening and the ways in which it proved challenging. As with investment in training, sustaining a shared understanding of Christian discernment with technology has been a challenge as the new has become the routine and time pressures have focused energies on the pragmatic. Even under constant vigilance, it is hard work to keep distinctive Christian understandings from being absorbed into broader societal or educational narratives. Yet the motivation among teachers and administrators to provide a genuine Christian nurture in the new pedagogical environment remains strong, even as some express a need to find time for the big-picture conversations that drove initial change.

A third key factor shaping Modern Christian Schools' responses to new technologies is the emphasis on building a culture of learning. We heard consistent comments on technology being used not simply because it is new and attractive, but rather in ways that would support learning within the parameters of the schools' mission. This entailed building a school culture in which teachers were free to play and experiment with technology and abandon tools and practices that did not enhance learning. It meant learning to live with a more dynamic curriculum, one crafted in part by teachers and informed by the unpredictability of the online environment. It meant allowing shifts in the implied authority and expertise structures in the classroom to push teachers and learners into more collaborative, differentiated, and inclusive patterns of teaching and learning. This third factor is closely tied to the first two. For the technology program to yield successful results, significant investment was needed not only in technological resources but also in training and in time for teachers to learn and experiment. This training and time were crucial if the ongoing process of change was to remain at all grounded in the schools' mission and faith commitments. Even with all the investments that took place, there was still a felt need among teachers and administrators for more time to reflect well on what was happening and how things were changing.

Faith and Practice

We described at the outset how we found in the Modern Christian Schools community not a single model of how faith shapes education but a complex tapestry of strategies. We found that many teachers at Modern Christian Schools were familiar with approaches to faith and learning that have influenced many other Christian schools. Some recalled a past emphasis on character and Bible knowledge. Many thought in terms of the importance of fostering a Christian perspective on subject matter and nurturing a Christian worldview. Various parts of the community had a clear concern for maintaining moral boundaries and wrestled with the question of how the boundaries of the school community might be both made more porous in the interests of missional outreach and kept safe in relation to nurturing students' personal and spiritual growth. As we have seen, none of these approaches have become irrelevant simply because learning devices have changed. What may have become more pressing, however, is the need to think beyond questions of belief and moral safety and consider both faith and technology as they relate to our practices.

We have noted in various parts of the book how strategies for tethering teaching and technology to faith were distributed unevenly. Parents were the most likely to talk about questions of moral purity, and also made reference to Christian perspectives. A focus on perspectives or worldview was also common among teachers, along with an emphasis on practices and relationships. Administrators were by far the most likely to appeal to mission categories, along with a focus on Christian perspectives and practices. This signals not so much disagreement or conflict as a variety of emphases.

Interestingly, while the idea of Christian perspectives or worldview was relatively common among all groups, it tended to be associated mostly with critiquing the content encountered through digital media rather than technological practices themselves. Yet many of the ways in which the schools were most clearly pushing back against the default tendencies of digital media had to do with practices. While it would be false to artificially separate beliefs and practices, it was when beliefs were embodied in shared practices such as worship, sabbath, slow reading, fasting, witness, and service that the schools were visibly shaping a learning environment oriented toward students living into discerning technology use. Conversely, the concerns explored in earlier chapters about student investment in shopping in class, poor time management, or digital distractions are matters of practice. Given how technology functions as a medium helping to shape our thinking and behavior, beliefs alone may well not be enough to create a countercurrent. Christian discernment with technology involves figuring out how to live together, not just what to believe.

Modern Christian Schools are working to build a pattern of shared Christian practice around digital technology. Other schools looking to do the same will need to consider not only how to manage the logistics of new devices and resources but how to build and sustain a schoolwide conversation about how faith informs practice. As we have seen, this may not be a tidy conversation; different sectors of the school community will bring their own concerns, perspectives, and understandings of faith and mission to the table. These varying perspectives can become resources if there is space for regular, thoughtful consideration of how learning practices and technology practices relate to basic faith commitments. The investment needed in technological change includes investment in communal discernment.

Individual and Community

The relationship between the individual and the community and the role of shared practices are themes that have echoed through several parts of the book. In the context of a deeply individualistic North American culture, it is not surprising to find a strong strand of thinking in the school community that focuses on individual autonomy. We see this, for instance, when students express the belief that making their own choices about when to disengage from learning and turn to digital entertainment should be acceptable, or that those who choose to be distracted should be left to take the consequences. We see it in the reluctance of students to intervene when others are making poor choices. We also see it in the similar inclination of some teachers to maximize freedom for students to face the consequences of their own failings, and in the tendency for school leaders to allow individual teachers to set many of their own boundaries with regard to technology rhythms. Even a term such as *sabbath*, which used to name a community-wide, socially enforced practice, is used mainly in the context of individual choice. Digital media themselves, with their powerful tools for authoring individual profiles, identities, and choices, exert pressure in the direction of individual autonomy.

Alongside this robust individualism we see a parallel instinct to affirm the importance of community and belonging. We found traces of periodic discussions of how to implement a sabbath, and of the need to partner with parents and churches. We see a community-oriented impulse in practices such as filtering and monitoring, regular communal worship, and a collective "PowerDown" time in which to spend time away from devices. Such practices were not offered as individual preferences but structured into everyone's week. Discussions of discernment revealed a desire to engage the whole community in helping students grow in wisdom, treating student work not simply as an individual creative product but as something addressed to a community audience. Teachers' investment in using digital technology to enhance differentiation in their teaching reflected not just a valuing of each individual student but a desire that each be included in the learning community. Digital media themselves, although they promise individual self-expression, draw us into a pattern of practices of interaction and communication that are shared society-wide and influence how we relate to others.

Exactly what the balance should be between individual responsibility and community norms is hardly a question that we can resolve here. Yet it is one that any school working through the shift to digital technology must implicitly or explicitly address in its pedagogy and technological practices, for it is a practical as well as a theological question. Schools have to figure out how much of the burden should be placed on individual student willpower when it comes to poor choices with high-distraction devices and how much of it should be placed on the supportive structure of shared practices. Schools would also do well to give explicit consideration to when allowing different classroom choices to be made by teachers reflects appropriate professional judgment and when it creates mixed messages that allow a drift toward less healthy patterns of practice, whether this is in terms of student device use or teacher workload. The impulse to create space for students to make their own choices, and to learn from the consequences of their failures, also has to be squared with the effect of individuals' choices on other students around them and with students' varied capacity for resisting temptation. Such considerations return us once more to the question of how a school might sustain a thoughtful, communal conversation about faith and technology practices amid the constant pressure to attend to the next task, the next message, the next change.

Such questions are partly practical, partly philosophical and theological, and partly constrained by the local culture of particular schools and communities. One-size-fits-all answers are therefore unlikely to work well. We do, however, come away from our research convinced that if Christian schools are to approach digital learning with discernment, then they must engage in some careful thinking and conversation on the individual's relationship to the community and the way in which shared practices can support individual growth.

Living with Discernment

As we have seen throughout, even given the massive investment of time, resources, and reflection, these questions are not fully resolved at Modern Christian Schools. This is not a criticism. Indeed, the schools' own awareness that the task of figuring out how to teach well with technology is complex and ongoing fueled their willingness to participate in our research. Throughout our study, school administrators, teachers, students, and parents were warmly welcoming and cooperative. They made themselves available inside and outside school hours for research conversations and were frank in their judgments about their own practices. Our goal has been neither to gloss over imperfections nor to foreground hidden faults, but to enter into their existing desire to continue to understand and improve their own practice. We met with a general readiness to learn from what we might discover, and we frequently heard expressions of thanks for taking the time to invest in the research. Our predominant experience when interacting with administrators, teachers, parents, and students was of eagerness to see the research succeed, gratitude for the information it might provide for school improvement, and openness to learning more about what was or was not working. In this sense Modern Christian Schools modeled well what it might mean to be modern Christian schools that are on a journey with no clear finish line and ill-defined boundaries but are committed to an ongoing investment in Christian discernment with technology.

Research Methods

This appendix extends chapter 4, providing a more substantive account of the methodological design used in the Technology and Educational Flourishing (TEF) project at a level of detail not needed by all readers. The overarching research design selected for this study was a fully integrated mixed design that engages both quantitative and qualitative data through all phases of the research process, from data collection through the processes of analysis and inference.[1] The benefit of such an approach is that both qualitative and quantitative methods drive and inform the ongoing research processes. A finding from the analysis of data from any particular method in year one, for instance, might lead to emergent findings and new research questions previously unconsidered. These may then shape in new ways the data collection or analysis in subsequent years. Choosing a dynamic and responsive methodological design offers a way to conduct a multiyear, longitudinal study with recognition that schools are constantly shifting systems.[2] It is certain that factors like changing personnel, ongoing professional development, shifts in curriculum or technological devices, and even the presence of the researchers are shaping changes in technology use and pedagogy over the course of time. We therefore leverage a method that provides a contextualized understanding of this change to understand not merely the outcomes of technology use but the processes and effects of such change.

Additionally, a fully integrated mixed design promotes an exploration of multiple perspectives (administrators, teachers, parents, students, and alumni) at multiple levels (school system, classroom, and individual). This design avoids limiting our understanding to a narrow view of technology in education by focusing on only specific perspectives, and instead widens our understanding to reveal a complex tapestry.[3] It reduces the limitations associated with the use of a single method and allows the research questions to drive the selection of methods.[4] It encourages reflexivity and promotes responsive changes during the research process.[5] Ultimately, this methodological choice allows researchers to develop a multifaceted understanding of the processes and outcomes of technological change within school communities. The fully integrated mixed design provided a valid and reliable empirical design for examining dynamic technological change over time in a faith-based school community.

The fully integrated mixed design included five distinct methods of data collection: classroom observations, surveys, focus groups, case studies, and documentary analysis of digital files. Using a multiphase design, the data was collected and analyzed in cycles. Table A.1 provides a general outline of the data collection and analysis phases. Phase 1 data collection included classroom observations, student and teacher surveys, focus groups, and archived digital artifacts. Phase 2 included additional focus groups; student, alumni, and teacher surveys; classroom observations; and case studies. Phase 3 concluded with focus groups and alumni and parent surveys. Each phase aligned with an academic school year, including the following summer (e.g., phase 1 = year 1 [fall through summer]).

Table A.1. Mixed methods design by phase

	Phase 1		Phase 2		Phase 3	
	Data collection	Analysis	Data collection	Analysis	Data collection	Analysis
Classroom observations						
Elementary	x	x	x	x		x
Middle school	x	x	x	x		x
High school	x	x	x	x		x
Surveys						
Students	x	x	x	x		x
Teachers	x	x	x	x		x
Alumni			x	x	x	x
Parents					x	x
Focus groups						
Students	x	x	x	x	x	x

	Phase 1		Phase 2		Phase 3	
	Data collection	Analysis	Data collection	Analysis	Data collection	Analysis
Teachers	x	x	x	x	x	x
Administrators	x		x	x	x	x
Parents			x	x	x	x
Documentary analysis						
All digital files	x	x		x		x
Case studies						
Elementary			x	x		x
Middle school			x	x		x
High school			x	x		x

The fully integrated mixed design acts as a methodological frame, a structure within which all particular methods take place. Each individual method is guided by best practices in empirical research. For this reason, we first describe the individual data collection methods and analysis steps particular to any single method, and then describe the mixed methods analytical procedures that supported the findings highlighted in this book.

Individual Methods

The five distinct methods of data collection (classroom observations, surveys, focus groups, case studies, and documentary analysis of digital files) were outlined briefly in chapter 4. Each is described in greater detail below.

Classroom Observations

Seventy-five classroom observations of randomly selected K–12 teachers for a period of 30–45 minutes (data collection: phases 1–2; analysis: phases 1–3)

Design and Collection

Observational methods have long been crucial for understanding pedagogical practices,[6] and they are an increasingly important method in educational technology research. They contribute to the development of a thick
description of actual practice in context, with attention to the complex
interactions of variables (e.g., participants, technologies, curricular content, physical space) within any given classroom. Given our intent to design
research focused more on the processes of change than a defined set of
outcomes like academic scores, observations offer contextualized glimpses
of classroom life. They target the intricacies of teaching and learning in
action and help move findings beyond oversimplified or deterministic understandings of technology in schools.[7] They also serve as a crucial point
of triangulation with other self-reported data (surveys and focus groups),
increasing validity for the entire methodological design.[8]

   In this study, random observations offered a way to develop a baseline
picture of teaching and learning in Modern Christian Schools. A sample
of seventy-five teachers was randomly selected from the entire school
system, and 30- to 45-minute observations of selected classrooms were
distributed across phases 1 and 2. This resulted in observations of thirty-
three high school, eleven middle school, and thirty-one elementary school
classrooms. With a desire to observe typical classroom practices, we provided teachers with limited notification of the observation timing to reduce
opportunities to consciously or unconsciously adjust lessons, thus limiting
response bias. The resulting observations shaped an evolving understanding of the interactions between technology and pedagogy in the everyday
life of the school.

   The observations were carried out by researchers trained to use both
running field notes and an observation protocol. The researchers designed
a classroom observation protocol that measured aspects of pedagogical
practices, technology use, and particular faith perspectives and practices.
The protocol structure also allowed researchers to account for multiple
activities simultaneously. For instance, the tool could account for classroom activities in which large or small groups interacted in different learning activities with varying types or levels of technology use. The protocol
was informed by scholarship, existing observation protocols,[9] and expert
consultation to ensure theoretical grounding and support validity.[10] Subsequent rounds of field testing and continued expert consultation led to

multiple revisions of the protocol and related training manual until final-ized. Using the final protocol and manual, six pilot observations served to establish interrater reliability at 84.67%.

Analysis

The primary analysis stemmed from the observation protocol data, which could be quantified. For example, protocol data provided discrete cate-gories of practices (direct instruction or lecture, nonacademic social in-teraction, etc.), format of participation (individual, whole class, etc.), and technology presence (digital tech in use, not in use, etc.). With this data, we could ask questions about specific relationships between variables. For example, how does student digital technology use compare in whole class versus small group learning activities? How does the duration of technol-ogy use compare from elementary to middle to high school? Do partic-ular faith practices come to the fore when teachers ask students to use one-to-one devices? Some questions were present from the outset of the research, while others emerged over time. Therefore, we used both uni-variate and descriptive analysis during phases 2 and 3 to examine a priori and emergent themes, described further in the mixed methods analytical procedures section.

The field notes served as narrative exemplars of particular types of practices, relevant for illustrating particular themes within the book, but were not analyzed in their own right. The field notes, originally handwrit-ten, were typed and then cleaned with an organization system that aligned with the protocol categories. They were then compiled in our data anal-ysis program, NVivo, using the protocol categories as identifying codes. As specific themes emerged across multiple methods and those themes were selected for inclusion in the book, the researchers returned at times to specific field notes (according to the organizational scheme and related codes) to provide examples of the theme from observations.

Surveys

Surveys of students, alumni, parents and teachers (data collection and analysis: phases 1–3)

Design and Collection

Surveys offer insight into the behavior, beliefs, and experiences of members of an educational community.[11] They provide the wide representative data from the study population that allow us to gauge community-wide agreement, disagreement, and frequencies. Our design included surveys of middle and high school students from Modern Christian Schools, high school students at Western Christian School, teachers from all grades at Modern Christian and from Western Christian, parents from all schools, alumni of both Modern Christian and Western Christian, and a sample of comparison college students at Liberal Arts College.[12] Student and teacher surveys were administered in two consecutive years in order to allow us to measure change in behaviors and attitudes across time, and many questions were administered to multiple groups of participants to allow comparison. For example, we asked many of the same questions about the impact of the technology program to all groups in order to be able to infer something about how attitudes about the one-to-one program differ between students, teachers, parents, and recent alumni.

Representative survey samples enable us to make three kinds of comparisons that are important to the study. First, we can compare results from other research methods, which come from a limited number of individuals, to a broader sample of the population. Second, we can compare between populations within a school, whether that is teachers and students or different age groups. Finally, we can compare between schools, and between the participants in our study and other nationwide studies. In each case, being able to draw inferences about the school population requires a broad sample of answers to the same questions. Moreover, comparisons between groups using survey data can include statistical controls for participant characteristics.

In this study, surveys were designed and administered with specific goals in mind. Surveys were designed to examine specific sets of variables: individual demographics, academic performance, within-school practices (with and without technology), outside-school practices (with and without technology), and the effects of technology on individual and communal beliefs and habits. Survey design drew on scholarship informing survey methodology, existing educational survey research, and scholarship associated with relevant variables for the study.

An overview of survey administration, timing, and response rates is provided in table A.2. Student and teacher surveys were administered in phase 1 and again in phase 2 to observe change over time. Minor survey revision occurred prior to phase 2 administrations in response to emerging findings and related questions that arose from the mixed methods data analysis at the end of phase 1. Alumni surveys were administered in phases 2 and 3. Parent surveys were administered in phase 3.

Table A.2. Survey Response Rates

Respondent	Phase	School[a]	Invited	Completed	Response rate
Alumni	2	MCHS	162	57	35.2%
	2	WCHS	155	48	31.0%
	3	MCHS	222	81	36.5%
	3	WCHS	144	48	33.3%
	3	LAC	407	201	49.4%[b]
		Total alumni	1,090	435	39.9%
Parents	3	MCHS, MCMS & WCHS	285	103	36.1%[b]
Students	1	MCHS & MCMS	717	434	60.5%
	1	WCHS	129	89	69.0%
	2	MCHS & MCMS	768	564	73.4%
	2	WCHS	449	161	35.9%
		Total students	2,063	1,248	60.5%
Teachers	1	MCHS & MCMS	70	55	78.6%
	2	MCHS & MCMS	110	68	61.8%
	2	WCHS	39	26	66.7%
		Total teachers	219	149	68.0%
Overall			3,657	1,935	52.9%

[a] MCHS = Modern Christian High School; WCHS = Western Christian High School; LAC = Liberal Arts College; MCMS = Modern Christian Middle School.
[b] The parent response rate and the LAC response rate are artificially low because the number of responses was capped for budget reasons.

Analysis

The survey data was analyzed at the conclusion of each phase to examine emerging findings and themes. This analysis proceeded in three steps. First, to test the validity of the survey questions, we measured the internal consistency of question groupings. This approach gave us an external method for checking whether the questions measured the underlying concepts that we were aiming for in the survey design. Because we expected variation in responses across survey participant groups (students, parents, teachers), we only tested within participant groups. Our instrument design largely held up. In the few cases where question groupings did not hold together, we used those questions sparingly and noted disagreement in the text.

The second step in data analysis was to examine descriptive statistics for each question within and between participant groups within years. We calculated t-statistics for difference in mean hypothesis tests between student participant groups. For the text in this book, we reported descriptive statistics in the form of "percent agree" or "percent disagree" for Likert-scale questions measuring agreement. For those measuring frequency we sometimes reported average frequency or time per day. These reported statistics aid the intuitive readability of the data. When comparing these created dichotomous outcomes, we also subjected them to mean-difference tests and reported statistically significant differences only when the p-value was below 0.05.

The final step when exploring differences between participant groups was to estimate linear regression models to make sure that observed differences between groups (i.e., Modern Christian Schools students and Western Christian School students) were not attributable to observable differences in the samples. Our samples between these two schools differ in important ways. We have a broader sample at Modern Christian, spanning a wider age/grade range and a wider range of reported academic performance. If we compare the raw averages between these two schools, we might falsely attribute differences between the schools to administrative decisions when in fact they are due to these sample differences. Using linear regression techniques to control for grade, gender, GPA, and other relevant observable characteristics proved important for making a number of the comparisons in this book.

Once the data from an individual phase was checked and cleaned and preliminary analysis was complete, we were able to match up data from other phases and from other participant groups for comparison. Most of the results reported in the text come from this pooled data which includes responses from multiple years and schools. In every case that was appropriate, we used linear regression methods to control for the school and grade that the students' or teachers' responses came from so that survey year, student age, and location did not drive the results. The findings were then triangulated with emerging results from other methods.

Focus Groups

Thirty-six focus groups with students, parents, and administrators (data collection and analysis: phases 1–3)

Design and Collection

Focus group interviews serve as a conduit for listening to a community's voices, their personal perspectives on a particular topic of study.[13] Focus groups, unlike individual interviews, draw together a group of people, typically selected on the basis of specific characteristics, to share their perspectives and insights. In this study they provided the opportunity to hear from the various groups that made up the Modern Christian Schools community. By design, focus groups invite interaction among group members, allowing them to hear from and build on or question one another's responses, thereby offering up important insight that is not gained from individual interviews.[14]

In this study, focus groups were purposefully spread across all three research phases. Focus groups in phase 1 and the beginning of phase 2 were leveraged to explore a priori themes, but the later focus groups proceeding through phase 3 were primarily used to probe emergent questions and themes. Our focus group design, guided by methodological scholarship,[15] included semi-structured interview questions beginning with a predesigned set of questions, while allowing for exploratory probes about interviewees' responses. Each focus group was conducted by a pair of researchers, and interviews were audio-recorded for transcription. Focus group participants were selected from a pool of candidates with a primary criterion in mind (see table A.3). If the pool of candidates exceeded twenty individuals, eight to fifteen randomly selected individuals were invited to participate, typically generating focus groups of approximately six to eight members.[16] Some groups, limited in size because of the selection criteria, like administrators or specific disciplinary teacher groups, were conducted with two to five participants. In all, we conducted thirty-six focus groups. An overview of groups with primary selection criteria is provided in the table.

Table A.3. Focus group selection criteria

Teachers (n = 16 groups)	Groups
Disciplinary subjects	
English language arts and Bible (mixed grades)	1
English language arts (mixed grades)	1
Science (mixed grades)	1
Math (mixed grades)	2
Languages (mixed grades)	2
Social studies/geography/history and psychology	1
Social studies	1
Art, music, band, and PE	1
Educational support services	1
Grade level	
Grades 7–12 teachers	1
Grades K–6 teachers	1
Duration of employment	
Teachers new to the school (mixed grades)	2
Random group selections	
Teachers (mixed grades)	1
Students (n = 12 groups)	
Grade level	
High school	7
Middle school	1
Elementary school (grade 6)	2
Academic subgroups	
At-risk learners or receiving student support (high school)	1
International students (high school)	1

Administrators (*n* = 4 groups)	
Principals, superintendents (current and former), and technology leaders	1
Principals (new to Modern Christian Schools in past two years)	1
Technology leaders (former)	2
Parents (*n* = 4 groups)	
Student grade level	
Middle and high school	1
Elementary	1
Random group selection	
Parents (students in K–12)	1
Duration of time at school	
Parents whose children are new to school	1

Analysis

Focus group transcription was informed by best practices ranging from organizing transcriptions to reviewing transcripts for accuracy.[17] The audio recordings were transcribed in full, capturing text verbatim by speaker. Owing to our emphasis on content of the dialogue and the need to set bounds to analysis time, nonlinguistic observations and other linguistic emphases (intonation, pause length, etc.) were not transcribed. For analysis, data were chunked into units by participant turn (starting when a participant began speaking and ending when they finished or were interrupted by another speaker). We then initiated a process of identifying codes based on recurring topics in the data using a selected set of focus group transcripts, beginning with deductive codes. This allowed the coding to begin with anticipated codes supported by a body of scholarship. With the same set of transcripts, the team continued with emergent codes, those derived from the data itself, allowing new codes to arise from the voices of school community members. Recursive cycles of data analysis through phases 1 and 2 allowed the team to refine codes, establish coding categories through constant comparison, develop a final coding manual, and achieve interrater reliability across multiple researchers.[18]

Upon completion of initial coding in phase 1, we added two analysis steps. The first was to explore a set of common words or phrases (e.g., image of God, God-glorifying, blessing) that were emerging frequently in focus groups. Qualitative keyword-in-context analysis was used to search the data for specific key terms with the goal of revealing emerging patterns about sets of terms themselves. This analysis complemented prior coding processes, and the analysis became part of the constant comparison process of thematic analysis. A second step included a clustering of codes into categories that were then counted by participant group. For instance, a selected set of codes (e.g., faith formation, intentional faith practices) were pooled into the category of *discernment-practices*. We could then explore the ways that the relationship between discernment and practices varied across parents, teachers, students, and administrators. Findings like these were used to identify whether a category was representative of all community members, or a select set.[19]

Thematic development occurred in phases 2 and 3 as researchers compared codes and emergent themes within similar groups (e.g., teacher groups to other teacher groups) and across groups (e.g., teacher groups with student groups). This analysis was crucial for understanding whether particular themes were present for particular groups or an entire school community.

Case Studies

Six unit-long case studies (data collection: phase 2; analysis: phases 2 and 3)

Design and Collection

Case studies are descriptive and particularistic, generating a thick description of a very specific phenomenon of study.[20] Drawing on ethnographic traditions, this method seeks to uncover deeper cultural knowledge about practices and beliefs through sustained immersion within a selected context, in this case classrooms.[21] Consider, for instance, the difference between the knowledge gained from spending an hour in a classroom and spending an entire month in the same classroom. We would undoubtedly gain a more substantive understanding of classroom practices in relationship to technology with an entire month to employ methods like observation, participant interviews, and collection of student or teacher work. Through these methodological means, case studies also uncover an understanding of practice that arises from the participants' perspectives. We can begin to probe participants' thinking by asking questions like the following: Why did a teacher make particular pedagogical choices? What drives student choice about the ways in which they use technology within a classroom? How do teachers or students understand the schools' mission in relation to classroom practice? What messages about Christian community are shaped by daily life in a specific classroom? Answers to these questions unveil the thinking behind the processes of technological change in action, thereby justifying case studies as a crucial method in this study.

We intentionally designed case studies, as one of the most in-depth and time-intensive methods of studying Modern Christian Schools, using best practices in the field.[22] Only a handful of case studies were possible, and so we selected classrooms by asking administrators and teacher-leaders within the community to recommend colleagues that were "thoughtful" in their use of technology. Six teachers were then selected from a pool of fifteen recommended participants in consideration of variables like years of experience, years at Modern Christian Schools, grade level, subject, post-secondary education level, and academic schedules. Teachers, in consultation with researchers, then each selected a unit of study that they believed reflected a high quality of technology integration (which did not necessarily mean a high quantity of use). The resulting units of study were the focus of case studies lasting the duration of a given unit, anywhere from three to six weeks. The following are the units studied:

- Second-grade social studies: How Do Communities Change? Our City's History
- Fourth-grade science: Animal Adaptations
- Seventh-grade math: Comparing, Scaling & Ratios
- High school chemistry: Chemical Equations
- High school English: Literature Research & Presentation (culminating unit)
- High school Bible: Corinth

We collected four distinct types of data within each case study.[23] First, we conducted observations of classrooms across the course of the unit, and simultaneously video-recorded classroom activities. The observations were conducted with the same use of field notes and observation protocol as the random classroom observations described previously. Unlike random classroom observations, where observations were limited to a 45-minute maximum, these observations extended for the duration of each class period regardless of its length, the goal being observation of the entire unit. The video and audio recordings served as a supplement, used for additional viewing to further clarify observation field notes or variables in the observation protocol.

Second, researchers collected a wide range of physical and digital materials developed by teachers and students over the course of the unit. The materials included lesson plans, classroom blogs, digital and nondigital content presented or provided by the teacher, student work samples, photographs of students in action, and physical classroom spaces. Together, these objects were a vital part of the cultural processes of teaching and learning within the classroom.[24] They were another window into the interaction between technology and the curriculum, teaching and learning process, and development of student knowledge.

The third and fourth data sets came from individual and focus group interviews. We interviewed teachers individually prior to, during, and after the unit of focus. Interviews were semi-structured, with a set of common questions for all teachers followed by open space for researcher questions about observed classroom practice. We also interviewed students, although in focus group format (three to six students each). These interviews were also semi-structured, beginning with a set of common questions and transitioning to researcher-developed questions in response to classroom observations.

Analysis

Analysis of case study data, conducted in phase 3, proceeded in stages. We first independently analyzed all data sources, with the exception of physical and digital artifacts. The analysis procedures for observational and interview data will not be repeated here, as they mirrored procedures described previously in the random classroom observations and focus group sections, with one exception. The coding process used the established reliable codes generated with the use of other data sets (focus groups and digital artifacts), and did not continue with emergent coding. In recognition of time limitations, we did not systematically analyze the physical and digital artifacts collected in the classroom. We analyzed a handful of selected artifacts on an individual basis in relation to the final rounds of thematic analysis to confirm or disconfirm themes or extend description of a classroom practice.

The second analysis stage consisted of constant comparison analysis to explore the interrelationship between codes or themes within the case study data itself. For example, we explored which observational codes arising in a particular teacher's classroom could be confirmed or disconfirmed by the interview codes, or which observational codes arising in one case study teacher's classroom could be confirmed or disconfirmed through observational codes in another case study teacher's classroom. This combination of data and methodological triangulation within the case studies themselves supported the validity of emerging themes.[25] Like all qualitative constant comparison analysis, recursive cycles of analysis led to the cohesion of themes within the case study data.

Documentary Analysis of Digital Files

Documentary analysis of the schools' digital files spanning twelve years (data collection: phase 2; analysis: phases 2 and 3)

Design and Collection

Document analysis, part of an ethnographic tradition of research, is a process of studying texts that sheds light on social and cultural knowledge, commitments, and changes in the history of a community.[26] The systematic analysis of documents is traditionally paired with other qualitative methods as a way of comparing and contrasting research findings. Our goal in this study was to uncover the social and cultural processes of technological change at the school, and reviewing a history of digital documents served a crucial role. The research process began nearly a decade into Modern Christian Schools' one-to-one program, but we were asking questions that probed technological change in the past as well as the present. A record of historical documents therefore presented a lens for looking back into the past to corroborate findings. To this end, we asked Modern Christian Schools administrators to provide any digital files from the pilot of the one-to-one program to the present. They provided 28,184 electronic files covering a twelve-year period.

Analysis

The initial phase of analysis in phase 1, data reduction, began with reviewing and coding files for relevance to the research. Included documents ranged from professional development plans and school handbooks to administrators' personal journals and teachers' individualized technology plans. Excluded documents ranged from receipts and device specifications to files having nothing to do with technology or the program at all. The resulting 815 relevant documents then proceeded to the next stage of coding. The transcripts were parsed into units of analysis based on meaning chunks delineated by breaks in the text. All images, figures, or other graphics were treated as a single unit. In phase 2, the documents were analyzed in a manner similar to focus group transcripts. Analysis began with deductive codes and then shifted to emergent codes. The refinement of codes occurred during phase 2 simultaneously with focus group transcript codes. Multiple iterations of code refinement led to the development of a final set of codes, with strong interrater reliability established on the documentary data.[27]

The research team then initiated a process of identifying codes based on recurring topics in the data using a selected set of focus group transcripts, beginning with deductive codes. This allowed the coding to begin with anticipated codes supported by a body of scholarship. With the same set of transcripts, the team continued with emergent codes, those derived from the data itself, allowing new codes to arise from the voices of school community members. Recursive cycles of data analysis through phases 1 and 2 allowed the team to refine codes, establish coding categories through constant comparison, develop a final coding manual, and achieve interrater reliability across multiple researchers. The process of qualitative keyword-in-context analysis was also applied to documents that could be digitally searched. The codes resulting from this analysis were then compiled with previous codes and integrated into the constant comparison process. The team used a final process of content analysis to group codes in a similar category and conduct counts of interest. This process of analyzing documents promoted comparison of emerging themes across time periods, community participants, and school trainings and other communications.

Mixed Methods Analytical Procedures

The above sections outlined the individual data collection and analysis procedures, while this section highlights the subsequent mixed methods procedures across sources. With multiple possible analytical strands owing to the vast set of data we collected, the research design demanded a systematic approach to yield valid findings.

Initial Phase

At the completion of phase 1 and the beginning of phase 2, individual method analyses were reaching various stages of completion. We first completed individual analysis of surveys, random classroom observations, and focus groups.[28] A primary purpose of the first surveys and classroom observations was to establish a baseline understanding of technological beliefs and practices, and so we prioritized analysis of these measures. This led to sequential analysis beginning with quantitative data.

First, we compared themes emerging from the quantitative analysis with one another. This process allowed us to probe, for example, whether a self-reported measure of ways participants used technology in classrooms (survey data) aligned with actual observations of that same technology use in classrooms (observation data). Second, we compared themes from quantitative analysis with qualitative focus group codes. The individual focus group analysis had not proceeded far enough for us to have confidence in emerging themes, but comparing the themes from quantitative data with developing codes and categories was still beneficial. It was here that we began to see the variations between deductive codes shaped by the very design of surveys and protocols and emergent codes uncovered as participants shared their thoughts.

Through these intricate processes of triangulation, we confirmed some themes across methods. Other emergent themes presented contrasting findings, thus requiring further exploration of extreme cases or sets of data. Additionally, analysis sometimes generated unanticipated or surprising emergent themes that we then followed up.[29] The use of additional strategies to examine themes in the early phases of research generally resulted in the following outcomes: (1) confirmation of an emergent theme, (2) recognition of disconfirmations as atypical or nonrepresentative cases, (3) designing or revising future methods to pursue unanswered questions,

(4) revisiting individual data sets for more detailed analysis, or similarly (5) revising or refining codes or entire themes. In the nascent phases of research, the two most valuable contributions from the analysis were the opportunity to further refine analytical codes and themes and the chance to refine future methods.

Intermediate Phase

By the end of phase 2, all but the case study and final round survey data was available for more integrated mixed methods analysis. The analysis proceeded concurrently at this stage, as we analyzed data from all available methods simultaneously. We compared individual survey findings from phase 2 with those from phase 1, with the goal of seeking confirmation or disconfirmation of trends between participants and across years.

Focus group and documentary analysis data also began to play a more significant role. The qualitative data from these methods was weighted more than quantitative data in phase 2 analysis, as it was a necessary step to establish the refined emergent codes and move toward broader themes and inferences. We reviewed codes and themes across data sources (e.g., focus group data, documentary analysis data), participant groups (e.g., teachers, parents, students), and stages of the laptop program (e.g., pilot years, launch years one to three, etc.). Each stage of comparison led to refinement of codes and categories, accompanied by clarifications in coding manuals. It was at this point, before a final comprehensive data coding process, that we performed interrater reliability checks with select focus groups and digital documents.

Next, we used the individual qualitative findings for the purposes of confirmation or disconfirmation and enhancement.[30] We compared them with findings and themes from methods in phases 1 and 2 generating quantitative data. Where themes were confirmed, the qualitative data generally enhanced or deepened understanding of phenomena explored through quantitative means. We pursued themes that were disconfirmed or not present in quantitative findings to gain further insight. For instance, were contrasting findings about teacher technology use due to factors like disciplinary expertise, years of teaching experience, or grade level? Were contrasting findings about the role of mission in the laptop program due to type of community member (e.g., teacher, parent), years at the school, or school trainings attended? It was this constant comparison followed by iterative cycles of analysis in one or more data sources that led to increased validity in the inferences about the ways technology affected the Modern Christian Schools community.

Concluding Phase

Phase 3 ushered in the end of data collection and individual analysis, now adding data from all methods to the analysis process. Analysis again proceeded concurrently in phase 3, similar to phase 2. Weight was now redistributed across methods, as the purpose was continued confirmation and enhancement of themes leading to empirically supported inferences. Methods for survey and focus group analysis were generally similar to those in phase 2, with one exception. With the coding scheme completed, focus group analysis was not used to refine codes but instead leveraged for further constant comparison around broader themes.

Case studies became the final data source available for mixed methods analysis in this phase. We viewed patterns in observation protocol data in relation to themes drawn from baseline measures like random observations or focus group descriptions. We also used case study focus group and interview data as a thematic point of corroboration with themes arising from both quantitative and qualitative analyses in previous phases. As larger inferences from other data sets emerged and case study data supported these inferences, researchers then returned to select case study observational field notes and artifacts to further expand, illustrate, or describe the findings.

As final inferences about the data took shape, we introduced further processes to assure credibility of the research findings.[31] We purposefully probed themes for outlying explanations, drawing now on the widest available range of analyzed data. We shared article sections or book chapters with members of the Modern Christian Schools community, a source of member-checking, and feedback was used to refine findings. An advisory board of scholars representing expertise in educational research, Christian education, and educational technology reviewed the findings as well. Each step in the mixed methods analysis process ensured that the final inferences shared in the book were built on confirmation through multiple data sources, participants, or years. Although mixed methods are inherently complex, a strong empirical design for data collection, analysis, and inferencing assured that we presented contextually rich and valid findings about the process of technological change at Modern Christian Schools.

Notes

Chapter 1

1. Throughout this book we will use "new" and "digital" technologies to refer to the digital tools and related techniques that have become increasingly ubiquitous in schools and daily life in the twenty-first century. A more thorough examination of technology and its meaning within this research is found in chapter 2.

2. Empirical research is based on measurable and observable phenomena and provides a crucial counterpoint to conceptual research that generates knowledge primarily from theory. The current balance of scholarship guiding Christian educators in a digital age leans to the conceptual, pointing to a need for empirical research like this study. See Kara Sevensma et al., "Seeking a Scholarship of Pedagogy, Technology, and Faith: A Literature Survey," *International Journal of Christianity and Education* 22, no. 3 (2018): 252–73.

3. The behaviors described in this opening vignette were not all observed at the same time or in the same classroom, but are drawn together from various facets of our data to create a general picture of some of the kinds of things happening in schools.

4. One-to-one technology programs refer to schools providing each student with a digital device (e.g., tablet or laptop).

5. See, among others, Albert Borgmann, *Power Failure: Christianity in the Culture of Technology* (Grand Rapids: Brazos, 2003); Andy Crouch, *The Tech-Wise Family: Everyday Steps for Putting Technology in Its Place* (Grand Rapids: Baker Books, 2017); Craig Detweiler, *iGods: How Technology Shapes Our Spiritual and Social Lives* (Grand Rapids: Brazos, 2013); John Dyer, *From the Garden to the City: The Redeeming and Corrupting Power of Technology* (Grand Rapids: Kregel, 2011); Stephen V. Monsma, ed., *Responsible Technology: A Christian Perspective* (Grand Rapids: Eerdmans, 1986); Derek C. Schuurman, *Shaping a Digital World: Faith, Culture and Computer Technology* (Downers Grove, IL: IVP Academic, 2013); Shannon Vallor, *Technology and the Virtues: A Philosophical Guide to a Future Worth Wanting* (New York: Oxford University Press, 2016).

Chapter 2

1. Heidi A. Campbell and Stephen Garner, *Networked Theology: Negotiating Faith in Digital Culture* (Grand Rapids: Baker Academic, 2016), 97.

2. See, e.g., Nathan F. Alleman, Perry L. Glanzer, and David S. Guthrie, "The Integration of Christian Theological Traditions into the Classroom: A Survey of CCCU Faculty," *Christian Scholar's Review* 45, no. 2 (2016): 103–24; Douglas Jacobsen and Rhonda Hustedt Jacobsen, *Scholarship and Christian Faith: Enlarging the Conversation* (Oxford: Oxford University Press, 2004); George M. Marsden, *The Outrageous Idea of Christian Scholarship* (Oxford: Oxford University Press, 1997); Todd C. Ream, Michael Beaty, and Larry Lion, "Faith and Learning: Toward a Typology of Faculty Views at Religious Research Universities," *Christian Higher Education* 3, no. 4 (2009): 349–72; Robert Sweetman, *Tracing the Lines: Spiritual Exercise and the Gesture of Christian Scholarship* (Eugene, OR: Wipf & Stock, 2016); Nicholas Wolterstorff, *Reason within the Bounds of Religion*, 2nd ed. (Grand Rapids: Eerdmans, 1988).

3. See, e.g., Sherry Turkle, *Alone Together: Why We Expect More from Technology and Less from Each Other* (New York: Basic Books, 2011); Turkle, *Reclaiming Conversation: The Power of Talk in a Digital Age* (New York: Penguin Books, 2016).

4. Cf. Sweetman, *Tracing the Lines*.

Chapter 3

1. On the optimistic side, see, e.g., Clayton M. Christensen, Michael B. Horn, and Curtis W. Johnson, *Disrupting Class: How Disruptive Innovation Will Change the Way the World Learns*, 2nd ed. (New York: McGraw-Hill, 2008); Tom Vander Ark, *Getting Smart: How Digital Learning Is Changing the World* (San Francisco: Jossey-Bass, 2012). On the pessimistic side, see, e.g., Todd Oppenheimer, *The Flickering Mind: Saving Education from the False Promise of Technology* (New York: Random House, 2004); Mark Bauerlein, *The Dumbest Generation: How the Digital Age Stupefies Young Americans and Jeopardizes Our Future (Or, Don't Trust Anyone under 30)* (New York: Jeremy P. Tarcher/Penguin, 2008).

2. See, e.g., Don Ihde, *Philosophy of Technology: An Introduction* (Saint Paul, MN: Paragon House, 1998).

3. A fascinating history of the technology of the bookshelf is provided in Henry Petroski, *The Book on the Bookshelf* (New York: Alfred A. Knopf, 1999).

4. Albert Borgmann, *Technology and the Character of Contemporary Life* (Chicago: University of Chicago Press, 1984); Jacques Ellul, *The Technological Society* (New York: Vintage, 1964); Andrew Feenberg, *Questioning Technology* (New York: Routledge, 1999); Martin Heidegger, *The Question Concerning Technology and Other Essays* (New York: Harper Torchbooks, 1977); Egbert Schuurman, *Faith and Hope in Technology* (Carlisle: Piquant Editions, 2003).

5. Cf. Ian G. Barbour, *Ethics in an Age of Technology: The Gifford Lectures 1989–1991*, vol. 2 (San Francisco: HarperSanFrancisco, 1993), 3–4; Heidi A. Campbell and Stephen Garner, *Networked Theology: Negotiating Faith in Digital Culture* (Grand Rapids: Baker Academic, 2016), 99–102.

6. For other ways of dividing up views of technology, see, e.g., Robert John Russell, "Five Attitudes toward Nature and Technology from a Christian Perspective," *Theology and Science* 1, no. 2 (2003): 149–59; Alexander J. Romiszowski, "Technology and Moral

or Ethical Values: Three Questions; Many More Answers," *Educational Technology* 52, no. 1 (2012): 10-17.

7. Donald A. Mackenzie and Judy Wajcman, *The Social Shaping of Technology*, 2nd ed. (Milton Keynes: Open University Press, 1999).

Chapter 4

1. For a review of existing literature, and the gaps in it, see Kara Sevensma et al., "Seeking a Scholarship of Pedagogy, Technology, and Faith: A Literature Survey," *International Journal of Christianity and Education* 22, no. 3 (2018): 252-73. The specific gaps in empirical research on technology in Christian schools are a subset of the limitations of existing empirical research on Christian schools in general. See, e.g., Elizabeth Green, *Mapping the Field: A Review of the Current Research Evidence on the Impact of Schools with a Christian Ethos* (London: Theos, 2009); David I. Smith, Joonyong Um, and Claudia D. Beversluis, "The Scholarship of Teaching and Learning in a Christian Context," *Christian Higher Education* 13, no. 1 (2014): 74-87.

2. For a survey of research on technology in religious communities more generally, see, e.g., Heidi A. Campbell and Stephen Garner, *Networked Theology: Negotiating Faith in Digital Culture* (Grand Rapids: Baker Academic, 2016).

3. Charles Teddlie and Abbas Tashakkori, *The Foundations of Mixed Methods Research: Integrating Quantitative and Qualitative Techniques in the Social and Behavioral Sciences* (Thousand Oaks, CA: SAGE, 2009).

4. John W. Creswell and Vicki L. Plano Clark, *Designing and Conducting Mixed Methods Research*, 2nd ed. (Thousand Oaks, CA: SAGE, 2011); R. Burke Johnson and Anthony J. Onwuegbuzie, "Mixed Methods Research: A Research Paradigm Whose Time Has Come," *Educational Researcher* 33, no. 7 (2004): 14-26.

Chapter 5

1. Modern Christian Schools' history is similar to that of Calvinistic schools described by Van Brummelen and Vryhof, from whose historical accounts we draw in what follows. Broader accounts of other kinds of faith-based private schooling can be found, e.g., in Alan Peshkin, *God's Choice: The Total World of a Fundamentalist Christian School* (Chicago: University of Chicago Press, 1986), and Anthony Bryk and Valerie Lee, *Catholic Schools and the Common Good* (Cambridge: Harvard University Press, 1993), though it should not be assumed that all the characteristics of the schools in those studies carry over to Modern Christian Schools. We also referred to sources focused specifically on the history of the community in which Modern Christian Schools are located, but we do not cite them here in order to preserve school anonymity. Peter De Boer and Donald Oppewal, "American Calvinist Day Schools," *Christian Scholar's Review* 13, no. 2 (1984): 120-40; Harro R. Van Brummelen, "Molding God's Children: The History of Curriculum in Christian Schools Rooted in Dutch Calvinism," PhD diss., University

of British Columbia, 1984, retrieved from https://open.library.ubc.ca/media/stream /pdf/831/1.0054665/1; Harro R. Van Brummelen, *Telling the Next Generation: Educational Development of North American Calvinist Christian Schools* (Lanham, MD: University Press of America, 1986); Steven C. Vryhof, *Between Memory and Vision: The Case for Faith-Based Schooling* (Grand Rapids: Eerdmans, 2004). For a more general overview of related school types, see, e.g., Deani Van Pelt et al., "Private Religious Protestant and Catholic Schools in the United States and Canada: Introduction, Overview, and Policy Implications," *Journal of School Choice* 6, no. 1 (2012): 1-19.

2. Van Brummelen, *Telling the Next Generation*; Vryhof, *Between Memory and Vision*.

3. James D. Bratt, ed., *Abraham Kuyper: A Centennial Reader* (Grand Rapids: Eerdmans, 1998).

4. The proposed amendment included society-based private Christian schools such as Modern Christian Schools.

5. This was significantly higher than the average for American adults during the same time period. John B. Horrigan, "Home Broadband Adoption 2006," Pew Research Center, May 28, 2006, http://www.pewinternet.org/2006/05/28/home-broadband -adoption-2006/.

6. School magazine, a regular publication for the Modern Christian Schools community.

Part 2 Introduction

1. Christian Smith, *Moral, Believing Animals: Human Personhood and Culture* (Oxford: Oxford University Press, 2009); Alasdair MacIntyre, *After Virtue*, 3rd ed. (Notre Dame, IN: University of Notre Dame Press, 2007).

2. Since this part of the book focuses on understanding the operation of the distinctive mission of Modern Christian Schools, it does not include data from our comparison sites.

Chapter 6

1. One factor affecting the wording was the desire to remove exclusive denominational references while retaining the distinctive emphases of the schools' Reformed tradition.

2. Some private school mission statements focus more on beliefs or services; the mission statement at Modern Christian Schools focuses on goals, with only the phrase "for Christ" indicating the beliefs that frame them. Cf. Albert J. Boerema, "An Analysis of Private School Mission Statements," *Peabody Journal of Education* 81, no. 1 (2006): 180-202, http://www.jstor.org/stable/25594702.

3. Christopher C. Morphew and Matthew Hartley, "Mission Statements: A Thematic Analysis of Rhetoric across Institutional Type," *Journal of Higher Education* 77 (2006): 456-71.

4. We examine how this worked out in part 3.

5. A mission focus on academics plus personal nurture is not in itself unique to Christian school mission statements. See, e.g., Kelly-Ann Allen et al., "Understanding the Priorities of Australian Secondary Schools through an Analysis of Their Mission and Vision Statements," *Educational Administration Quarterly* 54, no. 2 (2018): 249–74.

6. Ray Pennings et al., *CARDUS Education Survey* (Hamilton, ON: Cardus, 2011), 24–25.

7. See, e.g., Albert Wolters, *Creation Regained: Biblical Basics for a Reformational Worldview*, 2nd ed. (Grand Rapids: Eerdmans, 2005); Cornelius Plantinga Jr., *Engaging God's World: A Reformed Vision of Faith, Learning, and Living* (Grand Rapids: Eerdmans, 2002).

8. This emphasis is evident if we parse mission codes in focus group conversations. When mission-related phrases were coded in focus groups and compared to the total number of mission phrases, we find that bringing change to the world comprised 50.0%, preparing minds comprised 34.1%, and nurturing lives comprised 15.9% of the mission-specific discussion. Or, if we slice the data another way, we can ask, In how many focus groups did discussion of a particular phrase of the mission occur separate from discussion of the entire mission statement? Here we find bringing change to the world in thirteen focus groups, preparing minds in nine focus groups, and nurturing lives in four focus groups. These examples of data slices serve to highlight the ways in which the research team triangulated data to ensure that the findings above are valid, with recognition that there were more considerations in play (e.g., which coded utterances were prompted by the interviewer, whether a particular participant dominated a discussion, how long a coded utterance was) and other ways to examine the data. While such data is useful in ensuring the rigor of the research, it remains relegated to footnotes so as not to distract from the key points brought to the fore in the dialogue samples shared in chapters like this.

Chapter 7

1. Christopher C. Morphew and Matthew Hartley, "Mission Statements: A Thematic Analysis of Rhetoric across Institutional Type," *Journal of Higher Education* 77 (2006): 456–71.

2. Alongside official statements of mission are the "de facto school missions, visions, values, and goals" that can shape practice on the ground. D. Keith Gurley et al., "Mission, Vision, Values, and Goals: An Exploration of Key Organizational Statements and Daily Practice in Schools," *Journal of Educational Change* 16 (2015): 217–42.

3. See, e.g., Craig D. Jerald, *Defining a 21st Century Education* (Alexandria, VA: Center for Public Education, 2009), retrieved from http://www.centerforpubliceducation .org/LearnAbout/21st-Century/Defining-a-21st-CenturyEducation-Full-Report-PDF .pdf.

4. Cf. Michael Pelz and Kevin Den Dulk, "Looking Within or Reaching Out? The Effects of Religion on Private School Enrollments in an Era of School Choice," *Politics and Religion* 11, no. 1 (2018): 79–115.

5. Survey questions referred to the "school," singular, since participants were answering on the basis of their knowledge of whichever school in the Modern Christian Schools system they frequented.

6. Albert Boerema notes a tendency for faith-based schools to have "more diffuse" mission statements than other kinds of private schools, perhaps because of their attempt at a holistic focus on kinds of formation that go beyond academic development. Albert J. Boerema, "An Analysis of Private School Mission Statements," *Peabody Journal of Education* 81, no. 1 (2006): 198, http://www.jstor.org/stable/25594702.

Chapter 8

1. Peggy A. Ertmer, "Teacher Pedagogical Beliefs: The Final Frontier in Our Quest for Technology Integration?," *Educational Technology Research and Development* 53, no. 4 (2006): 25–39.

2. Peggy A. Ertmer and Anne Ottenbreit-Leftwich, "Removing Obstacles to the Pedagogical Changes Required by Jonassen's Vision of Authentic Technology-Enabled Learning," *Computers & Education* 64 (2013): 175–82; Everett M. Rogers, *Diffusion of Innovations*, 5th ed. (New York: Free Press, 2003).

3. Evan T. Straub, "Understanding Technology Adoption: Theory and Future Directions for Informal Learning," *Review of Educational Research* 79, no. 2 (2009): 625–49.

4. Coded focus group data reveals that when teachers spoke of recollections about the rationale for the one-to-one program, they referred to the mission itself or connected another rationale to the mission only 10.3% of the time.

5. International Society in Technology Education (ISTE), *ISTE Standards* (2008), retrieved from www.iste.org/standards/standards; Partnership for 21st Century Learning, *Reimagining Citizenship for the 21st Century: A Call for Action for Policy Makers and Educators* (2014), retrieved from http://www.P21.org.

6. Michael Fullan, *The New Meaning of Educational Change* (New York: Teachers College Press, 2015); Dianne L. Scouller, "From Philosophy to Practice: An Investigation of the Impact of a School's Philosophy on Policy and Classroom Practice," *Journal of Education and Christian Belief* 16, no. 1 (2012): 61–80.

7. Edgar H. Schein and Peter Schein, *Organizational Culture and Leadership*, 5th ed. (Hoboken, NJ: Wiley, 2017).

Chapter 9

1. This does not contradict the finding in previous chapters that community members varied in their perceptions of how the mission related to the launch of the technology program and in their interpretations of what the mission emphasis meant in practice. While the statistical data brought to the fore in this chapter lets us see overall levels of agreement with claims about the mission, the focus group data explored in the previous chapters reveals the texture of particular groups' and

individuals' interpretations, offering a sense of the range of stories at play in the community.

Chapter 10

1. We explore this further in part 4.

2. Cf. David I. Smith, Joonyong Um, and Claudia D. Beversluis, "The Scholarship of Teaching and Learning in a Christian Context," *Christian Higher Education* 13, no. 1 (2014): 74-87; Mary Taylor Huber and Sherwyn P. Morreale, eds., *Disciplinary Styles in the Scholarship of Teaching and Learning: Exploring Common Ground* (Washington, DC: American Association for Higher Education and the Carnegie Foundation for the Advancement of Teaching, 2002).

3. With our focus on a small group of teachers in one cluster of schools, the possibility that age and personality differences are shaping the culture of particular departments means that any conclusions on this point remain tentative.

4. This way of articulating a Reformed Christian approach to education and cultural engagement has been influentially articulated in the writings of Nicholas Wolterstorff. See, e.g., Nicholas Wolterstorff, *Until Justice and Peace Embrace* (Grand Rapids: Eerdmans, 1983); Clarence W. Joldersma and Gloria Goris Stronks, eds., *Educating for Shalom: Essays on Christian Higher Education* (Grand Rapids: Eerdmans, 2004). On the creation, fall, redemption framework mentioned by the teacher, see, e.g., Albert M. Wolters, *Creation Regained: Biblical Basics for a Reformational Worldview*, 2nd ed. (Grand Rapids: Eerdmans, 2005).

5. This shift was influenced by books such as James K. A. Smith, *Desiring the Kingdom: Worship, Worldview, and Cultural Formation* (Grand Rapids: Baker Academic, 2009); David I. Smith and James K. A. Smith, *Teaching and Christian Practices: Reshaping Faith and Learning* (Grand Rapids: Eerdmans, 2011); as well as by resources from other Christian school systems.

6. See, e.g., Perry L. Glanzer, "Why We Should Discard the Integration of Faith and Learning: Rearticulating the Mission of the Christian Scholar," *Journal of Education and Christian Belief* 12, no. 1 (2008): 41-51; Douglas Jacobsen and Rhonda Hustedt Jacobsen, *Scholarship and Christian Faith: Enlarging the Conversation* (New York: Oxford University Press, 2004); George Marsden, *The Outrageous Idea of Christian Scholarship* (New York: Oxford University Press, 1997); Todd C. Ream, Michael Beaty, and Larry Lion, "Faith and Learning: Toward a Typology of Faculty Views at Religious Research Universities," *Christian Higher Education* 3 (2004): 349-72; David L. Wolfe, "The Line of Demarcation between Integration and Pseudo-integration," in *The Reality of Christian Learning: Strategies for Faith-Discipline Integration*, ed. Harold Heie and David L. Wolfe (Grand Rapids: Christian University Press, 1987), 3-12.

7. This internal variety within a single school community offers an importantly different, complementary picture of how faith is worked out in schools from that gained by averaging across different school types. See, e.g., David Sikkink, "Religious School Differences in School Climate and Academic Mission: A Descriptive Overview of School Organization and Student Outcomes," *Journal of School Choice* 6, no. 1 (2012): 20-39;

Deani Van Pelt et al., "Private Religious Protestant and Catholic Schools in the United States and Canada: Introduction, Overview, and Policy Implications," *Journal of School Choice* 6, no. 1 (2012): 1–19.

Part 3 Introduction

1. Nicholas C. Burbules and Thomas A. Callister Jr., "The Risky Promises and Promising Risks of New Information Technologies for Education," *Bulletin of Science, Technology & Society* 19, no. 2 (1999): 105–12.

Chapter 11

1. Focus group participants noted that this support for learning technology had diminished in more recent years, which could pose a challenge for new teachers adjusting to the schools' technology use.

2. Frameworks and standards mentioned included SAMR, TPACK, and ISTE Standards. For further information, see International Society in Technology Education, *ISTE Standards* (2008), retrieved from www.iste.org/standards/standards; Matthew Koehler and Punya Mishra, "What Is Technological Pedagogical Content Knowledge (TPACK)?," *Contemporary Issues in Technology and Teacher Education* 9, no. 1 (2009): 60–70; Ruben R. Puentedura, "Building Transformation: An Introduction to the SAMR Model" (2014a), http://www.hippasus.com/rrpweblog/ar chives/2014/08/22/BuildingTransformation_AnIntroductionToSAMR.pdf; Ruben R. Puentedura, "Learning, Technology, and the SAMR Model: Goals, Processes, and Practice" (2014b), http://www.hippasus.com/rrpweblog/archives/2014/06/29/Learn ingTechnologySAMRModel.pdf.

3. We explore how these external frameworks that framed how teachers thought about teaching and learning related to the schools' Christian vision in part 4.

4. Doug Blomberg, *Wisdom and Curriculum: Christian Schooling after Postmodernity* (Sioux Center, IA: Dordt College Press, 2007); Danah Henriksen et al., "Play as a Foundational Thinking Skill and Transdisciplinary Habit of Mind," *TechTrends* 59, no. 3 (2015): 5–9.

5. Parker J. Palmer, *The Courage to Teach: Exploring the Inner Landscape of a Teacher's Life* (San Francisco: Jossey-Bass, 1997).

6. Rachel A. Vannatta and Nancy Fordham, "Teacher Dispositions as Predictors of Classroom Technology Use," *Journal of Research on Technology in Education* 36, no. 3 (2004): 253–71.

7. Danah Henriksen and Punya Mishra, "We Teach Who We Are," *Teachers College Record* 117, no. 7 (2015): 1–46; Punya Mishra, Matthew J. Koehler, and Danah Henriksen, "The Seven Trans-Disciplinary Habits of Mind: Extending the TPACK Framework Towards 21st Century Learning," *Educational Technology* 51, no. 2 (2011): 22–28.

Chapter 12

1. This sense of the tone of the early years is echoed in one teacher's response to an internal survey early in the program: "Have teachers think critically about the strengths, weaknesses, gains, and losses. Don't just sell the initiative as the end-all or as a panacea. Have teachers do some reflective analysis, some contextual, authentic thinking!"

2. On the possibilities of digital devices as imagined in the context of particular settings, see, e.g., Margaret Lloyd, "Imagining the Affordances of Mobile Devices as a Mechanism in Teaching and Learning," *International Journal of Educational Technology* 5, no. 1 (2018): 37–48.

3. See, e.g., Cindi May, "A Learning Secret: Don't Take Notes with a Laptop," *Scientific American*, June 3, 2014, https://www.scientificamerican.com/article/a-learning -secret-don-t-take-notes-with-a-laptop/; Pam A. Mueller and Daniel M. Oppenheimer, "The Pen Is Mightier Than the Keyboard: Advantages of Longhand over Laptop Note Taking," *Psychological Science* 25, no. 6 (2014): 1159–68.

4. Of course, in the natural sciences especially, technological mediation often intensifies the ability to perceive the material world, such as when a microscope or camera is used. Yet science teachers retained a sense of the authenticity of direct bodily experience and its proximity to spirituality.

5. Cf. Carrie B. Fried, "In-Class Laptop Use and Its Effects on Student Learning," *Computers & Education* 50, no. 3 (2008): 906–14.

6. This implies a more complex process than that revealed by more general studies of technology decision-making that focus more narrowly on effectiveness and achievement. See, e.g., Jung Lee, Frank A. Cerreto, and Jihyun Lee, "Theory of Planned Behavior and Teachers' Decisions Regarding Use of Educational Technology," *Journal of Educational Technology & Society* 13, no. 1 (2010): 152–64; William Sugar, Frank Crawley, and Bethann Fine, "Examining Teachers' Decisions to Adopt New Technology," *Educational Technology & Society* 7, no. 4 (2004): 201–13; Matthew M. Schmidt et al., "Implementing Project SIED: Special Education Teachers' Perceptions of a Simplified Technology Decision-Making Process for App Identification and Evaluation," *Journal of Special Education Technology* 32, no. 1 (2017): 12–22.

Chapter 13

1. The descriptions of transformational learning offered in focus groups often reflected constructivist, learner-centered pedagogical approaches that require sustained engagement from students. These approaches fall into categories such as experiential learning, discovery learning, or inquiry-based, project-based, and problem-based learning (hereafter collectively referred to as inquiry-based learning). There are multiple distinctions between inquiry-, project-, and problem-based learning. However, the differences were not clarified by Modern Christian Schools teachers, and terms seemed to be used interchangeably to refer to constructivist approaches. The end result was therefore to group X-based learning approaches together. More detailed descriptions than those included here would be needed to demonstrate full-fledged inquiry-based

learning, though we did observe instances that would qualify. See further W. S. Anthony, "Learning to Discover Rules by Discovery," *Journal of Educational Psychology* 64 (1973): 325–28; Brigid Barron and Linda Darling-Hammond, *Teaching for Meaningful Learning: A Review of Research on Inquiry-Based and Cooperative Learning; Book Excerpt* (N.p.: George Lucas Educational Foundation, 2008); David A. Kolb and Ronald Fry, "Towards an Applied Theory of Experiential Learning," in *Theories of Group Processes*, ed. Cary L. Cooper, 33–57 (New York: Wiley, 1975); John R. Savery and Thomas M. Duffy, "Problem-Based Learning: An Instructional Model and Its Constructivist Framework," in *Constructivist Learning Environments: Case Studies in Instructional Design*, ed. Brent G. Wilson, 135–48 (Englewood Cliffs, NJ: Educational Technology Publications, 1995).

2. Binbin Zheng et al., "Learning in One-to-One Laptop Environments: A Meta-Analysis and Research Synthesis," *Review of Educational Research* 86, no. 4 (2016): 1052–84; Filip Dochy et al., "Effects of Problem-Based Learning: A Meta-Analysis," *Learning and Instruction* 13, no. 5 (2003): 533–68; John W. Thomas, *A Review of Research on Project-Based Learning* (San Rafael, CA: The Autodesk Foundation, 2000).

3. Barron and Darling-Hammond, *Teaching for Meaningful Learning*.

4. The survey used the specific term *inquiry-based* in questions.

5. Inquiry-based learning in observations was defined as follows: Students work to explore a given problem or seek answers to questions. The problems or questions are complex, requiring information gathering, evaluation, interpretation, and synthesis. The goal of the inquiry is deep learning about complex concepts, not simply practicing how to use or apply concepts taught by the teacher. An additional goal is students learn how to guide their own learning process. Such work generally takes sustained time because the answers are complex and multifaceted. There may be variation in how much the teacher guides the inquiry process (e.g., defining the original question, providing appropriate resources), but students should be actively constructing knowledge. Students also develop a product of knowledge (e.g., lab report, skit, presentation, poem, paper). All activities contributing to answering the problem or question or reporting knowledge (e.g., reading, writing, discussion) will be coded as inquiry-based learning. Teaching and learning activities contributing to inquiry-based learning and coded as such will not also be coded as distinct, separate activities.

6. Our case studies were selected on the basis of several factors, including identification of the teachers concerned by their administrators as thoughtful in their integration of technology.

7. Barron and Darling-Hammond, *Teaching for Meaningful Learning*; David H. Jonassen et al., *Learning to Solve Problems with Technology: A Constructivist Perspective*, 2nd ed. (Upper Saddle River, NJ: Merrill Prentice Hall, 2003).

8. See note 5 above.

Chapter 14

1. Yong Zhao, *Catching Up or Leading the Way: American Education in the Age of Globalization* (Alexandria, VA: ASCD, 2009).

2. See, e.g., Steven M. Ross, Gary R. Morrison, and Deborah L. Lowther, "Educa-

tional Technology Research Past and Present: Balancing Rigor and Relevance to Impact School Learning," *Contemporary Educational Technology* 1, no. 1 (2010): 17–35.

3. Lower-order thinking skills and middle- or higher-order thinking skills were defined using the revised Bloom's taxonomy of educational objectives. In this study, lower-order skills aligned with categories of remembering and understanding; middle- and higher-order skills encompassed applying, analyzing, evaluating, and creating. See Lorin W. Anderson and David R. Krathwohl, *A Taxonomy for Learning, Teaching, and Assessing: A Revision of Bloom's Taxonomy of Educational Objectives* (New York: Longman, 2001).

4. The case study data do present a contrast worth noting. Compared to random observations, laptops and tablets in case study classrooms were present more frequently for lower-order learning tasks at the middle (58%) and high school levels (62%). When interpreting these findings, we must recall that case study teachers were selected for their "thoughtful use of technology" as regarded by peers and administrators, and re- searchers asked these teachers to self-select teaching units for observation. It may be that teachers, aware of the research aims and goals, selected units that were heavily imbued with technology despite being encouraged by researchers not to let that factor shape their choice. Even with this in mind, we can still point out that digital technologies were in use more of the time for middle- or higher-order thinking activities than lower- order thinking activities in all case study classrooms.

5. See, e.g., Fred M. Newmann, *Student Engagement and Achievement in American Secondary Schools* (New York: Teachers College Press, 1992).

6. J. Richard Middleton connects the idea of the image of God with responsibility for creating culture in *The Liberating Image: The Imago Dei in Genesis 1* (Grand Rapids: Brazos, 2005).

7. See David I. Smith, *On Christian Teaching: Practicing Faith in the Classroom* (Grand Rapids: Eerdmans, 2018).

Chapter 15

1. Carol A. Tomlinson, "Mapping a Route toward Differentiated Instruction," *Educational Leadership* 57 (1999): 12–17.

2. Timothy J. Landrum and Kimberly A. McDuffie, "Learning Styles in the Age of Differentiated Instruction," *Exceptionality* 18, no. 1 (2010): 6–17.

3. These areas are also the focus of Universal Design for Learning. For more infor- mation see http://www.cast.org.

4. Allan Collins and Richard Halverson, *Rethinking Education in the Age of Technology: The Digital Revolution and Schooling in America*, 2nd ed. (New York: Teachers College Press, 2018).

5. See Genesis 1:26–28. There are some risks here, theologically speaking, since the idea of humanity being made in the image of God appears only in a very small number of biblical passages, has been interpreted in various ways, and remains somewhat enig- matic. There is a recurring temptation when affirming human worth using "image of God" language to import our current sense of human identity and capacities back into

the biblical idea, and then use the biblical idea to back up current practice. An emphasis on individual creativity and individual difference has not always been how the image of God has been understood, but can be read as arising from a conversation between current cultural emphases and the biblical term.

6. A rich scholarship examines this relationship between image of God and implications about the nature of personhood, community, and notions of ability, particularly as related to disability. See, e.g., Nancy L. Eiesland, *The Disabled God: Toward a Liberatory Theology of Disability* (Nashville: Abingdon Press, 1994); Barbara J. Hedges-Goettl, "Thinking Theologically about Inclusion: Disability, Imago Dei and the Body of Christ," *Journal of Religion, Disability & Health* 6, no. 4 (2002): 7–30; John Swinton, "Who Is the God We Worship? Theologies of Disability; Challenges and New Possibilities," *International Journal of Practical Theology* 14, no. 2 (2011): 273–307.

7. For scholarship examining Christian concepts of inclusion, see, e.g., David W. Anderson, "Inclusion and Interdependence: Students with Special Needs in the Regular Classroom," *Journal of Education and Christian Belief* 10, no. 1 (2006): 43–59; Thomas E. Reynolds, *Vulnerable Communion: A Theology of Disability and Hospitality* (Grand Rapids: Brazos, 2008).

8. See, e.g., 1 Corinthians 12:12–27; Philippians 2:1–4.

Chapter 16

1. Efficiency in terms of speed was discussed by students as a benefit of technology in eight out of twelve student focus groups, whereas access, organization, and power were each explicitly discussed in four or fewer student focus groups.

2. Exceptions were typing and using calculators. It is no surprise that speed and access were voiced frequently in the school community, as they are among the factors most frequently noted as benefits by Americans who hold generally positive views of the internet in society. See Aaron Smith, "Declining Majority of Online Adults Say the Internet Has Been Good for Society," *Pew Research Center*, April 30, 2018, http://www.pewinternet.org/2018/04/30/declining-majority-of-online-adults-say-the-internet-has-been-good-for-society/.

3. The value placed on increasing student access to learning through technology is shared by teachers beyond Modern Christian Schools; see, e.g., Katherine McKnight et al., "Teaching in a Digital Age: How Educators Use Technology to Improve Student Learning," *Journal of Research on Technology in Education* 48, no. 3 (2016): 194–211.

4. Neil Postman, *Technopoly: The Surrender of Culture to Technology* (New York: Knopf, 1992).

5. Other studies of educational technology programs have confirmed students' recognition of the ways technology supports organization. See, e.g., Mark Warschauer, *Laptops and Literacy: Learning in the Wireless Classroom* (New York: Teachers College Press, 2006); David Kaufman and Swapna Kumar, "Student Perceptions of a One-to-One iPad Program in an Urban High School," *International Journal of Research in Education and Science* 4, no. 2 (2018): 454–70.

6. See, e.g., Qing Li, "Student and Teacher Views about Technology: A Tale of Two Cities?," *Journal of Research on Technology in Education* 39, no. 4 (2007): 377–97.

7. These successful teachers often spoke of the balance between three components central to a current educational technology framework (Technological Pedagogical Content Knowledge or TPACK), despite never referring to the framework by name. The TPACK framework suggests that Content, Pedagogy, and Technology are central to teaching with technology, and a teacher's knowledge of and ability to integrate the three will lead to effective teaching. To further explore the TPACK framework see: Matthew Koehler and Punya Mishra, "What Is Technological Pedagogical Content Knowledge (TPACK)?," *Contemporary Issues in Technology and Teacher Education* 9, no. 1 (2009): 60–70; Punya Mishra and Matthew J. Koehler, "Technological Pedagogical Content Knowledge (TPCK): Confronting the Wicked Problems of Teaching with Technology," in *Society for Information Technology & Teacher Education International Conference*, 2214–26 (Association for the Advancement of Computing in Education [AACE], 2007).

Chapter 17

1. Albert Borgmann, *Technology and the Character of Contemporary Life: A Philosophical Inquiry* (Chicago: University of Chicago Press, 1984).

2. We take a closer look at issues of distraction in chapter 32.

3. One study of moral reasoning in computer environments notes "the significant role of technology in enabling negative behavior and the relative inability of subjects' use of principled moral reasoning to overcome it," based on the finding that "IT productivity features such as copy-and-paste are positively related to task misconduct." Jeffrey A. Roberts and David M. Wasieleski, "Moral Reasoning in Computer-Based Task Environments: Exploring the Interplay between Cognitive and Technological Factors on Individuals' Propensity to Break Rules," *Journal of Business Ethics* 110, no. 3 (2012): 355–76, quotation from 355.

4. Specific comparisons are difficult given that existing studies have varied dramatically in which behaviors they surveyed, how clearly they indicated whether technology was in use, whether schools had technology programs, and more. For an examination of such scholarship, see, e.g., Mollie K. Galloway, "Cheating in Advantaged High Schools: Prevalence, Justifications, and Possibilities for Change," *Ethics and Behavior* 22, no. 5 (2012): 378–99; Dominic A. Sisti, "How Do High School Students Justify Internet Plagiarism?," *Ethics and Behavior* 17, no. 3 (2007): 215–31.

5. As noted previously, specific behavior comparisons are difficult given the various ways research defines cheating (e.g., copying homework, cheating on a test, plagiarizing), yet the amount or frequency of cheating or academic dishonesty can be compared here with caution. For studies reporting globally higher levels of cheating or academic dishonesty in either middle or high school, see, e.g., Lene Arnett Jensen et al., "It's Wrong, but Everybody Does It: Academic Dishonesty among High School and College Students," *Contemporary Educational Psychology* 27, no. 2 (2002): 209–28; Josephson Institute, *The 2012 Report Card on the Ethics of American Youth* (Los Angeles: Josephson Institute of Ethics, 2012).

6. See, e.g., Pam A. Mueller and Daniel M. Oppenheimer, "The Pen Is Mightier Than the Keyboard: Advantages of Longhand over Laptop Note Taking," *Psychological Science* 25, no. 6 (2014): 1159–68.

7. Alfie Kohn, "The Case Against Grades," *Educational Leadership* 69, no. 3 (2011): 28–33.

8. Borgmann, *Technology and the Character of Contemporary Life*; Jacques Ellul, *The Technological Society* (New York: Vintage Books, 1964).

Chapter 18

1. Binbin Zheng et al., "Learning in One-to-One Laptop Environments: A Meta-Analysis and Research Synthesis," *Review of Educational Research* 86, no. 4 (2016): 1052–84, https://doi.org/10.3102/0034654316628645.

2. See Jan Hábl, *Lessons in Humanity from the Life and Work of John Amos Comenius* (Bonn: Verlag für Kultur und Wissenschaft, 2011); David I. Smith, *John Amos Comenius: A Visionary Reformer of Schools* (Camp Hill, PA: Classical Academic Press, 2017).

3. John Amos Comenius, *Panegersia or Universal Awakening*, translated by A. M. O. Dobbie (Shipston-on-Stour: Peter Drinkwater, 1990), 18.

4. Material coded for the theme of discernment occurred in every focus group across all kinds of focus group participant. Material coded for the theme of discernment also occurred in 357 of the 815 school documents selected for detailed coding.

5. Cf. Dorothy C. Bass et al., *Christian Practical Wisdom: What It Is, Why It Matters* (Grand Rapids: Eerdmans, 2016).

6. Rowan D. Williams, "Interiority and Epiphany: A Reading in New Testament Ethics," *Modern Theology* 13, no. 1 (1997): 42. Williams argues elsewhere that for Christians, actions are not simply good or bad, but more or less suited for revealing God's life in us. Rowan Williams, afterword to *Blackwell Companion to Christian Ethics*, ed. Stanley Hauerwas and Samuel Wells (Oxford: Blackwell, 2004), 494–98.

7. Kees Waaijman, "Discernment and Biblical Spirituality: An Overview and Evaluation of Recent Research," in *The Spirit That Guides: Discernment in the Bible and Spirituality*, *Acta Theologica* Supplementum 17, ed. Pieter G. R. De Villiers, 1–12 (Bloemfontein: University of the Free State, 2013).

8. Henri Nouwen, *Discernment: Reading the Signs of Daily Life* (New York: HarperOne, 2013), 3.

9. Dennis J. Horton, "Discerning Spiritual Discernment: Assessing Current Approaches for Understanding God's Will," *Journal of Youth Ministry* 7, no. 2 (2009): 7–31; Edward Collins Vacek, "Discernment within a Mutual Love Relationship with God: A New Theological Foundation," *Theological Studies* 74 (2013): 683–710.

10. Peter Browning, "Moral Discernment and Mainline Protestantism: Toward a Collaborative Christian Ethic," *Journal of the Society of Christian Ethics* 28, no. 1 (2008): 109–32; Anthony Egan, "Conscience, Spirit, Discernment: The Holy Spirit, the Spiritual Exercises and the Formation of Moral Conscience," *Journal of Theology for Southern Africa* 138 (2008): 57–70.

11. Steven M. Nolt, "You Hold the Whole World in Your Hand: Cell Phones and

Discernment in Amish Churches," *Vision* (Fall 2015): 27–37; John W. Crossin, "Ecumenical Reflections on Moral Discernment," *Journal of Ecumenical Studies* 50, no. 4 (2015): 561–82.

12. Marlene Kropf, "Cultivating a Congregational Climate of Discernment," *Vision* 12, no. 2 (Fall 2011): 43–51.

Chapter 19

1. Mike S. Ribble, Gerald D. Bailey, and Tweed W. Ross, "Digital Citizenship: Addressing Appropriate Technology Behavior," *Learning & Leading with Technology* 32, no. 1 (2004): 6–11; Mike S. Ribble, *Digital Citizenship in Schools: Nine Elements All Students Should Know* (Eugene, OR: International Society for Technology in Education, 2015); Donna Young, "A 21st Century Model for Teaching Digital Citizenship," *Educational Horizons* 92, no. 3 (2014): 9–12.

2. Moonsun Choi, "A Concept Analysis of Digital Citizenship for Democratic Citizenship Education in the Internet Age," *Theory & Research in Social Education* 44, no. 4 (2016): 565–607; Moonsun Choi, Michael Glassman, and Dean Cristol, "What It Means to Be a Citizen in the Internet Age: Development of a Reliable and Valid Digital Citizenship Scale," *Computers & Education* 107 (2017): 100–112.

3. Choi, "Concept Analysis," 573.

4. The emphasis has been shifting over the past decade from individual compliance with norms such as copyright to how to create safe communities online. Choi, "Concept Analysis," 583.

5. Choi, "Concept Analysis," 577.

6. Choi, "Concept Analysis," 579.

7. Choi, "Concept Analysis," 581.

8. Choi, Glassman, and Cristol, "What It Means"; Susan M. Bearden, *Digital Citizenship: A Community-Based Approach* (Thousand Oaks, CA: Corwin, 2016); Nicole Krueger, "9 Resources for Teaching Digital Citizenship," *ISTE Blog*, December 23, 2014, https://www.iste.org/explore/articleDetail?articleid=242.

9. James K. A. Smith, *Awaiting the King: Reforming Public Theology* (Grand Rapids: Baker Academic, 2017), 3.

10. Cf. Shannon Vallor, *Technology and the Virtues: A Philosophical Guide to a Future Worth Wanting* (New York: Oxford University Press, 2016).

Chapter 20

1. Of the 28,184 electronic files covering a twelve-year period, 815 were identified as relevant to our research questions. As we reviewed the files, a provisional set of codes naming emergent themes were developed through research team discussions of recurring topics in the data. These, including a code for "discernment," were discussed, formalized with definitional criteria, and tested for interrater reliability with multiple

researchers. The research team met regularly to discuss border instances and clarify the boundaries of the code. Line-by-line coding with the discernment code achieved an interrater reliability of 90.4%. The coding process was complemented by text-string searches for key terms to ensure inclusion of all relevant data. All coded material was reviewed multiple times, and findings were reviewed and discussed by the research team. These processes are intended to ensure as far as possible that what we observed in the documentary archive was not just in the eye of the beholder. See the appendix on research methods for more details.

2. The fact that important statements of principle were sometimes carried over from year to year with the same typographic errors evidences direct copying from earlier documents. See n. 6 below.

3. The evidence discussed in this section includes notes from group brainstorming focused on discernment at two administrative and committee meetings as well as records of committee discussion of teacher feedback from internal surveys, all from the first five years of the technology program.

4. This material was included along with the rest of the documentary archive in the process of coding content for the presence of the discernment theme. The brainstorming documents were analyzed in further detail using emergent codes based on recurring topics in the data to establish the subthemes associated with discernment.

5. Formerly known as NETS (National Educational Technology Standards), the International Society for Technology in Education (ISTE) standards are published by a nonprofit membership association with the aim of setting basic standards for the use of technology in teaching and learning settings. Digital citizenship is an explicit organizing theme.

6. The fact that this recurs across the earliest sequence of documents as "Develop and apply a framework for discernment and ethic use of technology," before being corrected to "ethical" in subsequent documents, suggests that this goal was regularly copied and pasted into new training plans. A document laying out a three-year professional development plan in the seventh year of the program still includes the goal that teachers will "Learn to communicate appropriate legal, ethical, and discerning Christian behavior related to technology resources." An update two years later still refers to discernment as a "critical" overarching goal for school students. However, it is no longer mentioned in that update in the context of professional development for teachers, having been replaced by a focus on "Technology Literacy (as defined by ISTE NETS Standards along with the [State] Standards)."

7. An administrator in a focus group recalled that some of these sessions still included conversation about digital citizenship/discernment themes.

Chapter 21

1. Alan Noble, *Disruptive Witness: Speaking Truth in a Distracted Age* (Downers Grove, IL: IVP Books, 2018); Andy Crouch, *The Tech-Wise Family: Everyday Steps for Putting Technology in Its Proper Place* (Grand Rapids: Baker Books, 2017).

2. Council on Communications and Media, "Media Use in School-Aged Children

and Adolescents," *Pediatrics* 138, no. 5 (2016): e20162592, https://doi.org/10.1542/peds .2016-2592.

3. Oliviero Bruni et al., "Technology Use and Sleep Quality in Preadolescence and Adolescence," *Journal of Clinical Sleep Medicine* 11, no. 12 (2015): 1433–41, https://doi .org/10.5664/jcsm.5282; E. de Jong et al., "Association between TV Viewing, Computer Use and Overweight, Determinants and Competing Activities of Screen Time in 4- to 13-Year-Old Children," *International Journal of Obesity* 37, no. 1 (2013): 47–53, https://doi .org/10.1038/ijo.2011.244; Megan A. Moreno et al., "Problematic Internet Use among US Youth: A Systematic Review," *Archives of Pediatrics & Adolescent Medicine* 165, no. 9 (2011): 797–805, https://doi.org/10.1001/archpediatrics.2011.58.

4. Richard E. Bélanger et al., "A U-Shaped Association between Intensity of Internet Use and Adolescent Health," *Pediatrics* 127, no. 2 (2011): e330-335, https://doi .org/10.1542/peds.2010-1235; Jean M. Twenge et al., "Increases in Depressive Symptoms, Suicide-Related Outcomes, and Suicide Rates Among U.S. Adolescents After 2010 and Links to Increased New Media Screen Time," *Clinical Psychological Science* 6, no. 1 (2018): 3–17, https://doi.org/10.1177/2167702617723376.

5. Andrew K. Przybylski and Netta Weinstein, "A Large-Scale Test of the Goldilocks Hypothesis: Quantifying the Relations between Digital-Screen Use and the Mental Well-Being of Adolescents," *Psychological Science* 28, no. 2 (2017): 204–15, https://doi .org/10.1177/0956797616678438.

6. As noted in chapter 4, our survey data included high schoolers from an American Midwest, Protestant Christian school influenced by similar traditions as our focus school, and just a few years into a one-to-one technology program. We refer to this control group as Western Christian School. It is not part of the Modern Christian Schools system.

7. The methodological choice to observe overlapping activities within classrooms (e.g., two or more groups of students doing different types of activities) limits the ways average time on devices is reported. Rather than a fixed time, we can provide a range. The lower end of the range reflects average time on devices in classrooms with no overlapping activities, and the higher end of the range reflects average time with overlapping activities included.

8. Estimates are informed by the fact that an average school day at Modern Christian Schools is seven hours. Removing lunch, chapel, recesses, and/or passing periods leaves approximately six hours of instructional time. We can therefore multiply results from 45-minute observation blocks by eight to estimate screen time per day. These findings should be interpreted with caution as they are an extrapolation of data. They nonetheless provide useful data for comparison.

9. Vicky Rideout, *The Common Sense Census: Media Use by Tweens and Teens* (San Francisco: Common Sense Media, 2015), 17, retrieved from https://www.commonsense media.org/sites/default/files/uploads/research/census_researchreport.pdf.

10. Rideout, *Common Sense Census,* 82.

11. It is interesting to note that one 2016 study reports the average time parents spend on personal media use (not work related) nationally is over seven hours per day. It seems that the students are using devices at a rate similar to that of parents across the United States. See Alexis R. Lauricella et al., *The Common Sense Census: Plugged-In Parents of Tweens and Teens* (San Francisco: Common Sense Media, 2016).

12. We do not include time watching television or movies, since we did not measure this type of media consumption in a way that is comparable to this nationally representative study.

13. In our data, 48% of boys used social media more than an hour a day, while 63% of girls did the same. This same pattern shows up in Rideout, *The Common Sense Census* 62, retrieved from https://www.commonsensemedia.org/sites/default/files/uploads /research/census_researchreport.pdf.

14. Rideout, *Common Sense Census.*

15. L. Mark Carrier et al., "Causes, Effects, and Practicalities of Everyday Multitasking," *Developmental Review* 35 (2015): 64–78, https://doi.org/10.1016/j.dr.2014.12.005; Wade C. Jacobsen and Renata Forste, "The Wired Generation: Academic and Social Outcomes of Electronic Media Use among University Students," *Cyberpsychology, Behavior and Social Networking* 14, no. 5 (2011): 275–80, https://doi.org/10.1089/cyber.2010.0135.

16. Council on Communications and Media, "Media Use."

17. These differences were statistically significant in linear models controlling for school, gender, and grade.

18. Alexis R. Lauricella, Ellen Wartella, and Victoria J. Rideout, "Young Children's Screen Time: The Complex Role of Parent and Child Factors," *Journal of Applied Developmental Psychology* 36 (2015): 11–17.

Chapter 22

1. Survey data ($N = 54$).

2. This is in spite of the fact that examination of focus group transcripts showed that while the themes of Christian perspective and mission were prompted by interviewers a number of times, none of the interviewer questions prompted the purity theme.

3. Cf. Bruce Drake, Kristi Yuthas, and Jesse F. Dillard, "It's Only Words: Impacts of Information Technology on Moral Dialogue," *Journal of Business Ethics* 23, no. 1 (2000): 41–59; Jeffrey A. Roberts and David M. Wasieleski, "Moral Reasoning in Computer-Based Task Environments: Exploring the Interplay between Cognitive and Technological Factors on Individuals' Propensity to Break Rules," *Journal of Business Ethics* 110, no. 3 (2012): 355–76.

Chapter 23

1. Barna Group, "Teens and Young Adults Use Porn More Than Anyone Else," January 28, 2016, https://www.barna.com/research/teens-young-adults-use-porn-more -than-anyone-else/.

2. The filtering of some internet content is common across schools and libraries, in part because of federal regulations. This is not without controversy, as noted in Melissa D. Anderson, "How Internet Filtering Hurts Kids," *The Atlantic*, April 26, 2016, https://www.theatlantic.com/education/archive/2016/04/internet-filtering-hurts

-kids/479907/. Concerns about filtering that go beyond legal requirements are well represented by Kristen R. Batch, Trina Magi, and Michelle Luhtala, "Filtering Beyond CIPA: Consequences of and Alternatives to Overfiltering in Schools," *Knowledge Quest* 44, no. 1 (2015): 60–66.

3. While access of harmful material on school devices in school appears to be uncommon, technology administrators did anecdotally report dealing with cases of access at other times based on examination of device logs.

4. Barna Group, *The Porn Phenomenon: The Impact of Pornography in the Digital Age* (Ventura, CA: Barna Group, 2016).

5. By asking similar questions in many different ways, we can look for consistent results across questions and can be more confident of our conclusions.

6. These comparisons yielded no statistically significant differences in linear regression models that controlled for student grade, gender, and grade point average (GPA).

7. When surveying students about this kind of behavior, we worry about two kinds of bias. First, students might be nervous about admitting to being able to break the rules in a survey that is endorsed by the school administration. We gave strong assurances of privacy, but there still might be a social desirability effect that causes students to underreport these kinds of activities. Second, we worry that students might be overconfident whenever reporting on their own technological prowess, which would result in their overestimating their ability to bypass internet filtering. Overall, though, we have high confidence that the data are reliable and that our broader conclusions are well-founded, in part because we can favorably compare our survey data to the focus group conversations and classroom observations, and also because we can compare our results to other studies on similar topics.

8. These relationships proved strongly statistically significant in linear regression models even after controlling for the school, grade, and gender.

9. Other researchers have also found that filtering in schools had little effect on students' access to problematic content. Andrew K. Przybylski and Victoria Nash, "Internet Filtering Technology and Aversive Online Experiences in Adolescents," *Journal of Pediatrics* 184 (2017): 215–19, https://doi.org/10.1016/j.jpeds.2017.01.063; Andrew K. Przybylski and Victoria Nash, "Internet Filtering and Adolescent Exposure to Online Sexual Material," *Cyberpsychology, Behavior, and Social Networking* 21, no. 7 (2018): 405–10, https://doi.org/10.1089/cyber.2017.0466.

10. It is perhaps worth noting that in the Barna survey cited above, respondents aged thirty-one to fifty came across or sought out porn at rates very similar to, perhaps overall slightly higher than, teenagers, lending weight to Christian Smith's caution that many issues discussed as teen problems are in fact also adult problems, with teens often doing no worse and sometimes better than older generations. See Christian Smith and Melinda Lundquist Denton, *Soul Searching: The Religious and Spiritual Lives of American Teenagers* (New York: Oxford University Press, 2005), 187.

11. This difference is statistically significant in linear models including all students after controlling for gender and GPA.

12. Twenty-eight percent of Modern Christian alumni reported seeking out sexually explicit media at least a few times a month, compared to 35% of Western Christian alumni and 39% of Liberal Arts College students. The difference between Modern

Christian alumni and Liberal Arts College students was statistically significant in linear models that controlled for gender and GPA.

13. Cf. chapter 22.

Chapter 24

1. Christian Smith and Melinda Lundquist Denton, *Soul Searching: The Religious and Spiritual Lives of American Teenagers* (New York: Oxford University Press, 2005), 176.

2. Smith and Denton, *Soul Searching*, 178.

3. Adam Alter, *Irresistible: The Rise of Addictive Technology and the Business of Keeping Us Hooked* (New York: Penguin, 2017).

4. We explore this further in chapter 29.

Chapter 25

1. See, e.g., Mark A. Noll, *The Scandal of the Evangelical Mind* (Grand Rapids: Eerdmans, 1995); George M. Marsden, *The Outrageous Idea of Christian Scholarship* (New York: Oxford University Press, 1997); David K. Naugle Jr., *Worldview: The History of a Concept* (Grand Rapids: Eerdmans, 2002); J. P. Moreland and William Lane Craig, *Philosophical Foundations for a Christian Worldview* (Downers Grove, IL: IVP Academic, 2009).

2. This theme was emphasized less at the middle school and elementary school levels, being chosen by 63% of teachers, but was still in a tie for the most frequent response.

3. See David I. Smith and James K. A. Smith, "Practices, Faith, and Pedagogy," in *Teaching and Christian Practices: Reshaping Faith and Learning*, ed. David I. Smith and James K. A. Smith, 1–23 (Grand Rapids: Eerdmans, 2011).

4. Cf. Joshua J. Lewer, Nicholas R. Gerlich, and Lucas Doyle, "The Impact of Christian Education and Curriculum on Illegal Media File Sharing Attitudes and Behavior," *Christian Business Academy Review* 3 (2008): 70–79.

5. Cf. Craig Dykstra, *Growing in the Life of Faith: Education and Christian Practices*, 2nd ed. (Louisville: Westminster John Knox Press, 2005); Amy Plantinga-Pauw, "Attending to the Gaps between Beliefs and Practices," in *Practicing Theology: Beliefs and Practices in Christian Life*, ed. Miroslav Volf and Dorothy C. Bass, 33–48 (Grand Rapids: Eerdmans, 2002).

Part 4 Summary

1. Henri Nouwen, *Discernment: Reading the Signs of Daily Life* (New York: HarperOne, 2013), 3.

Chapter 26

1. Jean Lave and Etienne Wenger, *Situated Learning: Legitimate Peripheral Participation* (New York: Cambridge University Press, 1991); Etienne Wenger, *Communities of Practice: Learning, Meaning, and Identity* (New York: Cambridge University Press, 1999).

2. Craig Dykstra, *Growing in the Life of Faith: Education and Christian Practices*, 2nd ed. (Louisville: Westminster John Knox, 2005); Dorothy C. Bass, *Practicing Our Faith: A Way of Life for a Searching People*, 2nd ed. (San Francisco: Jossey-Bass, 2010). "Christian practices" here and throughout means practices that are normatively characteristic of Christianity, those that belong to its proper logic and biblical frame. This need not mean that Christians always succeed in practicing them or that they are not practiced by others.

3. Miroslav Volf, "Theology for a Way of Life," in *Practicing Theology: Beliefs and Practices in Christian Life*, ed. Miroslav Volf and Dorothy C. Bass, 245–63 (Grand Rapids: Eerdmans, 2002); Dykstra, *Growing*.

4. Alasdair C. MacIntyre, *After Virtue: A Study in Moral Theory*, 3rd ed. (Notre Dame, IN: University of Notre Dame Press, 2007).

5. This is of course a bare-bones definition. More complex definitions have been developed for more precise philosophical discussions, the most famous of which is that offered by Alasdair MacIntyre. According to MacIntyre, a practice is "any coherent and complex form of socially established cooperative human activity through which goods internal to that form of activity are realised in the course of trying to achieve those standards of excellence which are appropriate to, and partially definitive of, that form of activity, with the result that human powers to achieve excellence, and human conceptions to the ends and goods involved, are systematically extended." MacIntyre, *After Virtue*, 187.

6. James K. A. Smith, *Desiring the Kingdom: Worship, Worldview, and Cultural Formation* (Grand Rapids: Baker Academic, 2009); David I. Smith and James K. A. Smith, *Teaching and Christian Practices: Reshaping Faith and Learning* (Grand Rapids: Eerdmans, 2011).

7. Findings related to the themes of discernment and Christian perspectives are explored in part 4 of the book.

8. Cf. Leviticus 19:18, 33–34; Matthew 25:37–38; Hebrews 13:2. Some literature explores the connections between faith, hospitality, and education, including specifically language instruction. See, e.g., Irene Brouwer Konyndyk, "Direct and Explicit Instruction in the Foreign Language Classroom: Showing Hospitality to Students with Learning Disabilities," *Journal of Christianity and Foreign Languages* 12 (2011): 79–85; Amy G. Oden, *And You Welcomed Me: A Sourcebook on Hospitality in Early Christianity* (Nashville: Abingdon, 2001); Christine Pohl, *Making Room: Recovering Hospitality as a Christian Tradition* (Grand Rapids: Eerdmans, 1999); David I. Smith and Barbara Carvill, *The Gift of the Stranger: Faith, Hospitality, and Foreign Language Learning* (Grand Rapids: Eerdmans, 2000); Jacob Stratman, "What's in a Name: The Place of Recognition in a Hospitable Classroom," *International Journal of Christianity and Education* 19, no. 1 (2015): 26–36.

9. David I. Smith, "Hospitality, Language Pedagogy, and Communities of Practice," *Journal of Christianity and Foreign Languages* 12 (2011): 29–44.

Chapter 27

1. It should be noted that the examples discussed in this chapter and the next focus specifically on whether and how digital technology enhanced connection to the wider world. They took place in the context of various other learning activities that involved reaching out to audiences beyond the schools, but were less clearly tied to digital technology use.

2. These examples are drawn from focus group, case study, and classroom observation data.

3. Micah 6:8.

4. Allan Collins and Richard Halverson, *Rethinking Education in the Age of Technology: The Digital Revolution and Schooling in America* (New York: Teachers College Press, 2018).

Chapter 28

1. A substantive body of literature considers the social and psychological tensions arising from the connectivity of digital technologies. See, e.g., Craig Detweiler, *iGods: How Technology Shapes Our Spiritual and Social Lives* (Grand Rapids: Brazos, 2013); Sherry Turkle, *Alone Together: Why We Expect More from Technology and Less from Each Other* (New York: Basic Books, 2011); José Van Dijck, *The Culture of Connectivity: A Critical History of Social Media* (New York: Oxford University Press, 2013).

2. See, e.g., Sherry Turkle, *Reclaiming Conversation: The Power of Talk in a Digital Age* (New York: Penguin, 2016).

3. The data here can be compared to our finding in chapter 9 that teachers were more hesitant than other groups about whether use of laptops was supporting the "bring change to the world" element of the mission as well as had been hoped. Both sets of findings suggest some uncertainty in the school community on this score.

Chapter 29

1. See especially chapters 21 and 24.

2. See, e.g., Reynol Junco and Sheila R. Cotten, "No A 4 U: The Relationship between Multitasking and Academic Performance," *Computers & Education* 59, no. 2 (2012): 505–14; Jeffrey H. Kuznekoff, Stevie Munz, and Scott Titsworth, "Mobile Phones in the Classroom: Examining the Effects of Texting, Twitter, and Message Content on Student Learning," *Communication Education* 64, no. 3 (2015): 344–65, https://doi.org/10.1080/03634523.2015.1038727; Eyal Ophir, Clifford Nass, and Anthony D. Wagner, "Cognitive Control in Media Multitaskers," *Proceedings of the National Academy of Sciences* 106, no. 37 (2009): 15583–87; Antti Oulasvirta and Pertti Saariluoma, "Long-Term Working Memory and Interrupting Messages in Human–Computer Interaction," *Behaviour & Information Technology* 23, no. 1 (2004): 53–64.

3. Richard E. Mayer and Roxana Moreno, "Nine Ways to Reduce Cognitive Load in Multimedia Learning," *Educational Psychologist* 38, no. 1 (March 1, 2003): 43–52, https://doi.org/10.1207/S15326985EP3801_6.

4. American Psychological Association, *Stress in America: Coping with Change*, Stress in America™ Survey (2017); Kuznekoff, Munz, and Titsworth, "Mobile Phones in the Classroom," 344–65.

5. Jeffrey H. Kuznekoff and Scott Titsworth, "The Impact of Mobile Phone Usage on Student Learning," *Communication Education* 62, no. 3 (July 1, 2013): 233–52, https://doi.org/10.1080/03634523.2013.767917.

6. Carrie B. Fried, "In-Class Laptop Use and Its Effects on Student Learning," *Computers & Education* 50, no. 3 (April 1, 2008): 906–14, https://doi.org/10.1016/j.compedu.2006.09.006.

7. Faria Sana, Tina Weston, and Nicholas J. Cepeda, "Laptop Multitasking Hinders Classroom Learning for Both Users and Nearby Peers," *Computers & Education* 62 (2013): 24–31.

8. Some caveats are in order before exploring this data. Only observable behaviors (talking with peers about the school dance, shopping online, working on homework for another class, etc.) can be recorded. There is no way to actually capture the students daydreaming, zoning out, and so on. Given the challenges of observing individual students in whole-class settings, for reliability purposes the researchers recorded off-task behavior if any two or more students were engaged individually or collectively in a non-class-related activity and the duration lasted more than one minute.

9. Case study observation teachers were selected for their "thoughtful use of technology," and therefore reported time of technology use in these classrooms generally exceeded that in random classroom observations. In some units, like the middle school unit, technology use nearly tripled average reported use in random observations.

10. Larry D. Rosen, L. Mark Carrier, and Nancy A. Cheever, "Facebook and Texting Made Me Do It: Media-Induced Task-Switching While Studying," *Computers in Human Behavior* 29, no. 3 (2013): 948–58.

11. Amanda Lenhart et al., "Teens and Mobile Phones: Text Messaging Explodes as Teens Embrace It as the Centerpiece of Their Communication Strategies with Friends," *Pew Internet & American Life Project* (2010); Vicky Rideout, *Common Sense Census: Media Use by Tweens and Teens* (San Francisco: Common Sense Media, 2015), https://www.pewinternet.org/2010/04/20/teens-and-mobile-phones/.

12. This is a focus of practical resources such as Andy Crouch, *The Tech-Wise Family: Everyday Steps for Putting Technology in Its Proper Place* (Grand Rapids: Baker Books, 2017).

13. Laurel Felt and Michael Robb, *Technology Addiction: Concern, Controversy, and Finding Balance*, Research Brief (San Francisco: Common Sense Media, 2016).

14. Parents, and especially teachers, perhaps because they have longer experience without laptops and mobile phones, were more likely to believe that technology had fostered addiction for students.

15. Few students reported a negative impact on relationships, though only 8% of those with higher self-reported grades agreed with this statement while 16% of those with lower grades agreed. All of these differences are statistically significant in linear regression models controlling for gender and grade.

Chapter 30

1. Mary Budd Rowe, "Relation of Wait-Time and Rewards to the Development of Language, Logic, and Fate Control: Part II: Rewards," *Journal of Research in Science Teaching* 11, no. 4 (1974): 291–308; Mary Budd Rowe, "Wait Time: Slowing Down May Be a Way of Speeding Up!," *Journal of Teacher Education* 37 (1986): 43–50.

2. Ferris Jabr, "The Reading Brain in the Digital Age: The Science of Paper Versus Screens," *Scientific American*, April 11, 2013, https://www.scientificamerican.com/arti cle/reading-paper-screens/; Andrew Piper, *Book Was There: Reading in Electronic Times* (Chicago: University of Chicago Press, 2012).

3. See Paul J. Griffiths, *Religious Reading: The Place of Reading in the Practice of Religion* (New York: Oxford University Press, 1999); Griffiths, "Reading as a Spiritual Discipline," in *The Scope of Our Art: The Vocation of the Theological Teacher*, ed. L. Gregory Jones and Stephanie Paulsell, 32–47 (Grand Rapids: Eerdmans, 2002); Alan Jacobs, "Bakhtin and the Hermeneutics of Love," in *Bakhtin and Religion: A Feeling for Faith*, ed. Susan M. Felch and Paul J. Contino, 25–45 (Evanston, IL: Northwestern University Press, 2001); C. S. Lewis, *An Experiment in Criticism* (Cambridge: Cambridge University Press, 1961); Eugene H. Peterson, *Eat This Book: A Conversation in the Art of Spiritual Reading* (Grand Rapids: Eerdmans, 2006); David I. Smith, "Reading Practices and Christian Pedagogy: Enacting Charity with Texts," in *Teaching and Christian Practices: Reshaping Faith and Learning*, ed. David I. Smith and James K. A. Smith, 43–60 (Grand Rapids: Eerdmans, 2011).

4. David I. Smith, John Shortt, and John Sullivan, eds., *Teaching Spiritually Engaged Reading* (Nottingham: The Stapleford Center, 2007).

5. Cf. Milena I. Tsvetkova, "The Speed Reading Is in Disrepute: Advantages of Slow Reading for the Information Equilibrium," *European Journal of Contemporary Education* 6, no. 3 (2017): 593–603.

6. Cf. Wayne Au's account of curriculum as "complex environmental design" in Wayne Au, *Critical Curriculum Studies: Education, Consciousness, and the Politics of Knowing* (New York: Routledge, 2012).

7. Cf. Trevor Cooling and Elizabeth Green, "Competing Imaginations for Teaching and Learning: The Findings of Research into a Christian Approach to Teaching and Learning Called What If Learning," *International Journal of Christianity and Education* 19, no. 2 (2015): 96–107.

Chapter 31

1. See, e.g., Dallas Willard, *The Spirit of the Disciplines: Understanding How God Changes Lives* (New York: HarperOne, 1999).

2. Cf. Carolyne Call, "The Rough Trail to Authentic Pedagogy: Incorporating Hospitality, Fellowship, and Testimony into the Classroom," in *Teaching and Christian Practices: Reshaping Faith and Learning*, ed. David I. Smith and James K. A. Smith, 60–79 (Grand Rapids: Eerdmans, 2011); Amos Yong, *Hospitality and the Other: Pentecost, Christian Practices, and the Neighbor* (Maryknoll, NY: Orbis, 2008).

3. It could, of course, also be that devotional activity is somehow more conservative/ slower to change than classroom learning activities, which have been more the focus of professional development with technology. Some other findings, however, may tell against this, including the development of creative engagement with technology in Bible curriculum and the explicitness of the schools' efforts to connect technology to faith.

4. See, e.g., Abraham J. Heschel, *The Sabbath: Its Meaning for Modern Man* (New York: Farrar, Straus & Giroux, 1951); Dan B. Allender, *The Sabbath* (Nashville: Thomas Nelson, 2005); Marva J. Dawn, *Keeping the Sabbath Wholly: Ceasing, Resting, Embracing, Feasting* (Grand Rapids: Eerdmans, 1989).

5. Cf. Katrina C. Hoop, "Comte Unplugged: Using a 'Technology Fast' to Teach Sociological Theory," *Teaching Sociology* 40, no. 2 (2012): 158–65.

Chapter 32

1. Cf. David Kaufman and Swapna Kumar, "Student Perceptions of a One-to-One iPad Program in an Urban High School," *International Journal of Research in Education and Science* 4, no. 2 (2018): 454–70.

2. We are uncertain of the extent to which the reported teacher was intentional about the creation of this classroom expectation in relation to student responsibility, but such practices still convey messages.

3. Faria Sana, Tina Weston, and Nicholas J. Cepeda, "Laptop Multitasking Hinders Classroom Learning for Both Users and Nearby Peers," *Computers & Education* 62 (2013): 24–31.

4. Research suggests that peer group norms can significantly undermine school efforts to develop students' social attitudes and affect what behaviors students find acceptable. See, e.g., Luke McGuire, Adam Rutland, and Drew Nesdale, "Peer Group Norms and Accountability Moderate the Effect of School Norms on Children's Intergroup Attitudes," *Child Development* 86, no. 4 (2015): 1290–97; Kris Ojala and Drew Nesdale, "Bullying and Social Identity: The Effects of Group Norms and Distinctiveness Threat on Attitudes towards Bullying," *British Journal of Developmental Psychology* 22, no. 1 (2004): 19–35; Drew Nesdale and Michael J. Lawson, "Social Groups and Children's Intergroup Attitudes: Can School Norms Moderate the Effects of Social Group Norms?," *Child Development* 82, no. 5 (2011): 1594–1606.

5. Cf. Dominic Abrams et al., "Older but Wilier: Ingroup Accountability and the Development of Subjective Group Dynamics," *Developmental Psychology* 43, no. 1 (2007): 134–48.

6. Christian Smith and Melinda Lundquist Denton, *Soul Searching: The Religious and Spiritual Lives of American Teenagers* (New York: Oxford University Press, 2005), 176.

Chapter 33

1. See, e.g., Sherry Turkle, *Alone Together: Why We Expect More from Technology and Less from Each Other* (New York: Basic Books, 2011); Turkle, *Reclaiming Conversation:*

The Power of Talk in a Digital Age (New York: Penguin Books, 2016) ; Jean Twenge, *IGen: Why Today's Super-Connected Kids Are Growing Up Less Rebellious, More Tolerant, Less Happy—and Completely Unprepared for Adulthood—and What That Means for the Rest of Us* (New York: Atria Books, 2017).

2. Nathan Fisk, "'. . . when no one is hearing them swear'—Youth Safety and the Pedagogy of Surveillance," *Surveillance and Society* 12, no. 4 (2014): 566.

3. John Dyer, *From the Garden to the City: The Redeeming and Corrupting Power of Technology* (Grand Rapids: Kregel, 2011); Diane Hockridge, "What's the Problem? Spiritual Formation in Distance and Online Theological Education," *Journal of Christian Education* 54, no. 1 (2011): 25–38.

4. Hueth cautions against reducing the idea of distance to be traveled in online education to questions of physical proximity. In online, hybrid, and face-to-face learning communities, participants must cross many distances (cultural, ethical, linguistic, social, etc.) to meet each other. Alan C. Hueth, "E-Learning and Christian Higher Education: A War of the Worlds, or Lessons in Reductionism?," *Christian Scholar's Review* 33, no. 4 (2004): 527–46.

5. Matthew 7:12; Mark 12:29–31; 1 Corinthians 12–14.

6. 1 Corinthians 12:12–26; Ephesians 2:21; 1 Peter 2:5.

7. E.g., Romans 12:3–13; 14:20; 1 Corinthians 12:7; 13:1–13; 14:12; Ephesians 4:32; Philippians 2:3; 1 Thessalonians 5:11; James 5:16.

8. Helen M. Blier, "Webbing the Common Good: Virtual Environment, Incarnated Community, and Education for the Reign of God," *Teaching Theology & Religion* 11, no. 1 (2008): 24–31, doi:10.1111/j.1467-9647.2007.00393.x.

9. Amitai Etzioni, *The New Golden Rule: Community and Morality in a Democratic Society* (New York: Basic Books, 1996), 127.

10. Andrew Feenberg and Darin Barney, *Community in the Digital Age: Philosophy and Practice* (Lanham, MD: Rowman & Littlefield, 2004). We focus here on physically local community; the literature on digital technologies in Christian education has also increasingly examined the nature of online communities. See, e.g., Travis S. Hines et al., "Online Theological Education: A Case Study of Trinity School for Ministry," *Christian Higher Education* 8, no. 1 (2009): 32–41; Mark Nichols, "The Akademeia as Paradigm for Online Community in Theological Distance Education," *Journal of Christian Education* 54, no. 1 (2011): 5–23; Mary E. Quinn, Laura S. Foote, and Michele L. Williams, "Integrating a Biblical Worldview and Developing Online Courses for the Adult Learner," *Christian Scholar's Review* 41, no. 2 (2012): 163–73; Jay Rasmussen, "Online Instruction: Reflections of a Rookie Instructor," *Journal of Christian Education* 54, no. 1 (2011): 64–68; Alfred P. Rovai, Jason D. Baker, and William F. Cox Jr., "How Christianly Is Christian Distance Higher Education?," *Christian Higher Education* 7, no. 1 (2008): 1–22; Ros Stuart-Buttle, "Interrupting Adult Learning through Online Pedagogy," *Journal of Education and Christian Belief* 18, no. 1 (2014): 61–75; M. S. Yacapsin, "Graduate Student Preferences for Practicing Faith in Online Coursework," *Journal of Research on Christian Education* 23, no. 3 (2014): 271–82.

11. Material coded for the theme of community occurred in 91.6% of focus groups across all kinds of focus group participants. Material coded for the theme of community also occurred in 309 of the 815 school documents selected for detailed coding.

Chapter 34

1. Marc Prensky, "How to Teach with Technology: Keeping Both Teachers and Students Comfortable in an Era of Exponential Change," *Emerging Technologies for Learning* 2, no. 4 (2007): 40–46.
2. Cf. Ken Badley, *Curriculum Planning with Design Language: Building Elegant Courses and Units* (New York: Routledge, 2018); Mary Herring, Matthew Koehler, and Punya Mishra, *Handbook of Technological Pedagogical Content Knowledge (TPACK) for Educators* (New York: Routledge, 2016).
3. Richard S. Ascough, "Designing for Online Distance Education: Putting Pedagogy before Technology," *Teaching Theology & Religion* 5, no. 1 (2002): 17–29.
4. David I. Smith, *On Christian Teaching: Practicing Faith in the Classroom* (Grand Rapids: Eerdmans, 2018).
5. Dietrich Bonhoeffer, *Life Together and Prayerbook of the Bible*, Dietrich Bonhoeffer Works 5, trans. Daniel W. Bloesch and James H. Burtness (Minneapolis: Fortress Press, 1996); Neil Holm, "Classroom Formation & Spiritual Awareness Pedagogy Based on Bonhoeffer's *Life Together*," *Journal of Education and Christian Belief* 12, no. 2 (2008): 159–75; David I. Smith, "Teaching Bonhoeffer: Pedagogy and Peripheral Practices," *International Journal of Christianity & Education* 21, no. 2 (2017): 146–59.
6. Helen M. Blier, "Webbing the Common Good: Virtual Environment, Incarnated Community, and Education for the Reign of God," *Teaching Theology & Religion* 11, no. 1 (2008): 24–31.

Chapter 35

1. The number was even higher at Western Christian School, where 91% agreed that the technology program at their school had increased collaboration.
2. Partnership for 21st Century Learning, *P21 Framework Definitions* (2015), retrieved from http://www.p21.org/storage/documents/docs/P21_Framework_Definitions_New_Logo_2015.pdf.
3. Norma de Waal Malefyt and Howard Vanderwell, *Designing Worship Together: Models and Strategies for Worship Planning* (Herndon, VA: Alban Institute, 2005).
4. Cf. Robert Wuthnow, *Sharing the Journey: Support Groups and the Quest for a New Community* (New York: Free Press, 1994).
5. Gloria Goris Stronks and Doug Blomberg, eds., *A Vision with a Task: Christian Schooling for Responsive Discipleship* (Grand Rapids: Calvin Center for Christian Scholarship and Baker Books, 1993).
6. As a reminder, in random observations single lessons were observed and teachers were not notified until the day of the observation. In case study observations a smaller number of teachers were selected for being identified by peers and administrators as being particularly thoughtful in their approach to technology integration. These teachers' classes were observed over a longer period.
7. For the calculation of the amount of time collaboration occurred, each learning activity as a whole was evaluated by the above criteria. Furthermore, three noninstruc-

tional activities were removed from analysis: nonacademic social interaction, procedures and management, and technology management.

8. Max Lucado, *A Hat for Ivan* (Wheaton, IL: Crossway, 2004).

9. Studies examine the benefits of collaboration with technology, but do not determine an optimal amount. E.g., Juanjuan Chen Minhong Wang, Paul A. Kirschner, and Chin-Chung Tsai, "The Role of Collaboration, Computer Use, Learning Environments, and Supporting Strategies in CSCL: A Meta-Analysis," *Review of Educational Research* 88, no 6 (2018): 799–843.

10. Slicing the data in another direction lets us ask how much of the time students collaborated when using technology. If we look at all the activities in random observations where students were using individual technological devices, some or all of the students were collaborating 43% of this time. This figure was only 24% when no technology was in use. In the case study classrooms, collaborative screen time was higher, with some or all of the students engaged in collaboration 67% of the time when using screens, as opposed to 25% of the time when learning without technology. This reinforces the previous finding.

11. These responses were ranked from a list of eleven options, including school technology personnel and professional conferences. Options were ranked by teachers from most to least helpful.

Chapter 36

1. Steven C. Vryhof, *Between Memory and Vision: The Case for Faith-Based Schooling* (Grand Rapids: Eerdmans, 2004); Gary B. Arnold, "Parent Involvement in Our Schools," *Christian School Educator* 17, no. 2 (2014): 34–36. There is a pattern of higher parental participation in school-related activities in private schools in general: Amber Noel, Patrick Stark, and Jeremy Redford, *Parent and Family Involvement in Education, from the National Household Education Surveys Program of 2012: First Look* (Washington, DC: National Center for Education Statistics, Institute of Education Sciences, U.S. Department of Education, 2016).

2. See, e.g., Manya Whitaker and Kathleen Hoover-Dempsey, "School Influences on Parents' Role Beliefs," *The Elementary School Journal* 114, no. 1 (2013): 73–99; Virginia B. Bartel, "Home and School Factors Impacting Parental Involvement in a Title I Elementary School," *Journal of Research in Childhood Education* 24, no. 3 (2010): 209–28; Kellie J. Anderson and Kathleen M. Minke, "Parent Involvement in Education: Toward an Understanding of Parents' Decision Making," *Journal of Educational Research* 100, no. 5 (2007): 311, 323, 328; Steven B. Sheldon, "Improving Student Attendance with School, Family and Community Partnerships," *Journal of Educational Research* 100, no. 5 (2007): 267–75.

3. This may imply lack of clarity about how the commitment to discernment relates to the practical details, or it may indicate that the focus on meeting behavioral expectations was felt to be itself the most relevant outworking of Christian discernment.

4. Cf. Susan Bearden, *Digital Citizenship: A Community-Based Approach* (Thousand Oaks, CA: Corwin Press, 2016). Adult-youth mentorship allows space for reflection on what is posted and observed online, with the goal of cultivating "conscientious con-

nectivity." See Carrie James, *Disconnected: Youth, New Media, and the Ethics Gap* (Cambridge, MA: MIT Press, 2014).

5. Teachers also reflected critically on some such activities. In discussion with first-grade teachers about discipleship practices, they noted their realization that their prompt for student opinion papers focused on ego-centric desires, on what students wanted from their parents. The teachers discussed ways to steer students away from self-centered desires toward convincing someone to help make the world a better place.

6. The issues discussed in chapter 34 concerning the ways in which digital technology redefines authority and expertise structures directly affect parents as well as teachers. See, e.g., Anne C. Fletcher and Bethany L. Blair, "Maternal Authority Regarding Early Adolescents' Social Technology Use," *Journal of Family Issues* 35, no. 1 (2014): 54–74.

Chapter 37

1. Alexis R. Lauricella, Ellen Wartella, and Victoria J. Rideout, "Young Children's Screen Time: The Complex Role of Parent and Child Factors," *Journal of Applied Developmental Psychology* 36 (2015): 11–17; Anne C. Fletcher and Bethany L. Blair, "Implications of the Family Expert Role for Parental Rules Regarding Adolescent Use of Social Technologies," *New Media & Society* 18, no. 2 (2016): 239–56; Matthew S. Eastin, Bradley S. Greenberg, and Linda Hofschire, "Parenting the Internet," *Journal of Communication* 56, no. 3 (September 1, 2006): 486–504; Cory A. Kildare, "Impact of Parents' Mobile Device Use on Parent-Child Interaction: A Literature Review," *Computers in Human Behavior* 75 (October 2017): 579–93.

2. Compare this to the perceptions of responsibility for distraction explored in chapter 32. The tension between an emphasis on regulation, care, and intervention and an ethic based on leaving individuals to learn from negative natural consequences was a recurring theme that seemed to reflect unresolved attitudes within the community.

3. The idea of students checking their grades daily seems excessive and may play into the unhelpful effects of the task completion mentality explored in chapter 17.

4. Cf. Annika Andersson and Kalle Räisänen, "Using Class Blogs in 1:1 Schools—Searching for Unexplored Opportunities," *Computers in the Schools* 31, no. 3 (2014): 173–96.

5. It is worth noting that some teachers also expressed appreciation for how technology enabled them to better track and understand their own students' work—for instance, when students tracked their reading through online reading logs. Teachers could check them at any point and did not need to ask for the paper copy that might be in a backpack or tucked in a book at home. Some also noted the ease of taking the data and visualizing it, allowing students to examine their home reading habits and make plans to adjust to more effective practices.

6. This is a widely recognized problem. See, e.g., Steve Whittaker and Candace Sidner, "Email Overload: Exploring Personal Information Management of Email," in *Culture of the Internet*, ed. Sara Kiesler Lawrence, 277–95 (Mahwah, NJ: Erlbaum Associates Publishers, 1997); Rowena Brown, Julie Duck, and Nerina Jimmieson, "E-Mail in the Workplace: The Role of Stress Appraisals and Normative Response Pressure in

the Relationship between E-Mail Stressors and Employee Strain," *International Journal of Stress Management* 21, no. 4 (2014): 325–47; David Sumecki, Maxwell Chipulu, and Udechukwu Ojiako, "Email Overload: Exploring the Moderating Role of the Perception of Email as a 'Business Critical' Tool," *International Journal of Information Management* 31, no. 5 (2011): 407–14.

7. One study of parent-child cell phone communication suggested that increased frequency of calls was associated with decreased truthfulness. See Robert S. Weisskirch, "Parenting by Cell Phone: Parental Monitoring of Adolescents and Family Relations," *Journal of Youth and Adolescence* 38 (2009): 1123–39.

Chapter 38

1. Amitai Etzioni, *The New Golden Rule: Community and Morality in a Democratic Society* (New York: Basic Books, 1996), 127.

2. Scholarship exploring the ever-shifting temporal and spatial boundaries ushered in by digital communication technologies abounds. More broadly, these boundaries are explored in relation to organizational systems, although some scholars ask such questions of education specifically. See, e.g., Ronald Goodenow, "The Cyberspace Challenge: Modernity, Post-Modernity and Reflections on International Networking Policy," *Comparative Education* 32, no. 2 (1996): 197–216.

3. Tony Lawson and Chris Comber, "Introducing Information and Communication Technologies into Schools: The Blurring of Boundaries," *British Journal of Sociology of Education* 21, no. 3 (2000): 419–33.

Appendix

1. Charles Teddlie and Abbas Tashakkori, *The Foundations of Mixed Methods Research: Integrating Quantitative and Qualitative Techniques in the Social and Behavioral Sciences* (Thousand Oaks, CA: SAGE, 2009).

2. The need for longitudinal research that examines both process and outcomes is called for in a range of educational technology scholarship. See, e.g., Yong Zhao, Bo Yan, and Jing Lei, "The Logic and Logic Model of Technology Evaluation," in *International Handbook of Information Technology in Primary and Secondary Education*, ed. Joke Voogt and Gerald Knezek (Boston: Springer, 2008), 633–53.

3. John W. Creswell and Vicki L. Plano Clark, *Designing and Conducting Mixed Methods Research*, 2nd ed. (Thousand Oaks, CA: Sage, 2011).

4. R. Burke Johnson and Anthony J. Onwuegbuzie, "Mixed Methods Research: A Research Paradigm Whose Time Has Come," *Educational Researcher* 33, no. 7 (2004): 14–26.

5. Elizabeth G. Creamer, *An Introduction to Fully Integrated Mixed Methods Research* (Los Angeles: SAGE, 2017).

6. Observations have served as a central method for understanding and improving education for more than five decades. The uses of observations have ranged widely and

include improving pre-service and in-service teacher training, assessing quality teaching, promoting effective student learning, and more. For further exploration of classroom observations, see, e.g., Paul Atkinson and Martyn Hammersley, "Ethnography and Participant Observation," in *Handbook of Qualitative Research*, ed. Norman K. Denzin and Yvonna S. Lincoln, 248–61 (Thousand Oaks, CA: SAGE, 1994); Matt O'Leary, *Classroom Observation: A Guide to the Effective Observation of Teaching and Learning* (London: Routledge, 2013).

7. Neil Selwyn, "Looking Beyond Learning: Notes towards the Critical Study of Educational Technology," *Journal of Computer Assisted Learning* 26, no. 1 (2010): 65–73.

8. This research design relied on methods for using multiple sources to support validity of qualitative research. See, e.g., Anthony J. Onwuegbuzie and Nancy L. Leech, "Validity and Qualitative Research: An Oxymoron?," *Quality & Quantity* 41, no. 2 (2007): 233–49.

9. Existing protocols and scholarship related to observation protocol design were used to guide development of the current measure. Examples include E. M. Lewis, S. M. Ross, and M. J. Alberg, *School Observation Measure Reliability Analysis* (Memphis: University of Memphis, Center for Research in Educational Policy, 1999); D. L. Lowther, S. M. Ross, F. Clark, and A. Adcock, *Survey of Computer Use* (Memphis: University of Memphis, 1999); Jane A. Stallings and David H. Kaskowitz, *Follow Through Classroom Observation Evaluation 1972–1973*, SRI Project URU-7370 (Menlo Park, CA: Stanford Research Institute, 1974); Matthew T. Hora, Amanda Oleson, and Joseph J. Ferrare, *Teaching Dimensions Observation Protocol (TDOP) User's Manual* (Madison: Wisconsin Center for Education Research, 2013).

10. Janice M. Morse et al., "Verification Strategies for Establishing Reliability and Validity in Qualitative Research," *International Journal of Qualitative Methods* 1, no. 2 (2002): 13–22.

11. Floyd J. Fowler, *Improving Survey Questions: Design and Evaluation* (London: SAGE, 1995); Fowler, *Survey Research Methods* (London: SAGE, 2013); Peter H. Rossi, James D. Wright, and Andy B. Anderson, eds., *Handbook of Survey Research* (Orlando: Academic Press, 2013).

12. All of these school names have been changed to preserve the privacy of participants.

13. Andrea Fontana and James H. Frey, "Interviewing: The Art of Science," in *Handbook of Qualitative Research*, ed. Norman K. Denzin and Yvonna S. Lincoln, 361–76 (Thousand Oaks, CA: SAGE, 1994).

14. David L. Morgan, *Focus Groups as Qualitative Research* (Newbury Park, CA: SAGE, 1998).

15. Focus group designs were based on best practices in the field; see, e.g., Fontana and Frey, "Interviewing"; Anthony J. Onwuegbuzie et al., "A Qualitative Framework for Collecting and Analyzing Data in Focus Group Research," *International Journal of Qualitative Methods* 8, no. 3 (2009): 1–21; Robert S. Weiss, *Learning from Strangers: The Art and Method of Qualitative Interview Studies* (New York: Simon & Schuster, 1995).

16. An exception to focus group selection was necessary for students, as it became clear after phase 1 that they were more difficult to recruit through our email communication methods. Therefore, classroom teachers recruited willing participants for seven

focus groups (approximately eight students each) from within their homerooms and encouraged them to attend focus groups hosted during a nonacademic period.

17. Eleanor McLellan, Kathleen M. MacQueen, and Judith L. Neidig, "Beyond the Qualitative Interview: Data Preparation and Transcription," *Field Methods* 15, no. 1 (2003): 63–84.

18. All analysis was guided by scholarship about mixed methods research; see, e.g., Anselm Strauss and Juliet Corbin, *Basics of Qualitative Research Techniques* (Newbury Park, CA: SAGE, 1998); Eli Lieber and Thomas S. Weisner, "Meeting the Practical Challenges of Mixed Methods Research," in *SAGE Handbook of Mixed Methods in Social & Behavioral Research*, ed. Abbas Tashakkori and Charles Teddlie, 559–79 (Thousand Oaks, CA: SAGE, 2010); Matthew B. Miles, A. Michael Huberman, and Johnny Saldana, *Qualitative Data Analysis* (Thousand Oaks, CA: SAGE, 2013); Onwuegbuzie et al., "Qualitative Framework."

19. Both strategies provide greater analytical depth for focus group data. See, e.g., Onwuegbuzie et al., "Qualitative Framework."

20. Sharan B. Merriam, *Case Study Research in Education: A Qualitative Approach* (San Francisco: Jossey-Bass, 1988).

21. George Spindler and Louise Spindler, "Cultural Process and Ethnography: An Anthropological Perspective," in *The Handbook of Qualitative Research in Education*, ed. Margaret Diane LeCompte and Wendy L. Millroy, 53–92 (New York: Academic Press, 1992).

22. Robert E. Stake, "Qualitative Case Studies," in *Strategies of Qualitative Inquiry*, ed. Norman K. Denzin and Yvonna S. Lincoln, 119–49 (Thousand Oaks, CA: SAGE, 2008); Bedrettin Yazan, "Three Approaches to Case Study Methods in Education: Yin, Merriam, and Stake," *The Qualitative Report* 20, no. 2 (2015): 134–52.

23. The observation and focus group interview methods used in the case studies mirrored to a large extent those in the random classroom observations and focus group sections, described in detail previously in the appendix. The detail of methodological description here will not be repeated. See prior appendix sections for further detail.

24. Norman K. Denzin, *Collecting and Interpreting Qualitative Materials*, 3rd ed. (Thousand Oaks, CA: SAGE, 2008).

25. Onwuegbuzie and Leech, "Validity."

26. Glenn A. Bowen, "Document Analysis as a Qualitative Research Method," *Qualitative Research Journal* 9, no. 2 (2009): 27–40; Denzin, *Collecting and Interpreting*.

27. See the focus group analysis section in this appendix for additional detail about constant comparative and methodological scholarship guiding this type of analysis.

28. Given transcription time, focus groups were only beginning to enter coding at the end of phase 1. The emerging codes and themes played a more significant role by the end of phase 2.

29. Both strategies are opportunities to enhance validity in mixed methods studies. See Onwuegbuzie and Leech, "Validity."

30. Creamer, *Introduction*, 21–40.

31. Creswell and Plano Clark, *Designing and Conducting*; Onwuegbuzie and Leech, "Validity."

Index